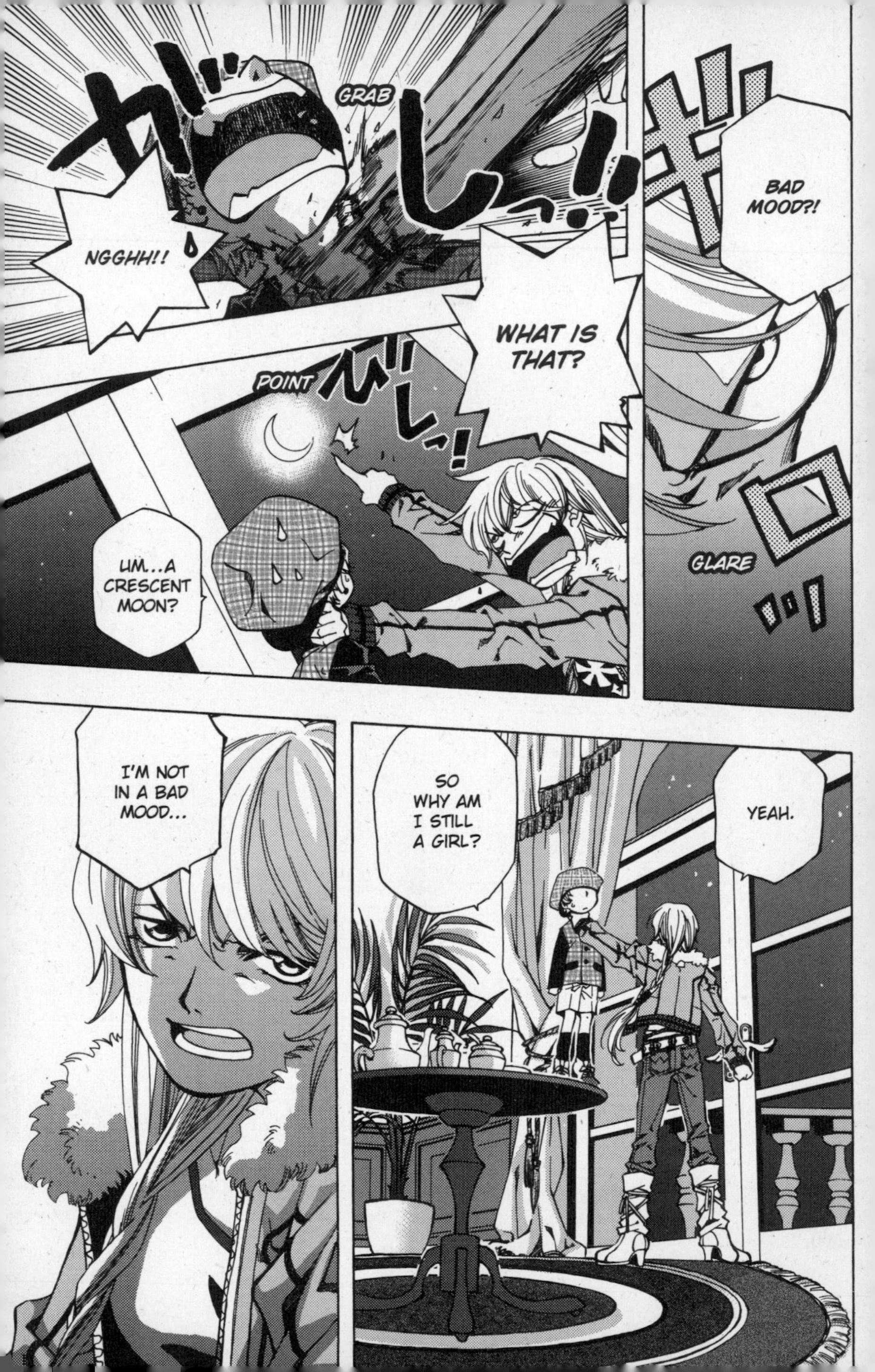
BAD MOOD?!
GLARE
GRAB
NGGHH!!
WHAT IS THAT?
POINT
UM...A CRESCENT MOON?
YEAH.
SO WHY AM I STILL A GIRL?
I'M NOT IN A BAD MOOD...

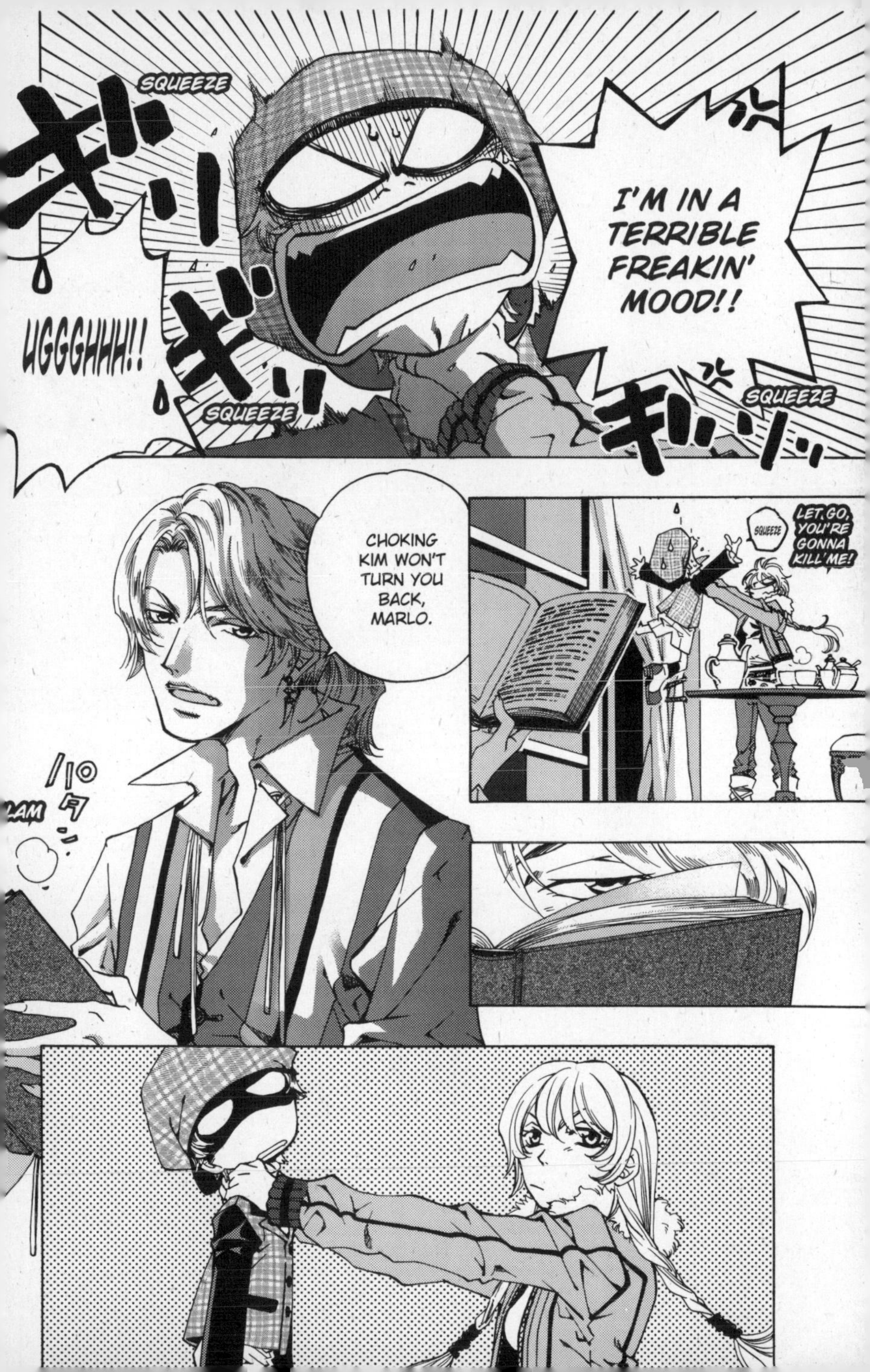
I'M IN A TERRIBLE FREAKIN' MOOD!!
SQUEEZE
SQUEEZE
UGGGHHH!!
SQUEEZE
SQUEEZE
LET GO, YOU'RE GONNA KILL ME!
CHOKING KIM WON'T TURN YOU BACK, MARLO.
LAM

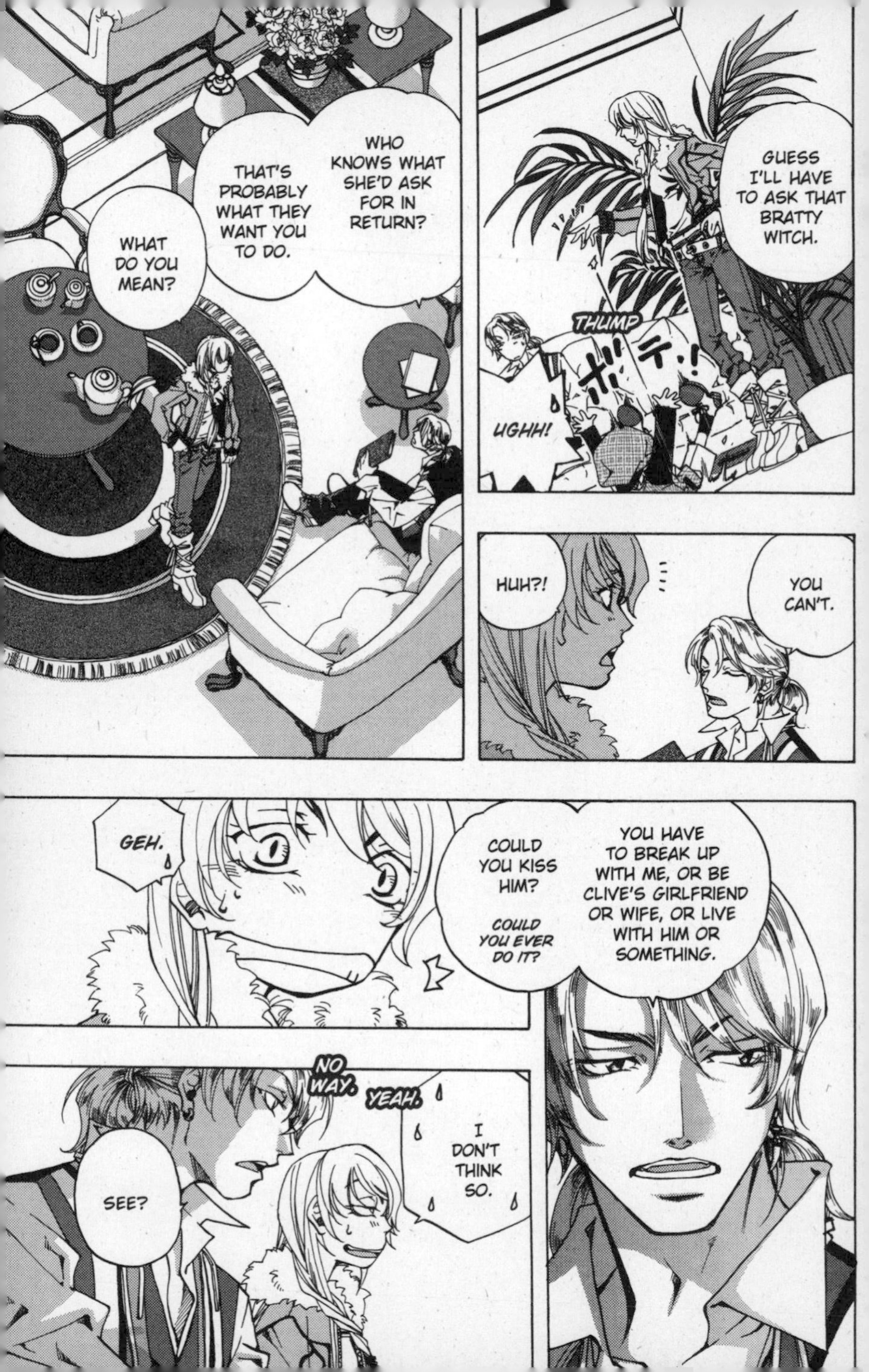
GUESS I'LL HAVE TO ASK THAT BRATTY WITCH.
THUMP
ボテッ!
UGHH!
YOU CAN'T.
HUH?!
WHO KNOWS WHAT SHE'D ASK FOR IN RETURN?
THAT'S PROBABLY WHAT THEY WANT YOU TO DO.
WHAT DO YOU MEAN?
YOU HAVE TO BREAK UP WITH ME, OR BE CLIVE'S GIRLFRIEND OR WIFE, OR LIVE WITH HIM OR SOMETHING.
COULD YOU KISS HIM?
COULD YOU EVER DO IT?
GEH.
NO WAY.
YEAH.
I DON'T THINK SO.
SEE?

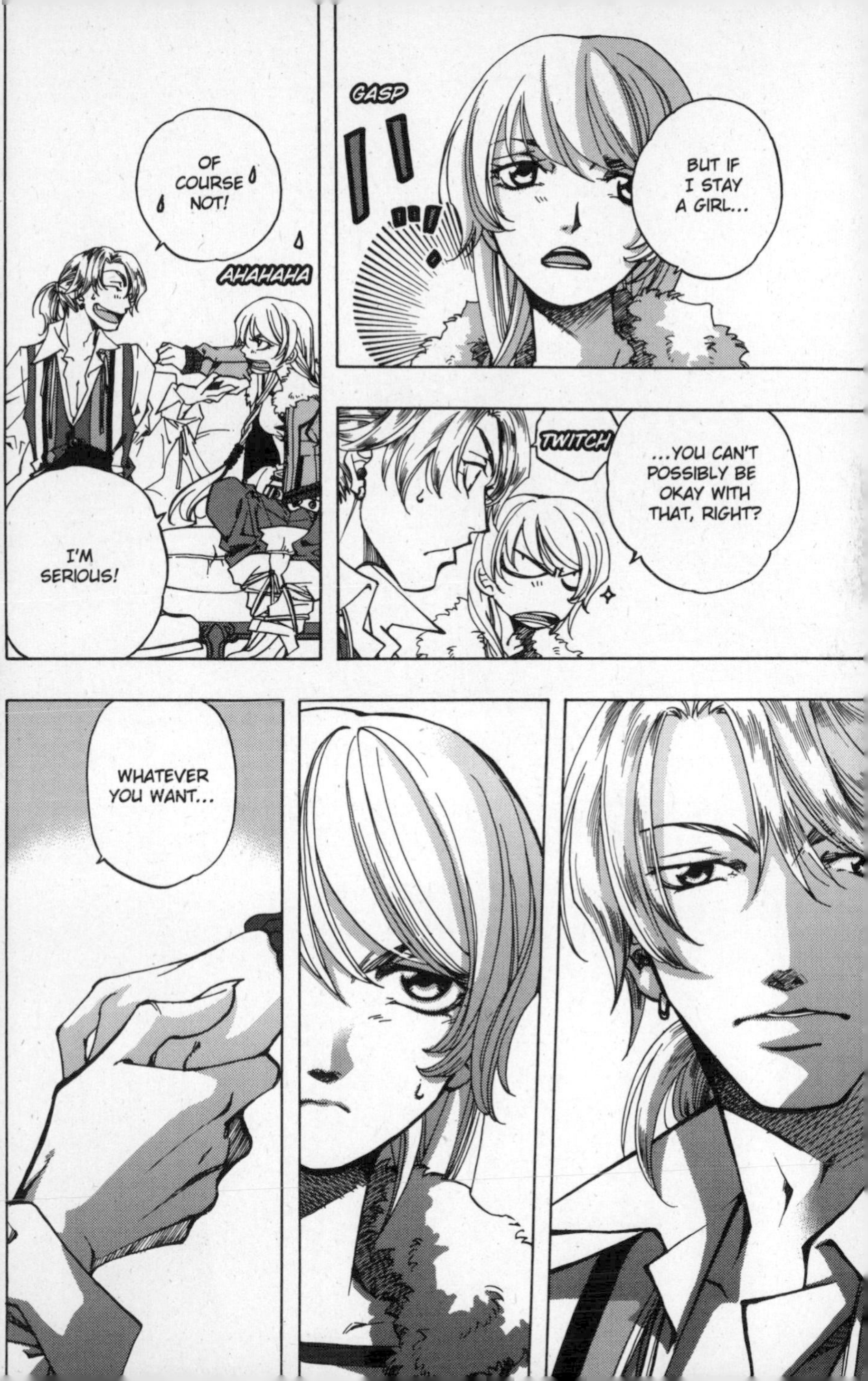
GASP
BUT IF I STAY A GIRL...
...YOU CAN'T POSSIBLY BE OKAY WITH THAT, RIGHT?
TWITCH
AHAHAHA
OF COURSE NOT!
I'M SERIOUS!
WHATEVER YOU WANT...

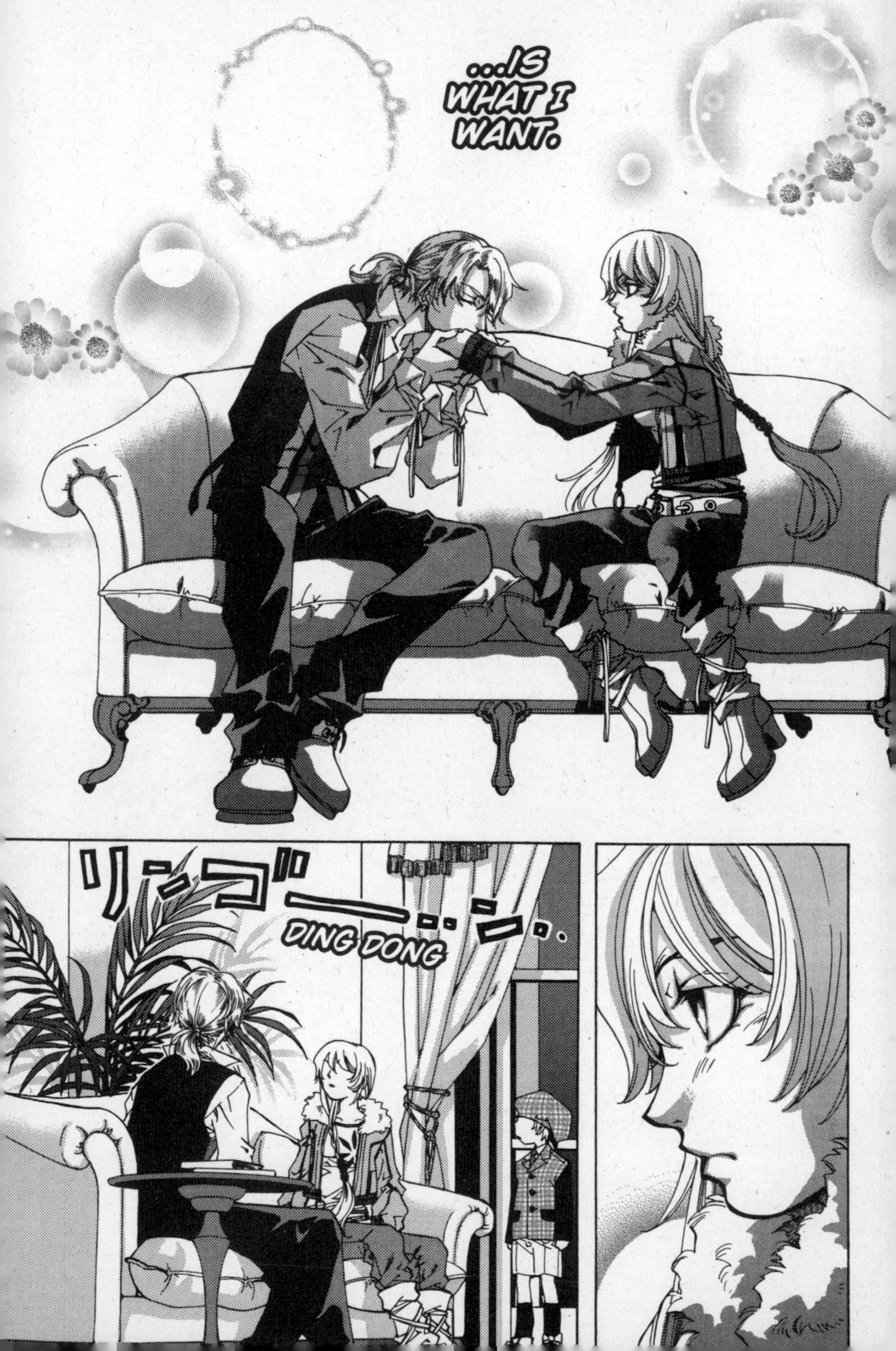
...IS WHAT I WANT.
DING DONG

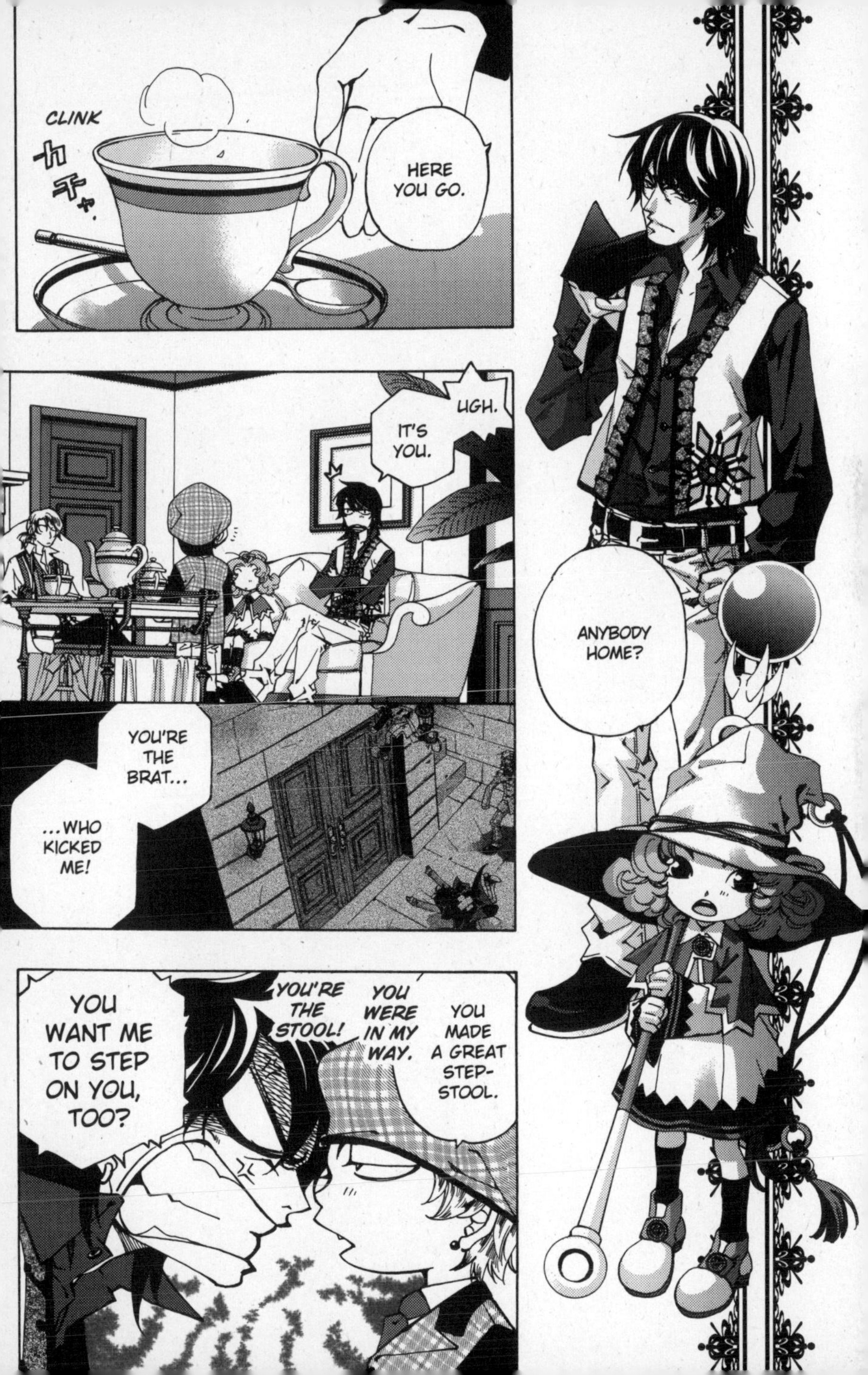
ANYBODY HOME?
HERE YOU GO.
CLINK
UGH.
IT'S YOU.
YOU'RE THE BRAT...
...WHO KICKED ME!
YOU MADE A GREAT STEP-STOOL.
YOU WERE IN MY WAY.
YOU'RE THE STOOL!
YOU WANT ME TO STEP ON YOU, TOO?

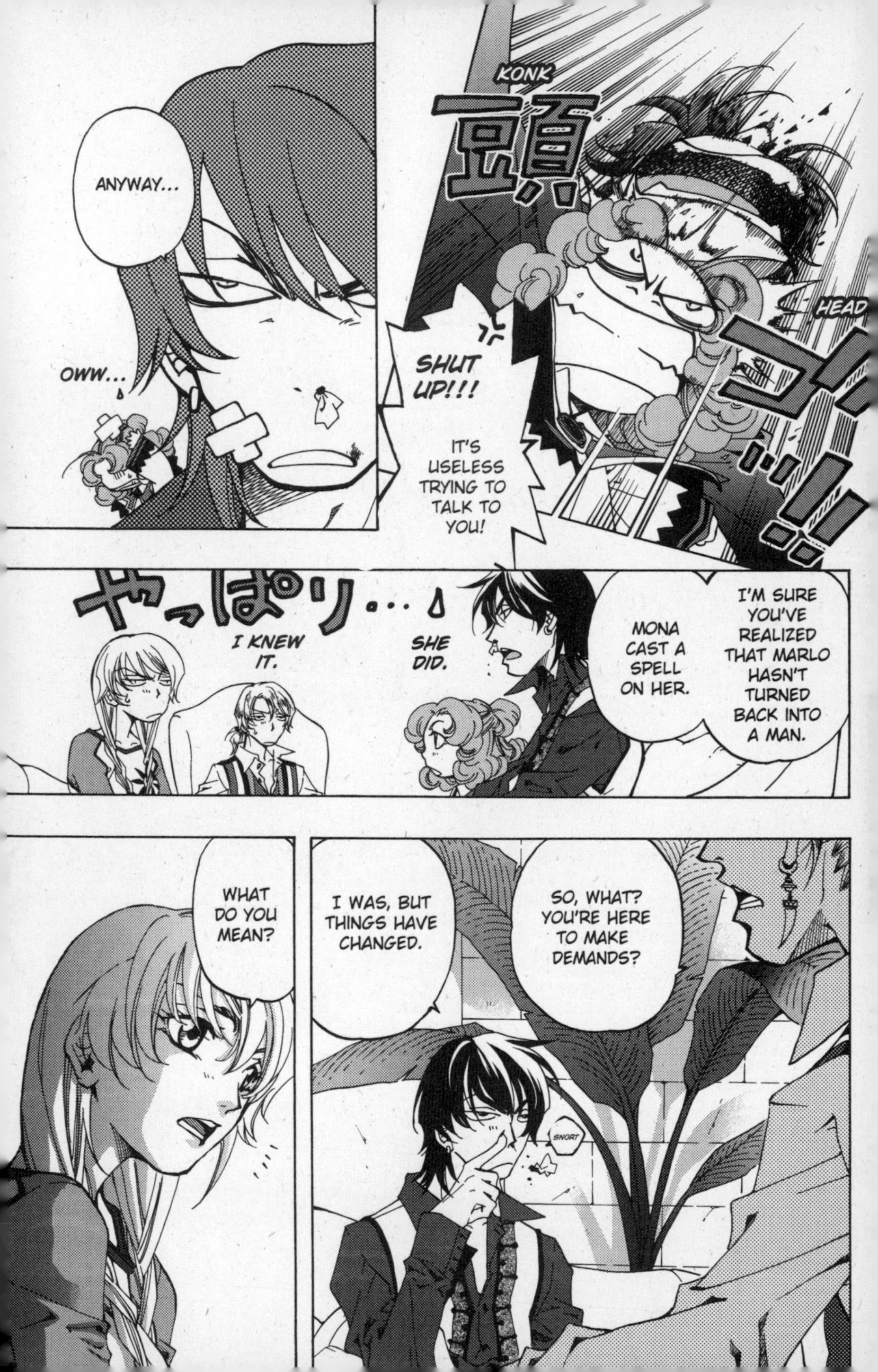
HEAD
ゴッ!!!
KONK
頭
SHUT UP!!!
IT'S USELESS TRYING TO TALK TO YOU!
ANYWAY...
OWW...
I'M SURE YOU'VE REALIZED THAT MARLO HASN'T TURNED BACK INTO A MAN.
MONA CAST A SPELL ON HER.
SHE DID.
I KNEW IT.
やっぱり...
SO, WHAT? YOU'RE HERE TO MAKE DEMANDS?
SNORT
I WAS, BUT THINGS HAVE CHANGED.
WHAT DO YOU MEAN?

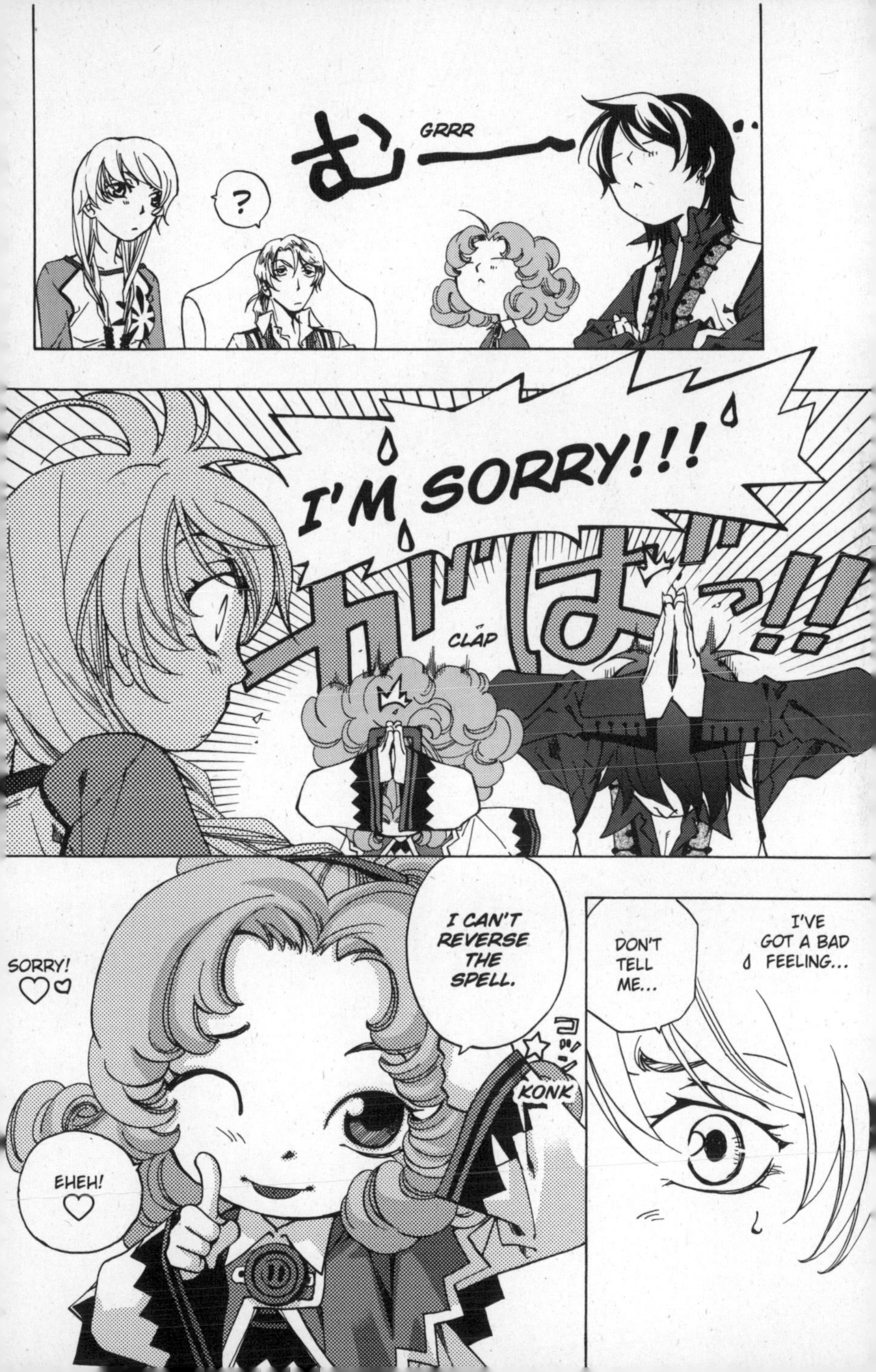

むー
GRRR
?
I'M SORRY!!!
がばっ!!
CLAP
I'VE GOT A BAD FEELING...
DON'T TELL ME...
I CAN'T REVERSE THE SPELL.
KONK
SORRY!
EHEH!

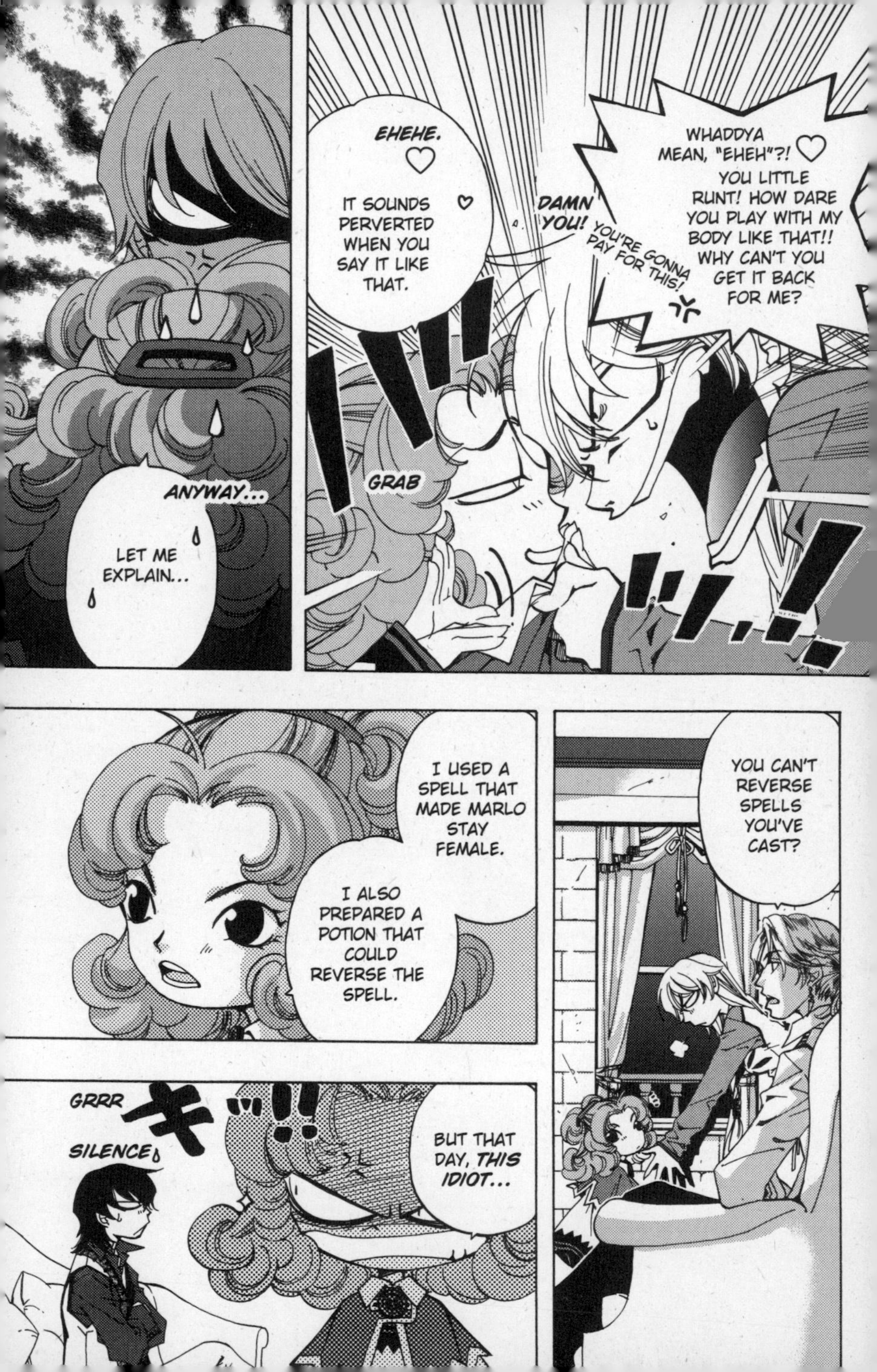
WHADDYA MEAN, "EHEH"?! ♡ YOU LITTLE RUNT! HOW DARE YOU PLAY WITH MY BODY LIKE THAT!! WHY CAN'T YOU GET IT BACK FOR ME?
YOU'RE GONNA PAY FOR THIS!
DAMN YOU!
EHEHE. ♡
IT SOUNDS PERVERTED WHEN YOU SAY IT LIKE THAT. ♡
GRAB
ANYWAY...
LET ME EXPLAIN...
YOU CAN'T REVERSE SPELLS YOU'VE CAST?
I USED A SPELL THAT MADE MARLO STAY FEMALE.
I ALSO PREPARED A POTION THAT COULD REVERSE THE SPELL.
BUT THAT DAY, *THIS IDIOT*...
GRRR
SILENCE

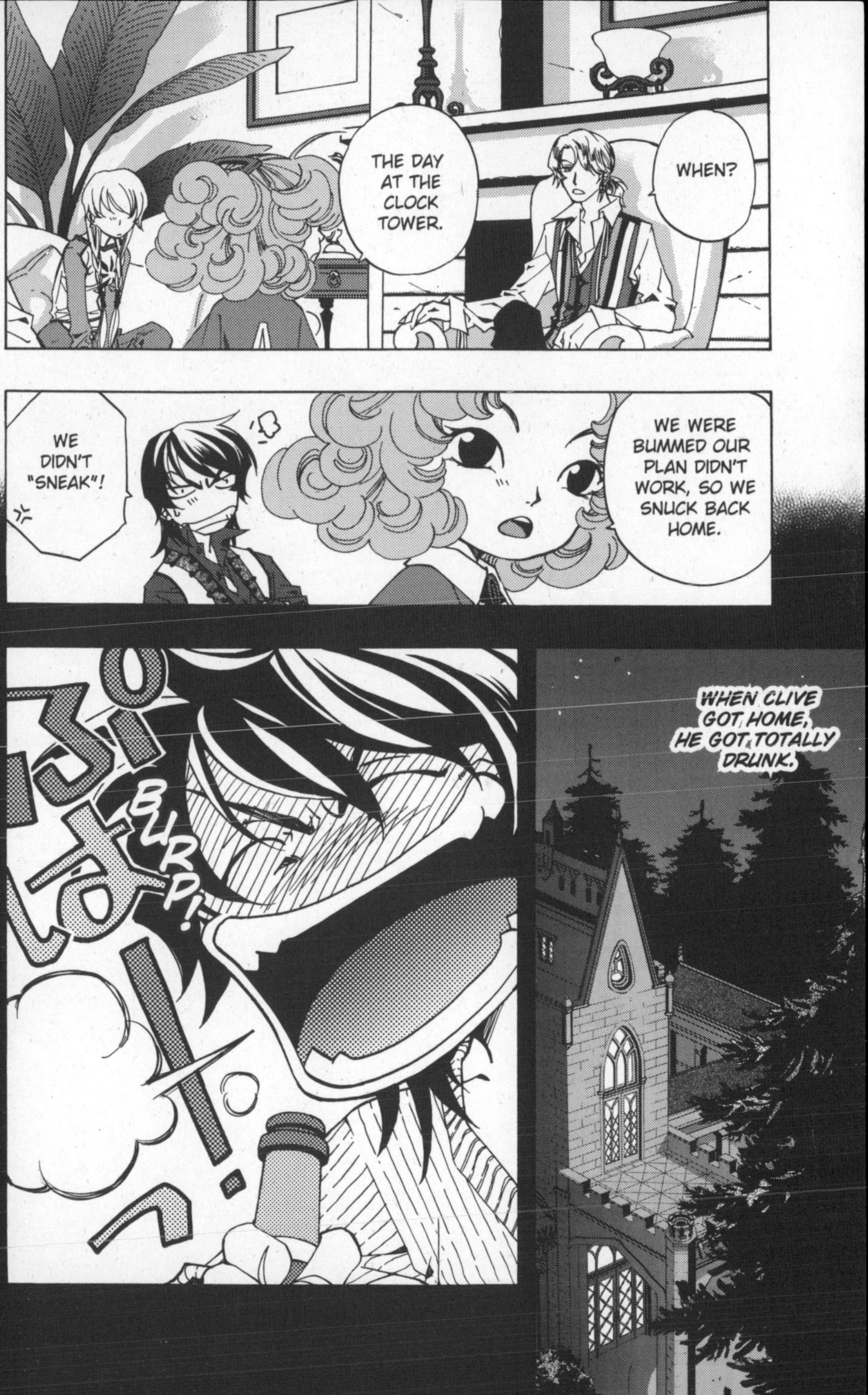
WHEN?
THE DAY AT THE CLOCK TOWER.
WE WERE BUMMED OUR PLAN DIDN'T WORK, SO WE SNUCK BACK HOME.
WE DIDN'T "SNEAK"!
WHEN CLIVE GOT HOME, HE GOT TOTALLY DRUNK.
BURP!

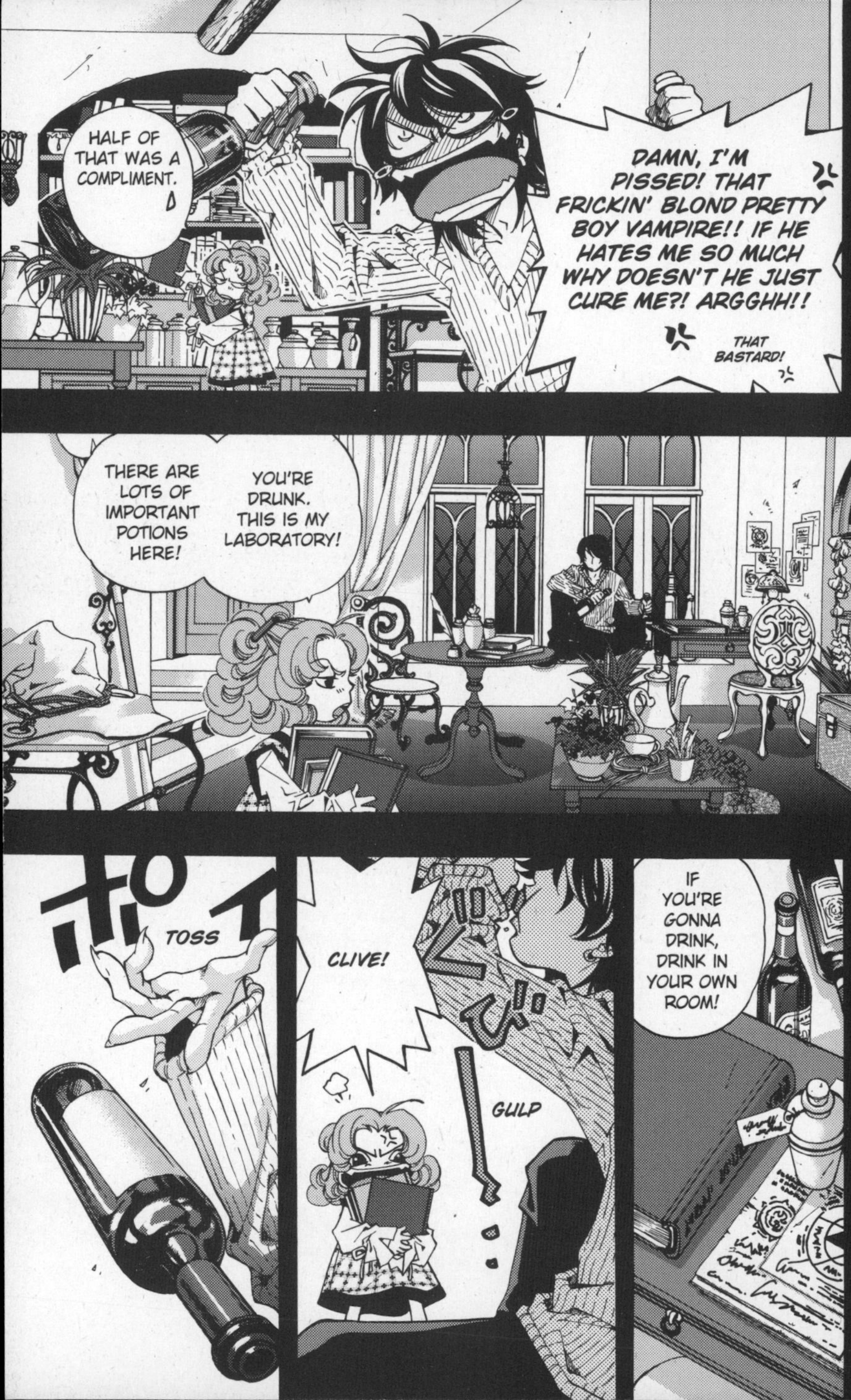
DAMN, I'M PISSED! THAT FRICKIN' BLOND PRETTY BOY VAMPIRE!! IF HE HATES ME SO MUCH WHY DOESN'T HE JUST CURE ME?! ARGGHH!!
THAT BASTARD!
HALF OF THAT WAS A COMPLIMENT.
YOU'RE DRUNK. THIS IS MY LABORATORY!
THERE ARE LOTS OF IMPORTANT POTIONS HERE!
IF YOU'RE GONNA DRINK, DRINK IN YOUR OWN ROOM!
CLIVE!
GULP
TOSS

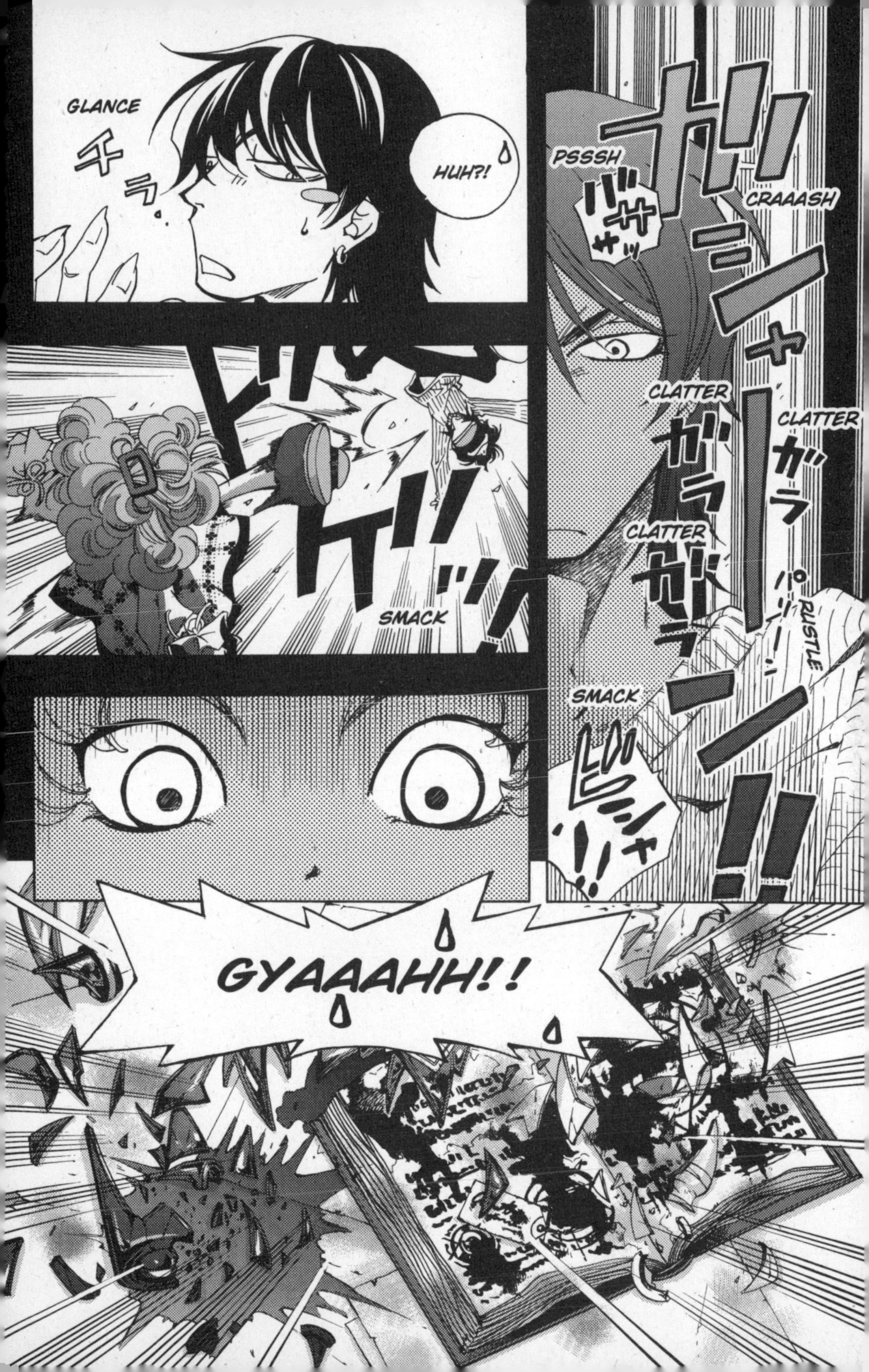
PSSSH
CRAAASH
CLATTER
CLATTER
CLATTER
RUSTLE
SMACK
HUH?!
GLANCE
SMACK
GYAAAHH!!

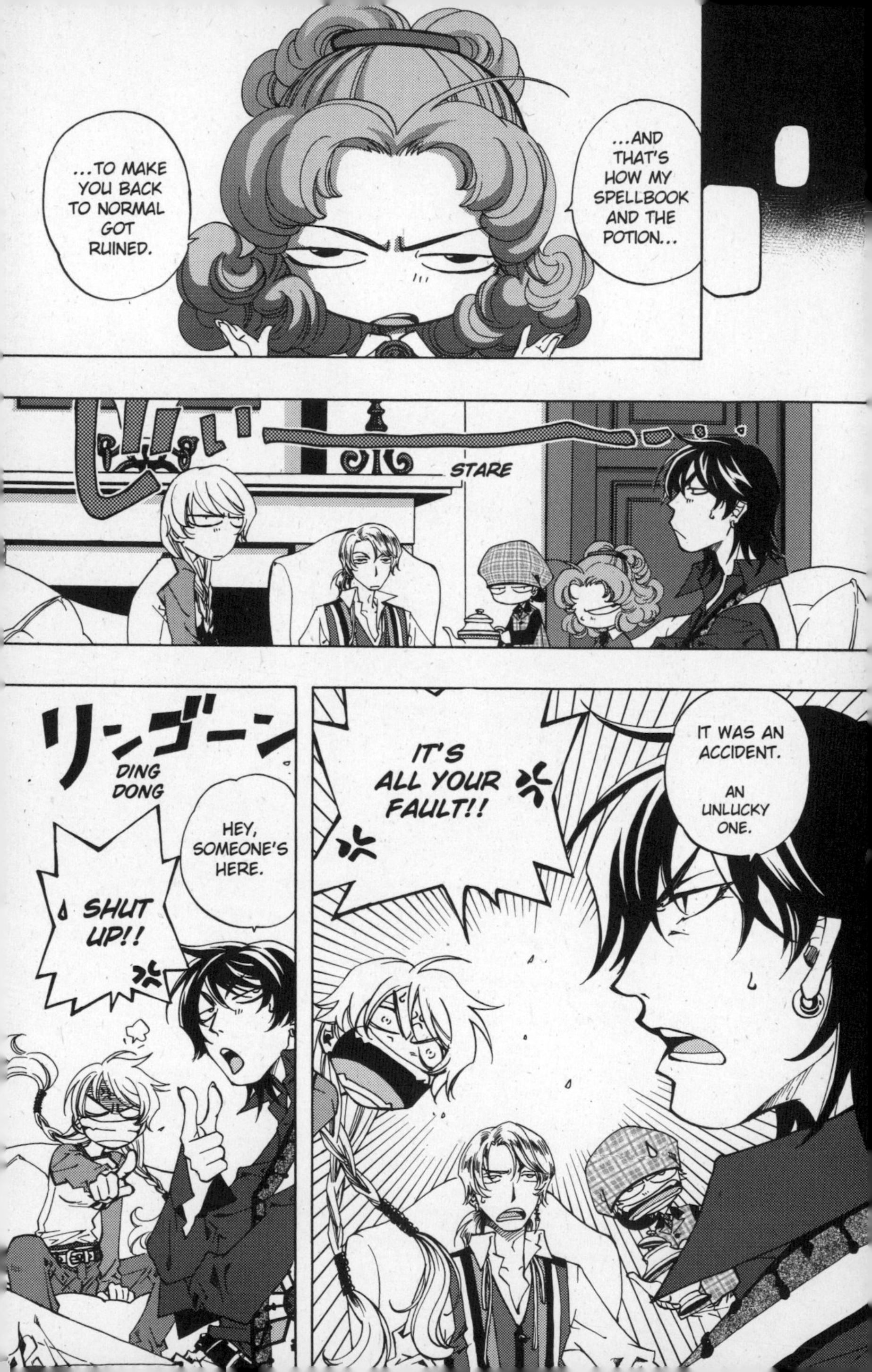
...AND THAT'S HOW MY SPELLBOOK AND THE POTION...
...TO MAKE YOU BACK TO NORMAL GOT RUINED.
STARE
IT WAS AN ACCIDENT. AN UNLUCKY ONE.
IT'S ALL YOUR FAULT!!
リンゴーン
DING DONG
HEY, SOMEONE'S HERE.
SHUT UP!!

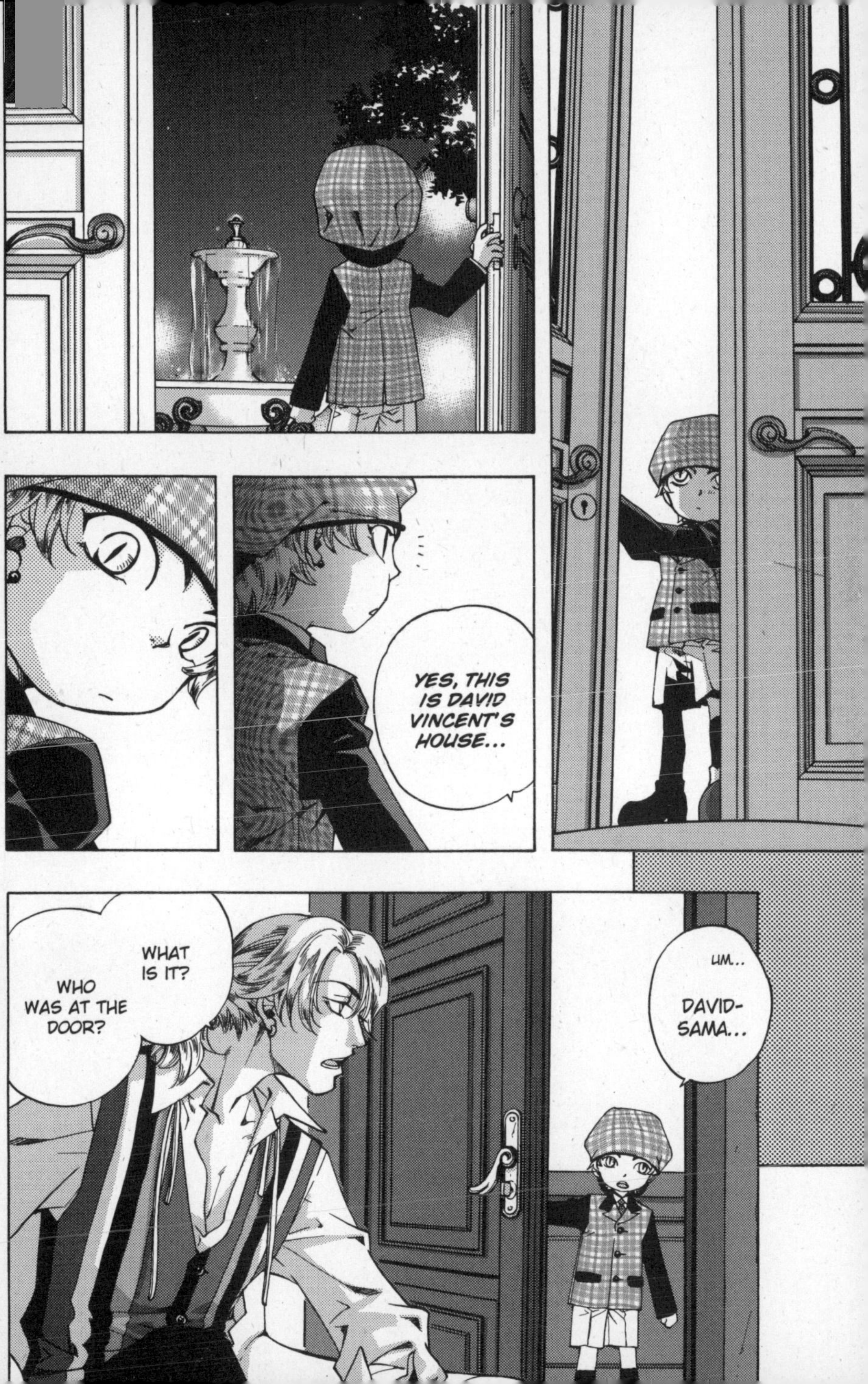
YES, THIS IS DAVID VINCENT'S HOUSE...
UM...
DAVID-SAMA...
WHAT IS IT?
WHO WAS AT THE DOOR?

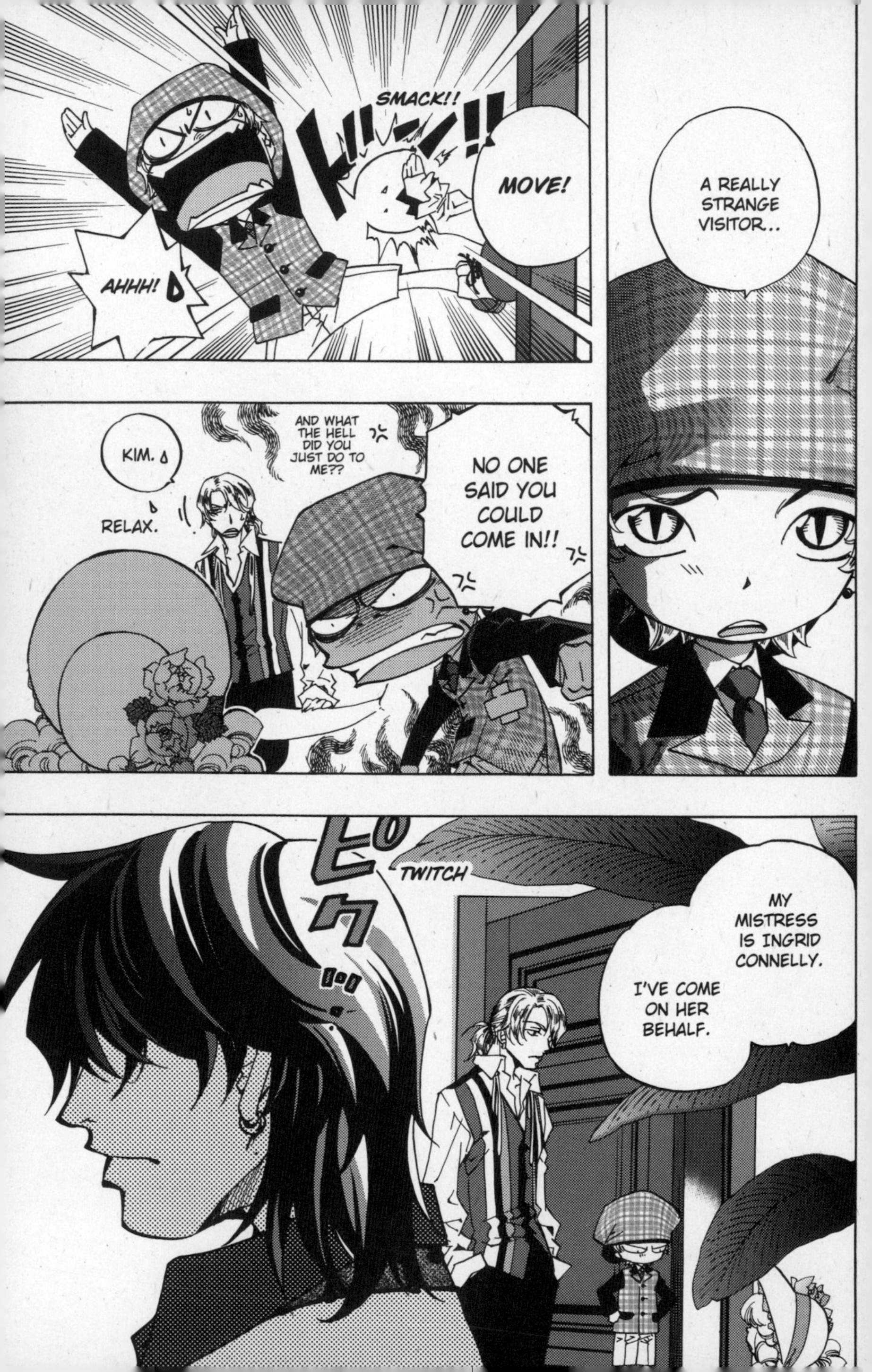
A REALLY STRANGE VISITOR...
MOVE!
SMACK!!
AHHH!
NO ONE SAID YOU COULD COME IN!!
AND WHAT THE HELL DID YOU JUST DO TO ME??
KIM.
RELAX.
TWITCH
MY MISTRESS IS INGRID CONNELLY.
I'VE COME ON HER BEHALF.

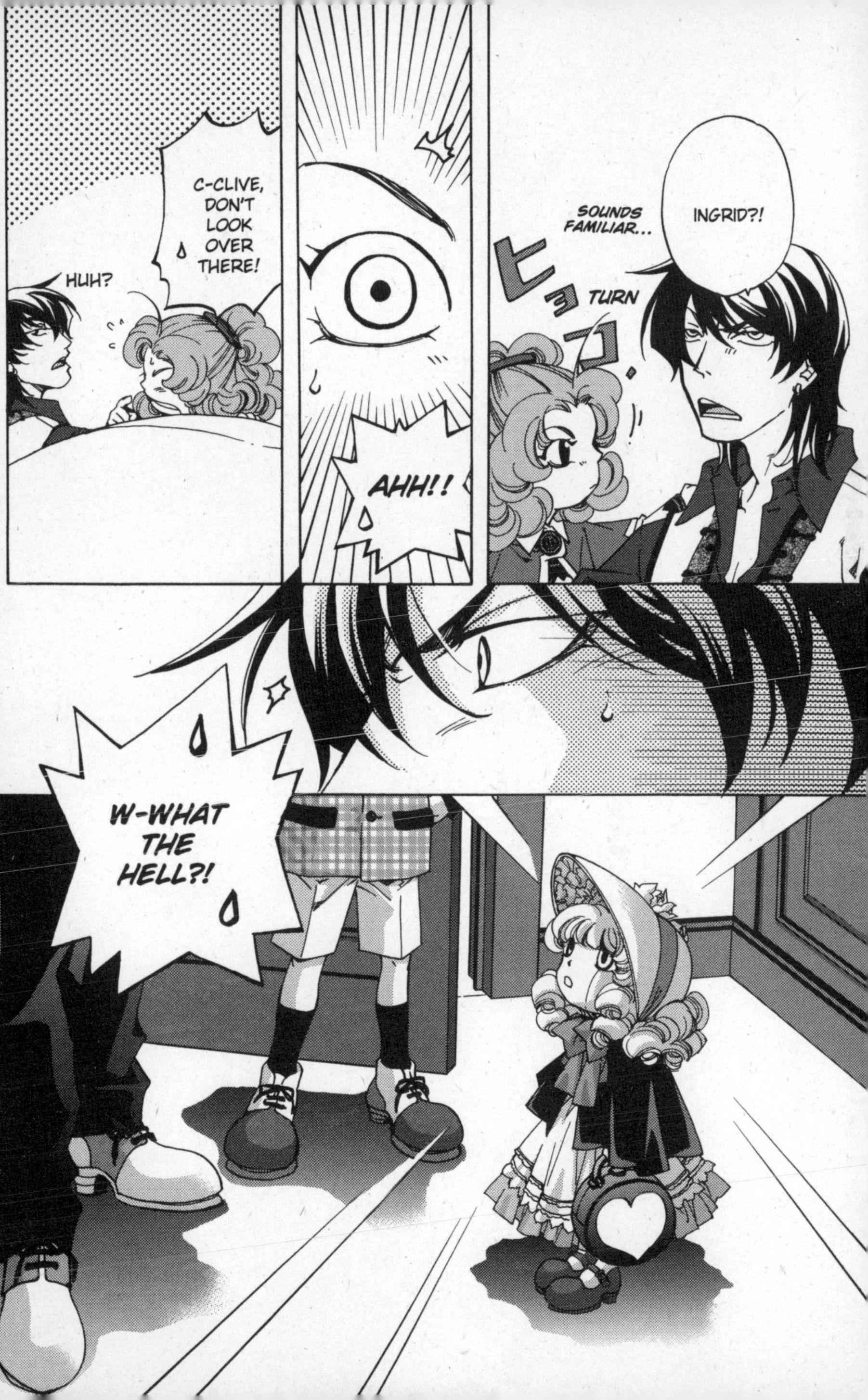
INGRID?!
SOUNDS FAMILIAR...
TURN
ヒョコ
AHH!!
C-CLIVE, DON'T LOOK OVER THERE!
HUH?
W-WHAT THE HELL?!

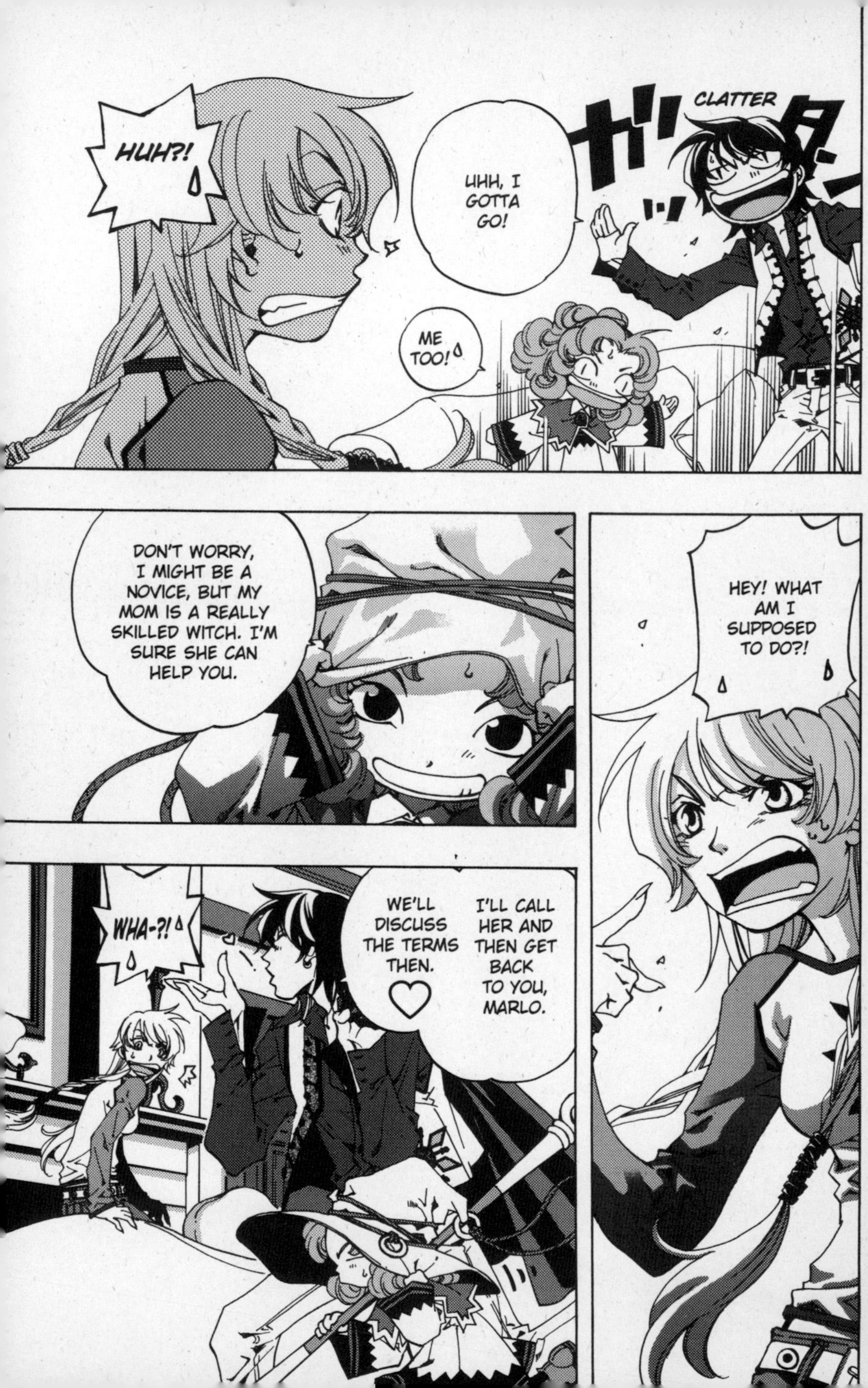
CLATTER
UHH, I GOTTA GO!
ME TOO!
HUH?!
HEY! WHAT AM I SUPPOSED TO DO?!
DON'T WORRY, I MIGHT BE A NOVICE, BUT MY MOM IS A REALLY SKILLED WITCH. I'M SURE SHE CAN HELP YOU.
I'LL CALL HER AND THEN GET BACK TO YOU, MARLO.
WE'LL DISCUSS THE TERMS THEN.
WHA-?!

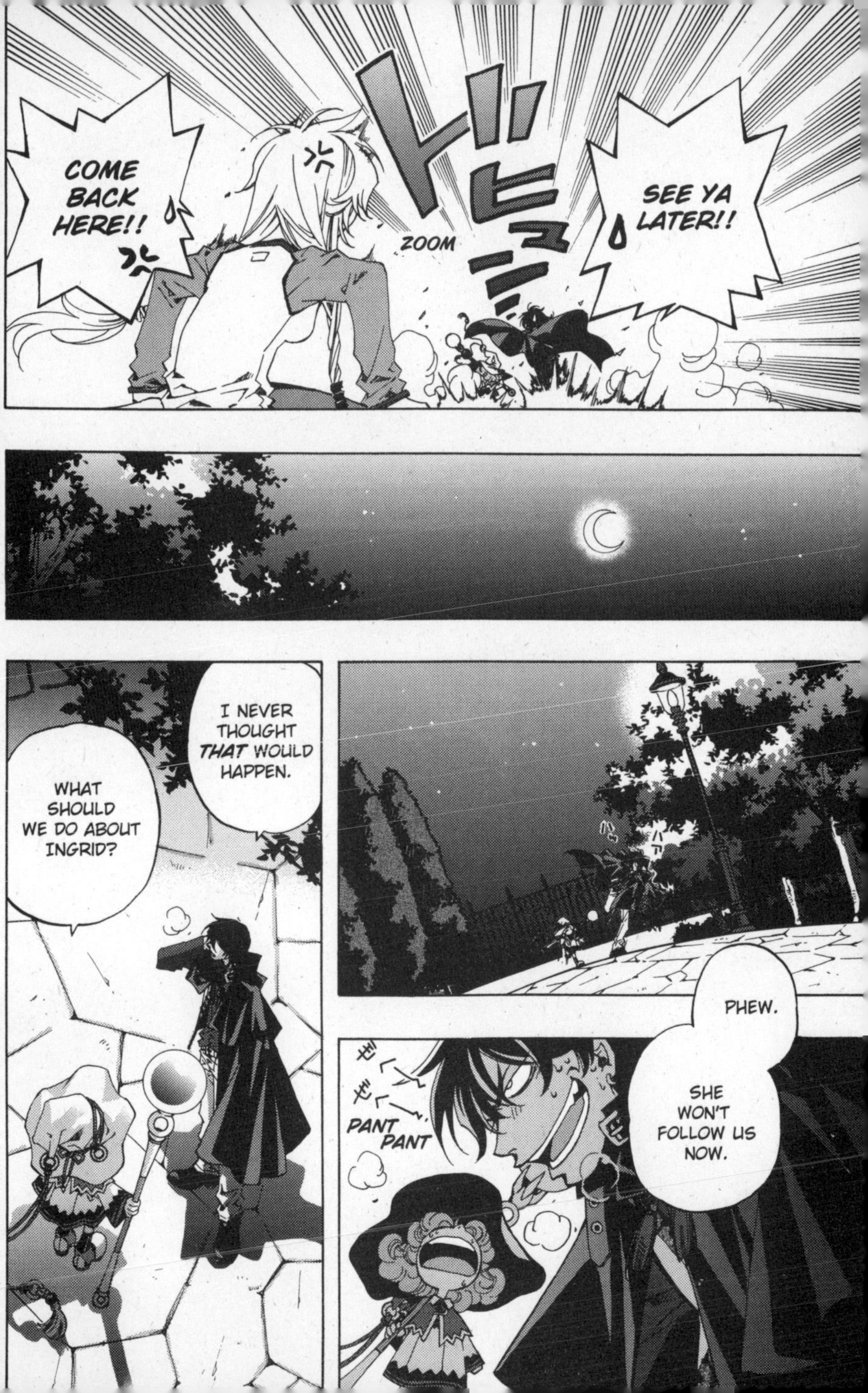
SEE YA LATER!!
ZOOM
COME BACK HERE!!
PHEW.
SHE WON'T FOLLOW US NOW.
PANT PANT
I NEVER THOUGHT *THAT* WOULD HAPPEN.
WHAT SHOULD WE DO ABOUT INGRID?

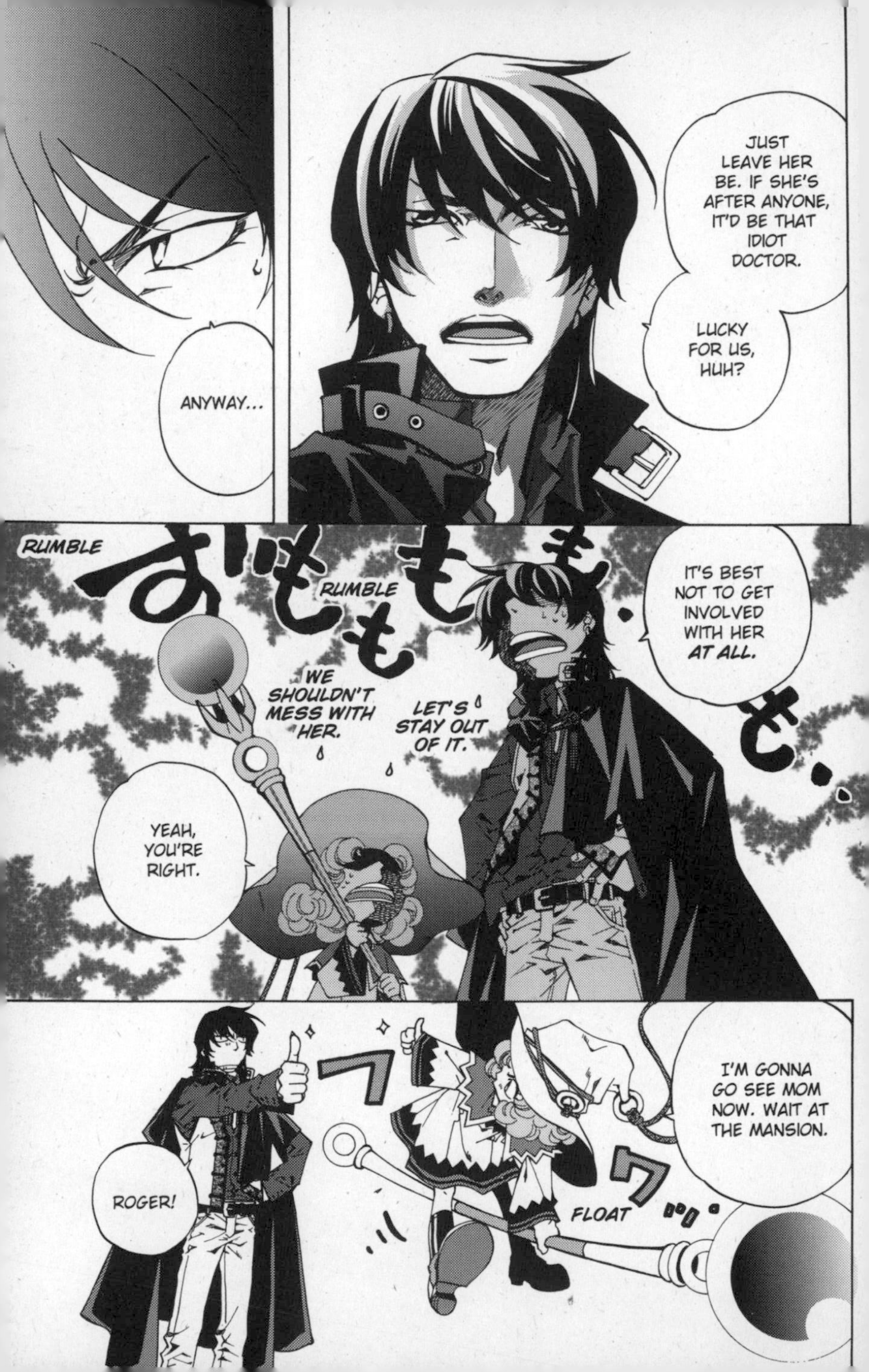
JUST LEAVE HER BE. IF SHE'S AFTER ANYONE, IT'D BE THAT IDIOT DOCTOR.
LUCKY FOR US, HUH?
ANYWAY...
IT'S BEST NOT TO GET INVOLVED WITH HER AT ALL.
RUMBLE
RUMBLE
LET'S STAY OUT OF IT.
WE SHOULDN'T MESS WITH HER.
YEAH, YOU'RE RIGHT.
I'M GONNA GO SEE MOM NOW. WAIT AT THE MANSION.
フワ
FLOAT
ROGER!

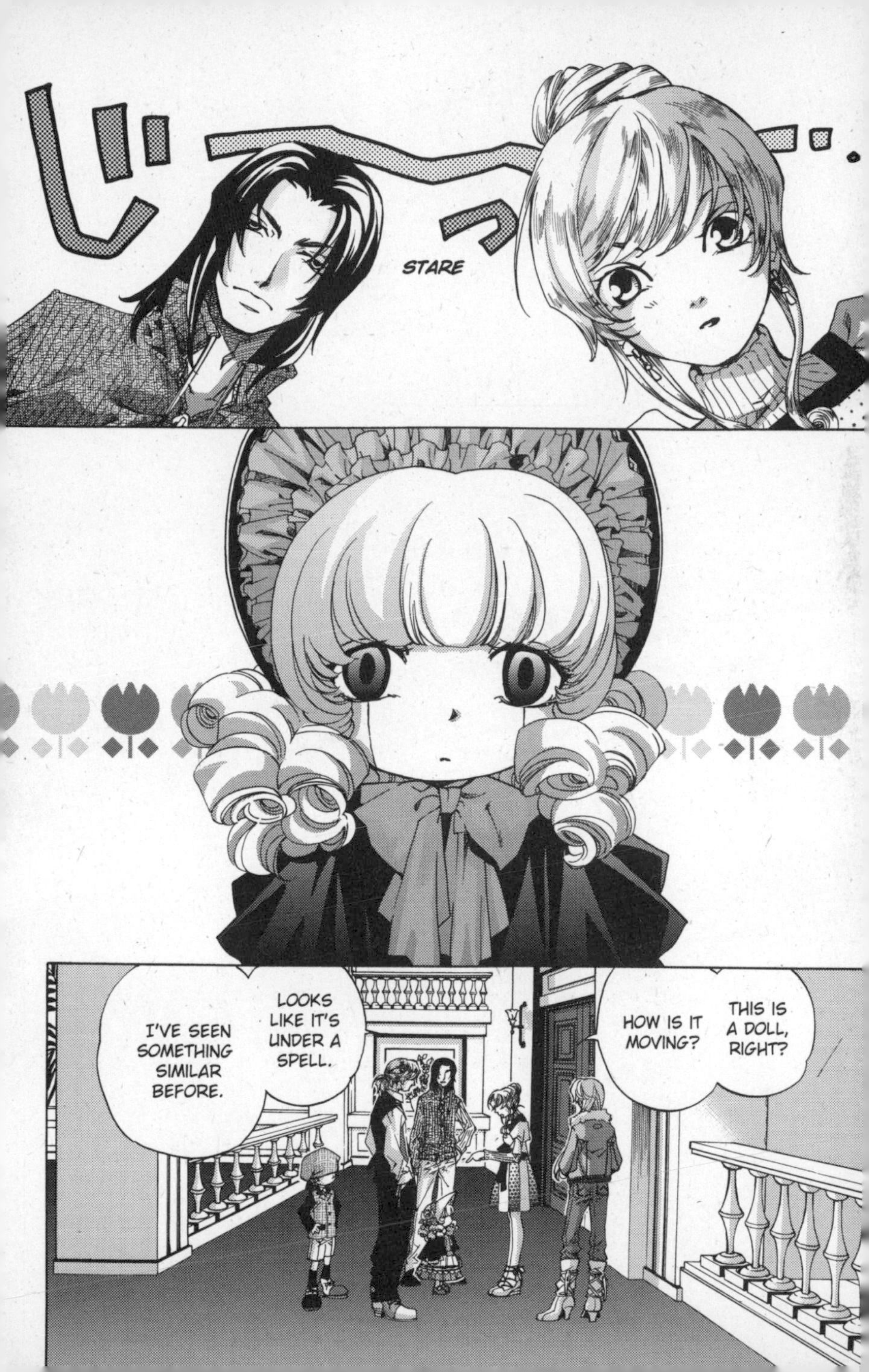
じ〜っ…
STARE
THIS IS A DOLL, RIGHT?
HOW IS IT MOVING?
LOOKS LIKE IT'S UNDER A SPELL.
I'VE SEEN SOMETHING SIMILAR BEFORE.

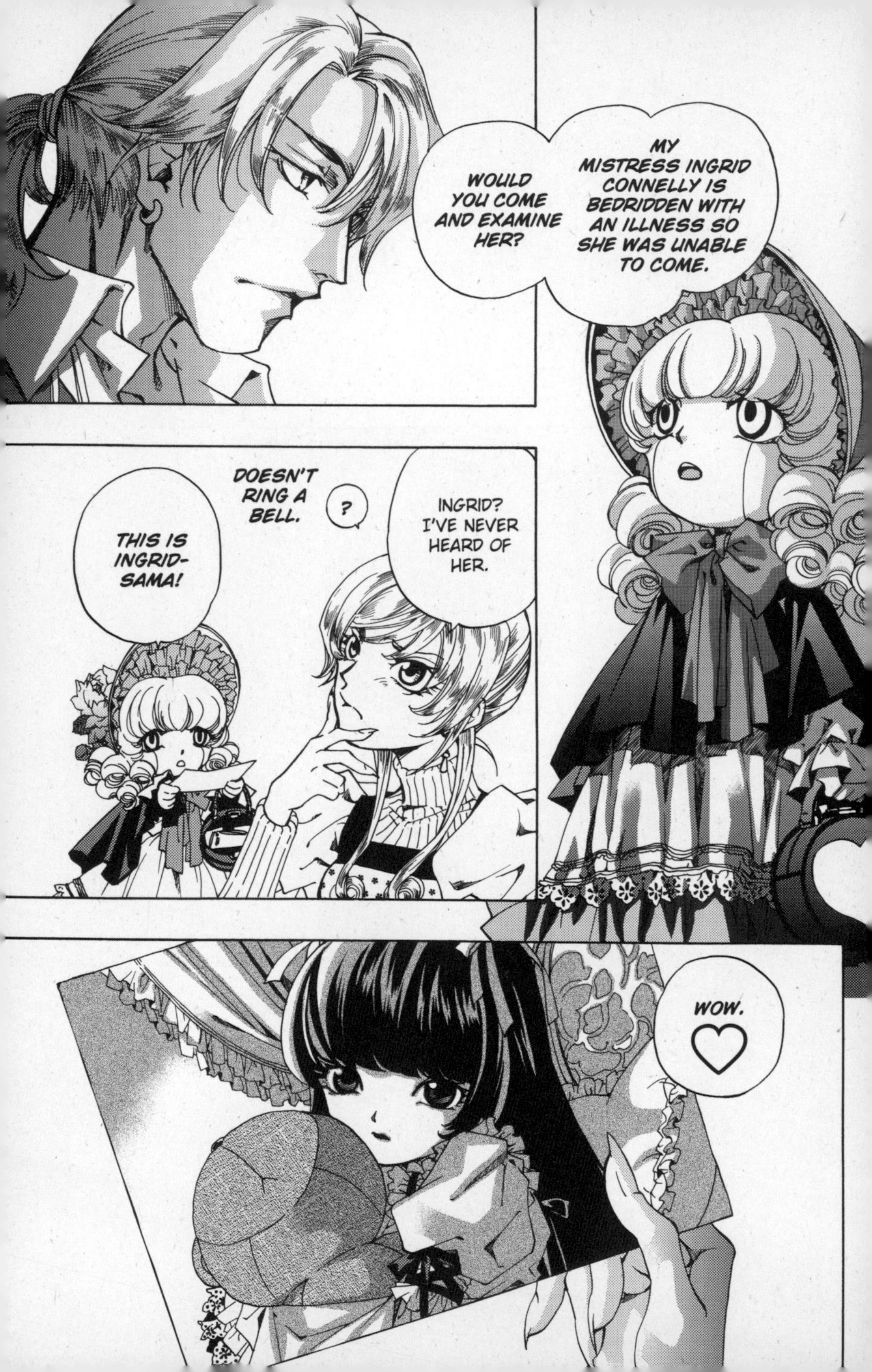
MY MISTRESS INGRID CONNELLY IS BEDRIDDEN WITH AN ILLNESS SO SHE WAS UNABLE TO COME.
WOULD YOU COME AND EXAMINE HER?
INGRID? I'VE NEVER HEARD OF HER.
?
DOESN'T RING A BELL.
THIS IS INGRID-SAMA!
WOW. ♡

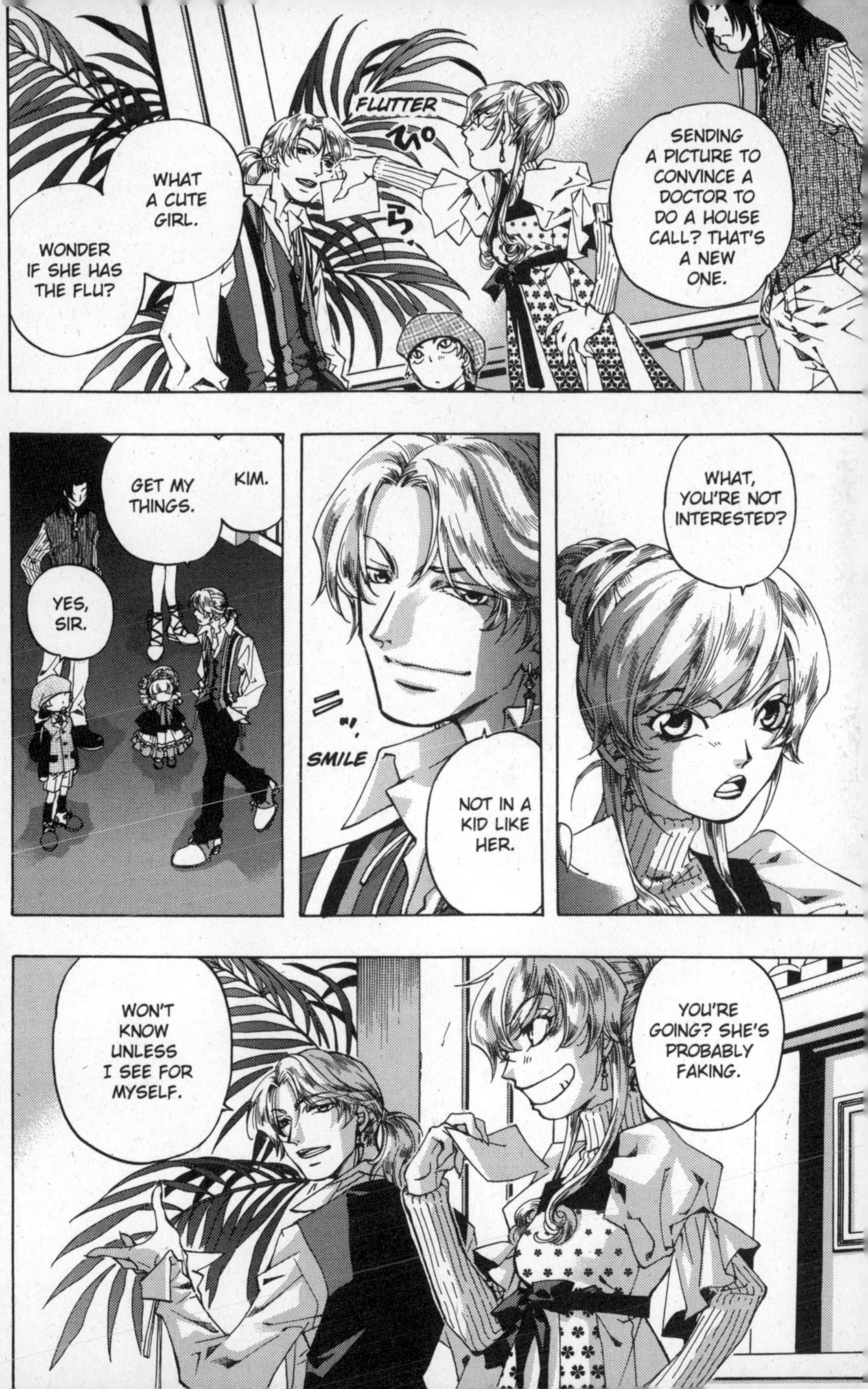
SENDING A PICTURE TO CONVINCE A DOCTOR TO DO A HOUSE CALL? THAT'S A NEW ONE.
FLUTTER
WHAT A CUTE GIRL.
WONDER IF SHE HAS THE FLU?
WHAT, YOU'RE NOT INTERESTED?
SMILE
NOT IN A KID LIKE HER.
KIM.
GET MY THINGS.
YES, SIR.
YOU'RE GOING? SHE'S PROBABLY FAKING.
WON'T KNOW UNLESS I SEE FOR MYSELF.

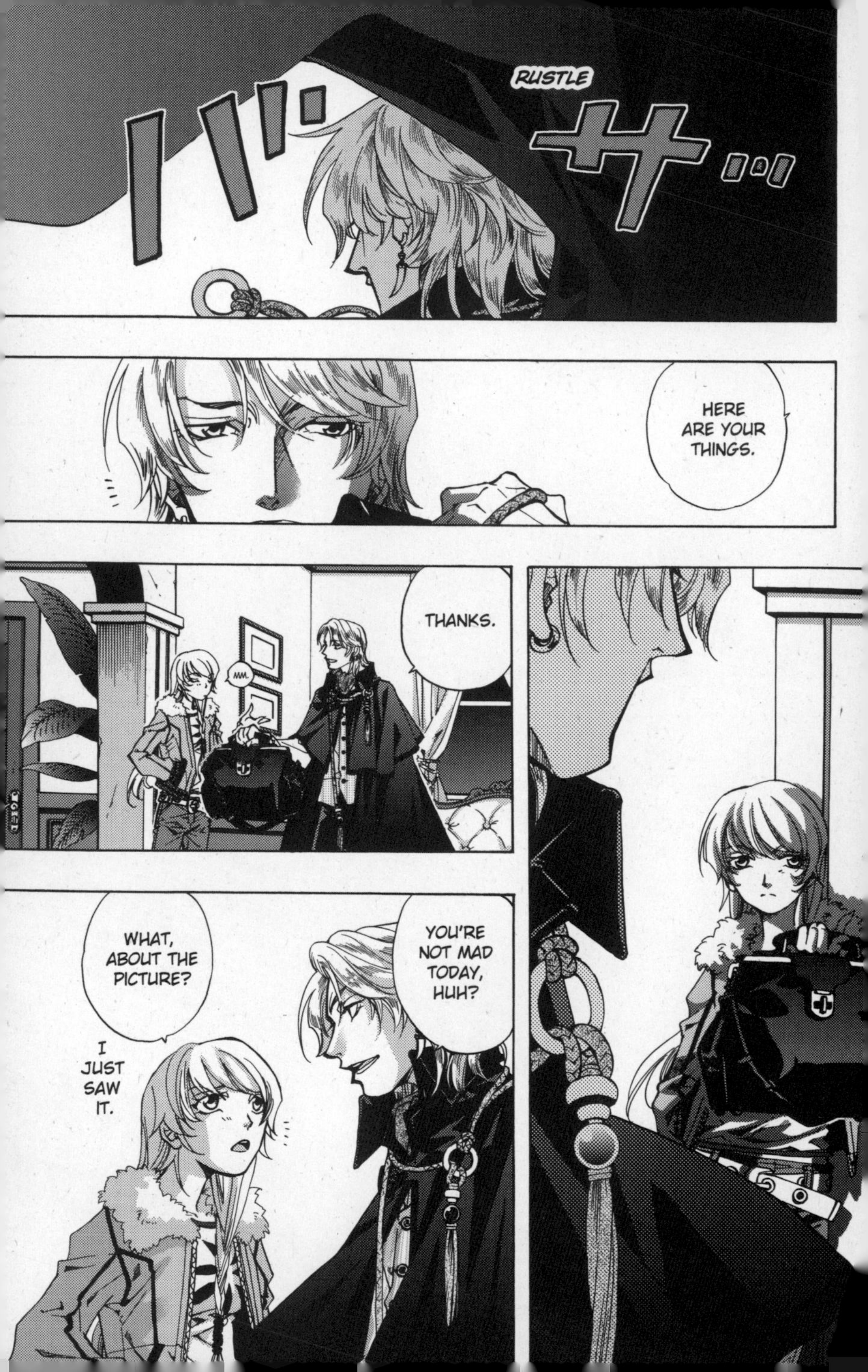
RUSTLE
HERE ARE YOUR THINGS.
THANKS.
MM.
YOU'RE NOT MAD TODAY, HUH?
WHAT, ABOUT THE PICTURE?
I JUST SAW IT.

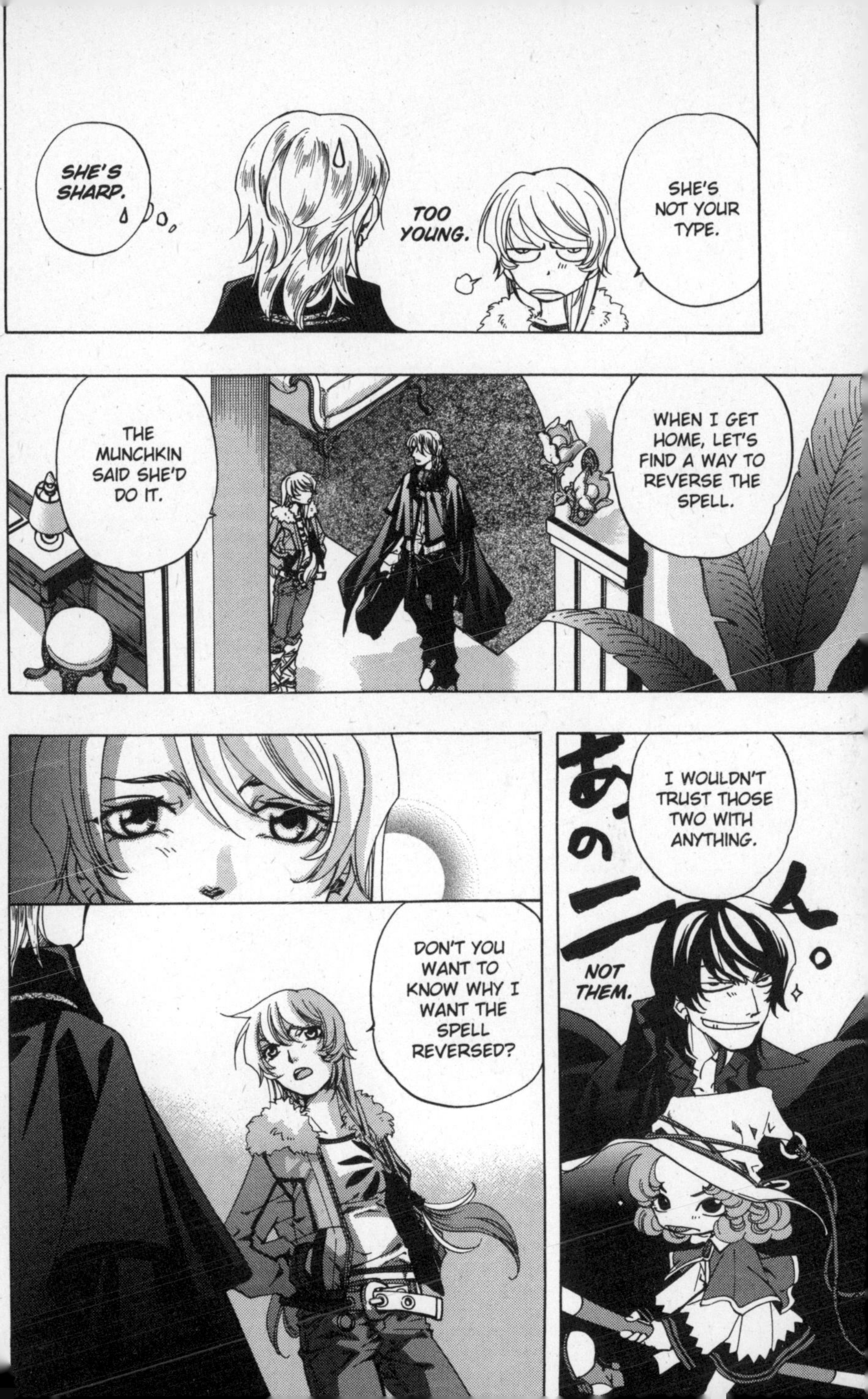
SHE'S NOT YOUR TYPE.
TOO YOUNG.
SHE'S SHARP.
WHEN I GET HOME, LET'S FIND A WAY TO REVERSE THE SPELL.
THE MUNCHKIN SAID SHE'D DO IT.
あの二人。
I WOULDN'T TRUST THOSE TWO WITH ANYTHING.
NOT THEM.
DON'T YOU WANT TO KNOW WHY I WANT THE SPELL REVERSED?

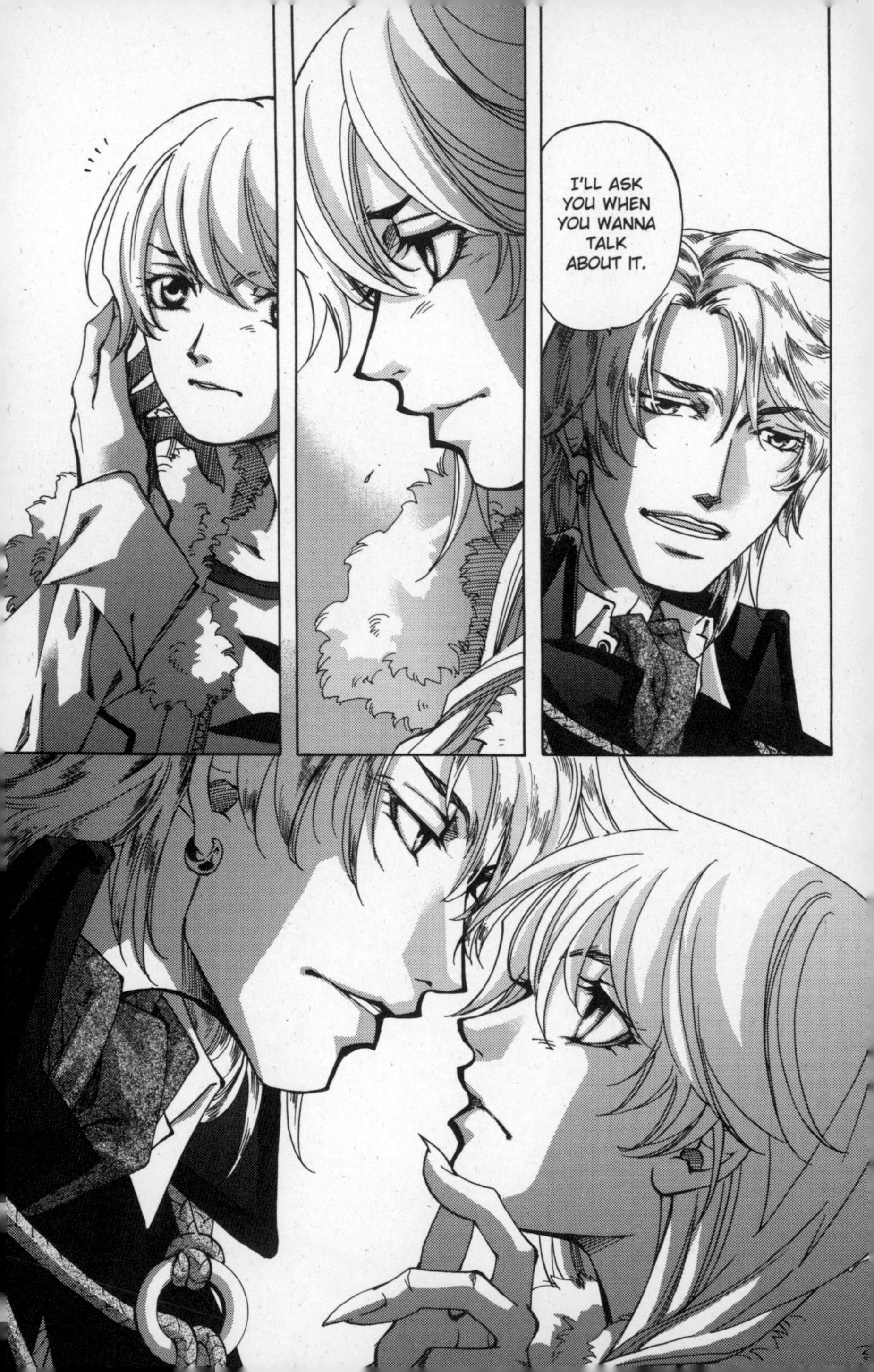
I'LL ASK YOU WHEN YOU WANNA TALK ABOUT IT.

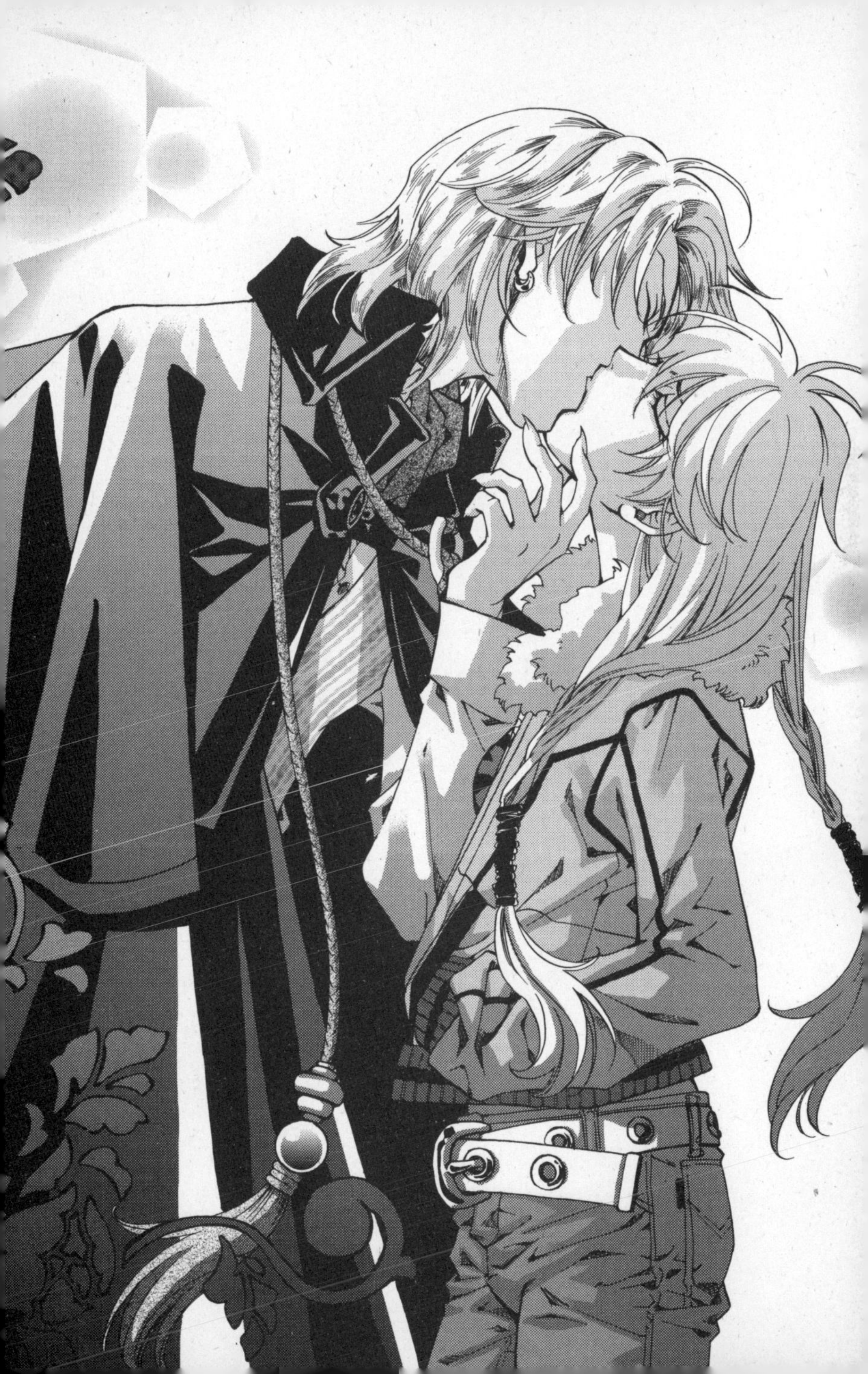

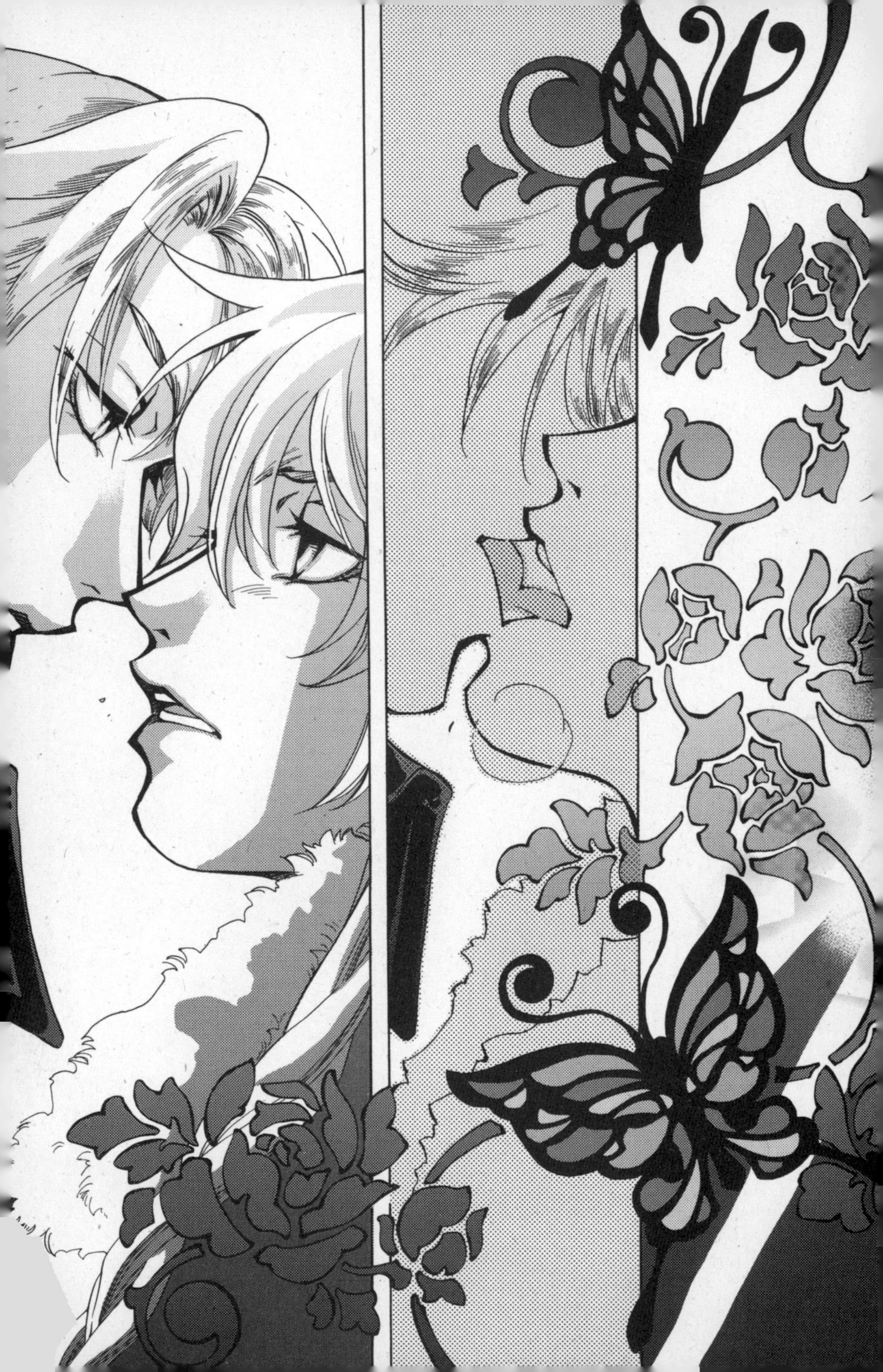

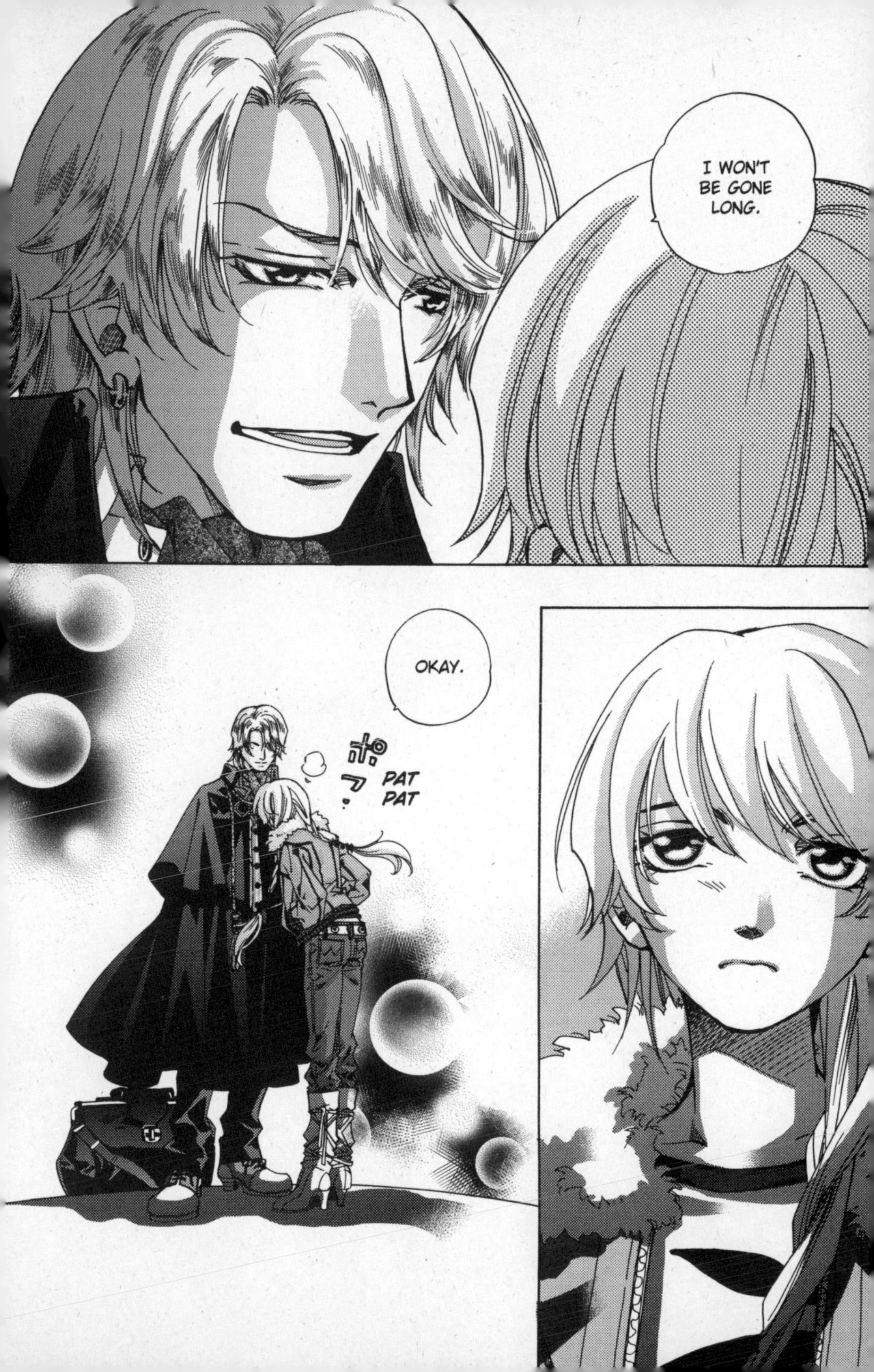
I WON'T BE GONE LONG.
OKAY.
PAT PAT

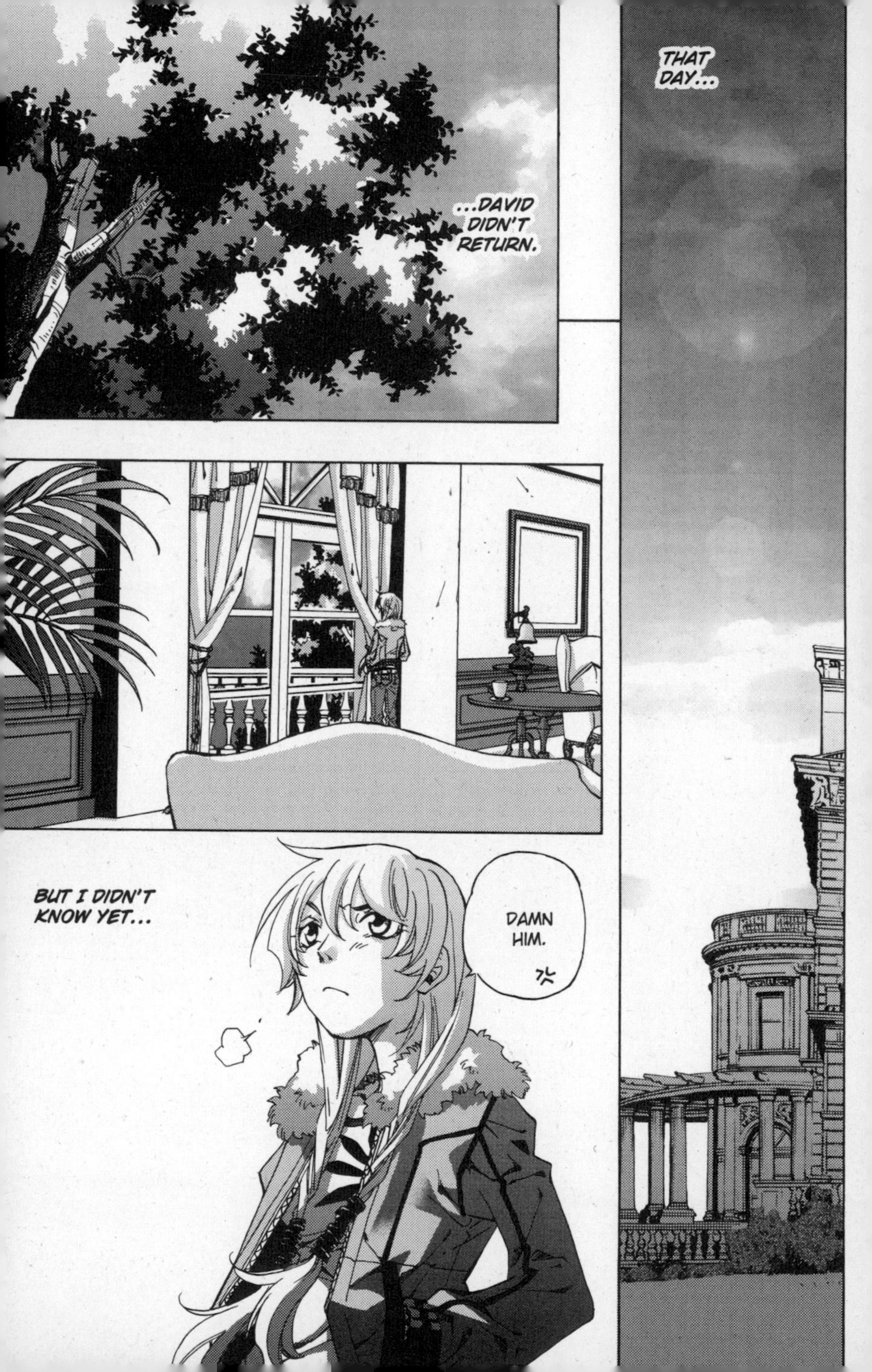
THAT DAY...
...DAVID DIDN'T RETURN.
DAMN HIM.
BUT I DIDN'T KNOW YET...

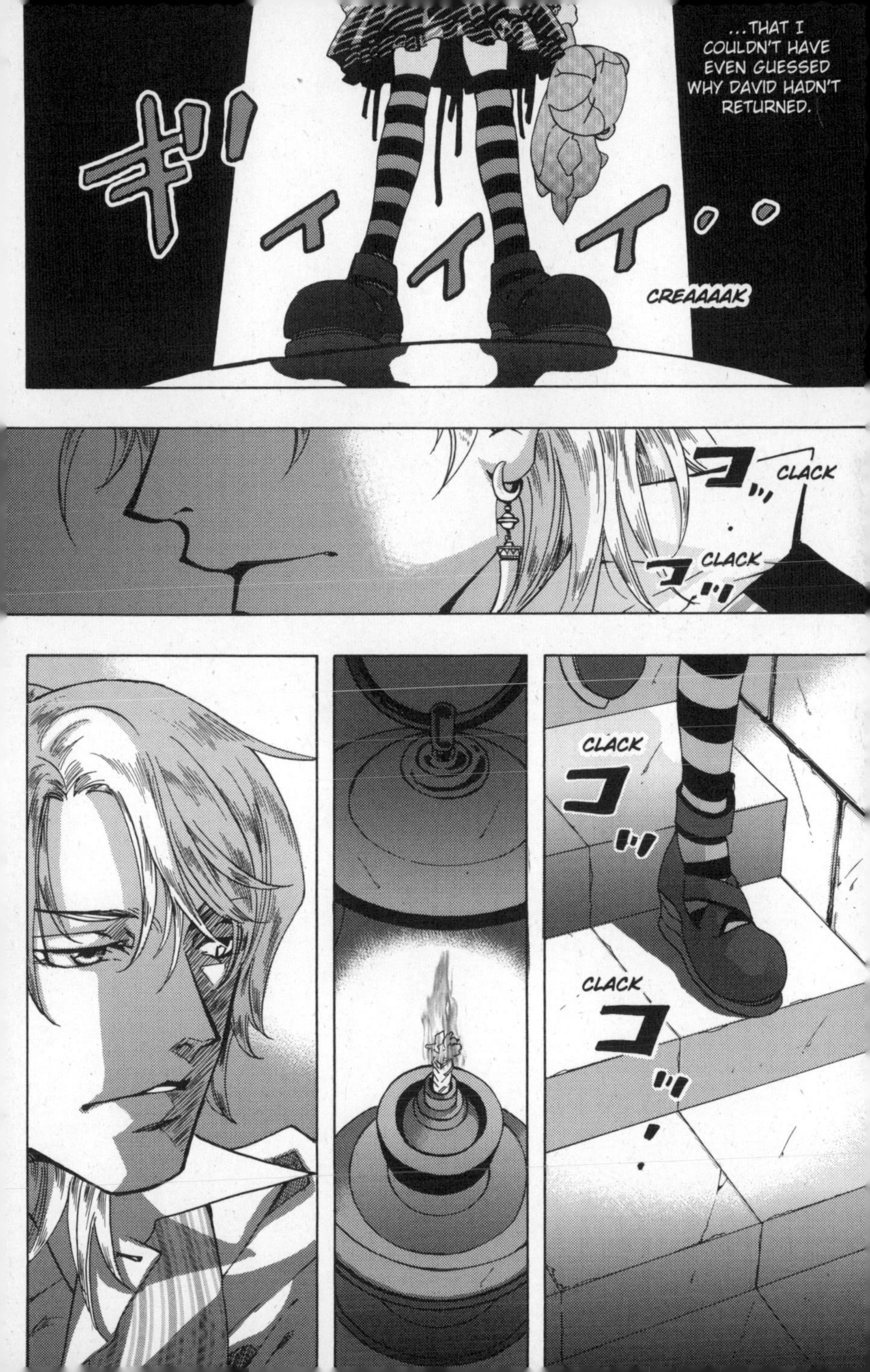
...THAT I COULDN'T HAVE EVEN GUESSED WHY DAVID HADN'T RETURNED.
ギイイ・・
CREAAAAK
コッ
CLACK
コッ
CLACK
CLACK
コッ
CLACK
コッ

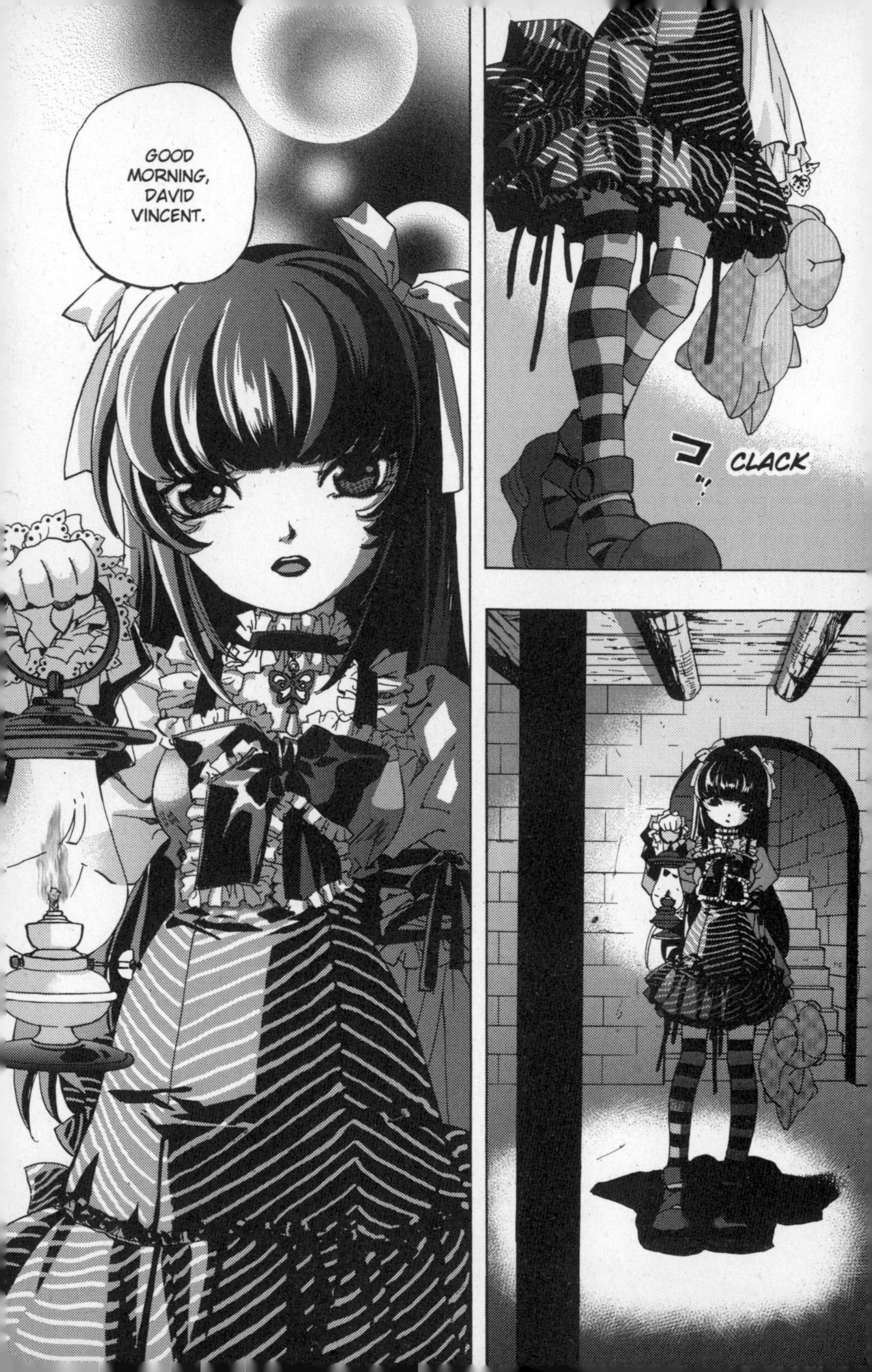
CLACK
GOOD MORNING, DAVID VINCENT.

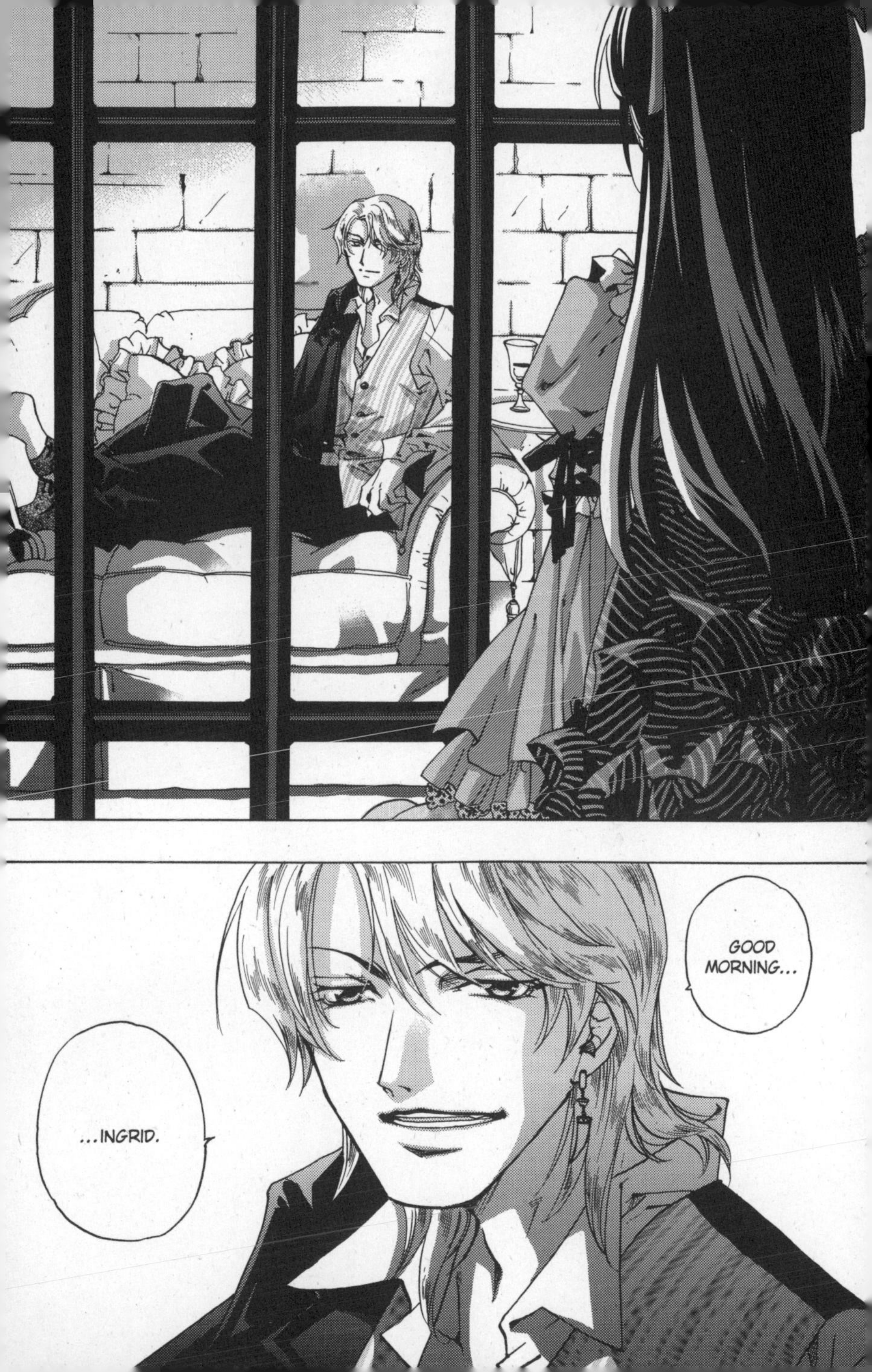
GOOD MORNING...
...INGRID.

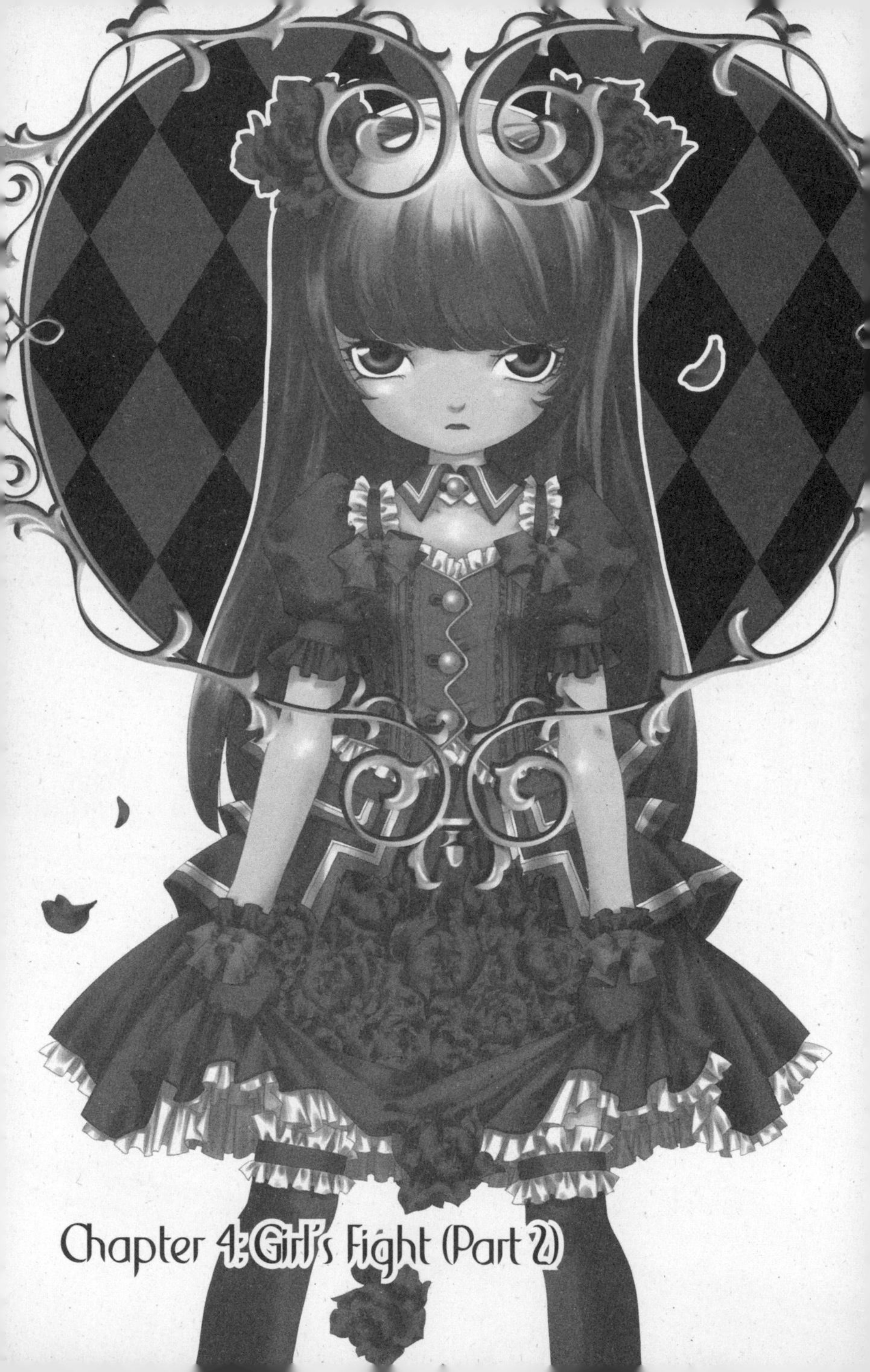

Chapter 4: Girl's Fight (Part 2)

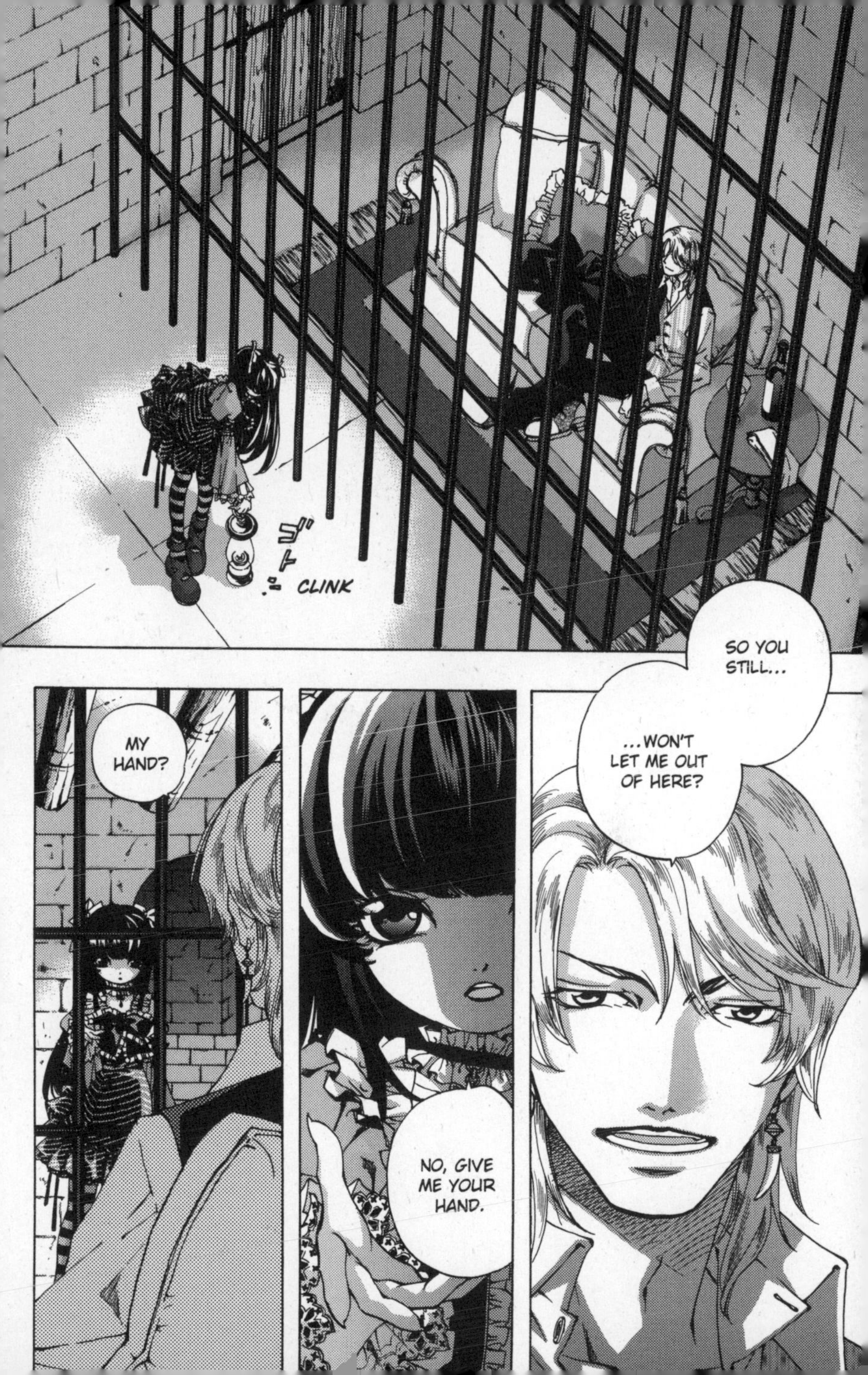
ゴト
CLINK
SO YOU STILL...
...WON'T LET ME OUT OF HERE?
NO, GIVE ME YOUR HAND.
MY HAND?

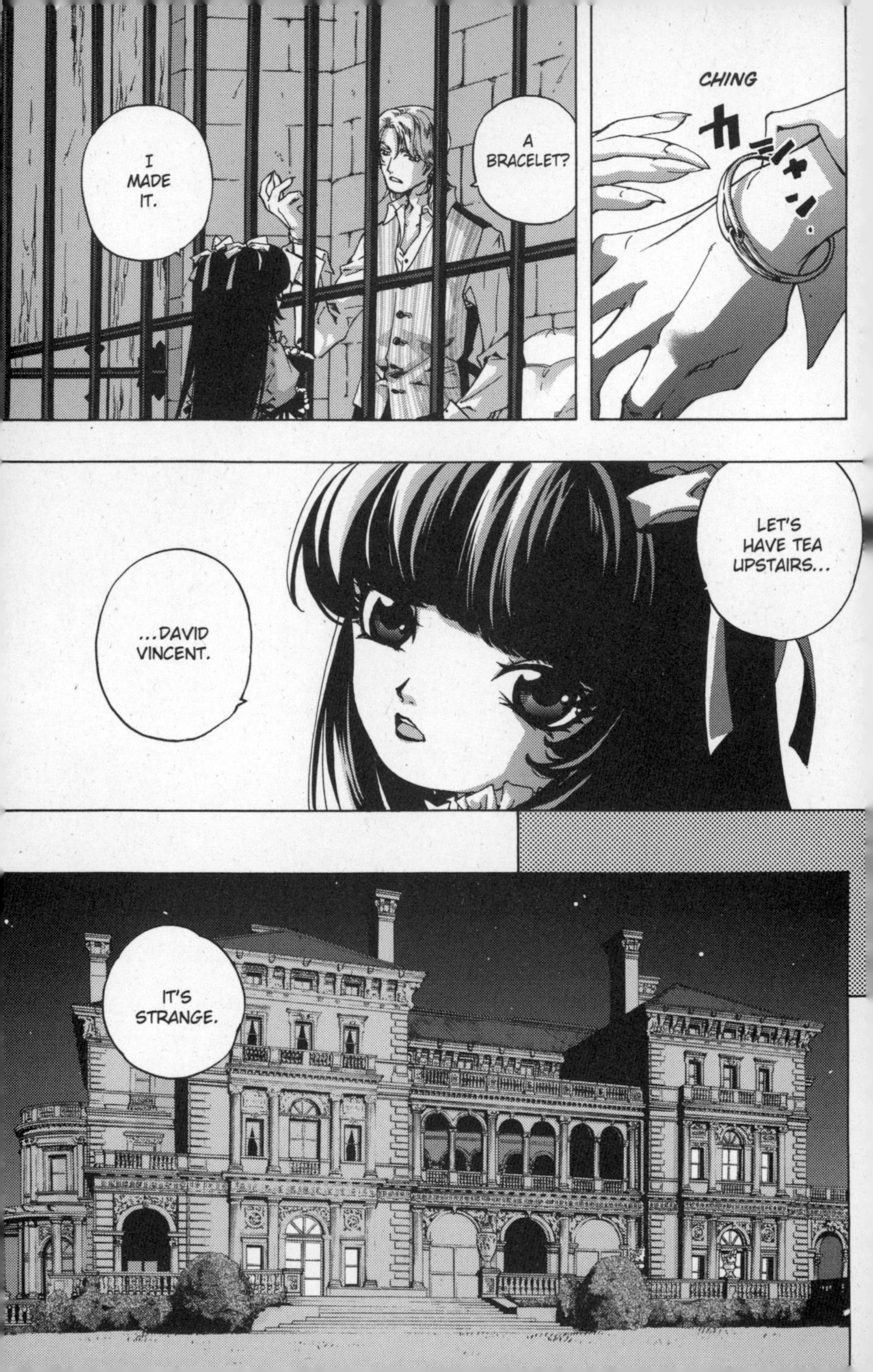
CHING
A BRACELET?
I MADE IT.
LET'S HAVE TEA UPSTAIRS...
...DAVID VINCENT.
IT'S STRANGE.

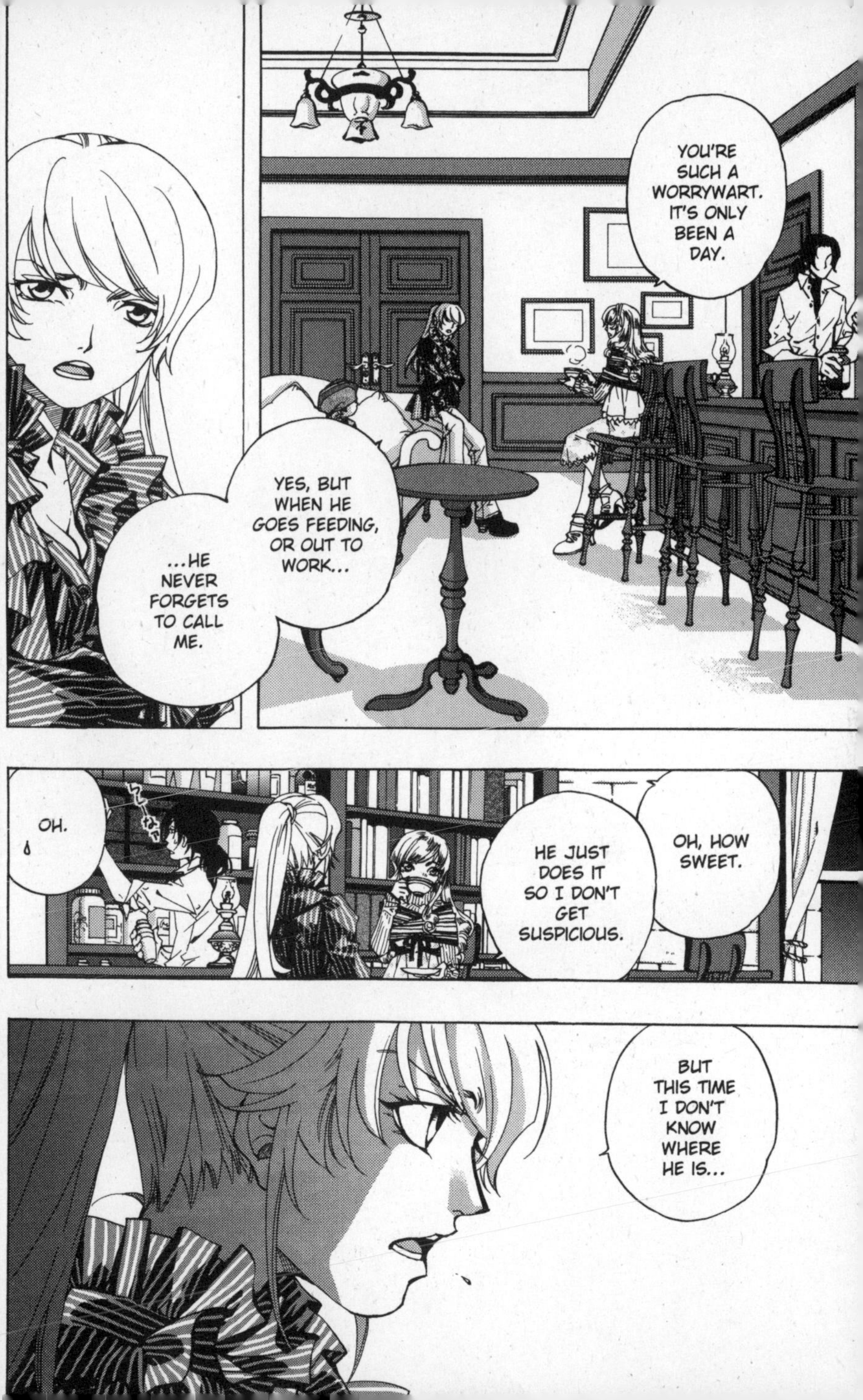
YOU'RE SUCH A WORRYWART. IT'S ONLY BEEN A DAY.
YES, BUT WHEN HE GOES FEEDING, OR OUT TO WORK...
...HE NEVER FORGETS TO CALL ME.
OH, HOW SWEET.
HE JUST DOES IT SO I DON'T GET SUSPICIOUS.
OH.
BUT THIS TIME I DON'T KNOW WHERE HE IS...

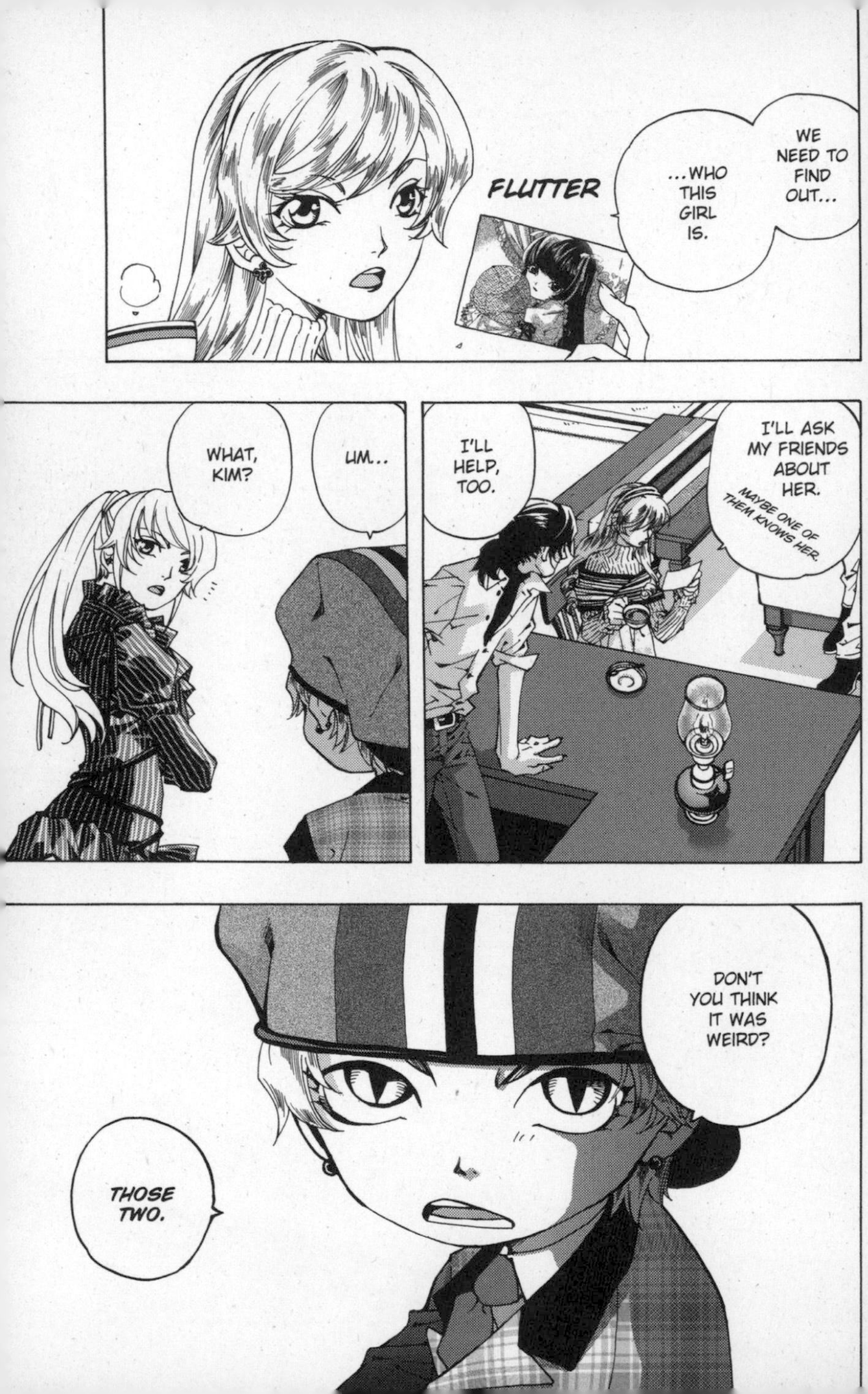
WE NEED TO FIND OUT…
…WHO THIS GIRL IS.
FLUTTER
I'LL ASK MY FRIENDS ABOUT HER.
MAYBE ONE OF THEM KNOWS HER.
I'LL HELP, TOO.
UM…
WHAT, KIM?
DON'T YOU THINK IT WAS WEIRD?
THOSE TWO.

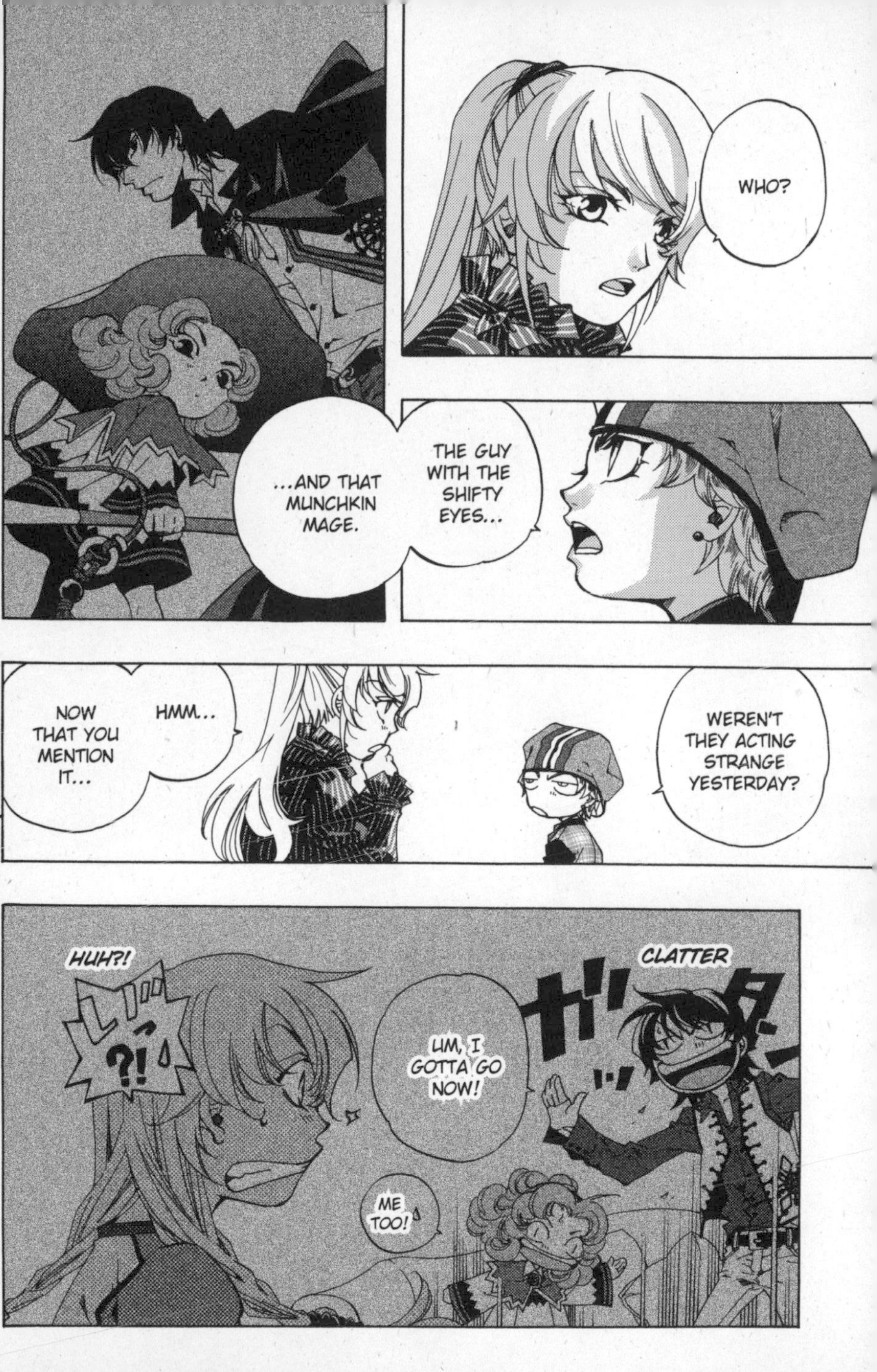
WHO?
THE GUY WITH THE SHIFTY EYES...
...AND THAT MUNCHKIN MAGE.
WEREN'T THEY ACTING STRANGE YESTERDAY?
HMM...
NOW THAT YOU MENTION IT...
CLATTER
UM, I GOTTA GO NOW!
HUH?!
?!
ME TOO!

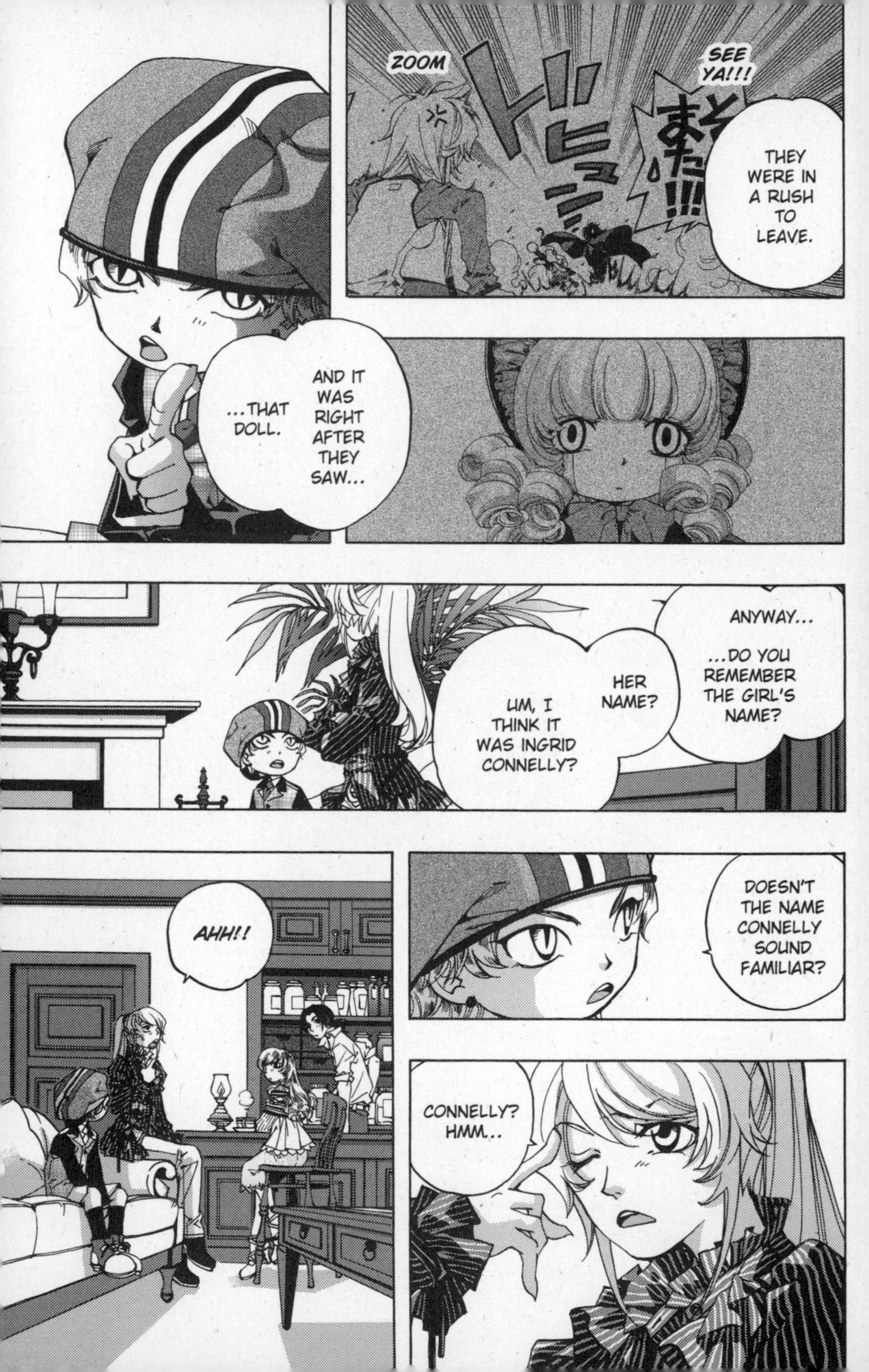
SEE YA!!!
ZOOM
THEY WERE IN A RUSH TO LEAVE.
AND IT WAS RIGHT AFTER THEY SAW...
...THAT DOLL.
ANYWAY...
...DO YOU REMEMBER THE GIRL'S NAME?
HER NAME?
UM, I THINK IT WAS INGRID CONNELLY?
DOESN'T THE NAME CONNELLY SOUND FAMILIAR?
CONNELLY? HMM...
AHH!!

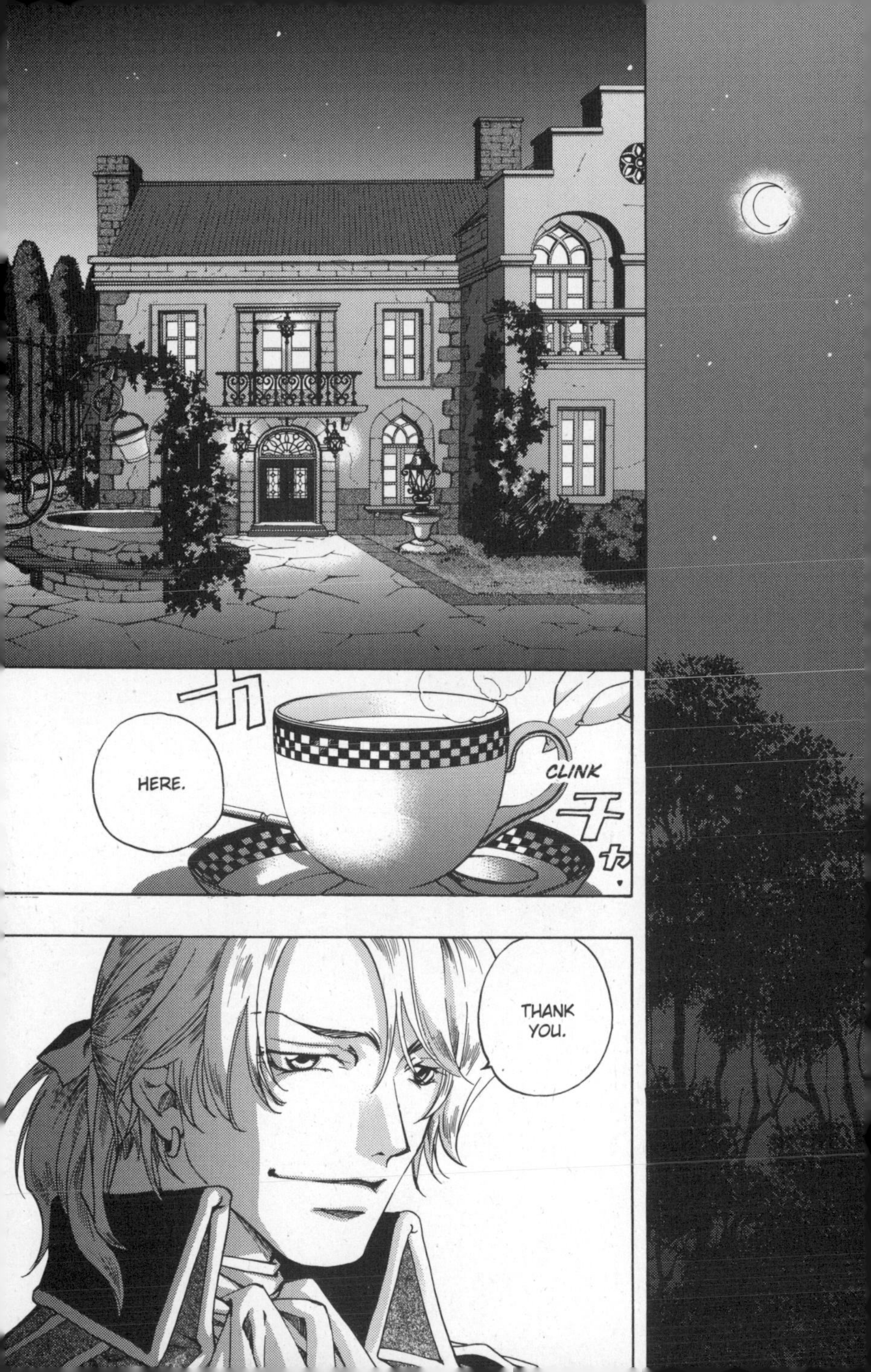
チャ
CLINK
HERE.
カ
THANK YOU.

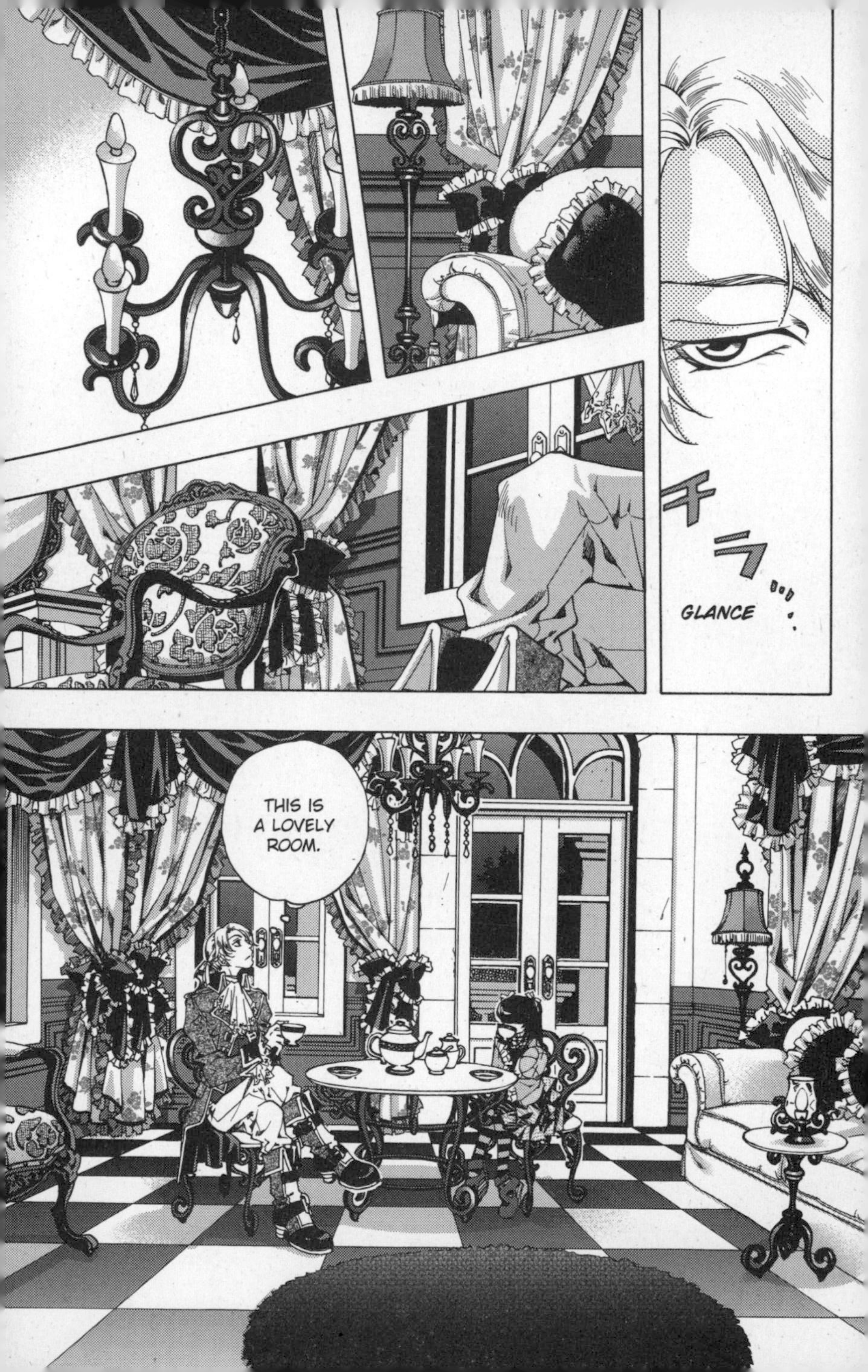
チラ
GLANCE
THIS IS A LOVELY ROOM.

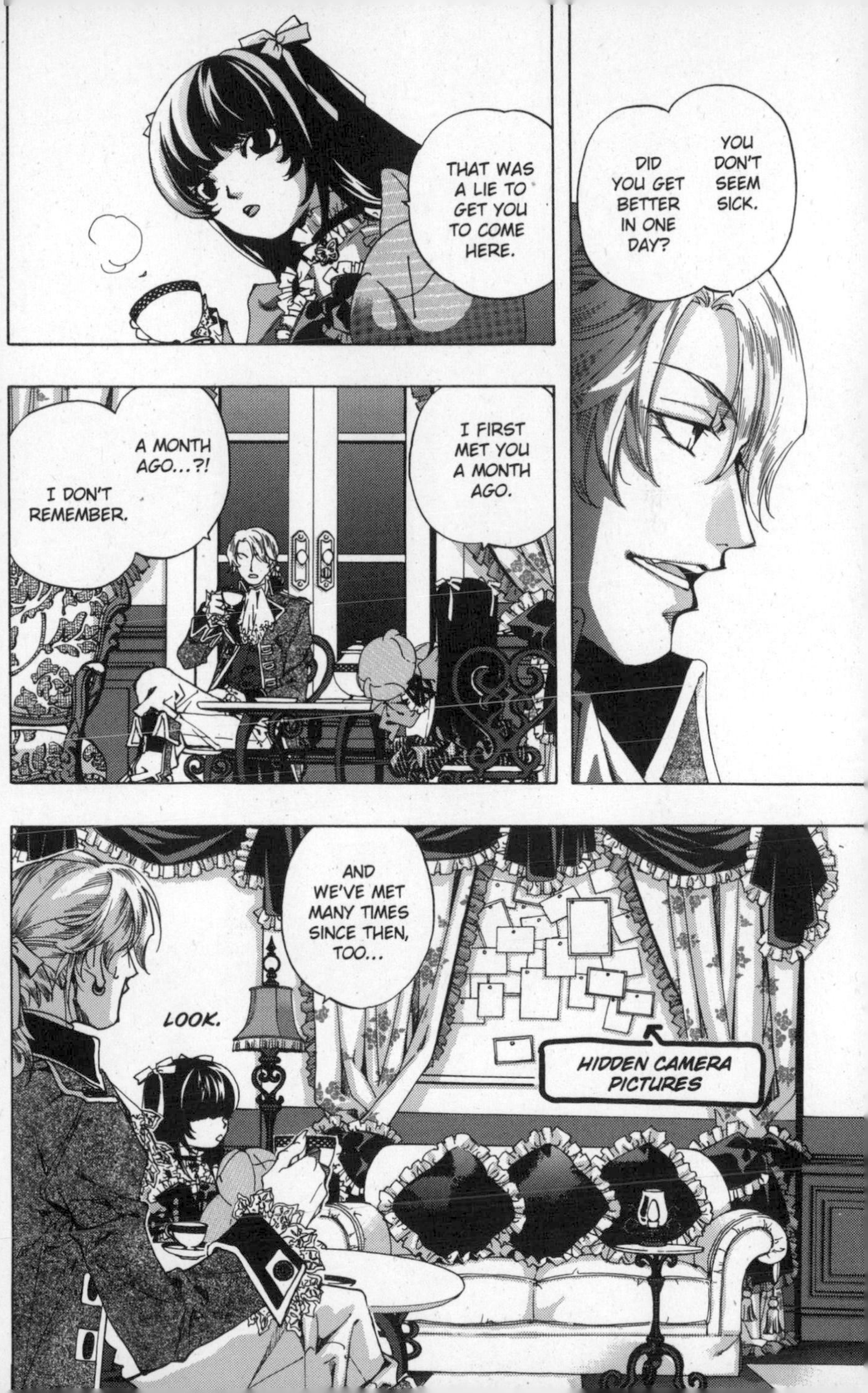
YOU DON'T SEEM SICK.
DID YOU GET BETTER IN ONE DAY?
THAT WAS A LIE TO GET YOU TO COME HERE.
I FIRST MET YOU A MONTH AGO.
A MONTH AGO...?!
I DON'T REMEMBER.
AND WE'VE MET MANY TIMES SINCE THEN, TOO...
LOOK.
HIDDEN CAMERA PICTURES

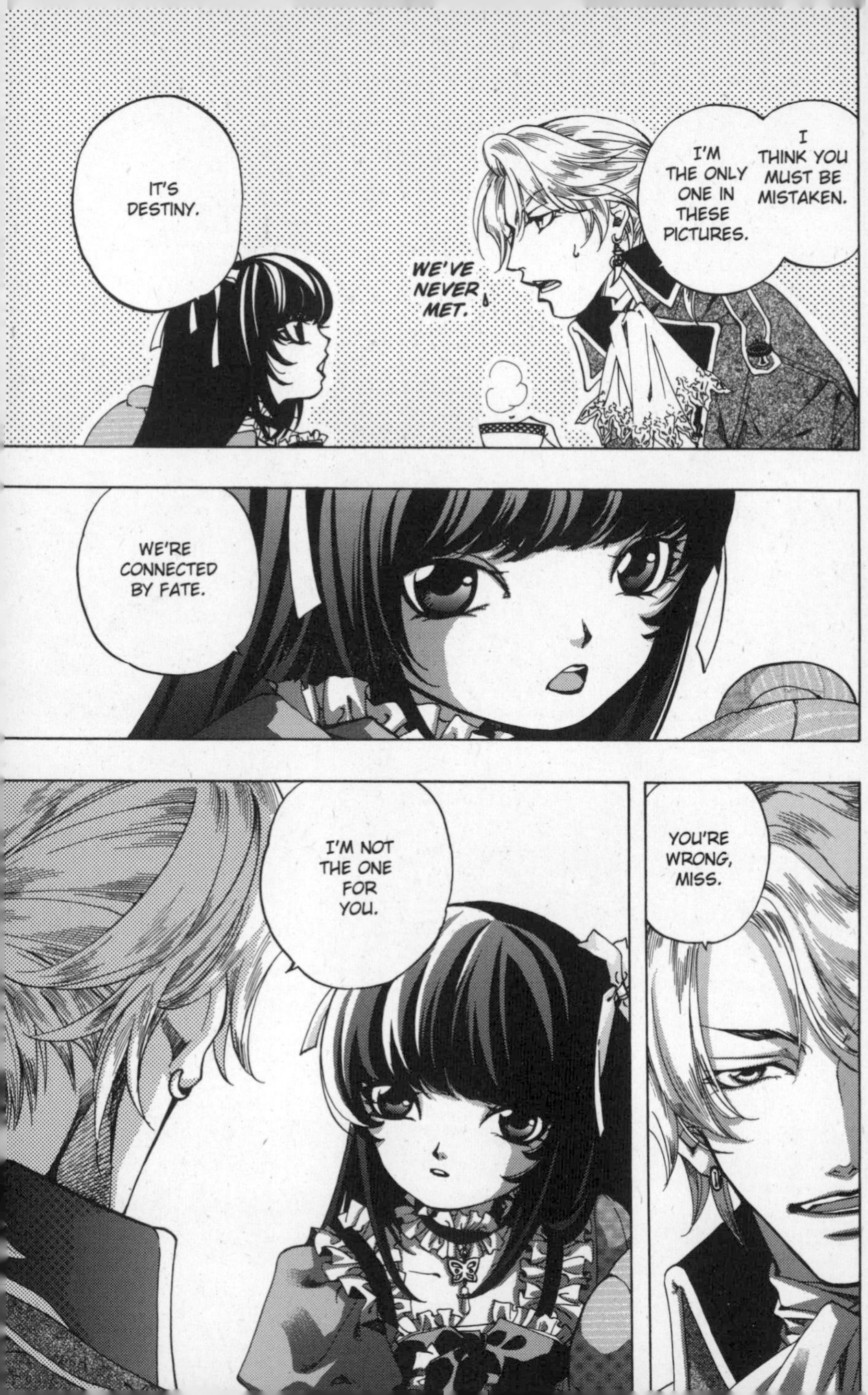
I THINK YOU MUST BE MISTAKEN.
I'M THE ONLY ONE IN THESE PICTURES.
WE'VE NEVER MET.
IT'S DESTINY.
WE'RE CONNECTED BY FATE.
YOU'RE WRONG, MISS.
I'M NOT THE ONE FOR YOU.

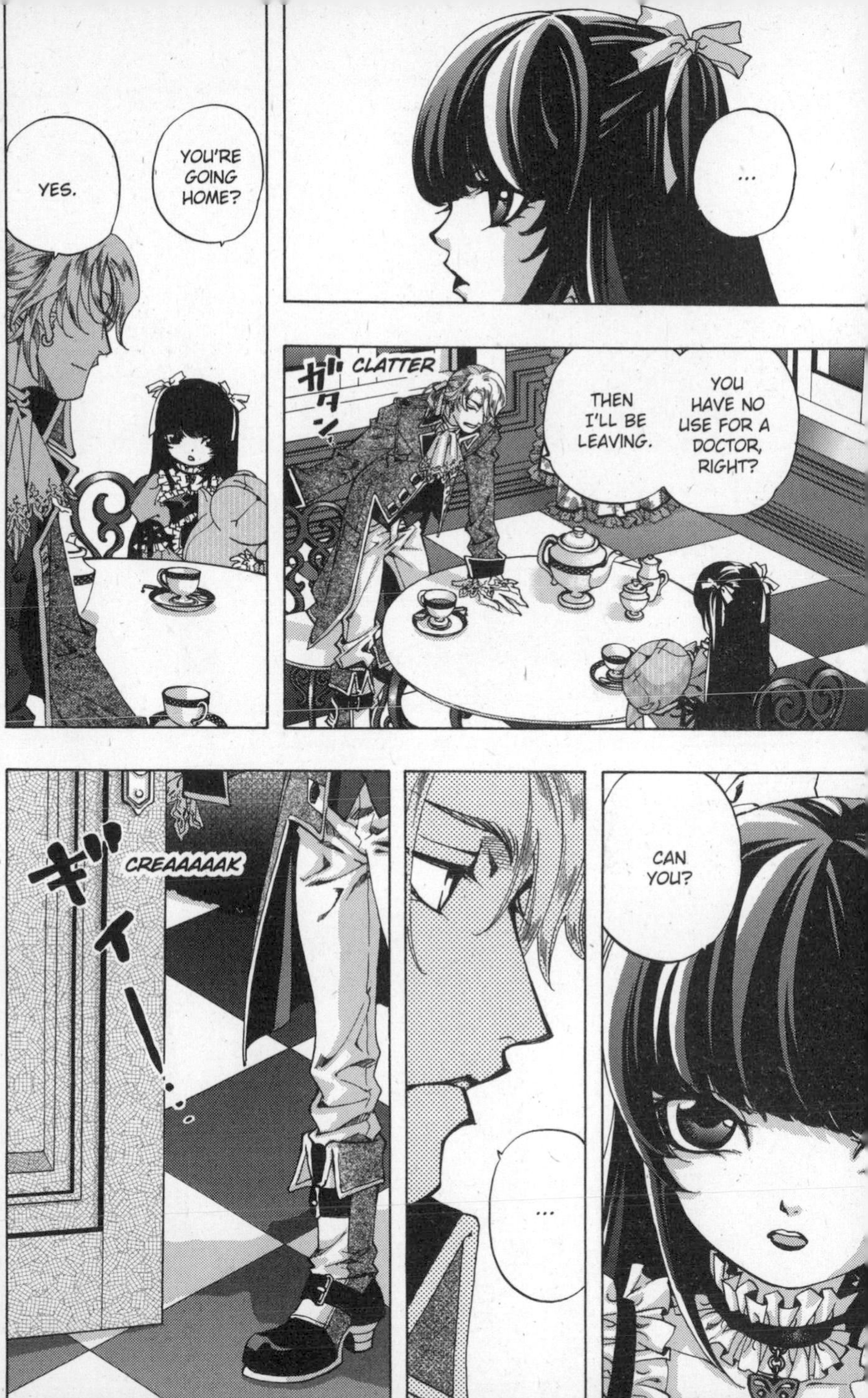
...
YOU HAVE NO USE FOR A DOCTOR, RIGHT?
THEN I'LL BE LEAVING.
ガタン
CLATTER
YOU'RE GOING HOME?
YES.
CAN YOU?
...
ギィー
CREAAAAAK

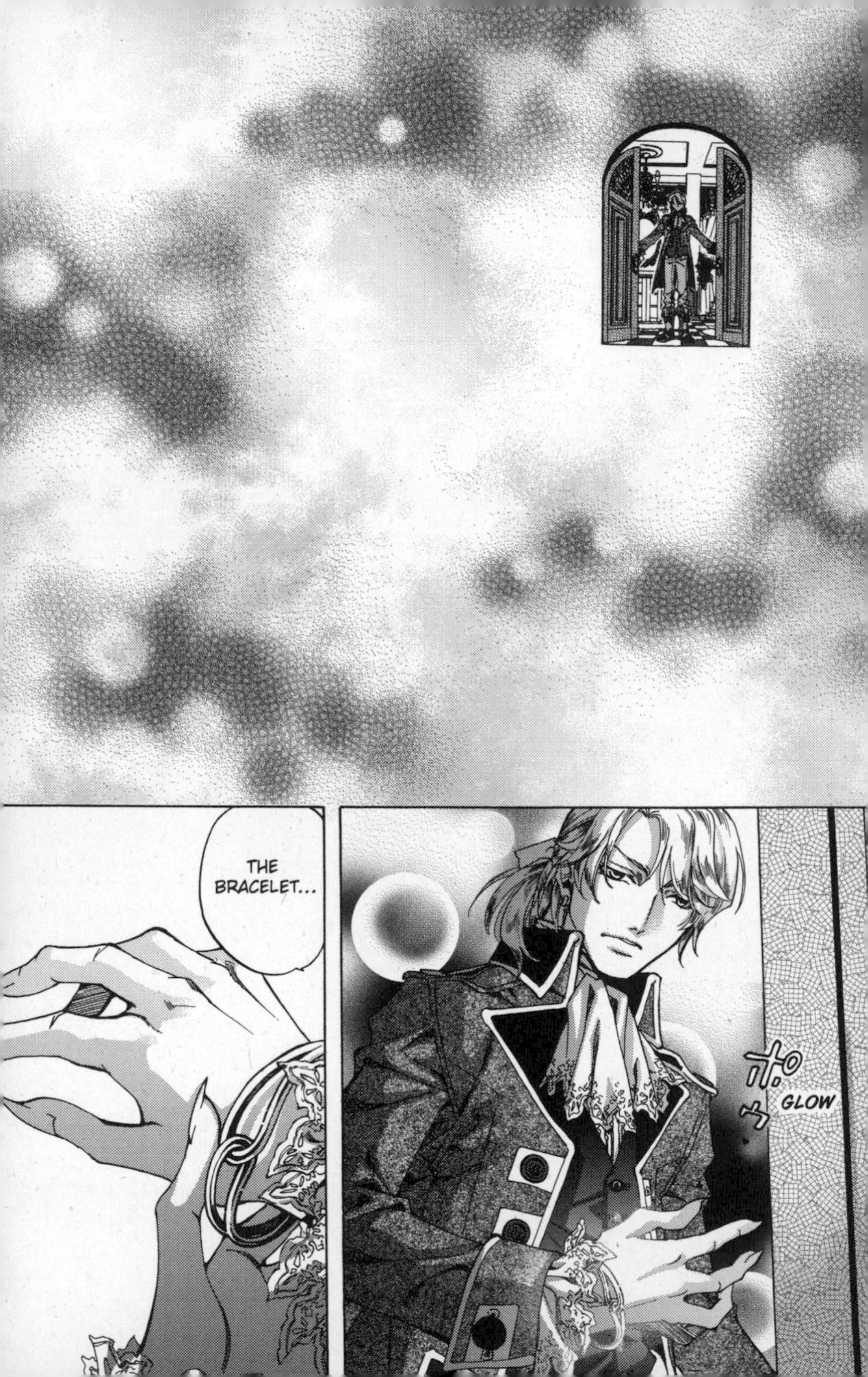
ポッ
GLOW
THE BRACELET...

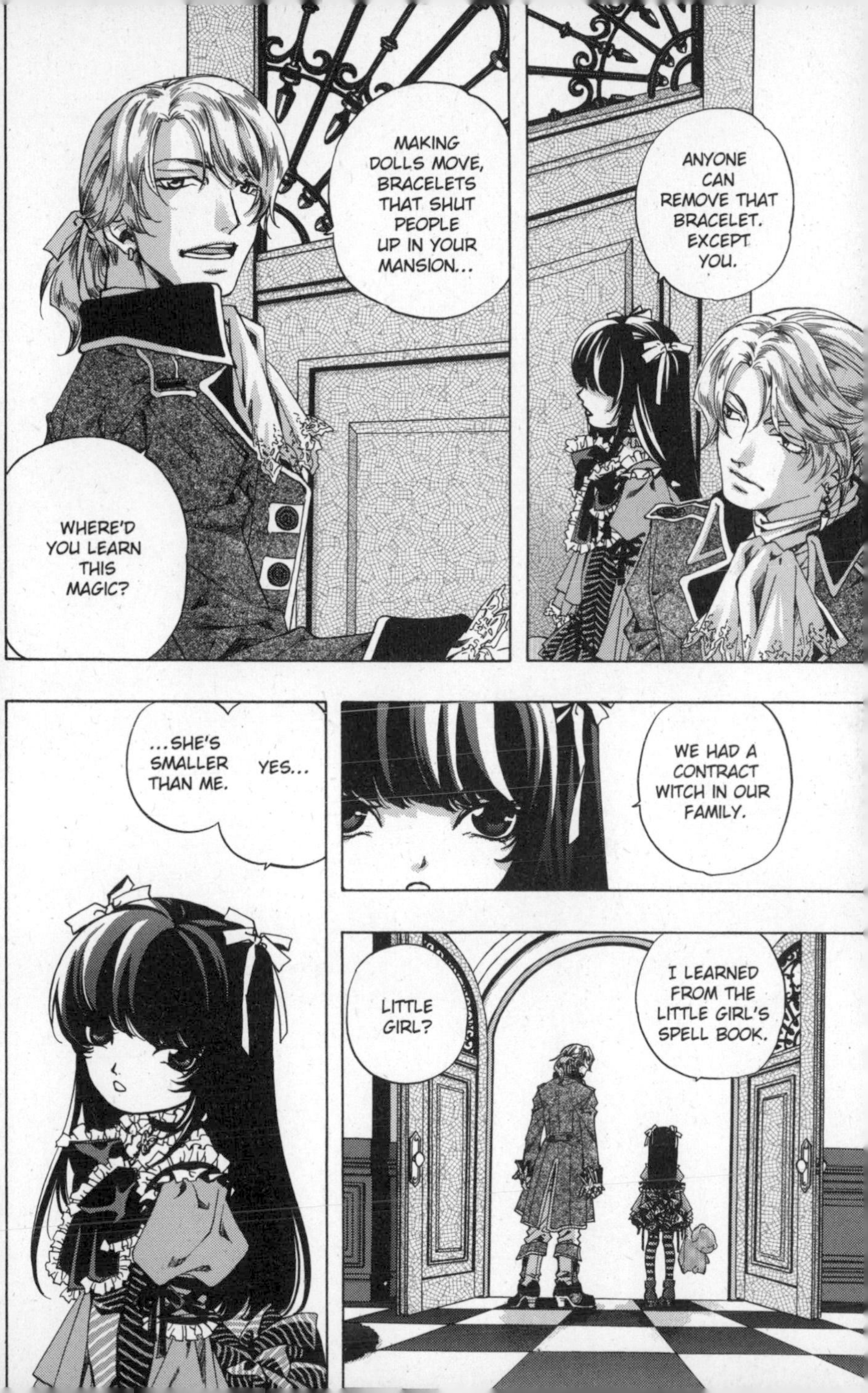
ANYONE CAN REMOVE THAT BRACELET. EXCEPT YOU.
MAKING DOLLS MOVE, BRACELETS THAT SHUT PEOPLE UP IN YOUR MANSION...
WHERE'D YOU LEARN THIS MAGIC?
WE HAD A CONTRACT WITCH IN OUR FAMILY.
I LEARNED FROM THE LITTLE GIRL'S SPELL BOOK.
LITTLE GIRL?
YES...
...SHE'S SMALLER THAN ME.

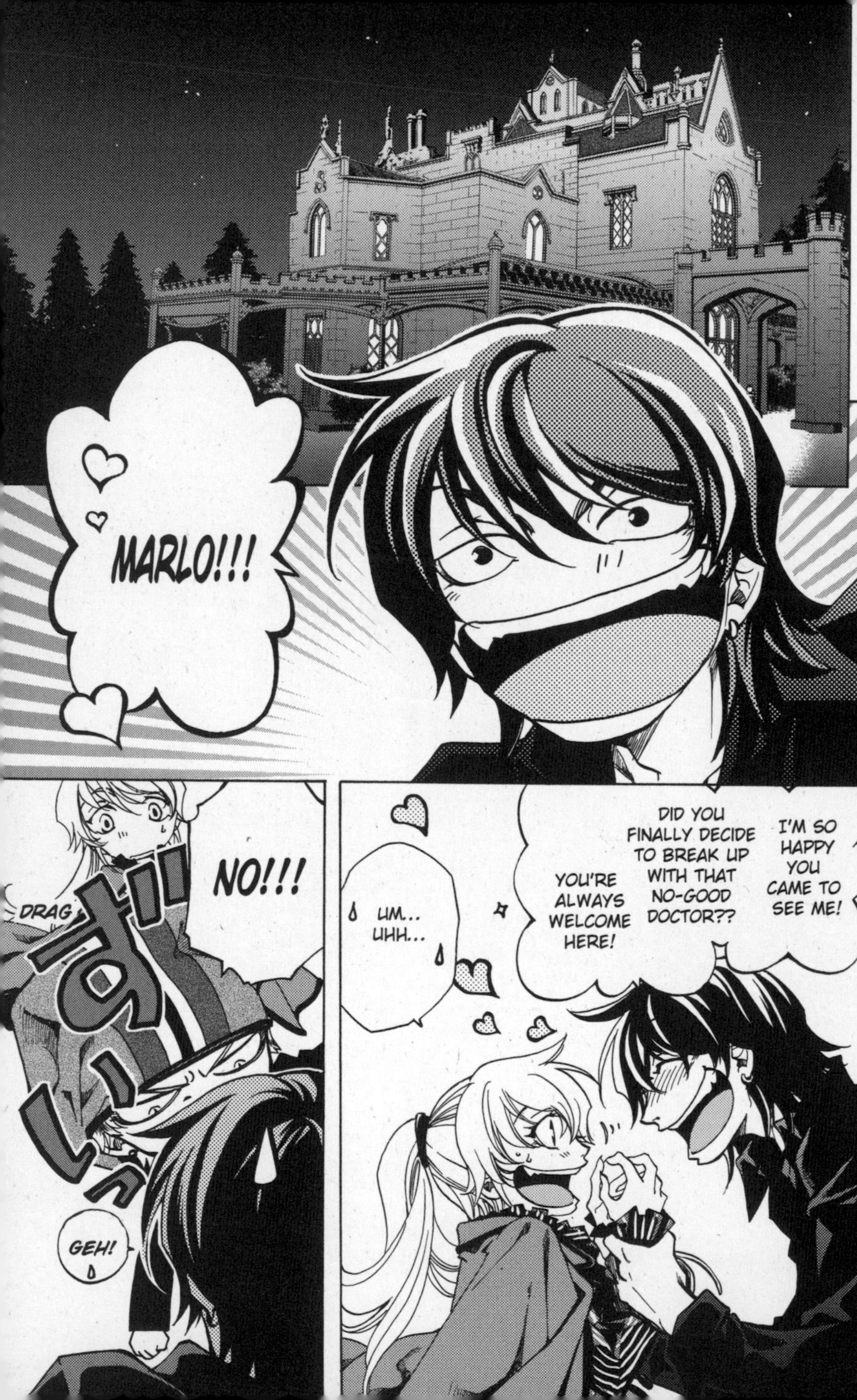
MARLO!!!
I'M SO HAPPY YOU CAME TO SEE ME!
DID YOU FINALLY DECIDE TO BREAK UP WITH THAT NO-GOOD DOCTOR??
YOU'RE ALWAYS WELCOME HERE!
UM... UHH...
NO!!!
DRAG
GEH!

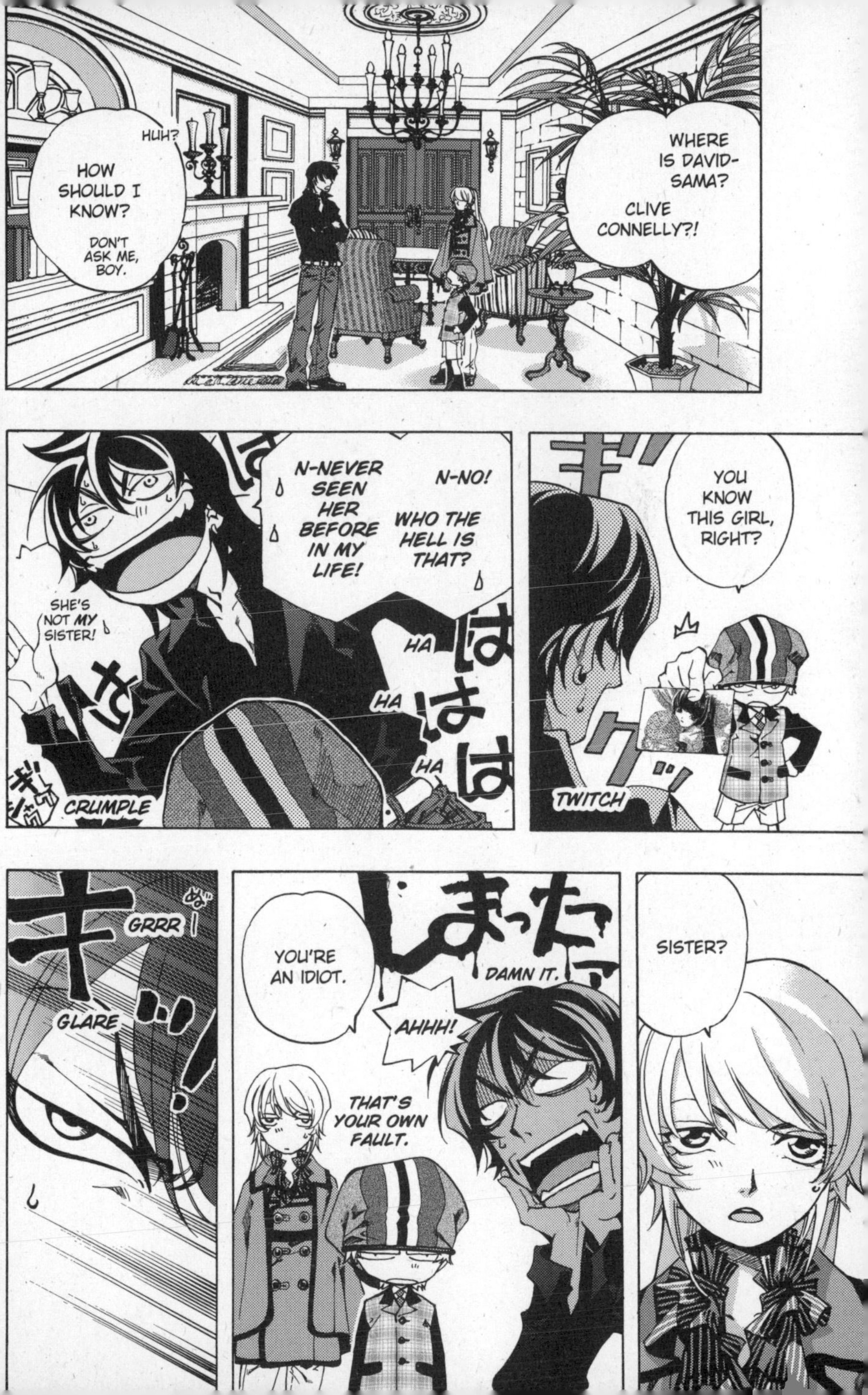
WHERE IS DAVID-SAMA?
CLIVE CONNELLY?!
HUH?
HOW SHOULD I KNOW?
DON'T ASK ME, BOY.
YOU KNOW THIS GIRL, RIGHT?
TWITCH
N-NO!
WHO THE HELL IS THAT?
N-NEVER SEEN HER BEFORE IN MY LIFE!
HA
HA
HA
SHE'S NOT MY SISTER!
CRUMPLE
SISTER?
DAMN IT.
AHHH!
YOU'RE AN IDIOT.
THAT'S YOUR OWN FAULT.
GRRR
GLARE

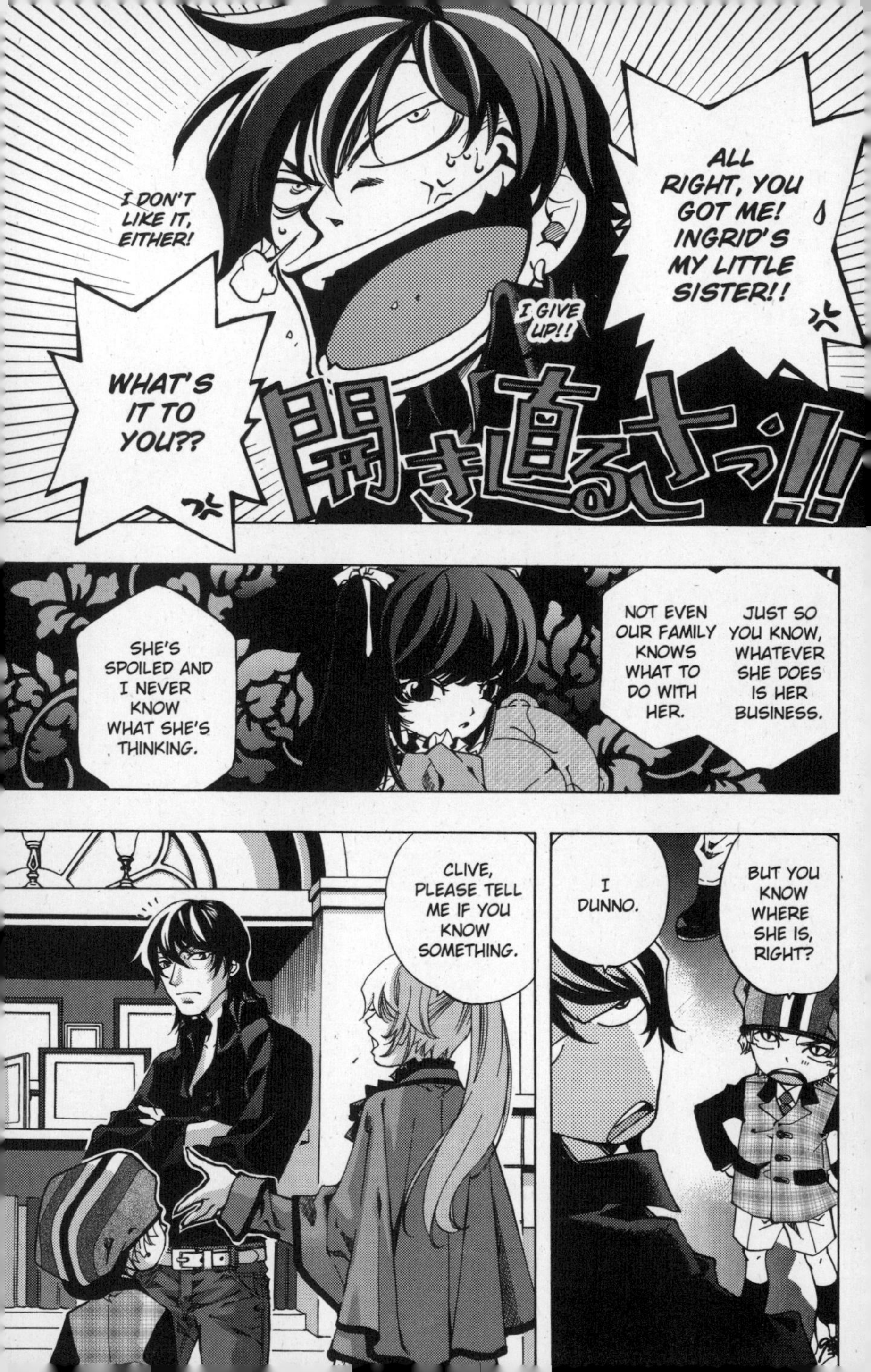
ALL RIGHT, YOU GOT ME! INGRID'S MY LITTLE SISTER!!
I GIVE UP!!
I DON'T LIKE IT, EITHER!
WHAT'S IT TO YOU??
開き直るさっ!!
JUST SO YOU KNOW, WHATEVER SHE DOES IS HER BUSINESS.
NOT EVEN OUR FAMILY KNOWS WHAT TO DO WITH HER.
SHE'S SPOILED AND I NEVER KNOW WHAT SHE'S THINKING.
BUT YOU KNOW WHERE SHE IS, RIGHT?
I DUNNO.
CLIVE, PLEASE TELL ME IF YOU KNOW SOMETHING.

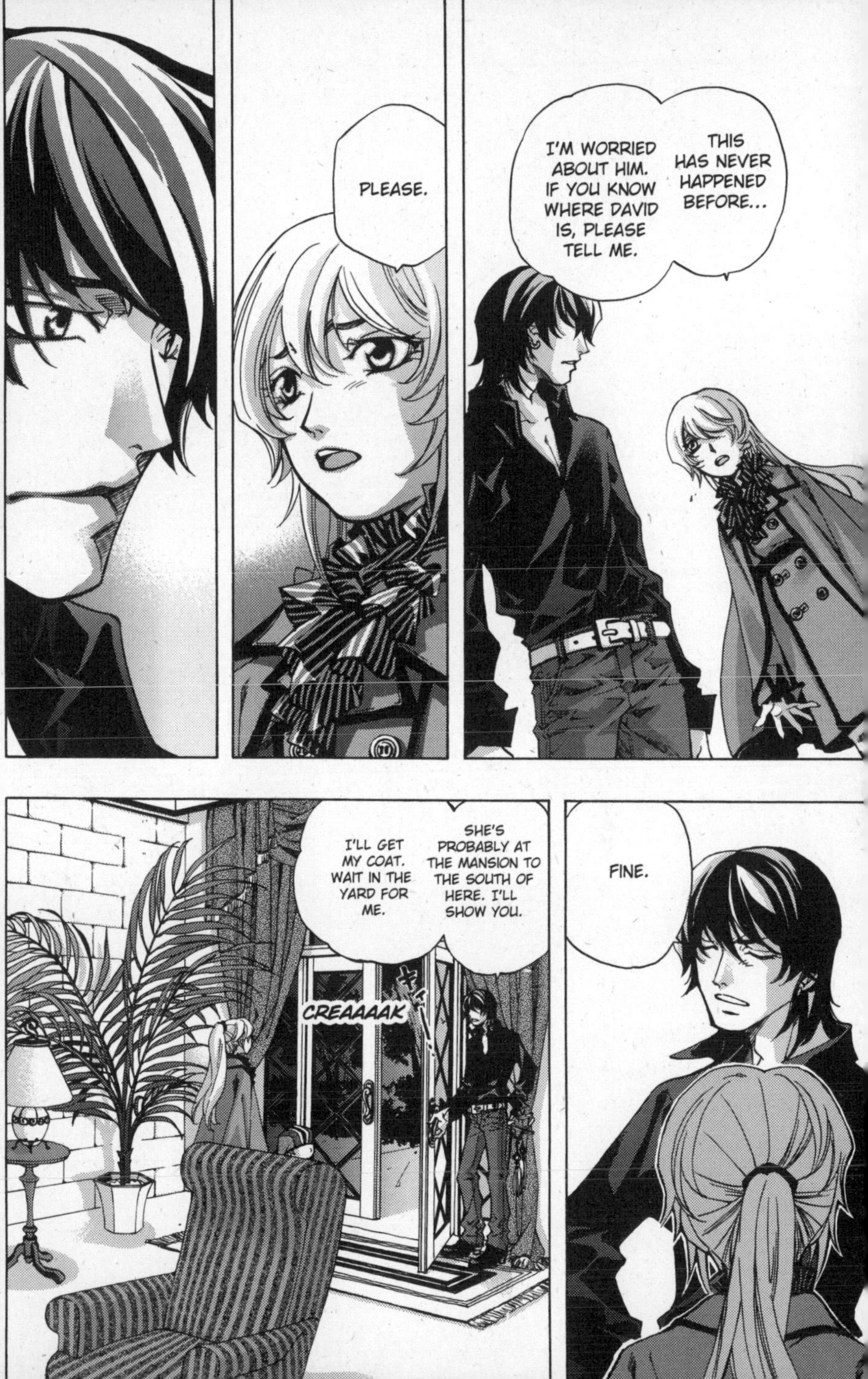
THIS HAS NEVER HAPPENED BEFORE...
I'M WORRIED ABOUT HIM. IF YOU KNOW WHERE DAVID IS, PLEASE TELL ME.
PLEASE.
FINE.
SHE'S PROBABLY AT THE MANSION TO THE SOUTH OF HERE. I'LL SHOW YOU.
I'LL GET MY COAT. WAIT IN THE YARD FOR ME.
CREAAAAK

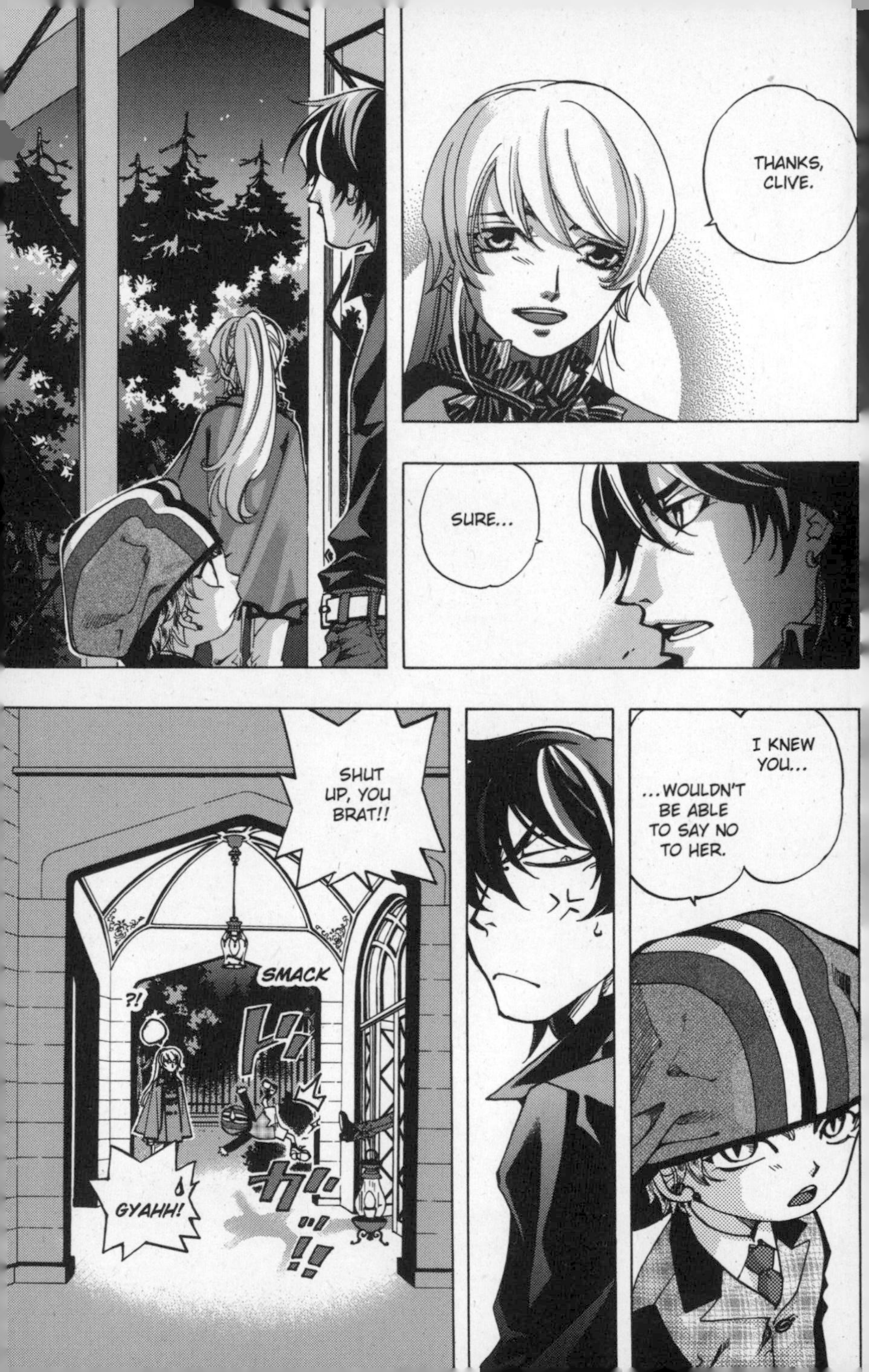
THANKS, CLIVE.
SURE...
I KNEW YOU...
...WOULDN'T BE ABLE TO SAY NO TO HER.
SHUT UP, YOU BRAT!!
SMACK
?!
GYAHH!

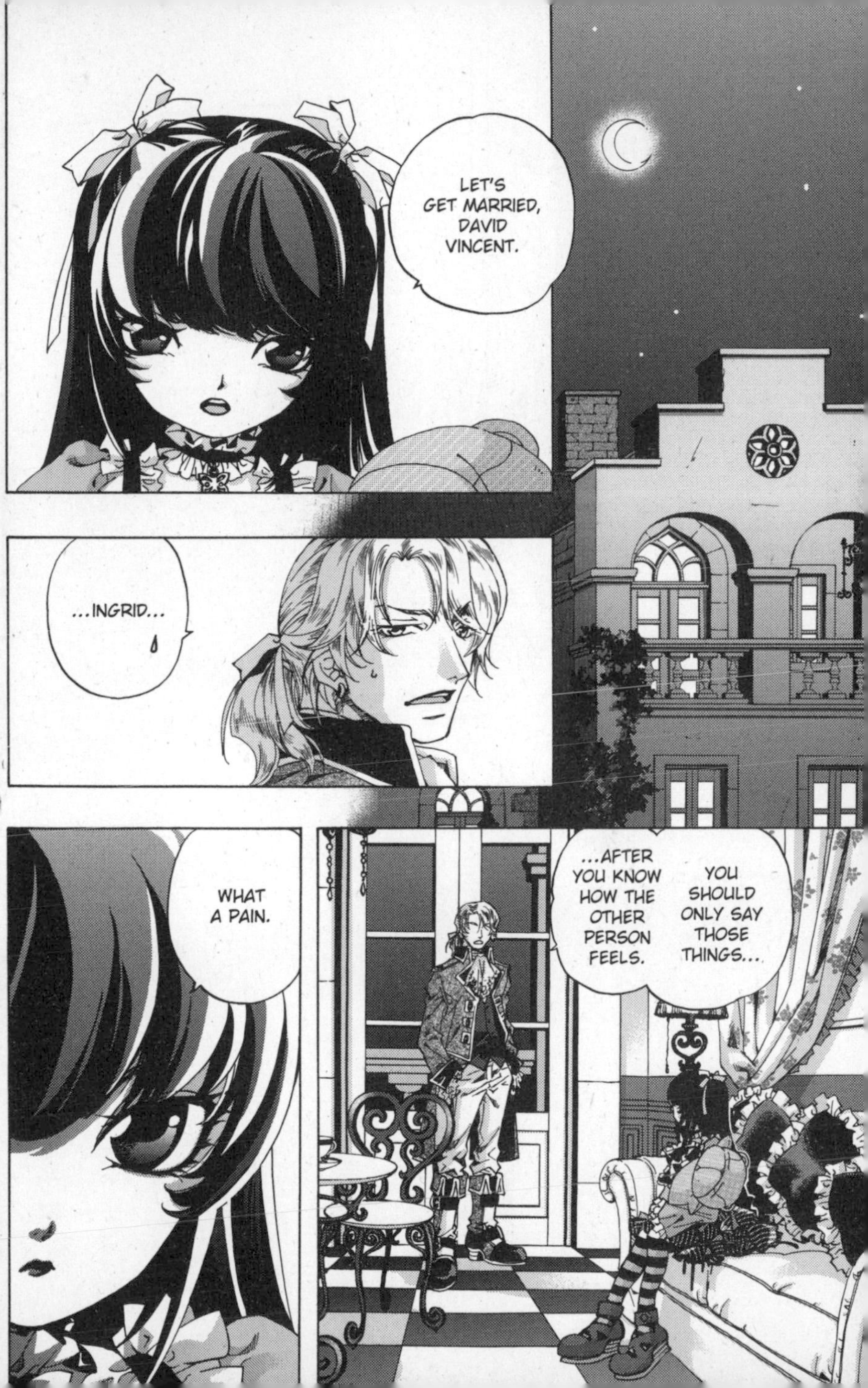
LET'S GET MARRIED, DAVID VINCENT.
...INGRID...
YOU SHOULD ONLY SAY THOSE THINGS...
...AFTER YOU KNOW HOW THE OTHER PERSON FEELS.
WHAT A PAIN.

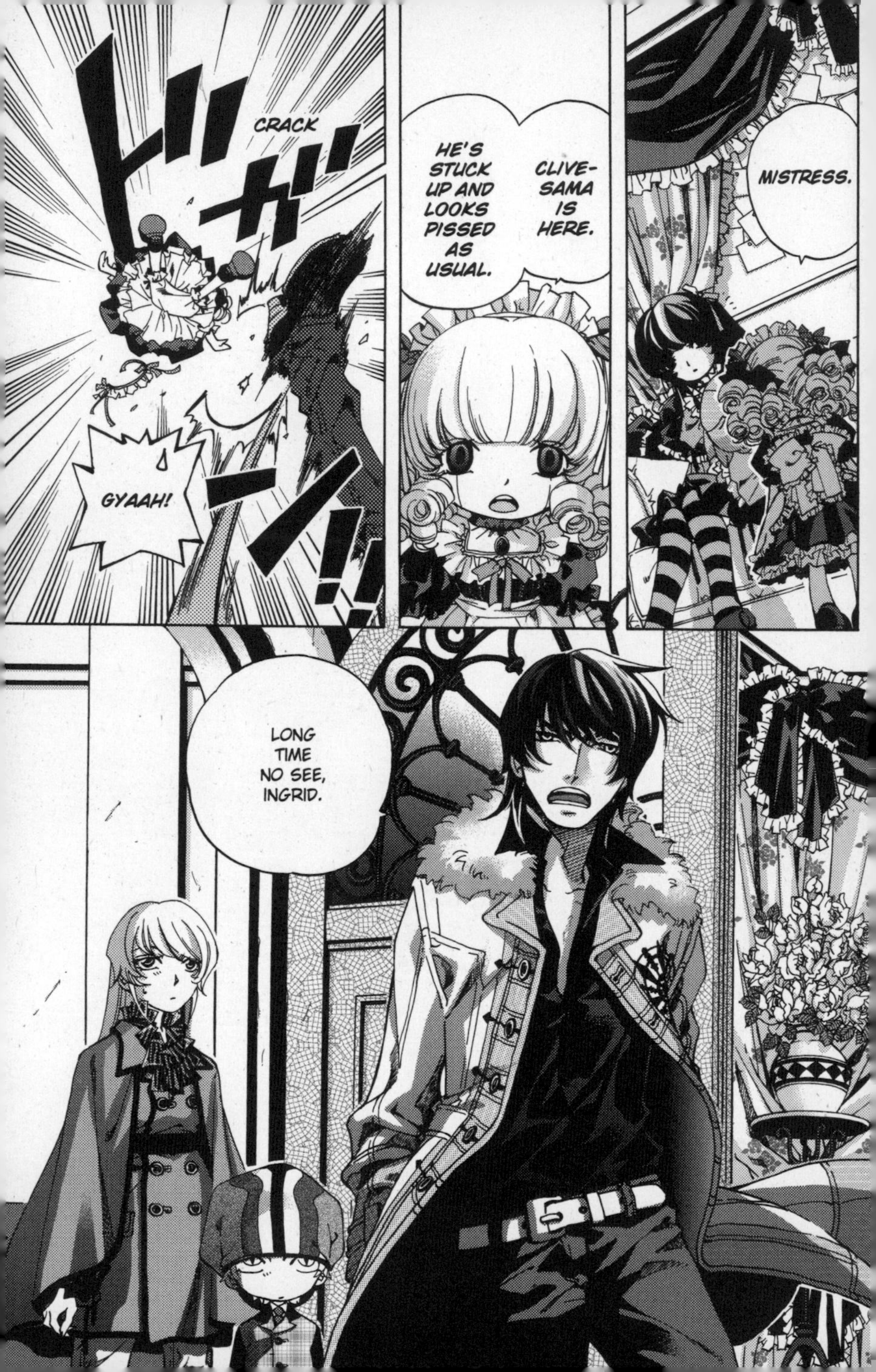
MISTRESS.
CLIVE-SAMA IS HERE.
HE'S STUCK UP AND LOOKS PISSED AS USUAL.
CRACK
GYAAH!
LONG TIME NO SEE, INGRID.

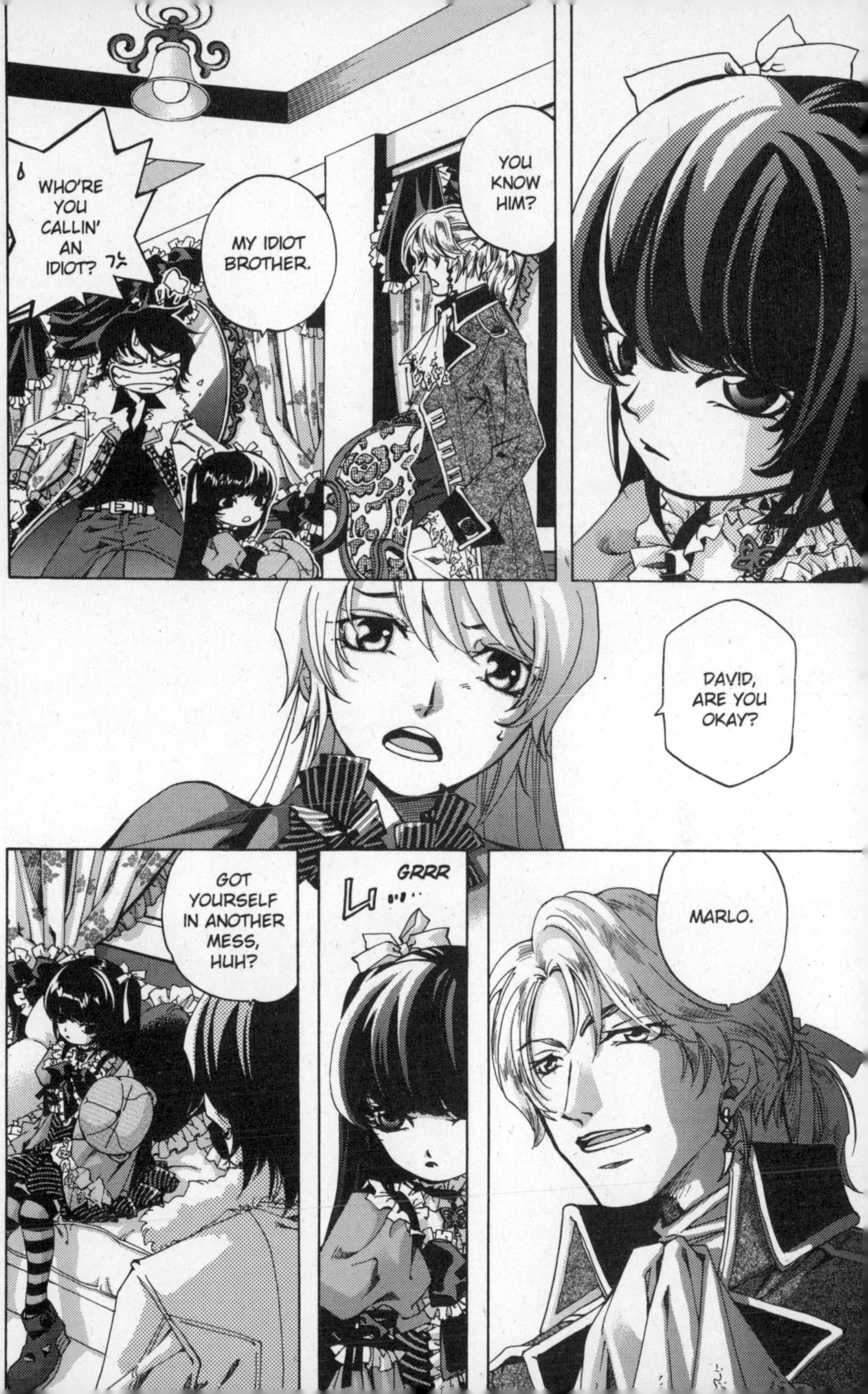
YOU KNOW HIM?
MY IDIOT BROTHER.
WHO'RE YOU CALLIN' AN IDIOT?
DAVID, ARE YOU OKAY?
MARLO.
GRRR
GOT YOURSELF IN ANOTHER MESS, HUH?

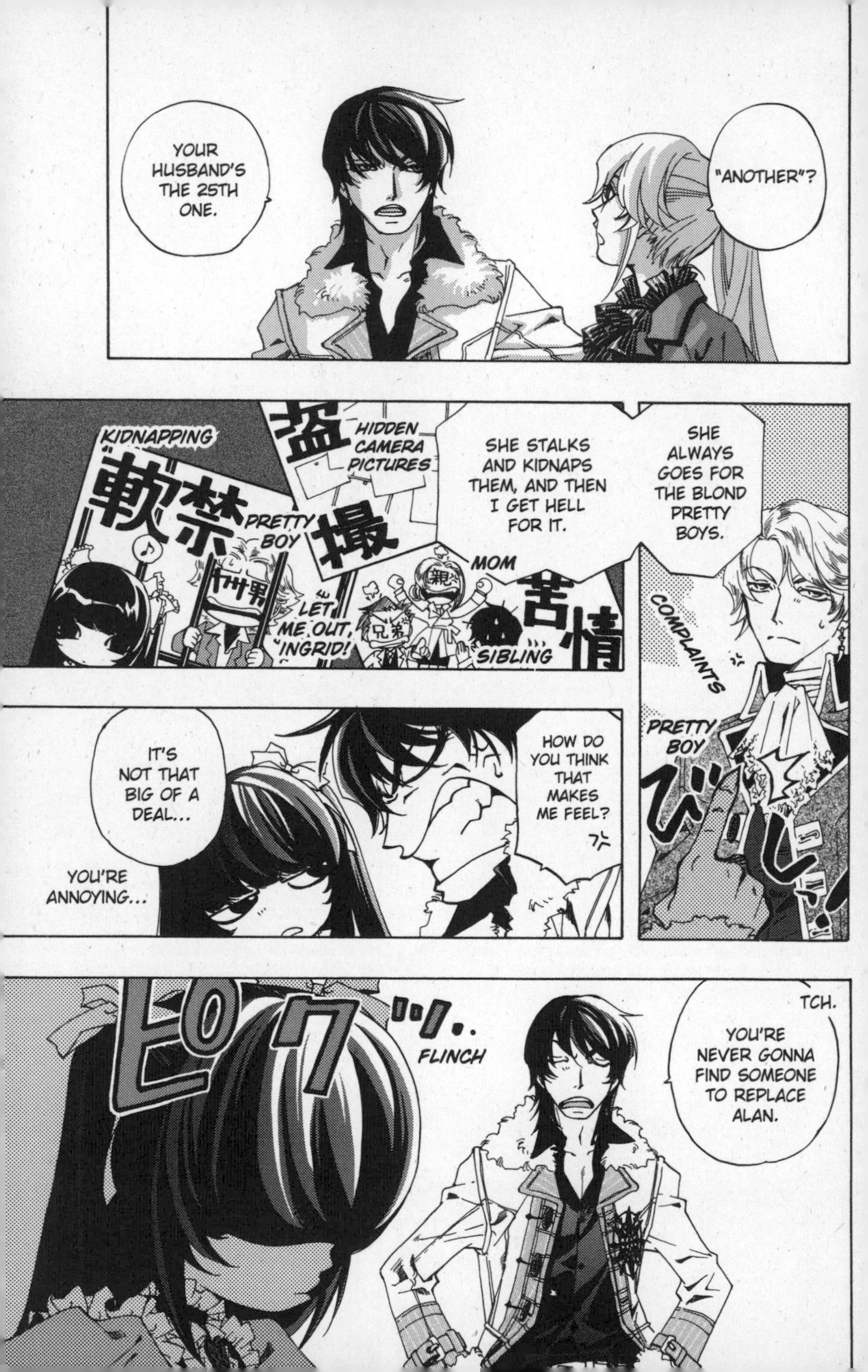
"ANOTHER"?
YOUR HUSBAND'S THE 25TH ONE.
SHE ALWAYS GOES FOR THE BLOND PRETTY BOYS.
COMPLAINTS
PRETTY BOY
SHE STALKS AND KIDNAPS THEM, AND THEN I GET HELL FOR IT.
盗撮
HIDDEN CAMERA PICTURES
KIDNAPPING
軟禁
PRETTY BOY
LET ME OUT, INGRID!
MOM
苦情
SIBLING
HOW DO YOU THINK THAT MAKES ME FEEL?
IT'S NOT THAT BIG OF A DEAL...
YOU'RE ANNOYING...
TCH.
YOU'RE NEVER GONNA FIND SOMEONE TO REPLACE ALAN.
ビクッ..
FLINCH

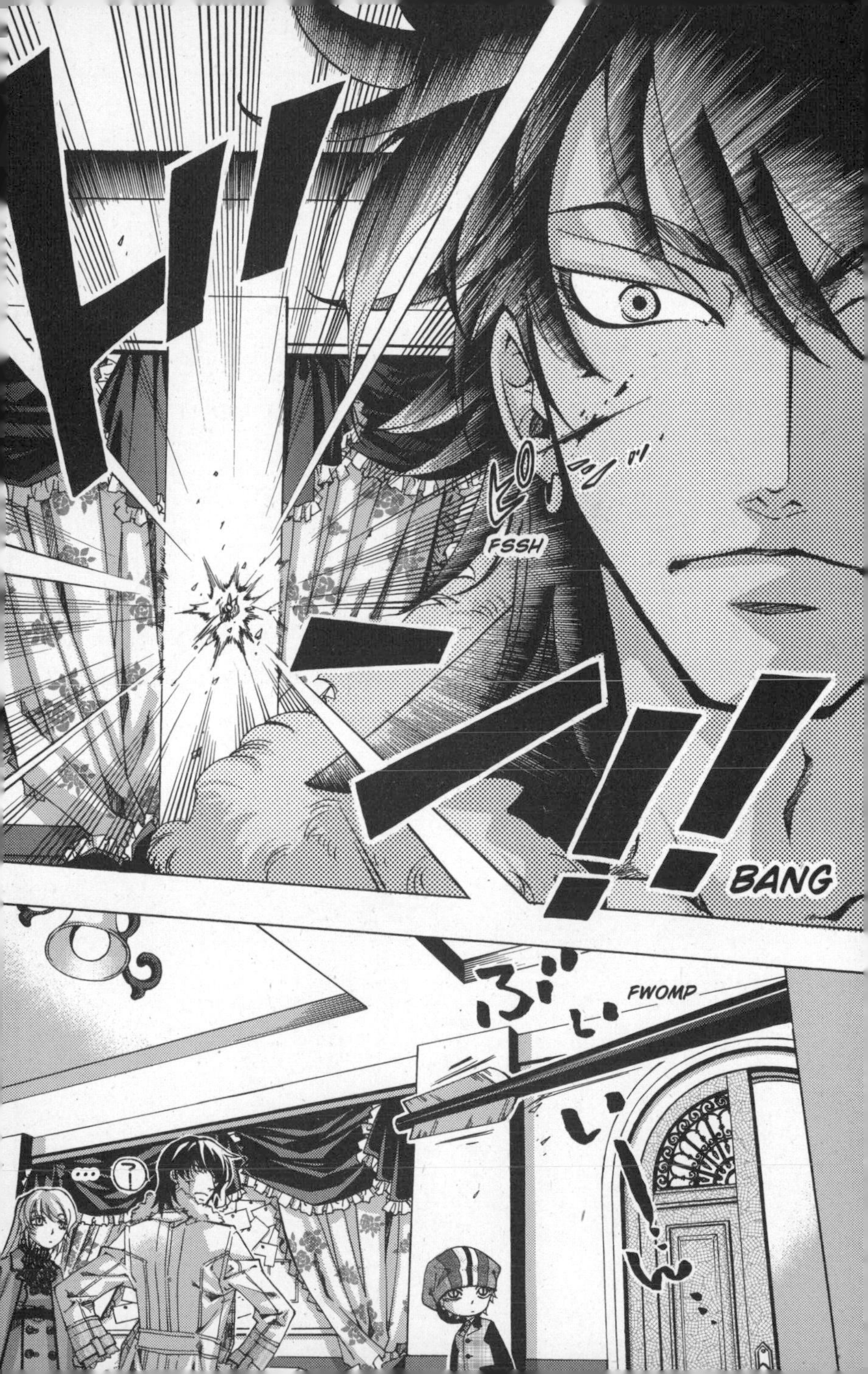
FSSH
BANG
FWOMP
...
?

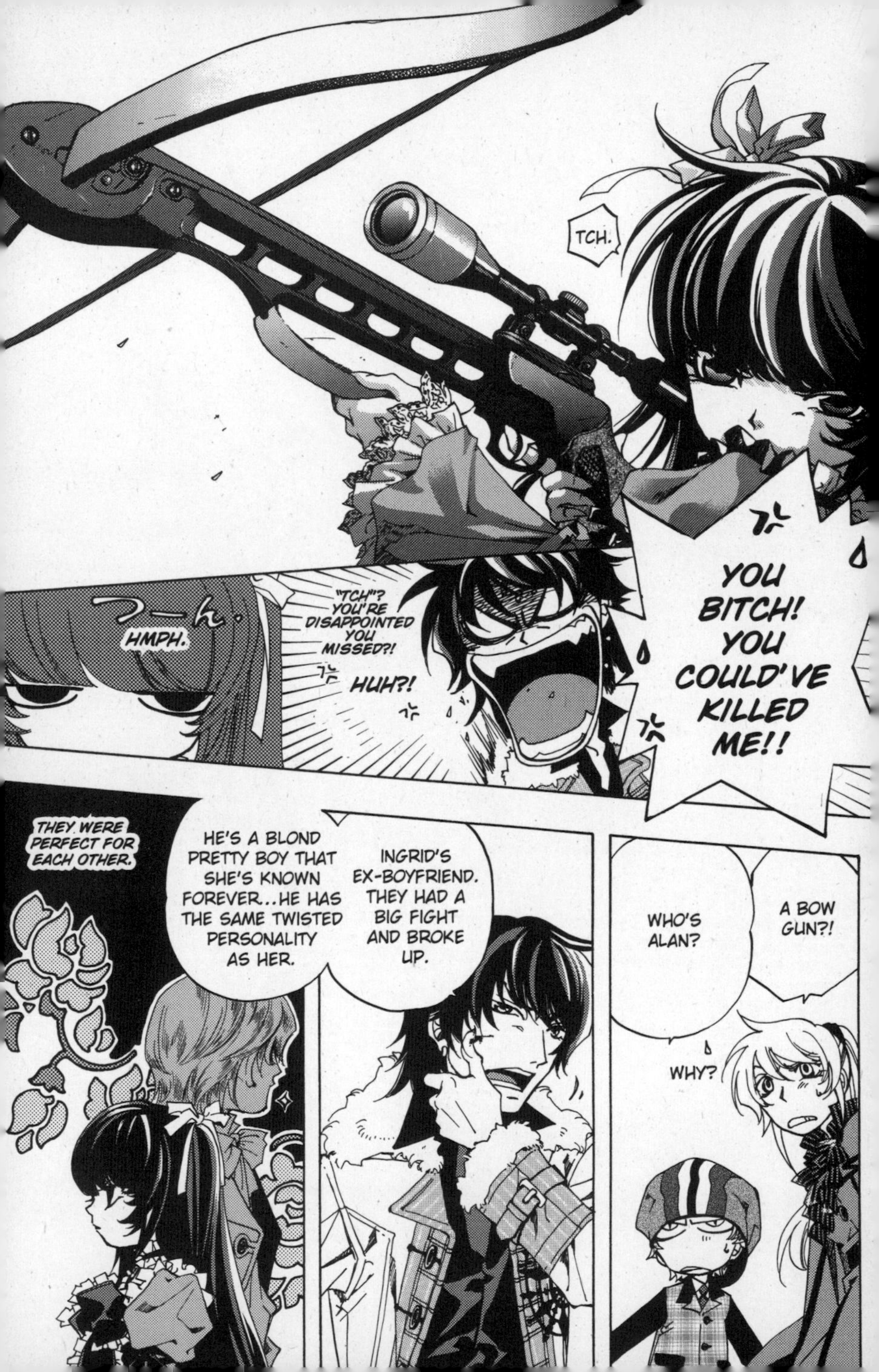
TCH.
YOU BITCH! YOU COULD'VE KILLED ME!!
"TCH"? YOU'RE DISAPPOINTED YOU MISSED?!
HUH?!
つーん.
HMPH.
A BOW GUN?!
WHO'S ALAN?
WHY?
INGRID'S EX-BOYFRIEND. THEY HAD A BIG FIGHT AND BROKE UP.
HE'S A BLOND PRETTY BOY THAT SHE'S KNOWN FOREVER...HE HAS THE SAME TWISTED PERSONALITY AS HER.
THEY WERE PERFECT FOR EACH OTHER.

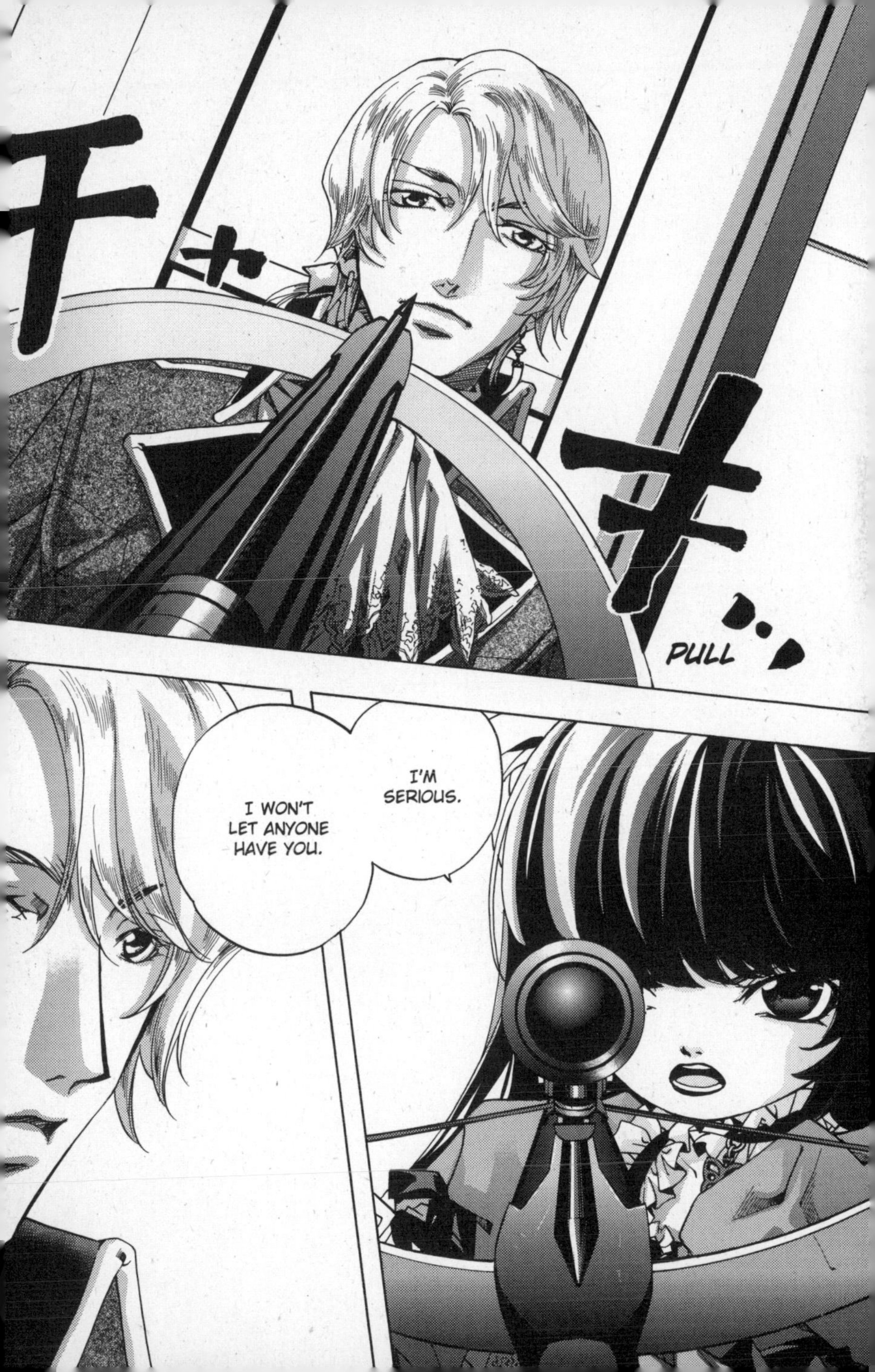
チャキ
PULL
I'M SERIOUS.
I WON'T LET ANYONE HAVE YOU.

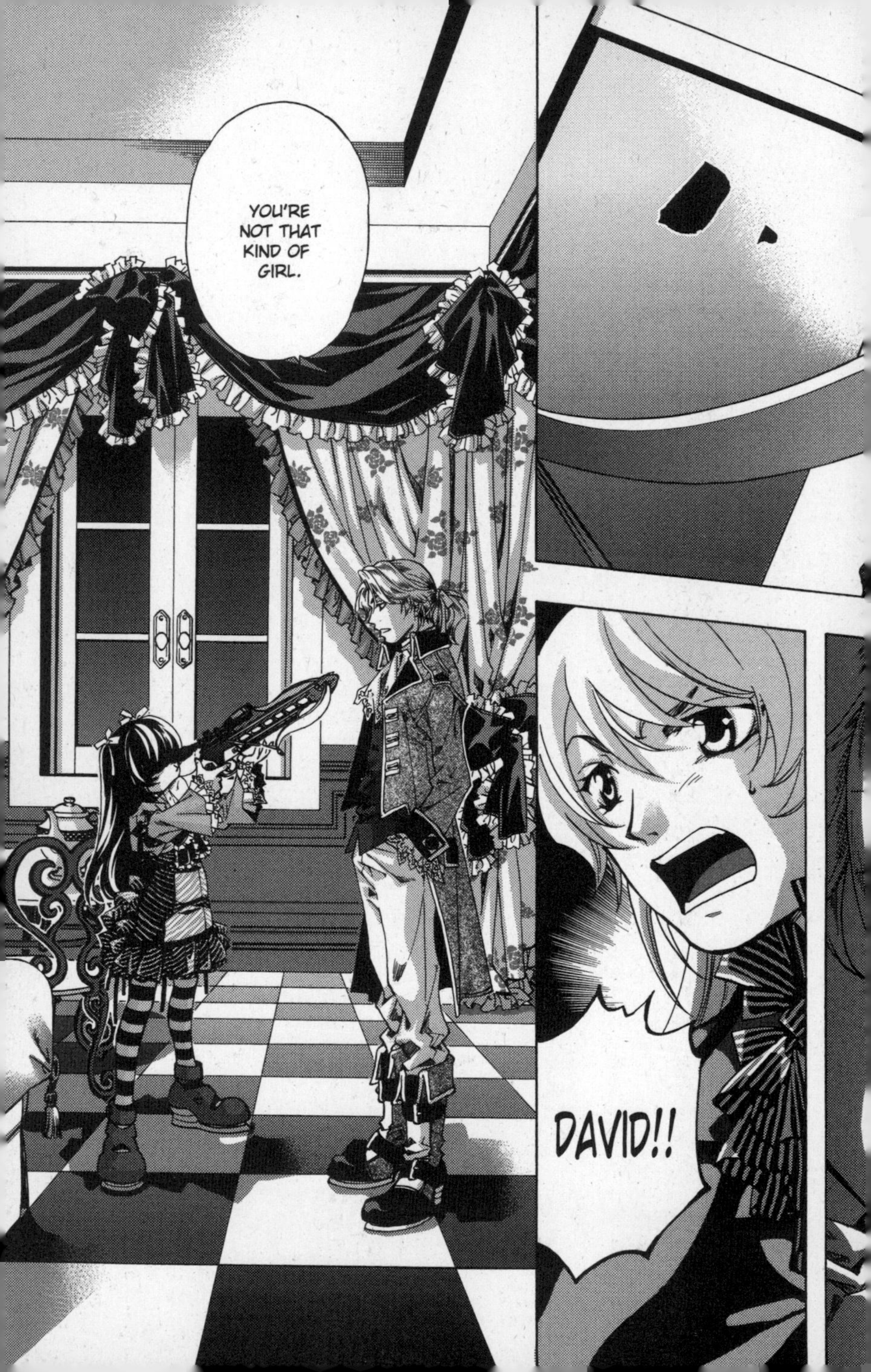
DAVID!!
YOU'RE NOT THAT KIND OF GIRL.

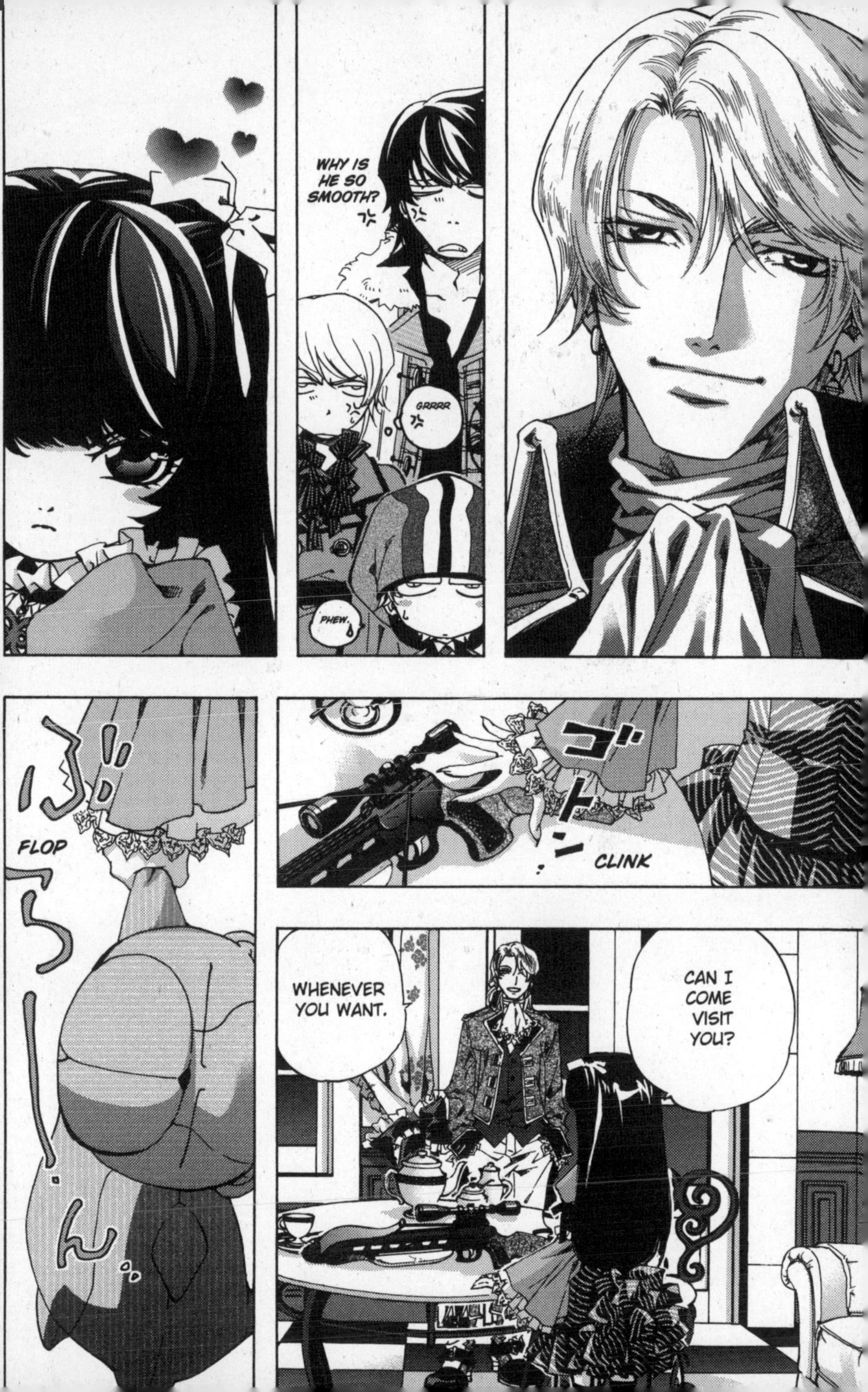
WHY IS HE SO SMOOTH?
GRRRR
PHEW.
CLINK
CAN I COME VISIT YOU?
WHENEVER YOU WANT.
FLOP

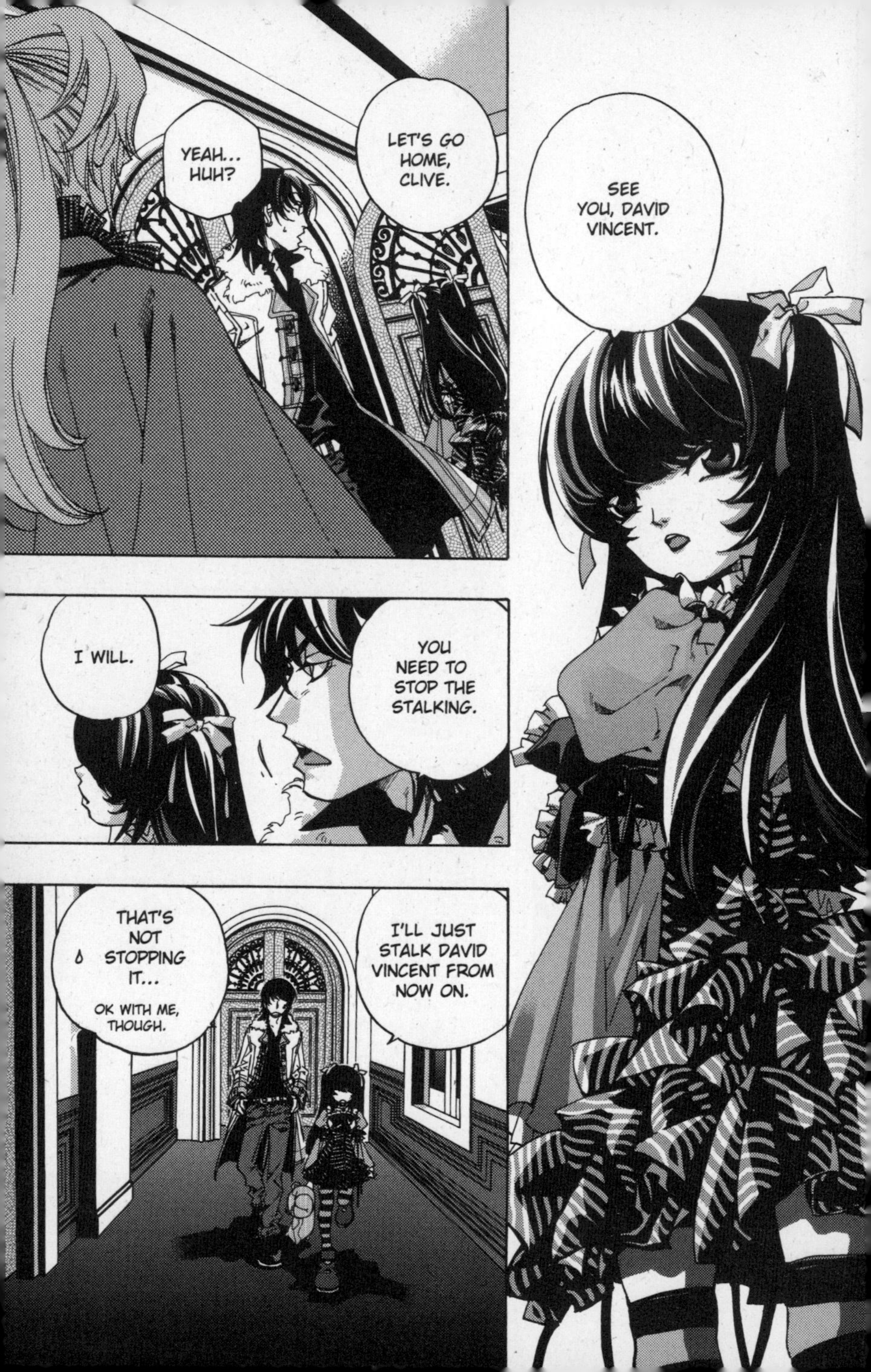
SEE YOU, DAVID VINCENT.
LET'S GO HOME, CLIVE.
YEAH... HUH?
YOU NEED TO STOP THE STALKING.
I WILL.
I'LL JUST STALK DAVID VINCENT FROM NOW ON.
THAT'S NOT STOPPING IT...
OK WITH ME, THOUGH.

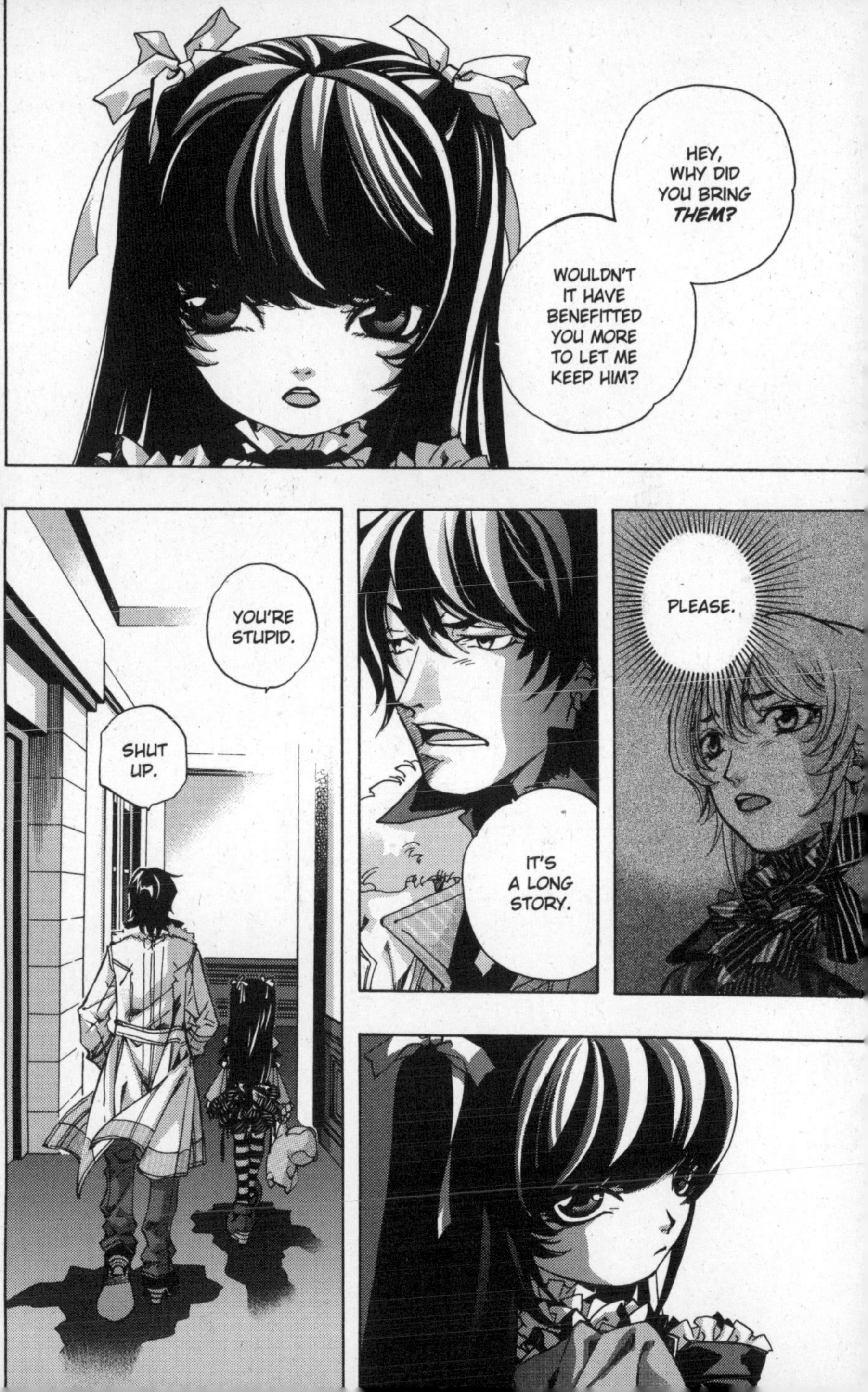
HEY, WHY DID YOU BRING *THEM?*
WOULDN'T IT HAVE BENEFITTED YOU MORE TO LET ME KEEP HIM?
PLEASE.
IT'S A LONG STORY.
YOU'RE STUPID.
SHUT UP.

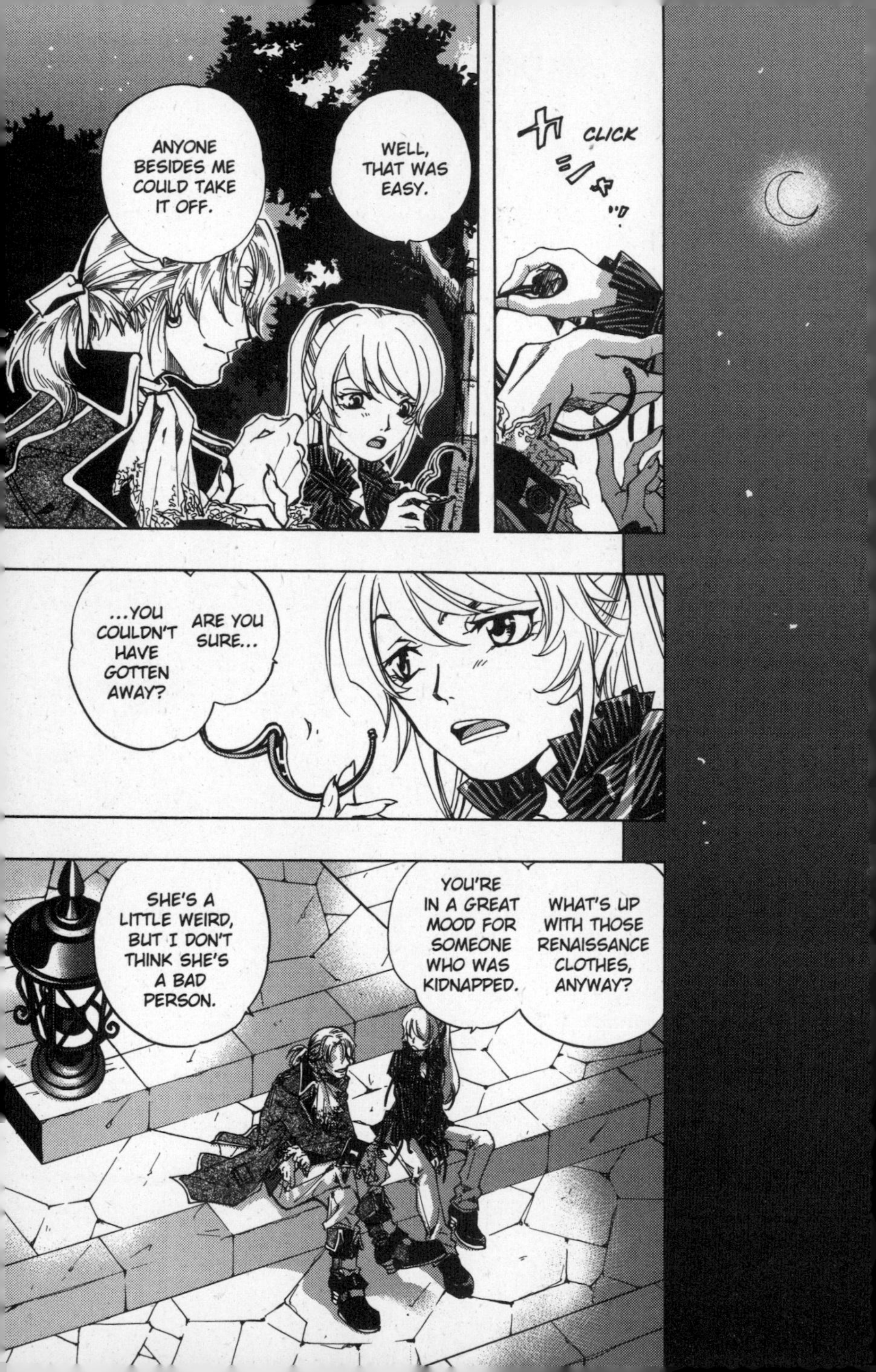
CLICK
WELL, THAT WAS EASY.
ANYONE BESIDES ME COULD TAKE IT OFF.
ARE YOU SURE...
...YOU COULDN'T HAVE GOTTEN AWAY?
WHAT'S UP WITH THOSE RENAISSANCE CLOTHES, ANYWAY?
YOU'RE IN A GREAT MOOD FOR SOMEONE WHO WAS KIDNAPPED.
SHE'S A LITTLE WEIRD, BUT I DON'T THINK SHE'S A BAD PERSON.

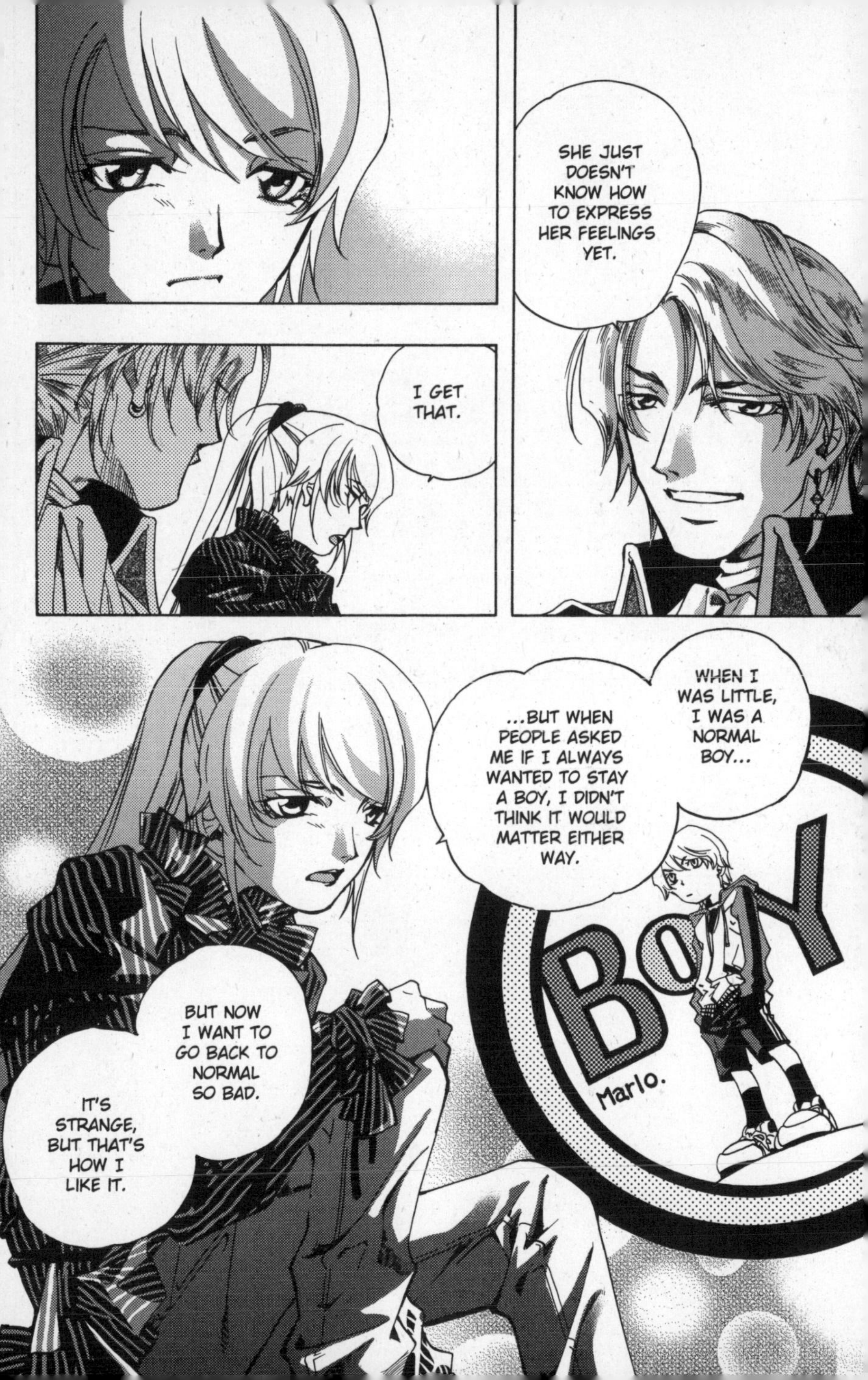
SHE JUST DOESN'T KNOW HOW TO EXPRESS HER FEELINGS YET.
I GET THAT.
WHEN I WAS LITTLE, I WAS A NORMAL BOY...
...BUT WHEN PEOPLE ASKED ME IF I ALWAYS WANTED TO STAY A BOY, I DIDN'T THINK IT WOULD MATTER EITHER WAY.
BOY
Marlo.
BUT NOW I WANT TO GO BACK TO NORMAL SO BAD.
IT'S STRANGE, BUT THAT'S HOW I LIKE IT.

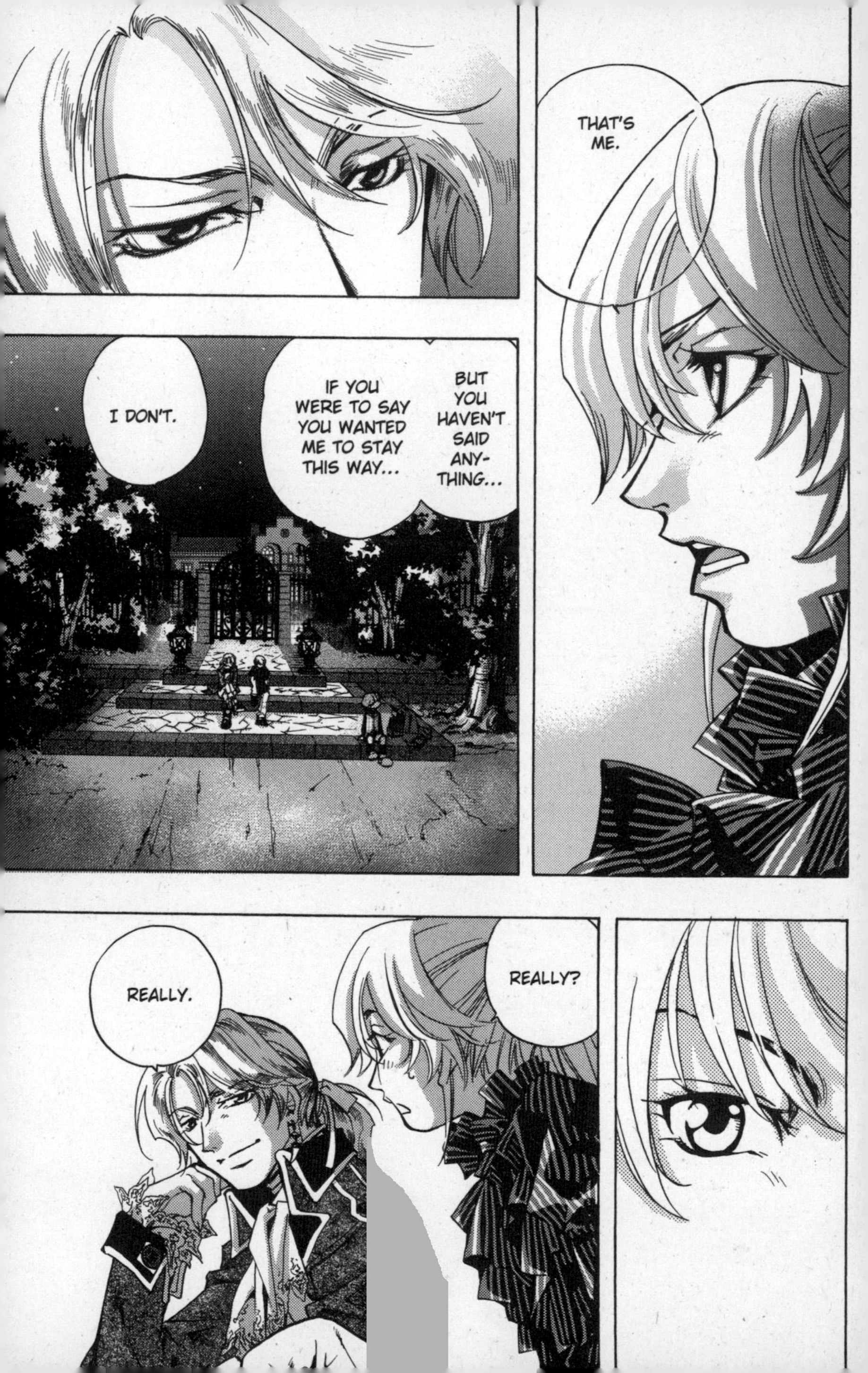
THAT'S ME.
IF YOU WERE TO SAY YOU WANTED ME TO STAY THIS WAY...
BUT YOU HAVEN'T SAID ANYTHING...
I DON'T.
REALLY?
REALLY.

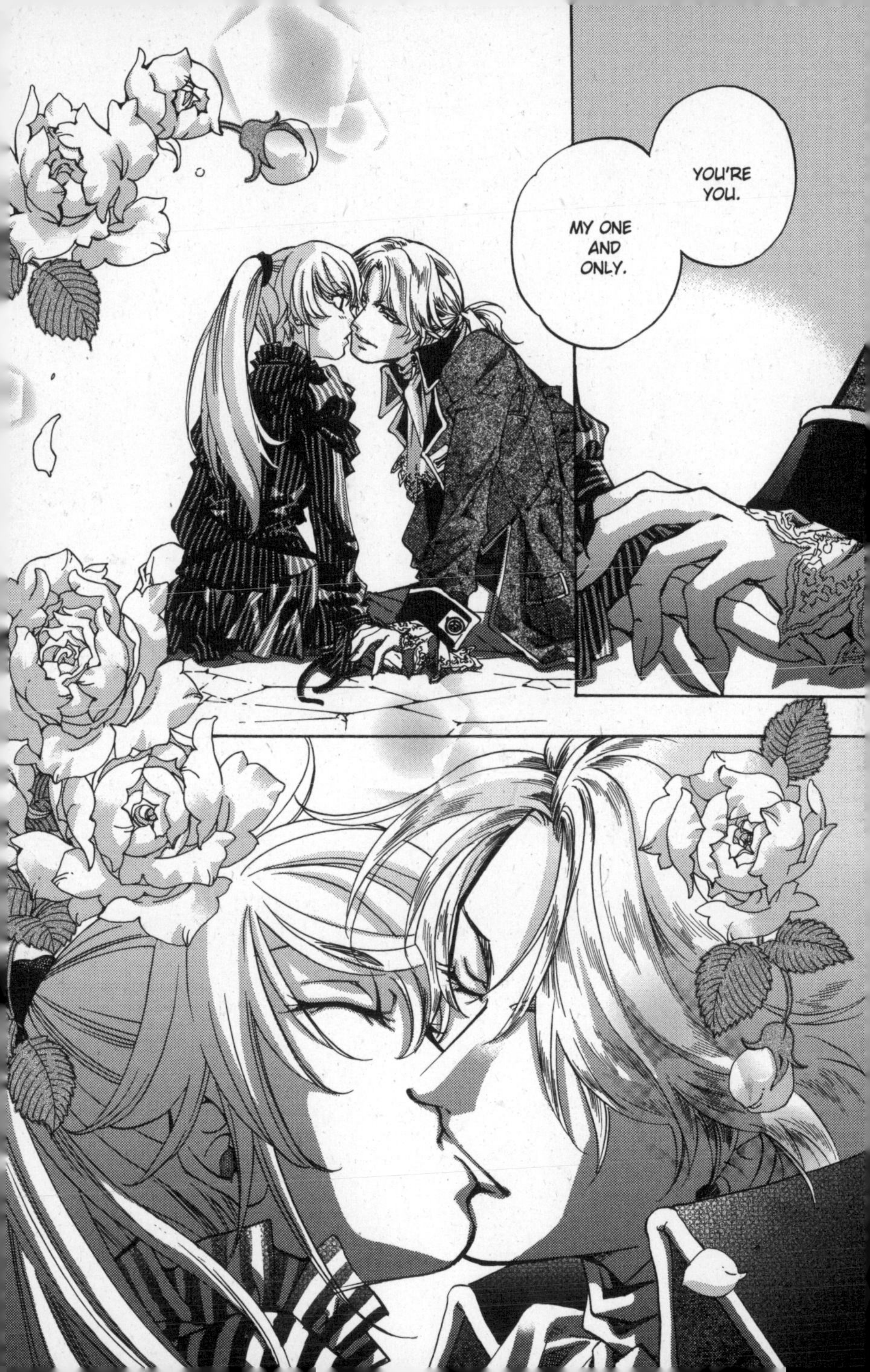
YOU'RE YOU.
MY ONE AND ONLY.

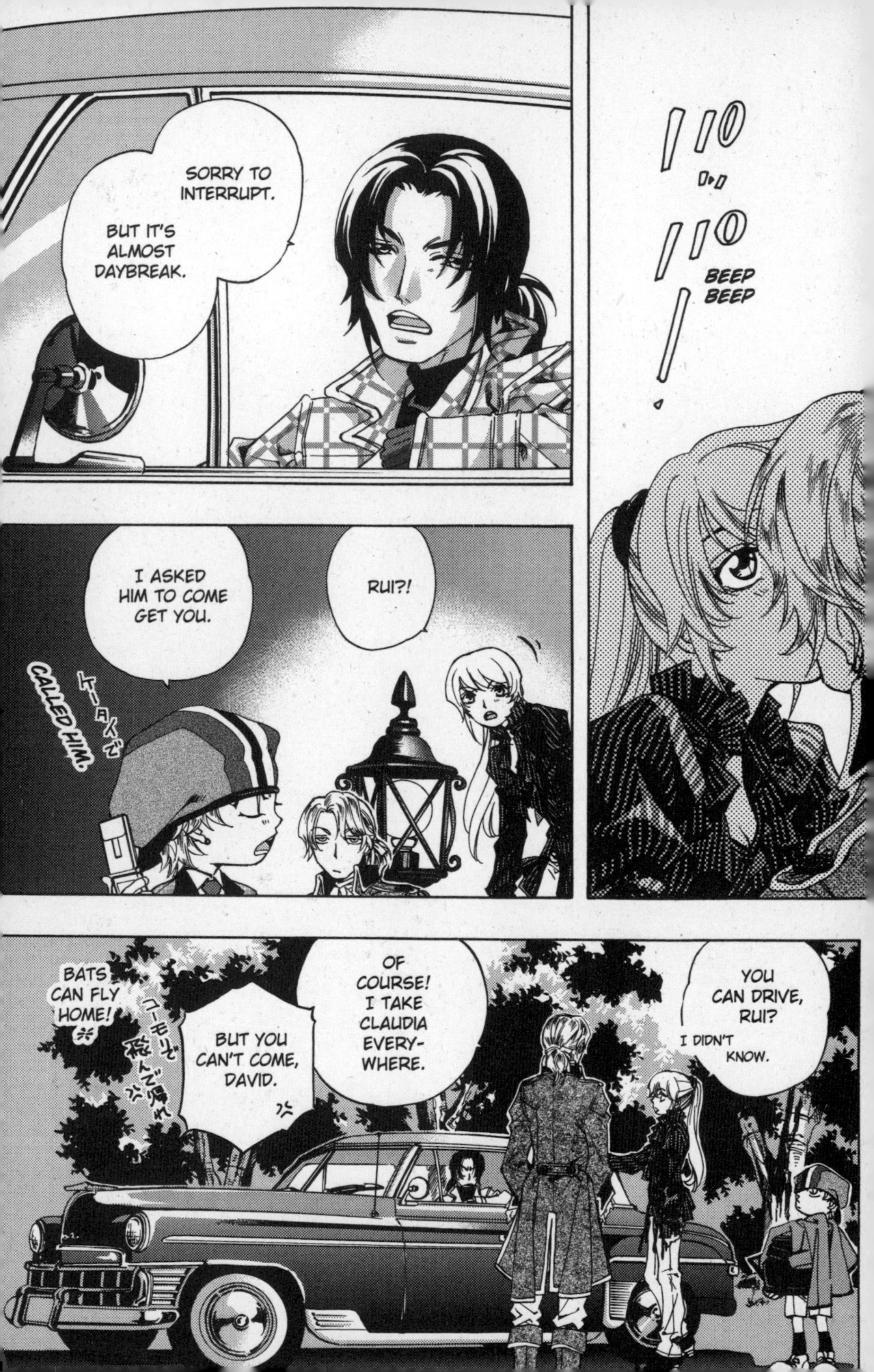

BEEP BEEP
SORRY TO INTERRUPT.
BUT IT'S ALMOST DAYBREAK.
RUI?!
I ASKED HIM TO COME GET YOU.
ケータイで
CALLED HIM.
YOU CAN DRIVE, RUI?
I DIDN'T KNOW.
OF COURSE! I TAKE CLAUDIA EVERY-WHERE.
BUT YOU CAN'T COME, DAVID.
コーモリで飛んで帰れ
BATS CAN FLY HOME!

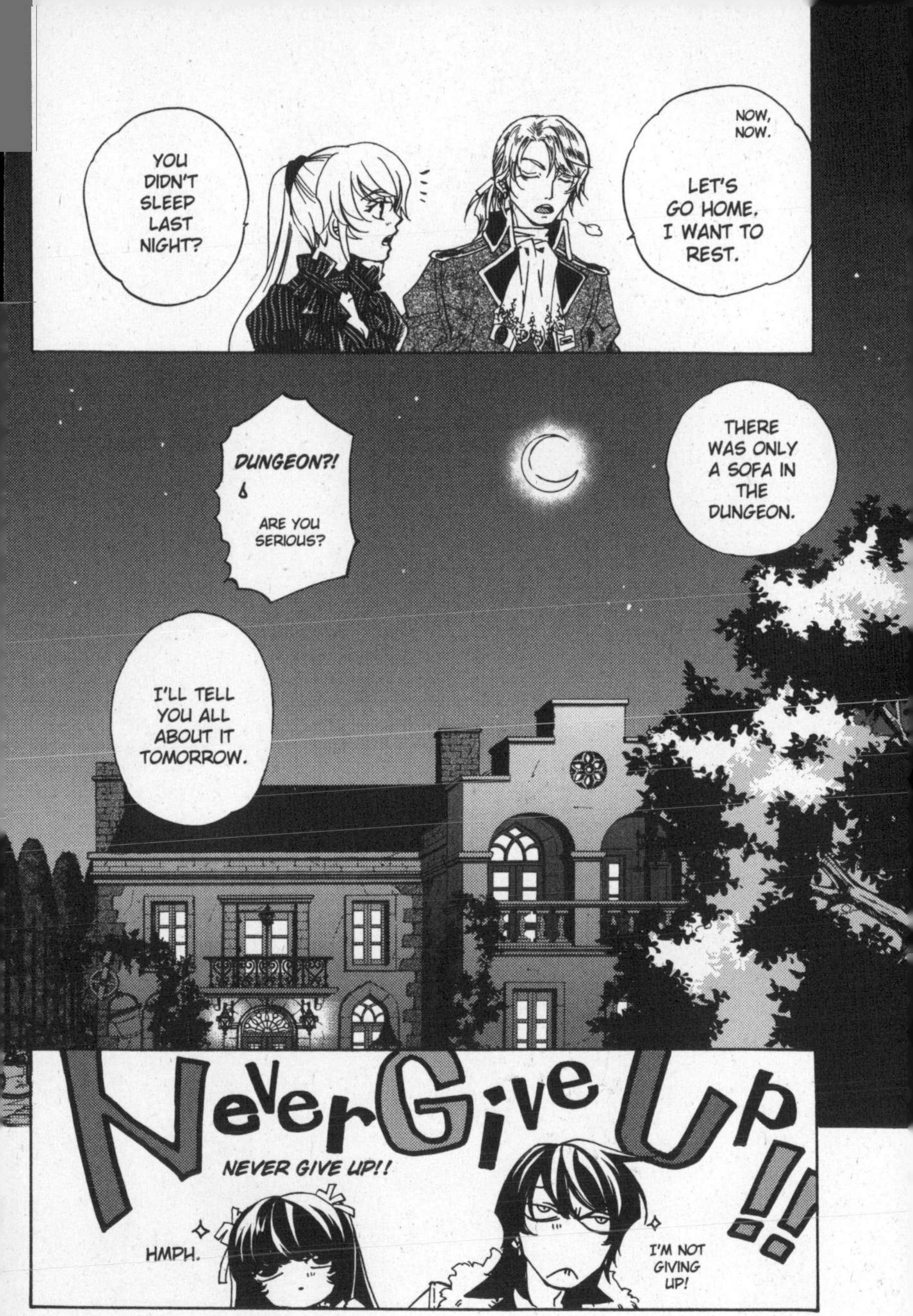
NOW, NOW.
LET'S GO HOME. I WANT TO REST.
YOU DIDN'T SLEEP LAST NIGHT?
THERE WAS ONLY A SOFA IN THE DUNGEON.
DUNGEON?!
ARE YOU SERIOUS?
I'LL TELL YOU ALL ABOUT IT TOMORROW.
NeverGiveUp!!
NEVER GIVE UP!!
I'M NOT GIVING UP!
HMPH.

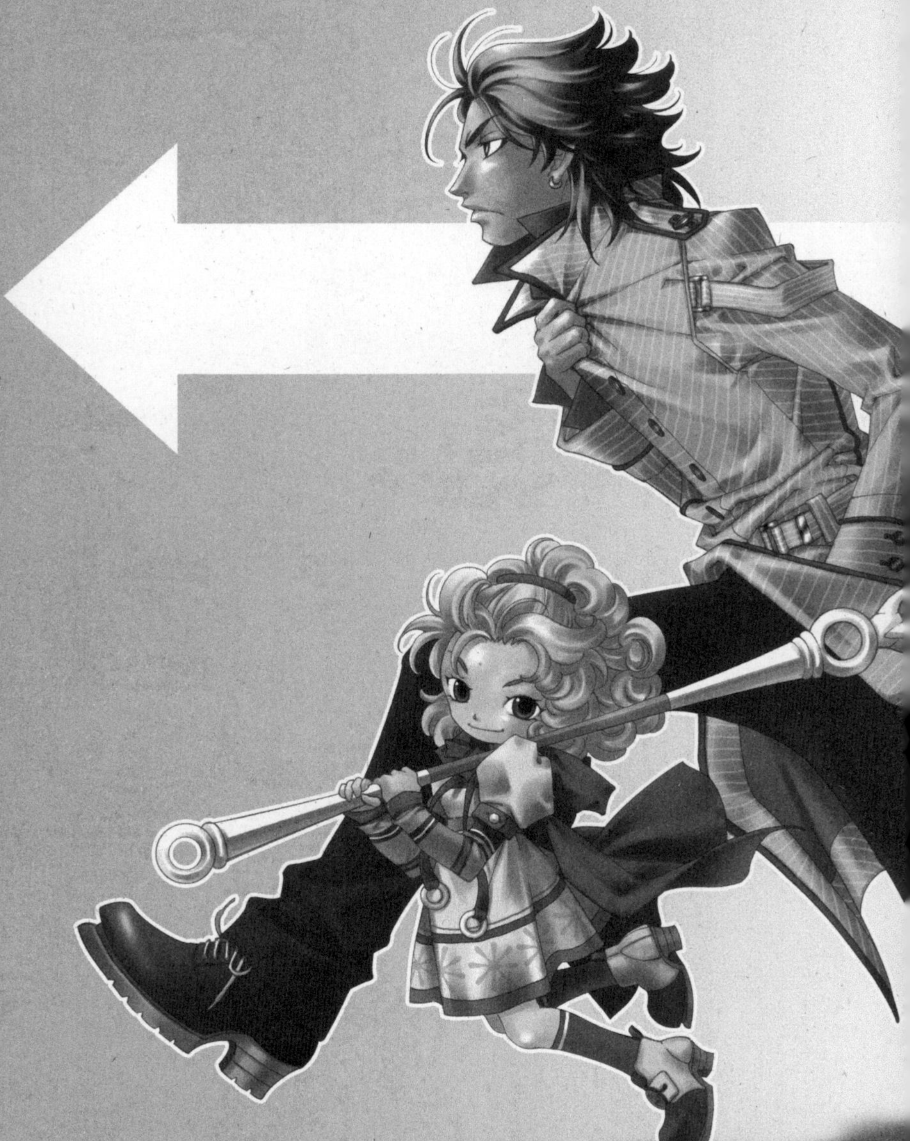

Chapter 5: Mona and Clive

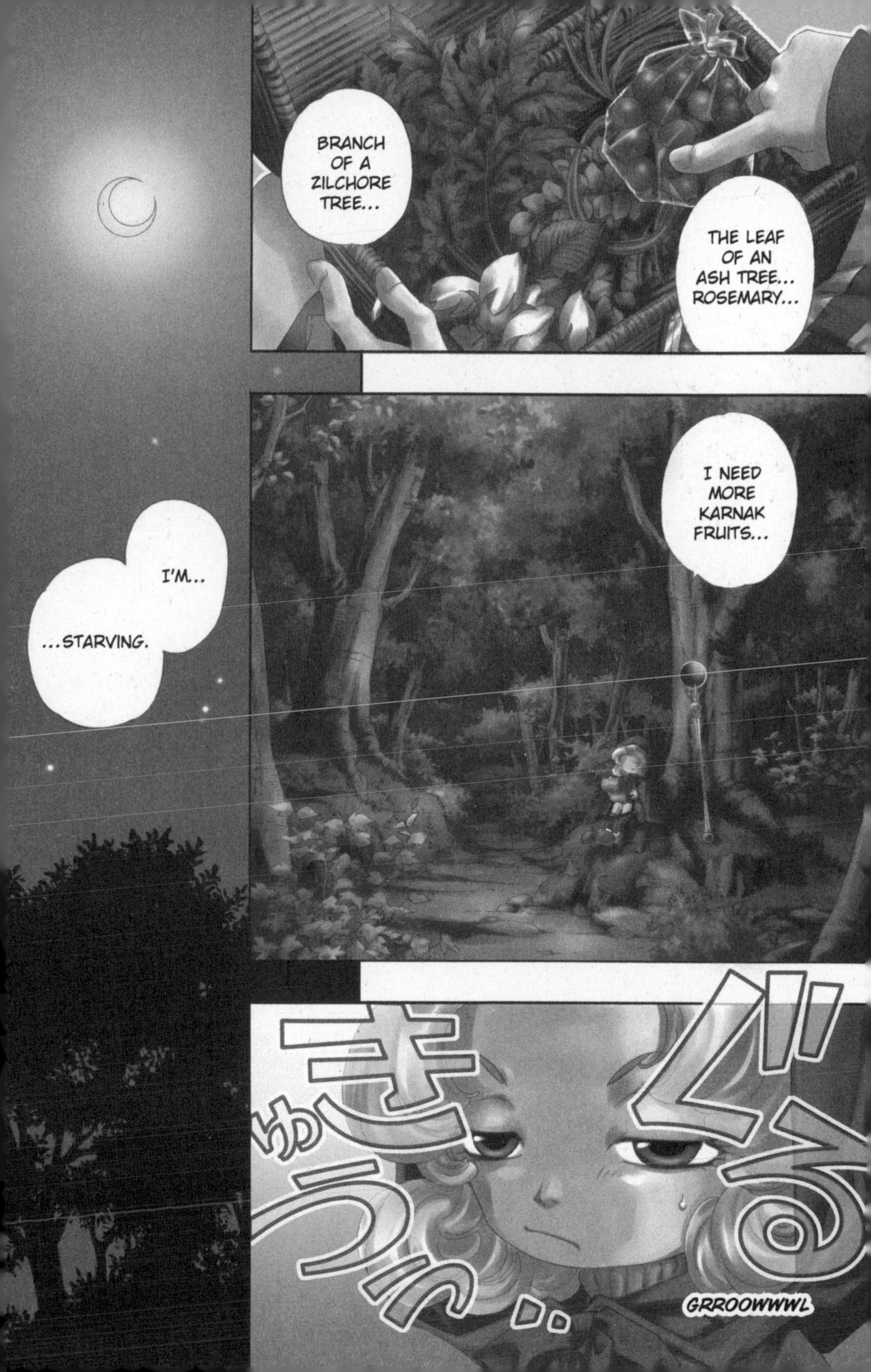
BRANCH OF A ZILCHORE TREE...
THE LEAF OF AN ASH TREE... ROSEMARY...
I NEED MORE KARNAK FRUITS...
GRROOWWWL
I'M...
...STARVING.

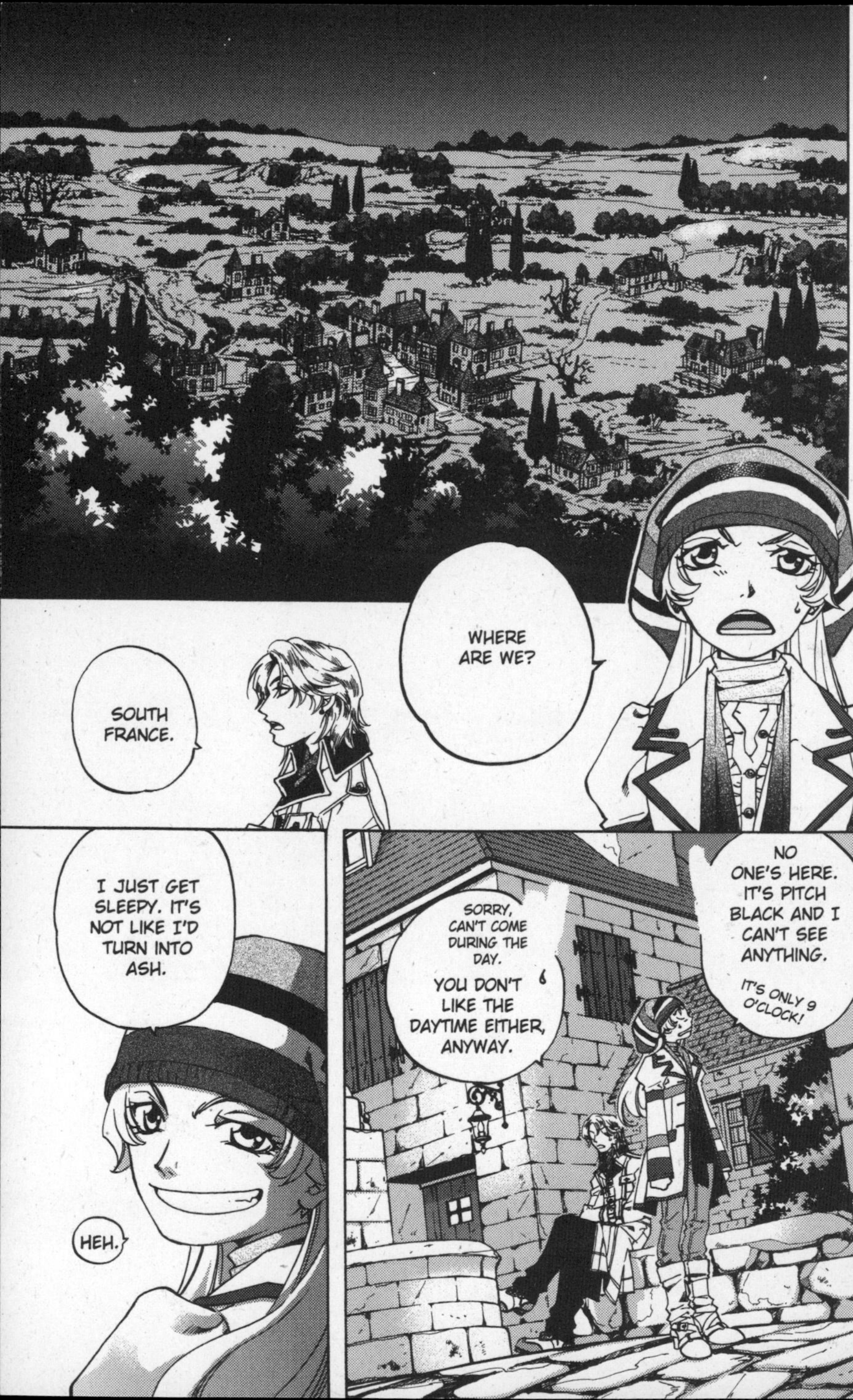
WHERE ARE WE?
SOUTH FRANCE.
NO ONE'S HERE. IT'S PITCH BLACK AND I CAN'T SEE ANYTHING.
IT'S ONLY 9 O'CLOCK!
SORRY, CAN'T COME DURING THE DAY.
YOU DON'T LIKE THE DAYTIME EITHER, ANYWAY.
I JUST GET SLEEPY. IT'S NOT LIKE I'D TURN INTO ASH.
HEH.

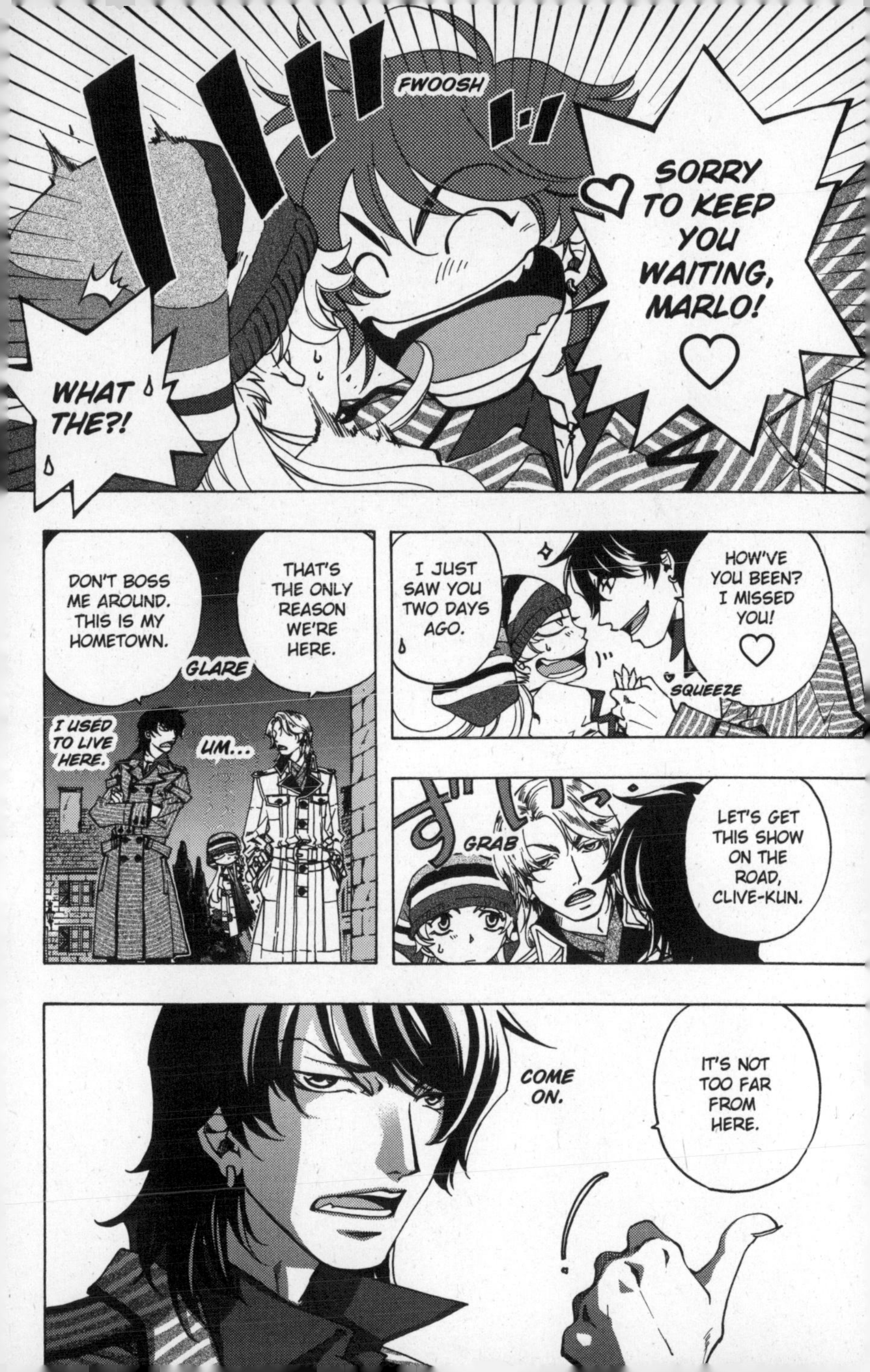
FWOOSH
SORRY TO KEEP YOU WAITING, MARLO!
WHAT THE?!
HOW'VE YOU BEEN? I MISSED YOU!
SQUEEZE
I JUST SAW YOU TWO DAYS AGO.
LET'S GET THIS SHOW ON THE ROAD, CLIVE-KUN.
GRAB
THAT'S THE ONLY REASON WE'RE HERE.
DON'T BOSS ME AROUND. THIS IS MY HOMETOWN.
GLARE
UM...
I USED TO LIVE HERE.
IT'S NOT TOO FAR FROM HERE.
COME ON.

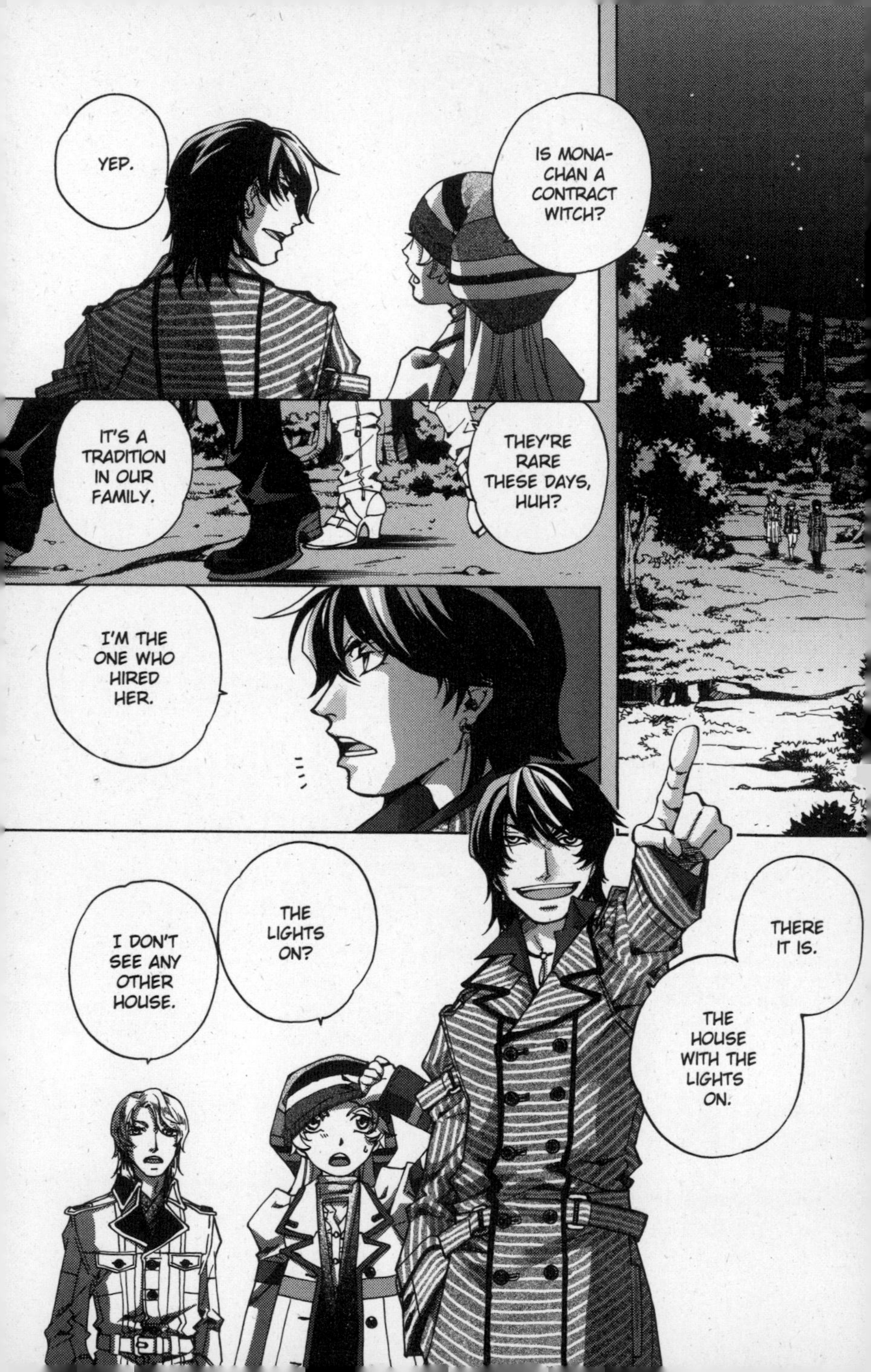
IS MONA-CHAN A CONTRACT WITCH?
YEP.
THEY'RE RARE THESE DAYS, HUH?
IT'S A TRADITION IN OUR FAMILY.
I'M THE ONE WHO HIRED HER.
THERE IT IS.
THE HOUSE WITH THE LIGHTS ON.
THE LIGHTS ON?
I DON'T SEE ANY OTHER HOUSE.

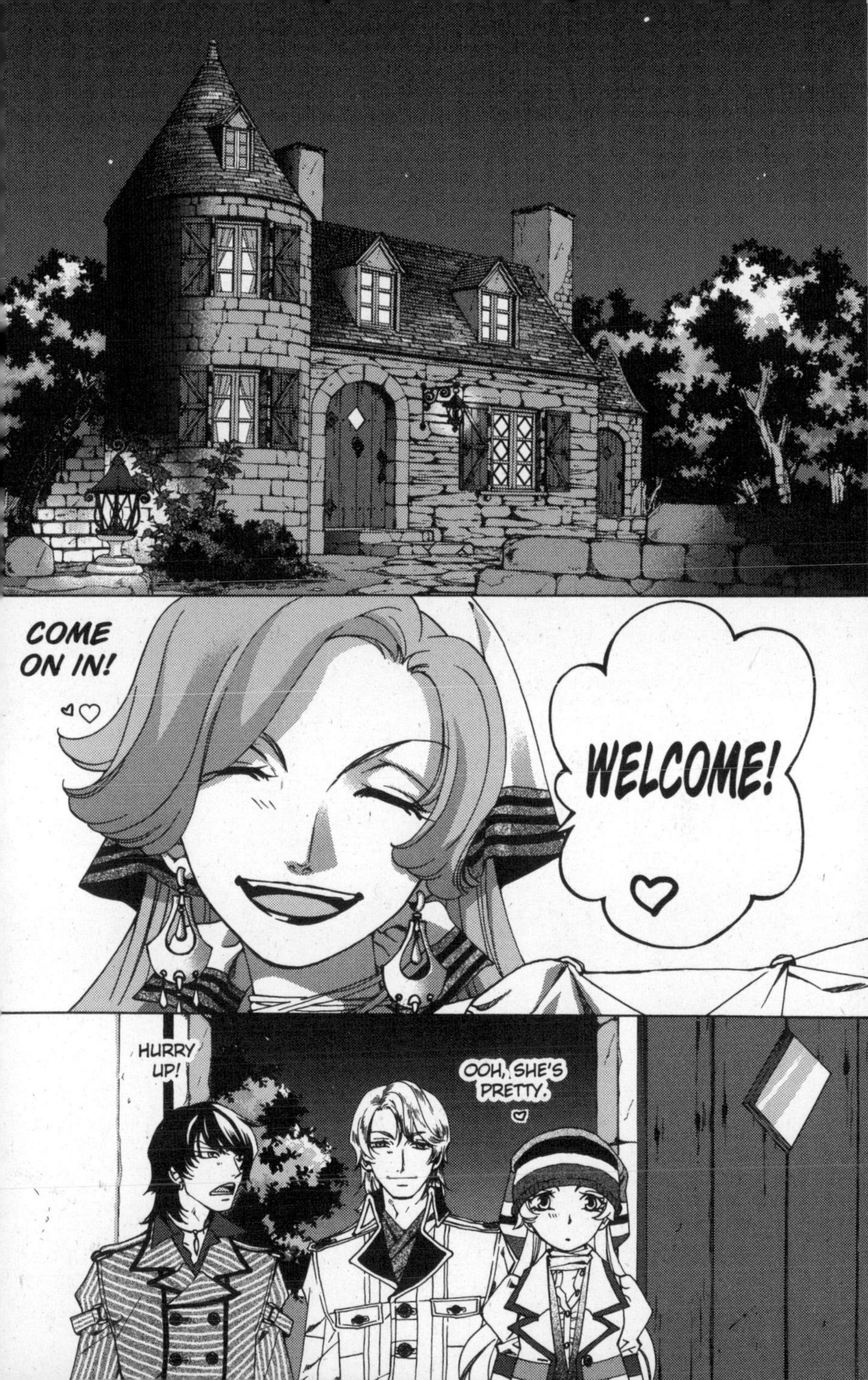
WELCOME!
COME ON IN!
OOH, SHE'S PRETTY.
HURRY UP!

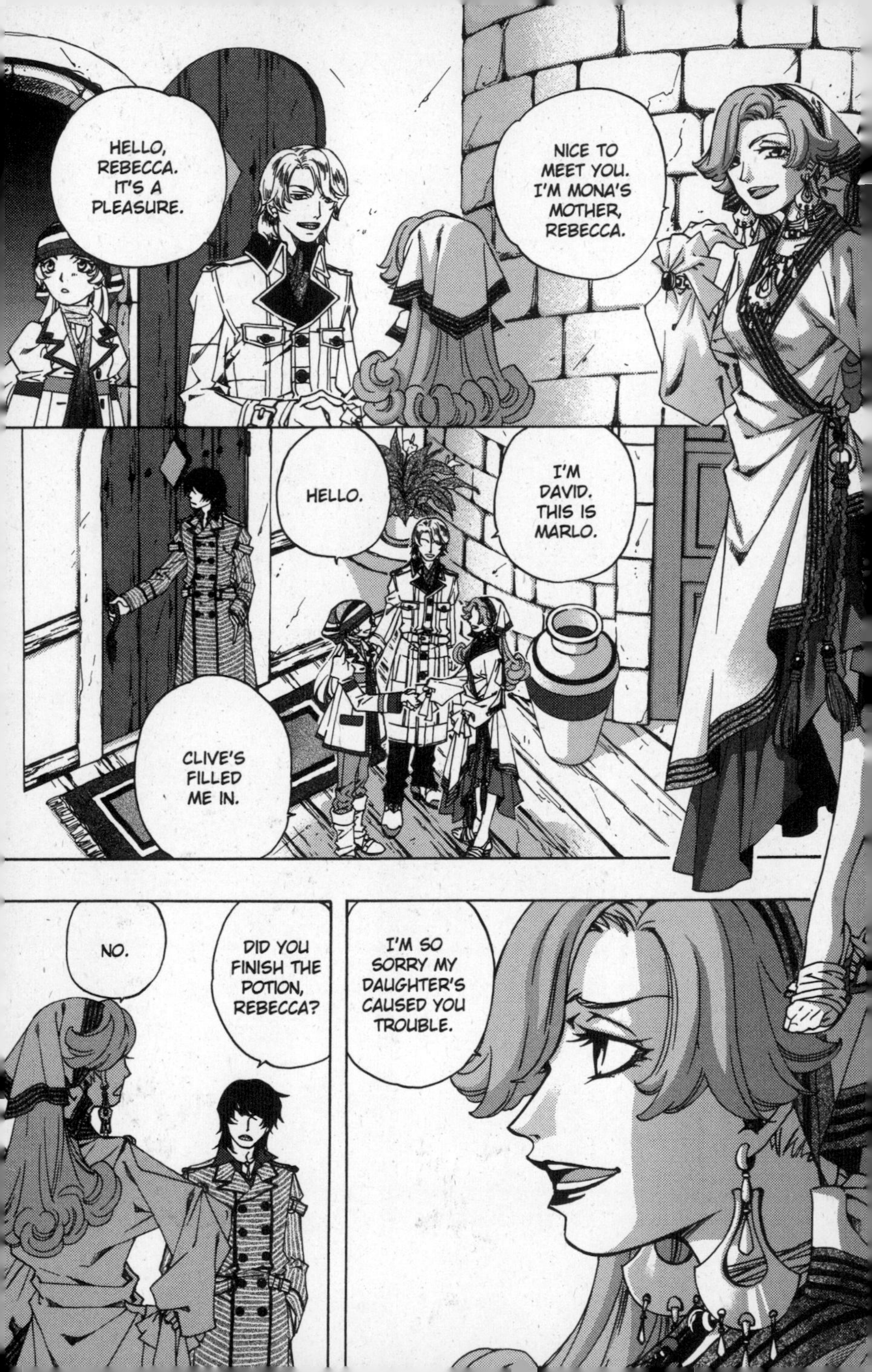
NICE TO MEET YOU. I'M MONA'S MOTHER, REBECCA.
HELLO, REBECCA. IT'S A PLEASURE.
I'M DAVID. THIS IS MARLO.
HELLO.
CLIVE'S FILLED ME IN.
I'M SO SORRY MY DAUGHTER'S CAUSED YOU TROUBLE.
DID YOU FINISH THE POTION, REBECCA?
NO.

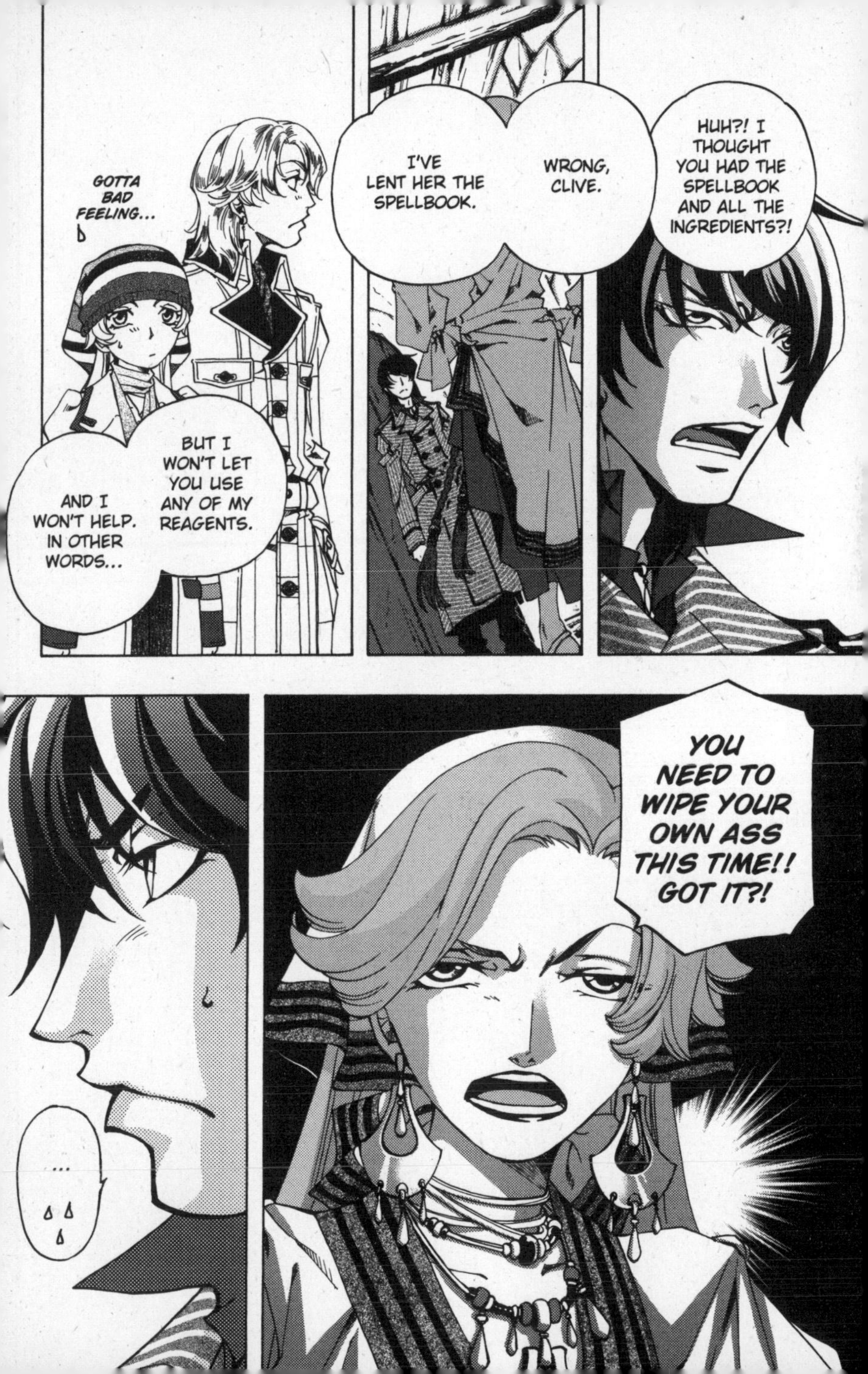
HUH?! I THOUGHT YOU HAD THE SPELLBOOK AND ALL THE INGREDIENTS?!
WRONG, CLIVE.
I'VE LENT HER THE SPELLBOOK.
GOTTA BAD FEELING...
BUT I WON'T LET YOU USE ANY OF MY REAGENTS.
AND I WON'T HELP. IN OTHER WORDS...
YOU NEED TO WIPE YOUR OWN ASS THIS TIME!! GOT IT?!
...

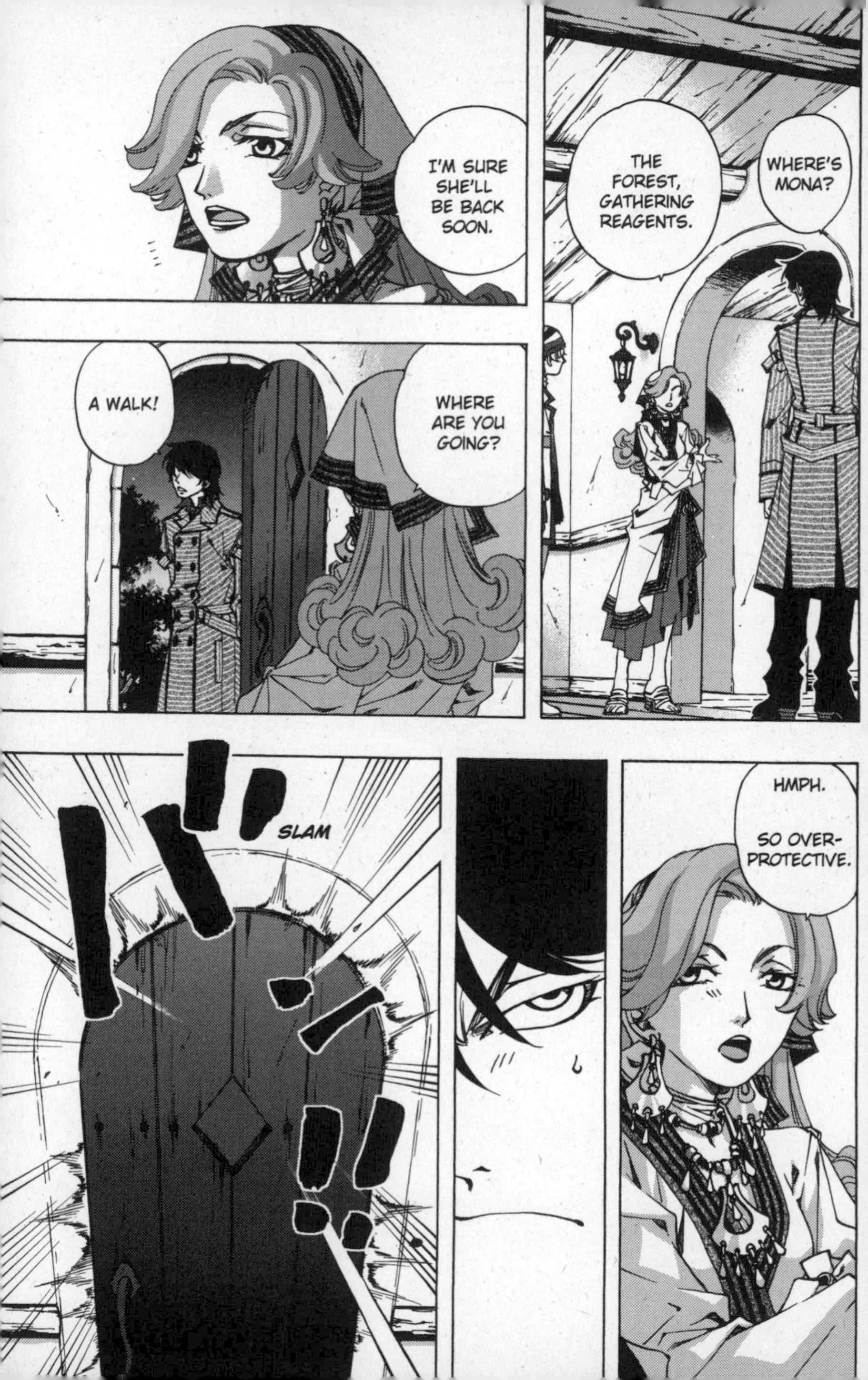
WHERE'S MONA?
THE FOREST, GATHERING REAGENTS.
I'M SURE SHE'LL BE BACK SOON.
WHERE ARE YOU GOING?
A WALK!
HMPH.
SO OVER-PROTECTIVE.
SLAM

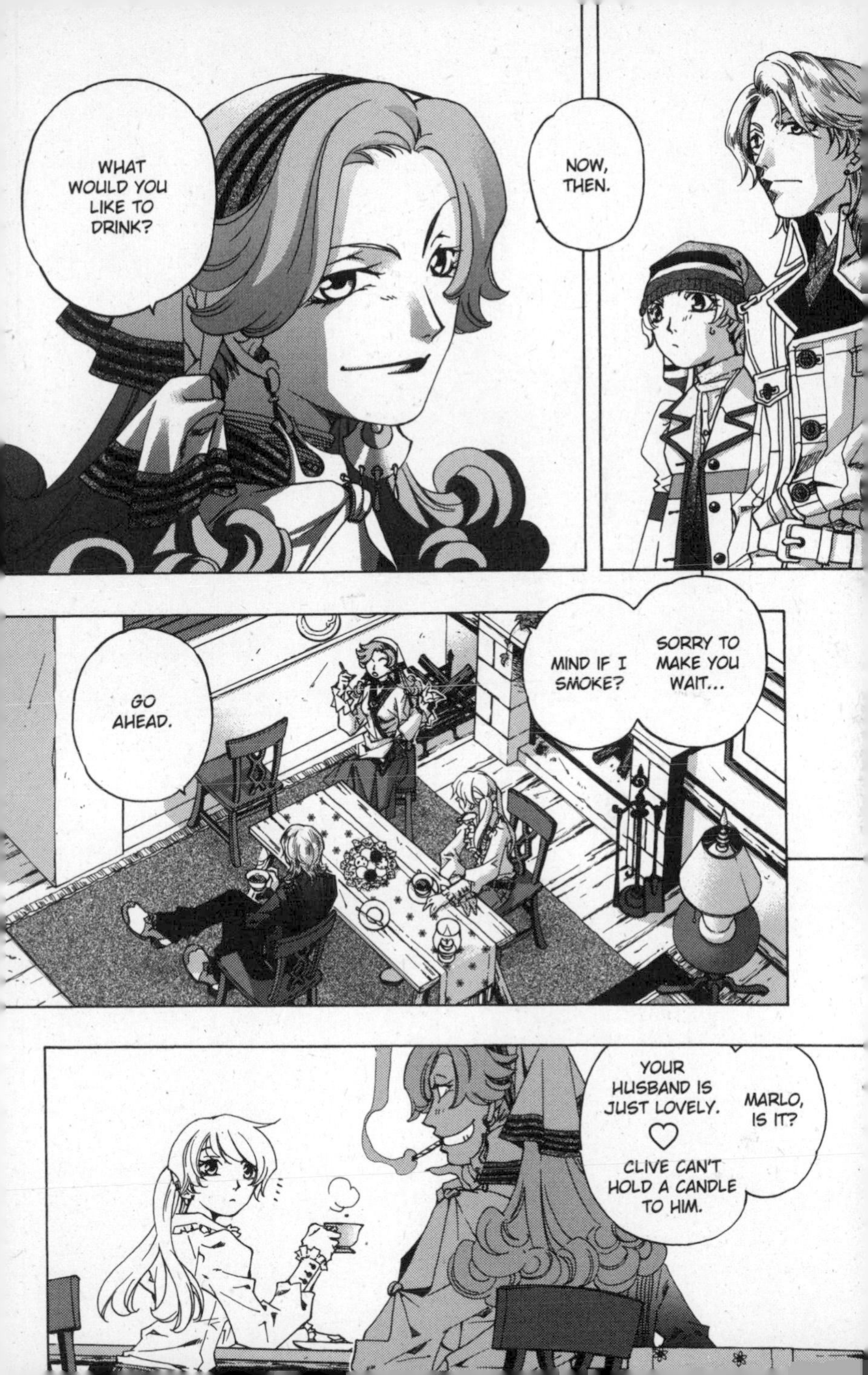
NOW, THEN.
WHAT WOULD YOU LIKE TO DRINK?
SORRY TO MAKE YOU WAIT...
MIND IF I SMOKE?
GO AHEAD.
MARLO, IS IT?
YOUR HUSBAND IS JUST LOVELY. ♡
CLIVE CAN'T HOLD A CANDLE TO HIM.

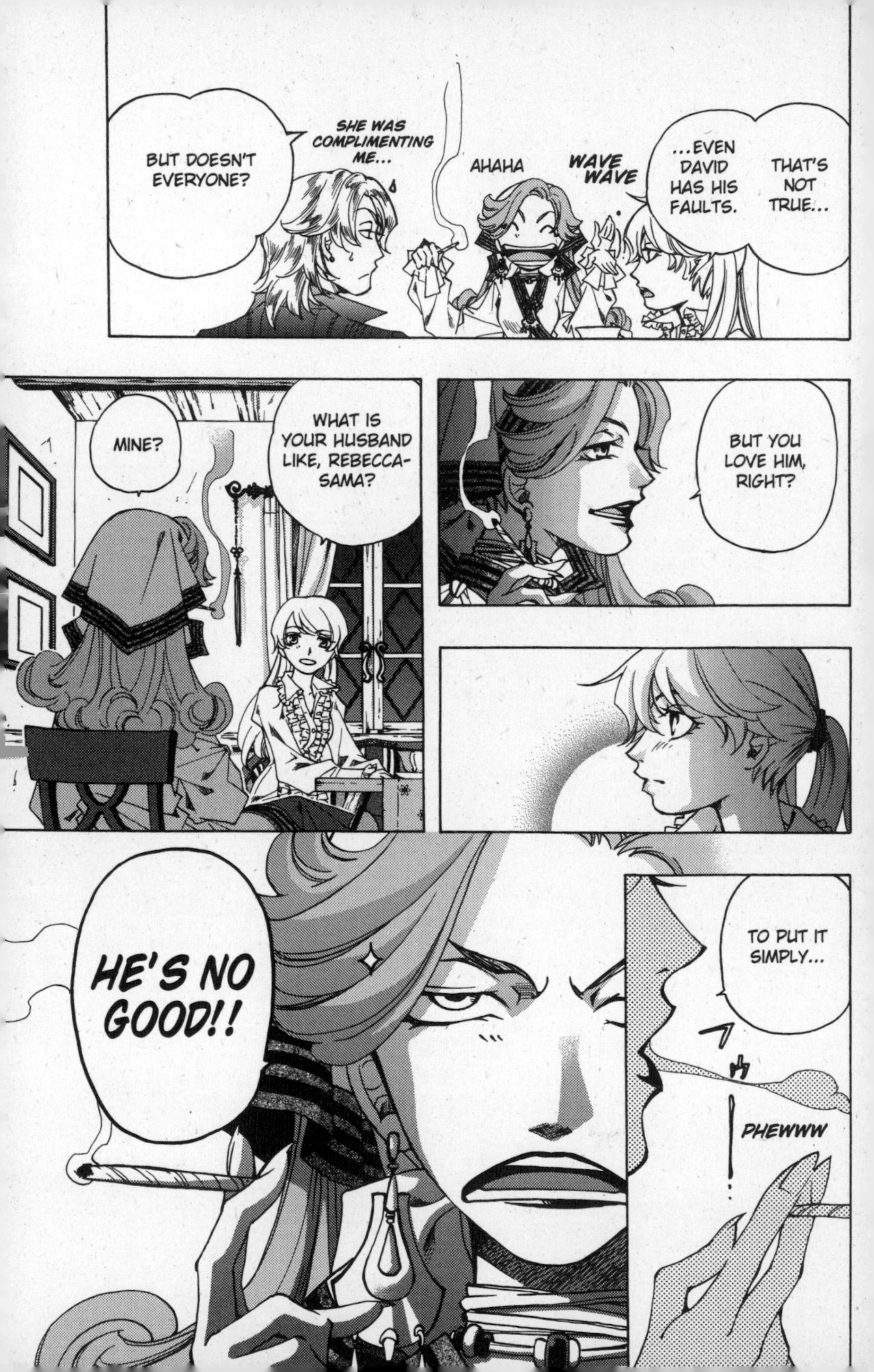
THAT'S NOT TRUE...
...EVEN DAVID HAS HIS FAULTS.
WAVE WAVE
AHAHA
SHE WAS COMPLIMENTING ME...
BUT DOESN'T EVERYONE?
BUT YOU LOVE HIM, RIGHT?
WHAT IS YOUR HUSBAND LIKE, REBECCA-SAMA?
MINE?
TO PUT IT SIMPLY...
PHEWWW
HE'S NO GOOD!!

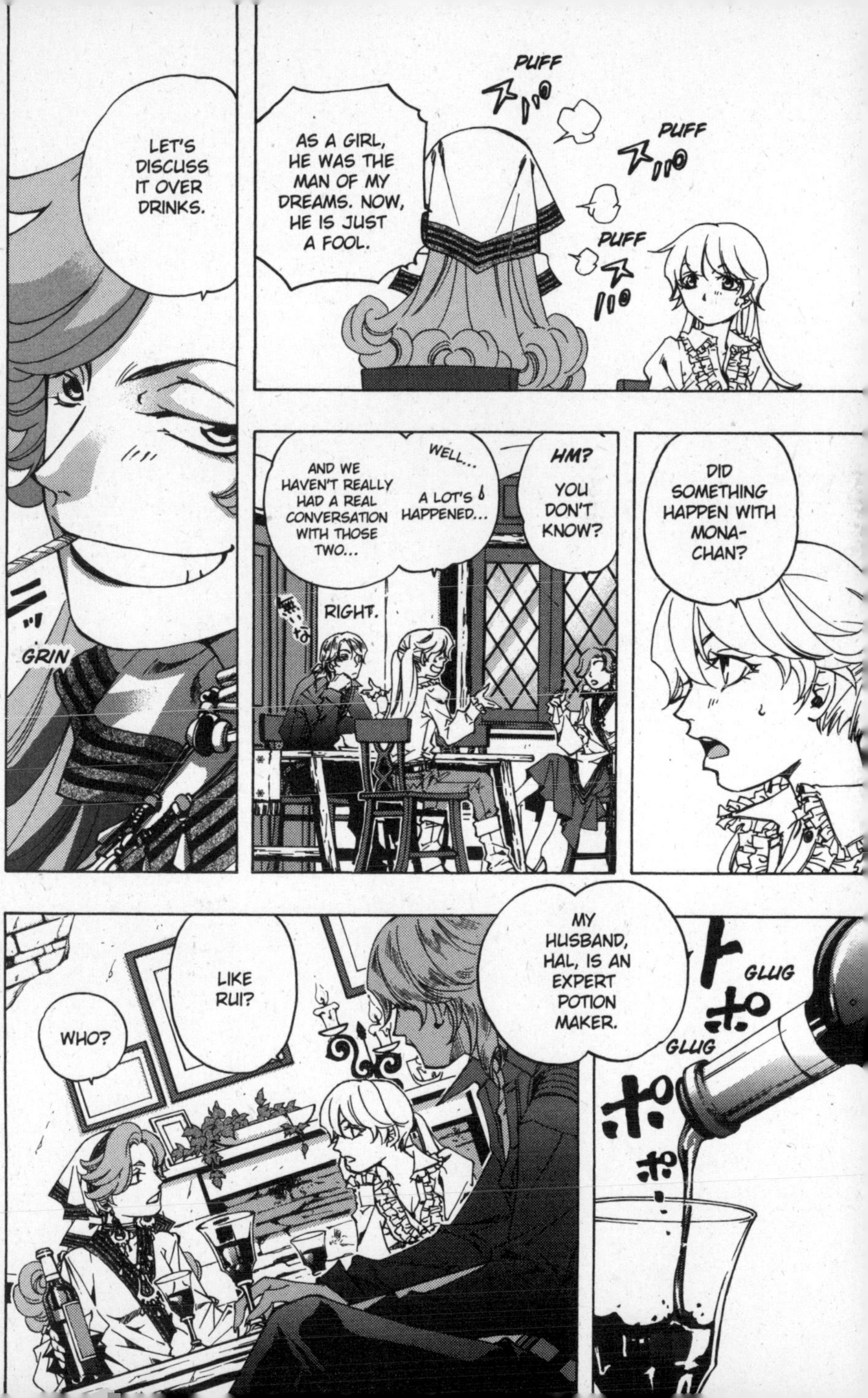
PUFF
PUFF
PUFF
AS A GIRL, HE WAS THE MAN OF MY DREAMS. NOW, HE IS JUST A FOOL.
DID SOMETHING HAPPEN WITH MONA-CHAN?
HM? YOU DON'T KNOW?
WELL... A LOT'S HAPPENED...
AND WE HAVEN'T REALLY HAD A REAL CONVERSATION WITH THOSE TWO...
RIGHT.
LET'S DISCUSS IT OVER DRINKS.
GRIN
GLUG
GLUG
MY HUSBAND, HAL, IS AN EXPERT POTION MAKER.
LIKE RUI?
WHO?

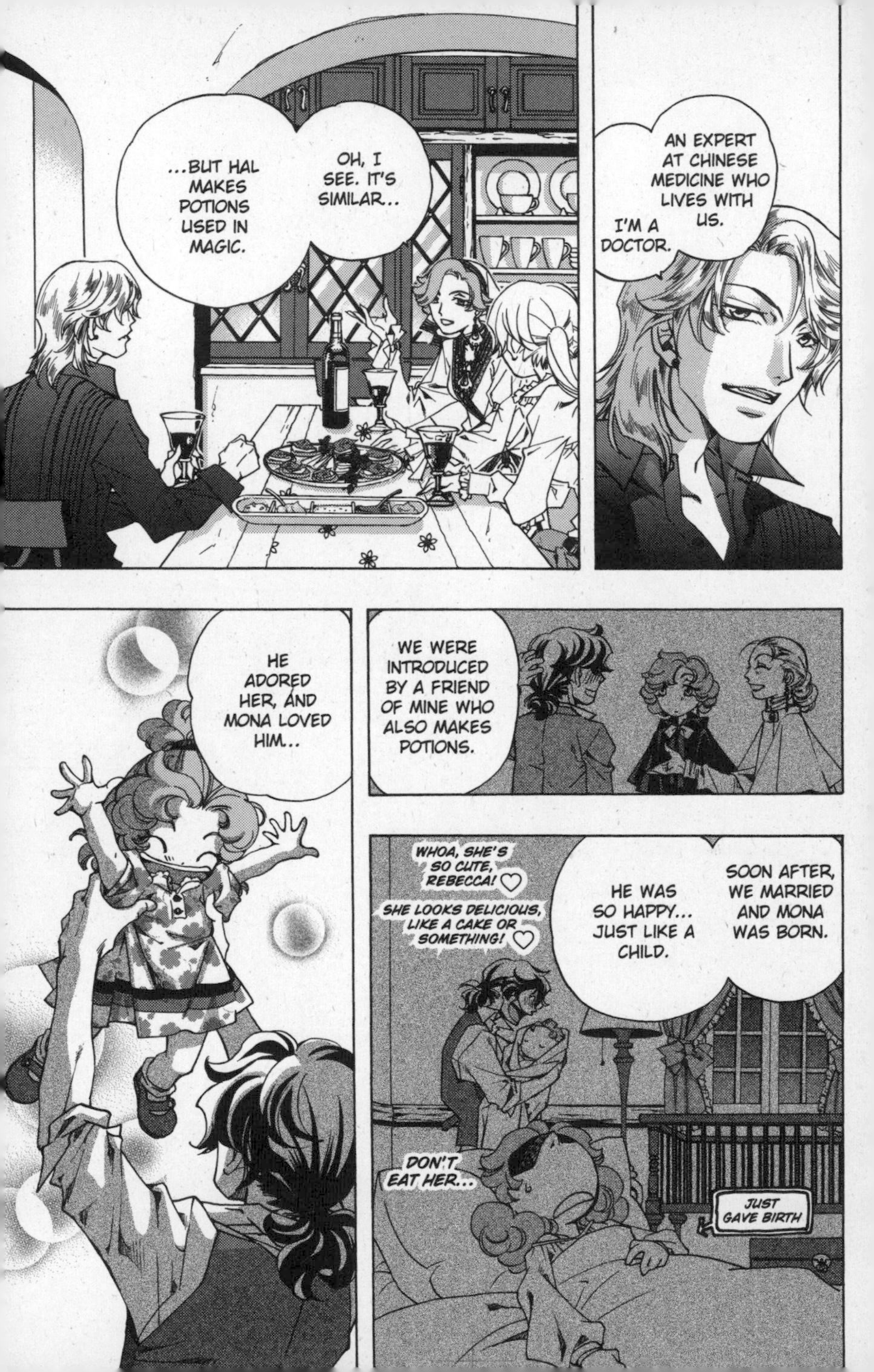
AN EXPERT AT CHINESE MEDICINE WHO LIVES WITH US.
I'M A DOCTOR.
OH, I SEE. IT'S SIMILAR...
...BUT HAL MAKES POTIONS USED IN MAGIC.
WE WERE INTRODUCED BY A FRIEND OF MINE WHO ALSO MAKES POTIONS.
SOON AFTER, WE MARRIED AND MONA WAS BORN.
HE WAS SO HAPPY... JUST LIKE A CHILD.
WHOA, SHE'S SO CUTE, REBECCA! ♡
SHE LOOKS DELICIOUS, LIKE A CAKE OR SOMETHING! ♡
DON'T EAT HER...
JUST GAVE BIRTH
HE ADORED HER, AND MONA LOVED HIM...

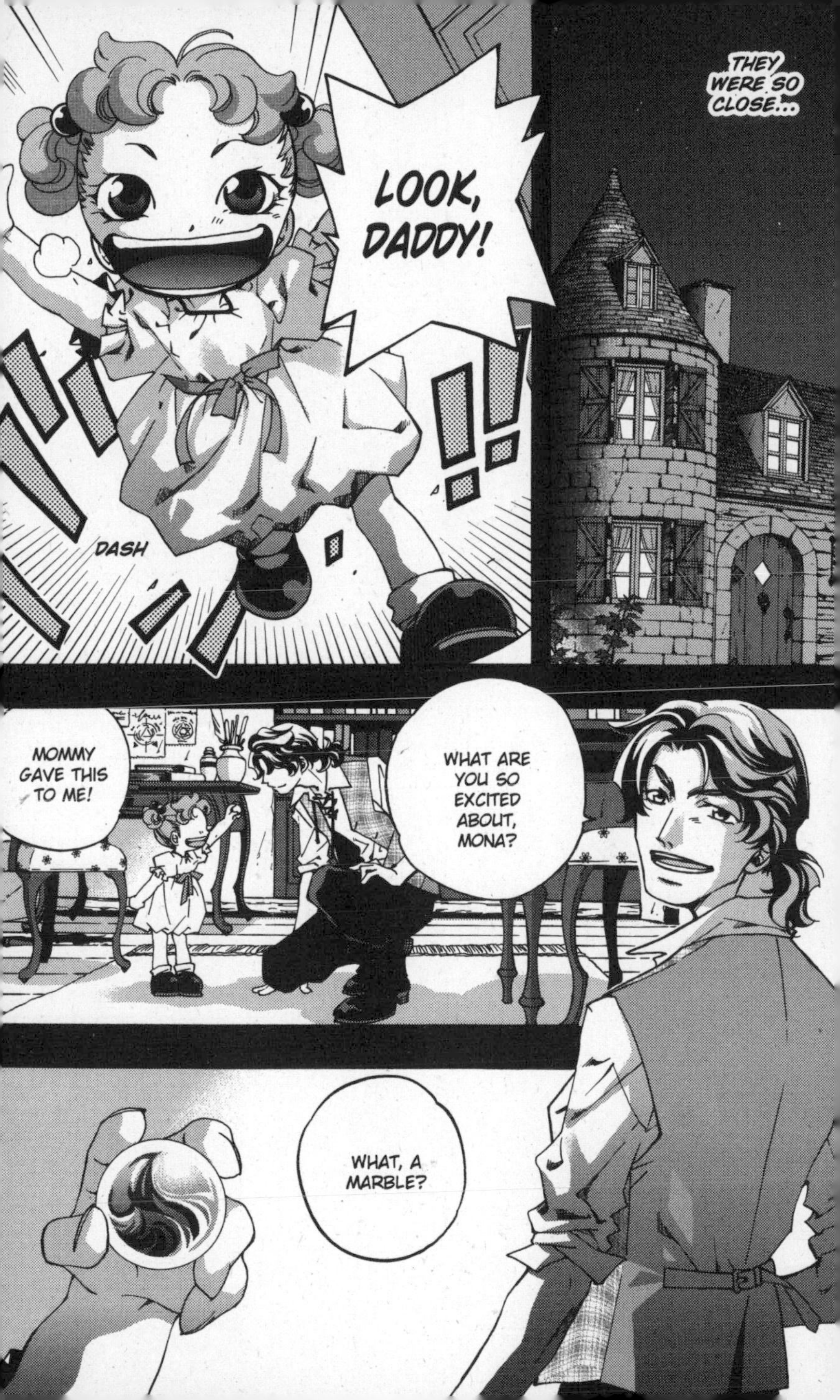
THEY WERE SO CLOSE...
LOOK, DADDY!
DASH
WHAT ARE YOU SO EXCITED ABOUT, MONA?
MOMMY GAVE THIS TO ME!
WHAT, A MARBLE?

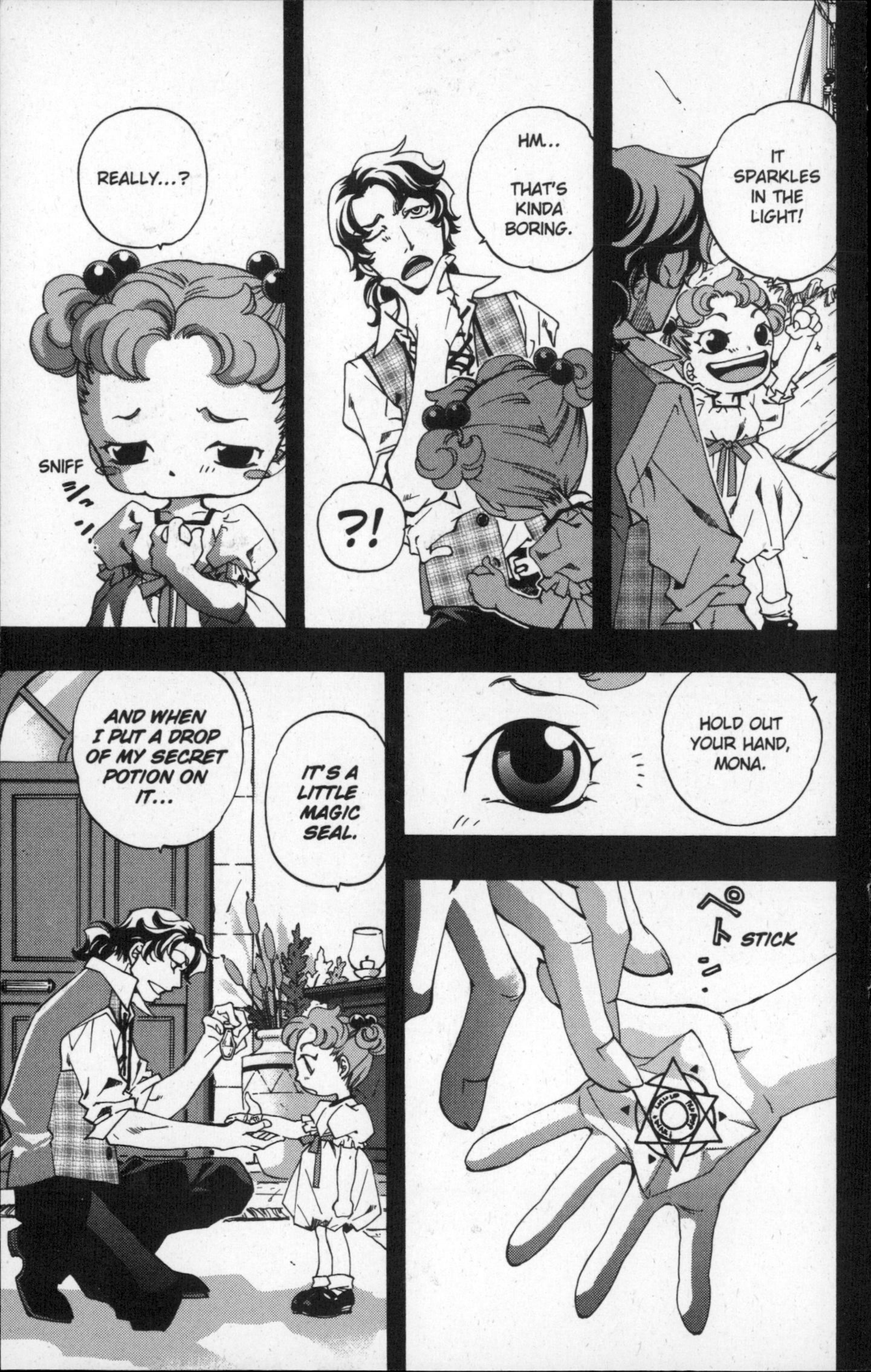
IT SPARKLES IN THE LIGHT!
HM... THAT'S KINDA BORING.
?!
REALLY...?
SNIFF
HOLD OUT YOUR HAND, MONA.
STICK
IT'S A LITTLE MAGIC SEAL.
AND WHEN I PUT A DROP OF MY SECRET POTION ON IT...

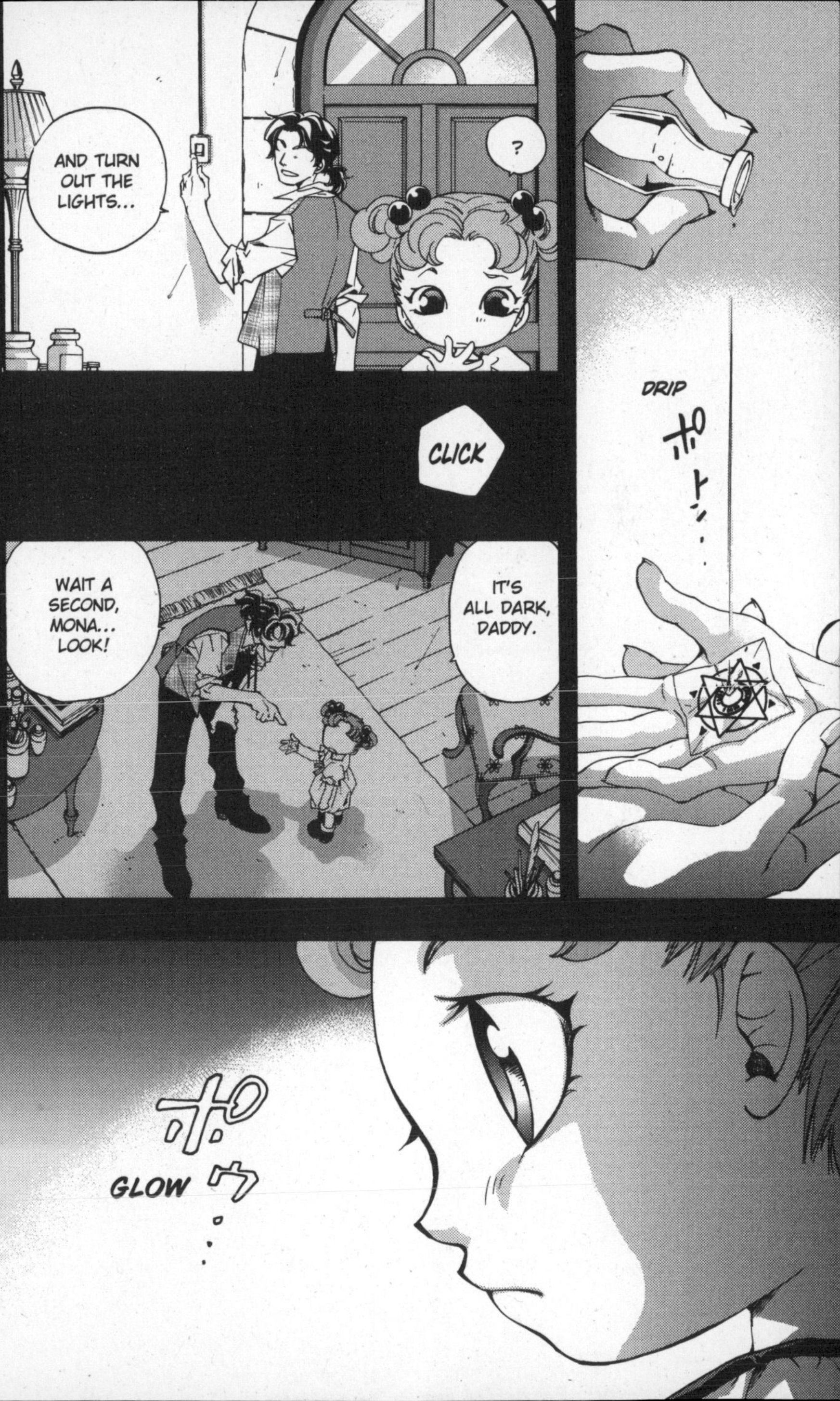
DRIP
ポトッ…
?
AND TURN OUT THE LIGHTS...
CLICK
IT'S ALL DARK, DADDY.
WAIT A SECOND, MONA... LOOK!
GLOW
ポウ…

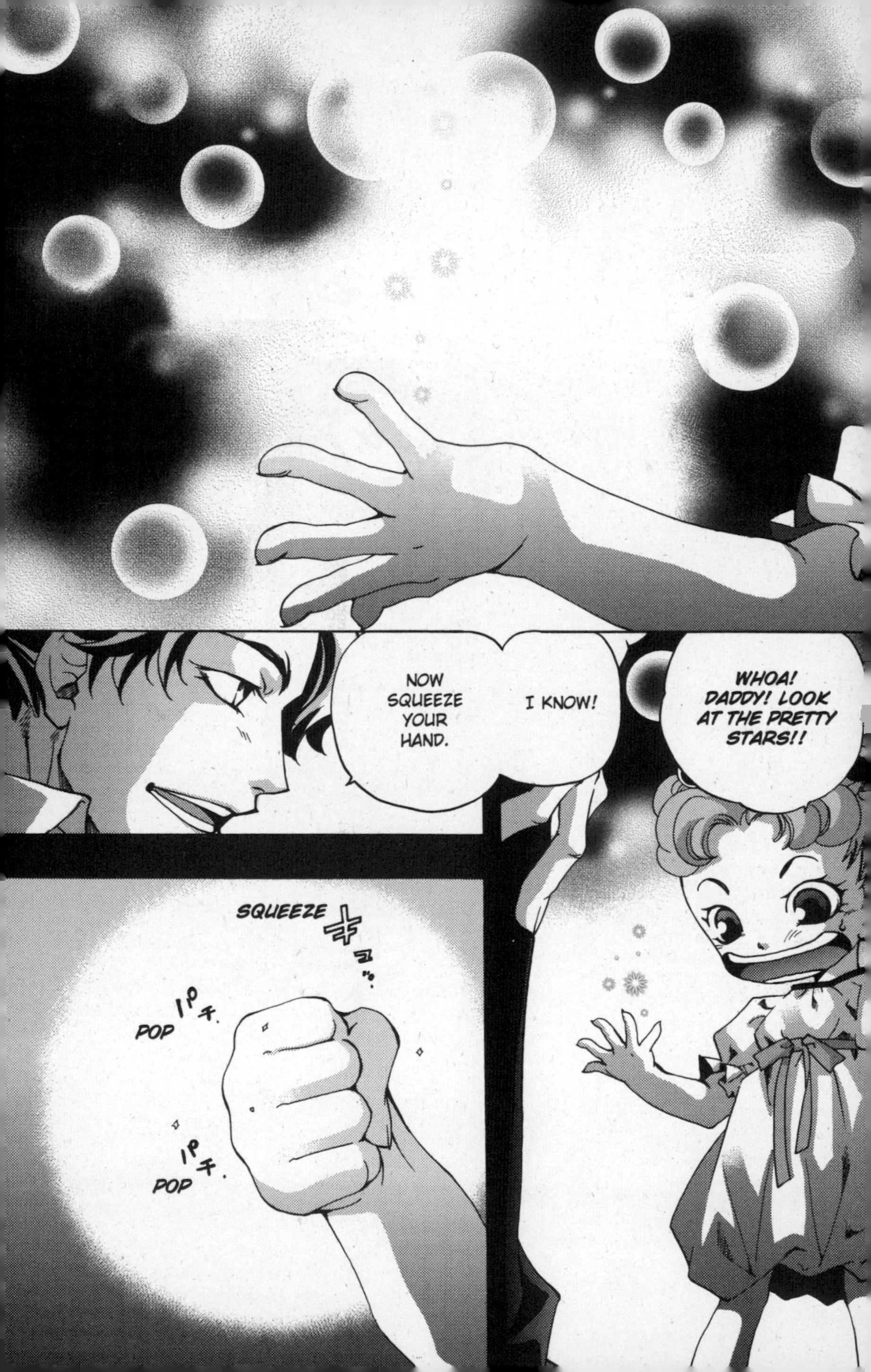
WHOA! DADDY! LOOK AT THE PRETTY STARS!!
I KNOW!
NOW SQUEEZE YOUR HAND.
SQUEEZE
POP
POP

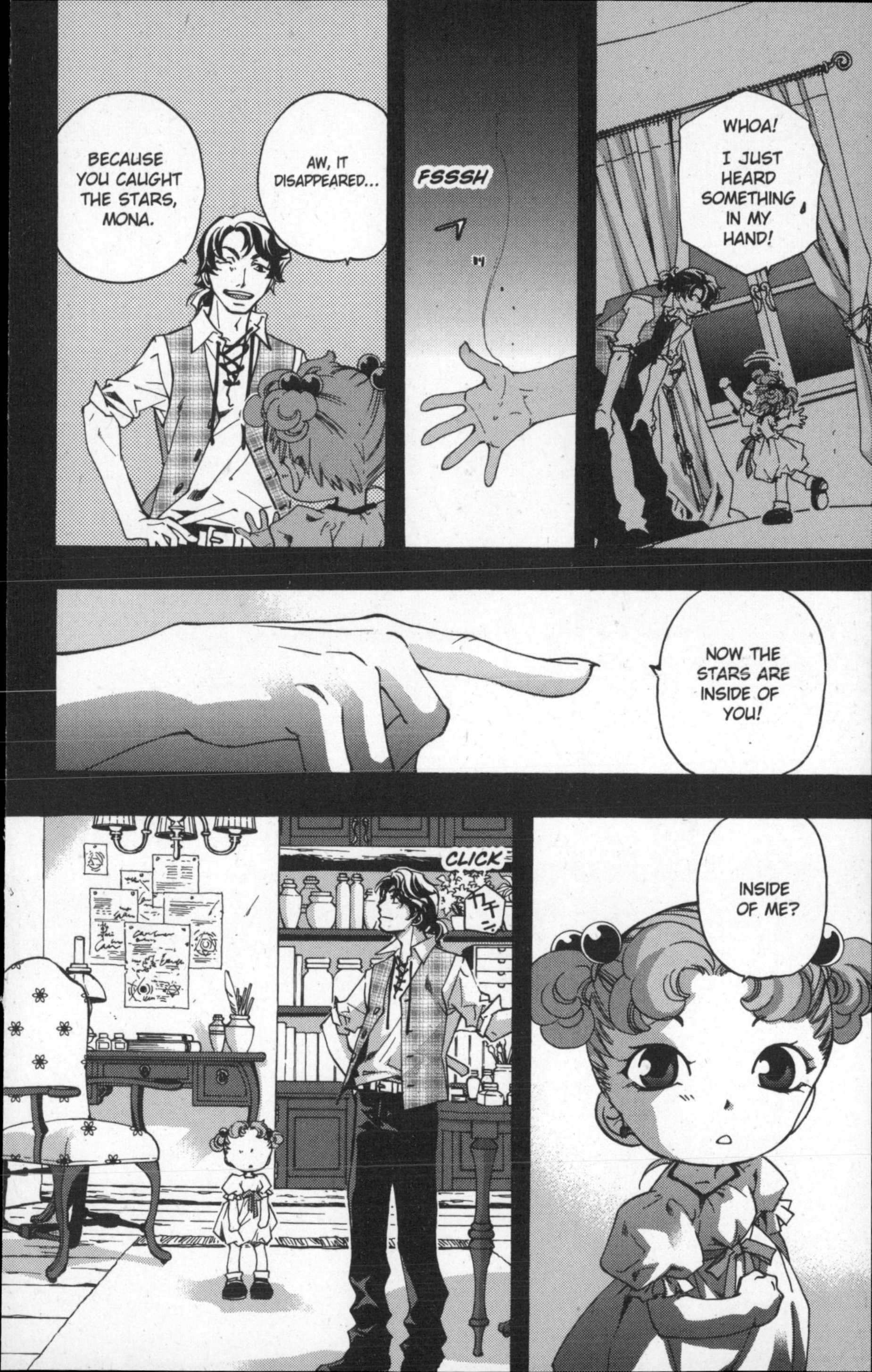
WHOA!
I JUST HEARD SOMETHING IN MY HAND!
FSSSH
AW, IT DISAPPEARED...
BECAUSE YOU CAUGHT THE STARS, MONA.
NOW THE STARS ARE INSIDE OF YOU!
INSIDE OF ME?
CLICK

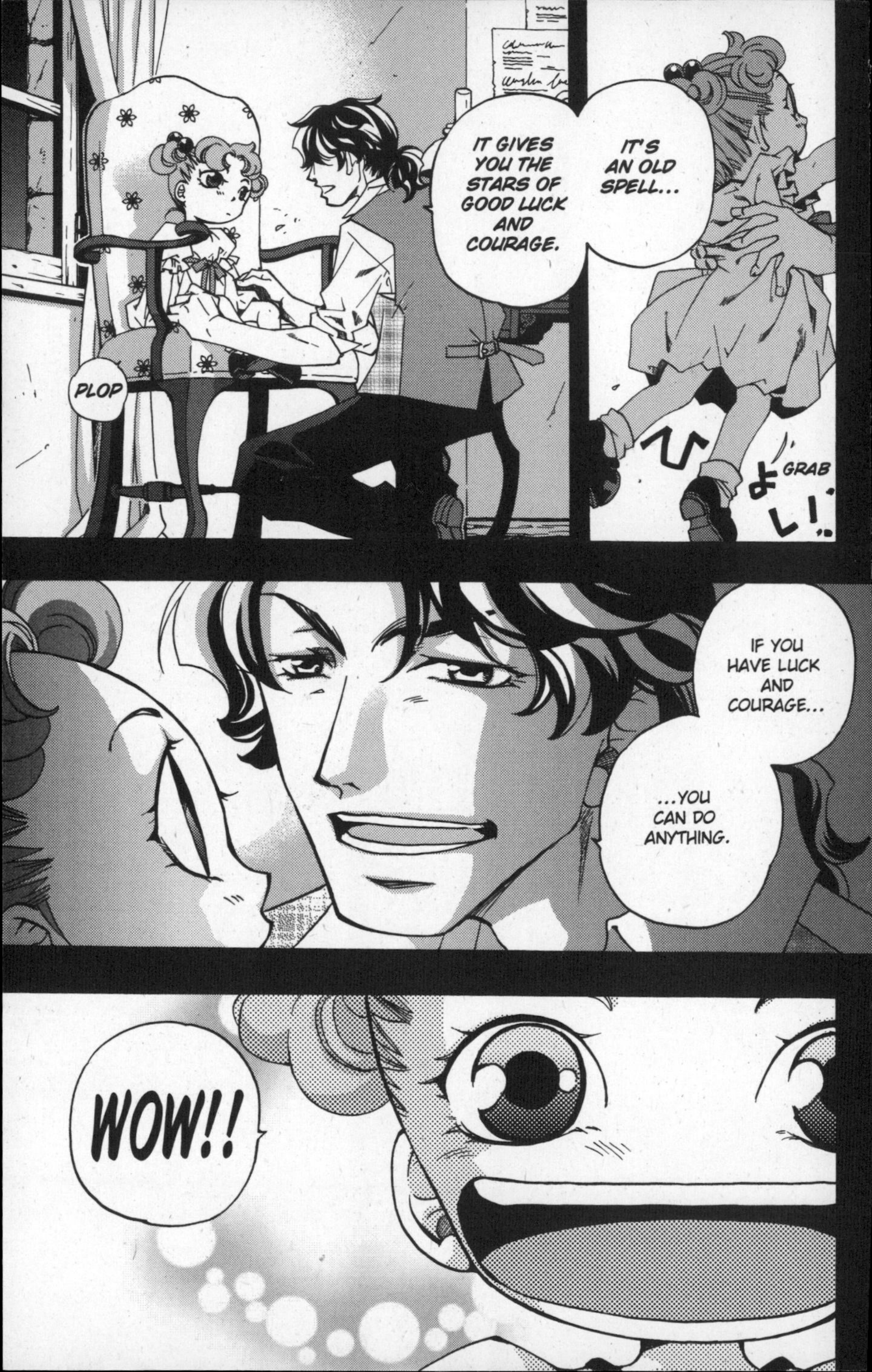

ひょい!
GRAB
IT'S AN OLD SPELL...
IT GIVES YOU THE STARS OF GOOD LUCK AND COURAGE.
PLOP
IF YOU HAVE LUCK AND COURAGE...
...YOU CAN DO ANYTHING.
WOW!!

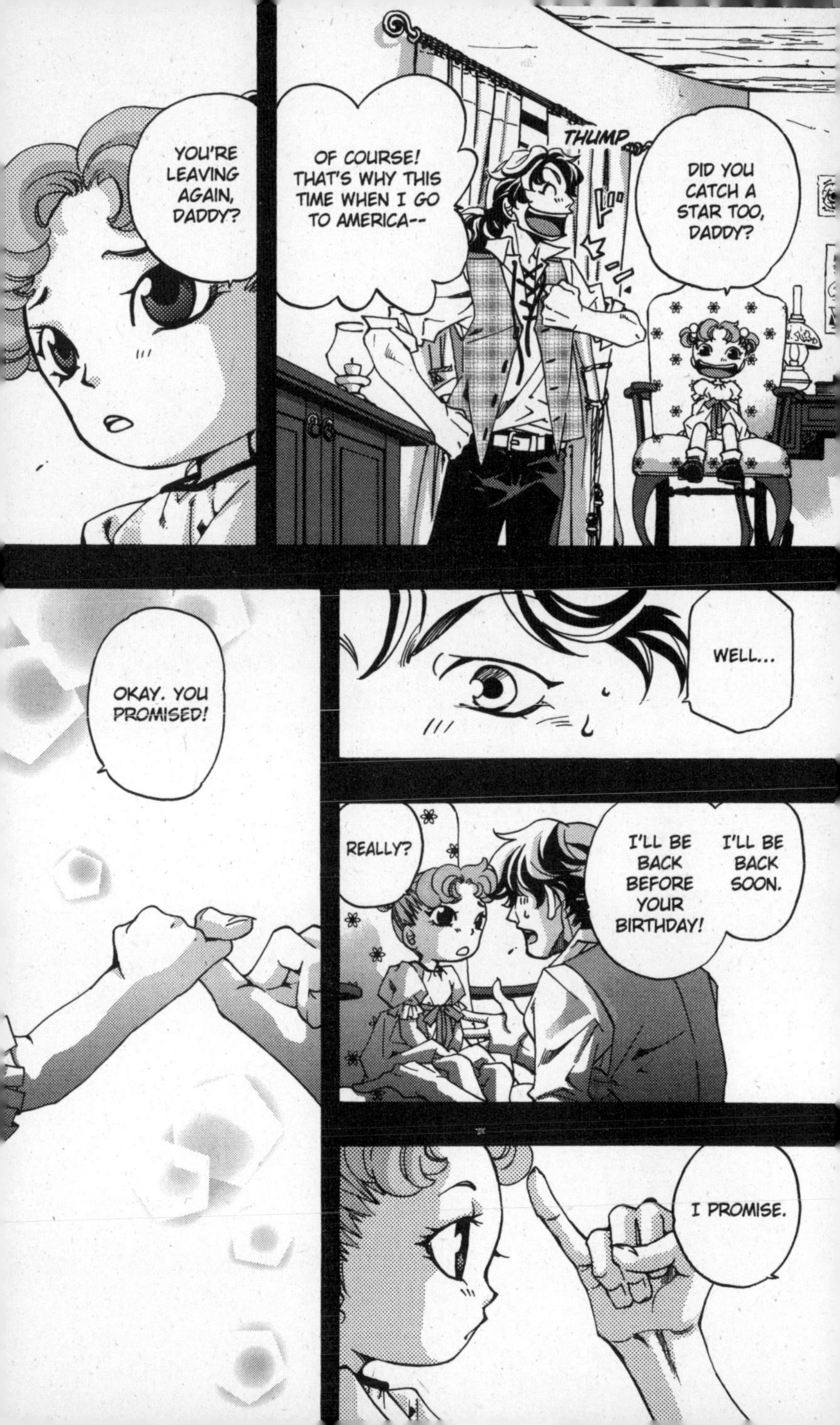
THUMP
DID YOU CATCH A STAR TOO, DADDY?
OF COURSE! THAT'S WHY THIS TIME WHEN I GO TO AMERICA--
YOU'RE LEAVING AGAIN, DADDY?
WELL...
I'LL BE BACK SOON.
I'LL BE BACK BEFORE YOUR BIRTHDAY!
REALLY?
I PROMISE.
OKAY. YOU PROMISED!

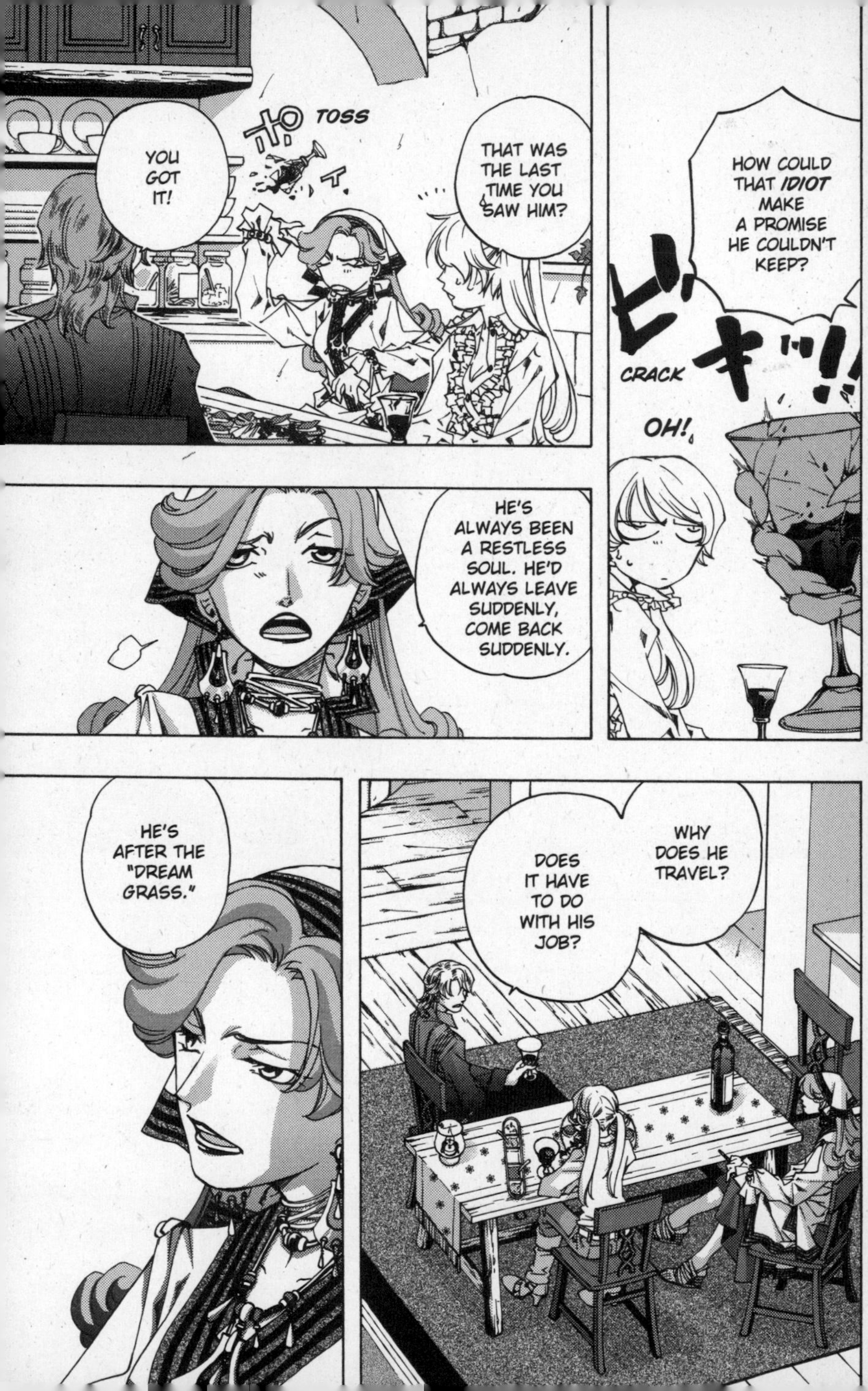
HOW COULD THAT *IDIOT* MAKE A PROMISE HE COULDN'T KEEP?
CRACK
OH!
THAT WAS THE LAST TIME YOU SAW HIM?
TOSS
YOU GOT IT!
HE'S ALWAYS BEEN A RESTLESS SOUL. HE'D ALWAYS LEAVE SUDDENLY, COME BACK SUDDENLY.
WHY DOES HE TRAVEL?
DOES IT HAVE TO DO WITH HIS JOB?
HE'S AFTER THE "DREAM GRASS."

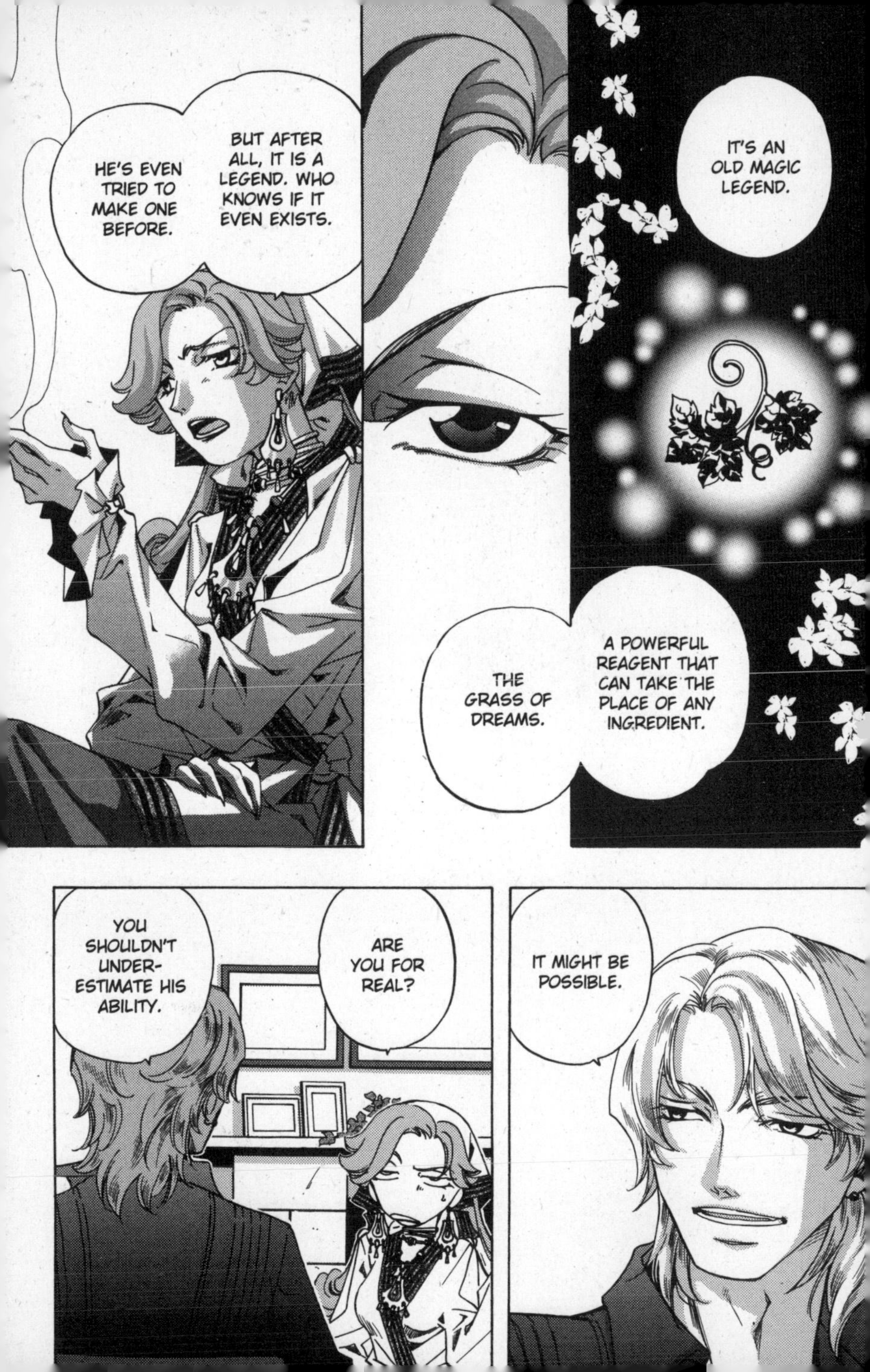
IT'S AN OLD MAGIC LEGEND.
THE GRASS OF DREAMS. A POWERFUL REAGENT THAT CAN TAKE THE PLACE OF ANY INGREDIENT.
HE'S EVEN TRIED TO MAKE ONE BEFORE. BUT AFTER ALL, IT IS A LEGEND. WHO KNOWS IF IT EVEN EXISTS.
IT MIGHT BE POSSIBLE.
ARE YOU FOR REAL?
YOU SHOULDN'T UNDER-ESTIMATE HIS ABILITY.

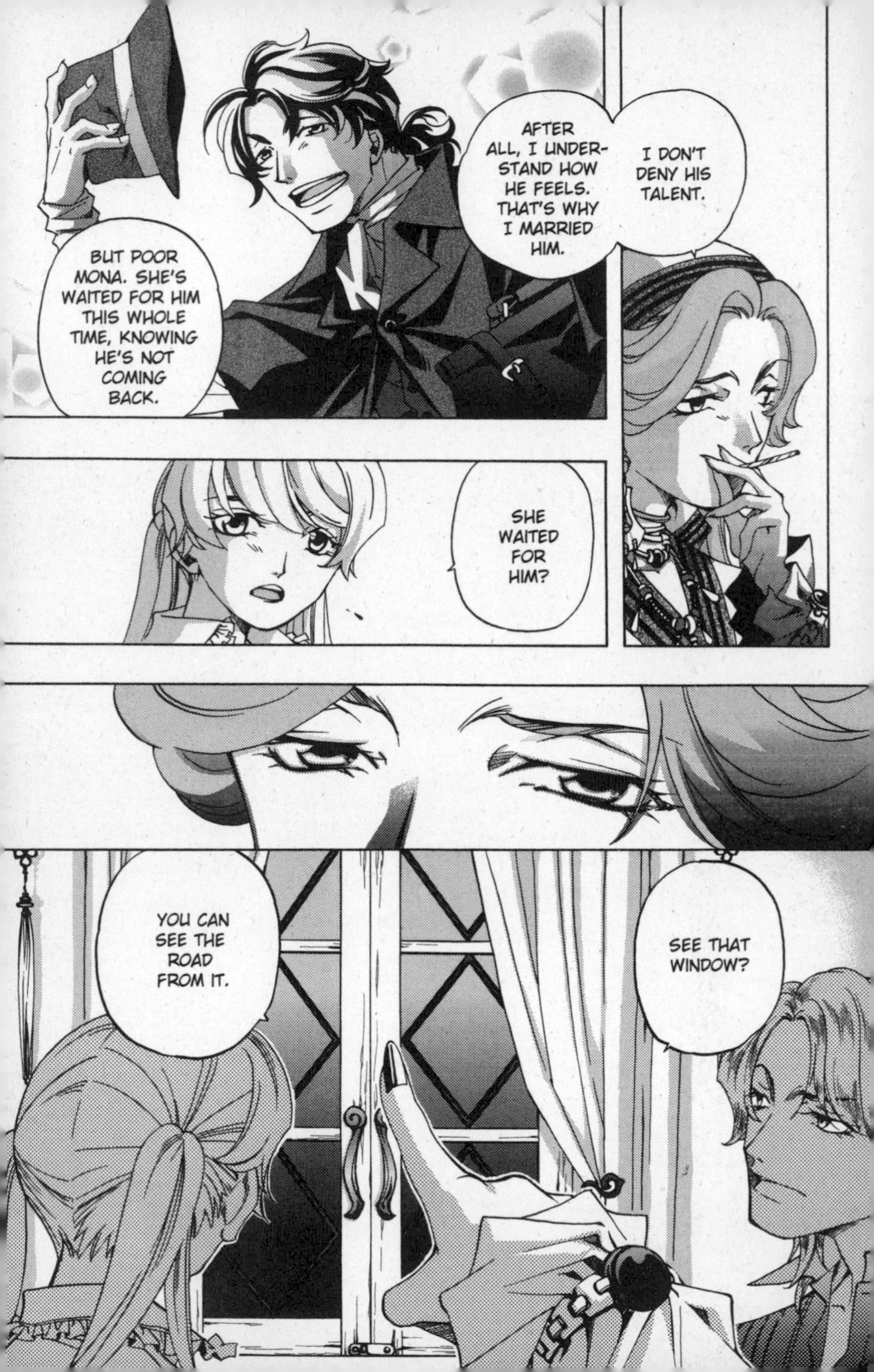
I DON'T DENY HIS TALENT.
AFTER ALL, I UNDERSTAND HOW HE FEELS. THAT'S WHY I MARRIED HIM.
BUT POOR MONA. SHE'S WAITED FOR HIM THIS WHOLE TIME, KNOWING HE'S NOT COMING BACK.
SHE WAITED FOR HIM?
SEE THAT WINDOW?
YOU CAN SEE THE ROAD FROM IT.

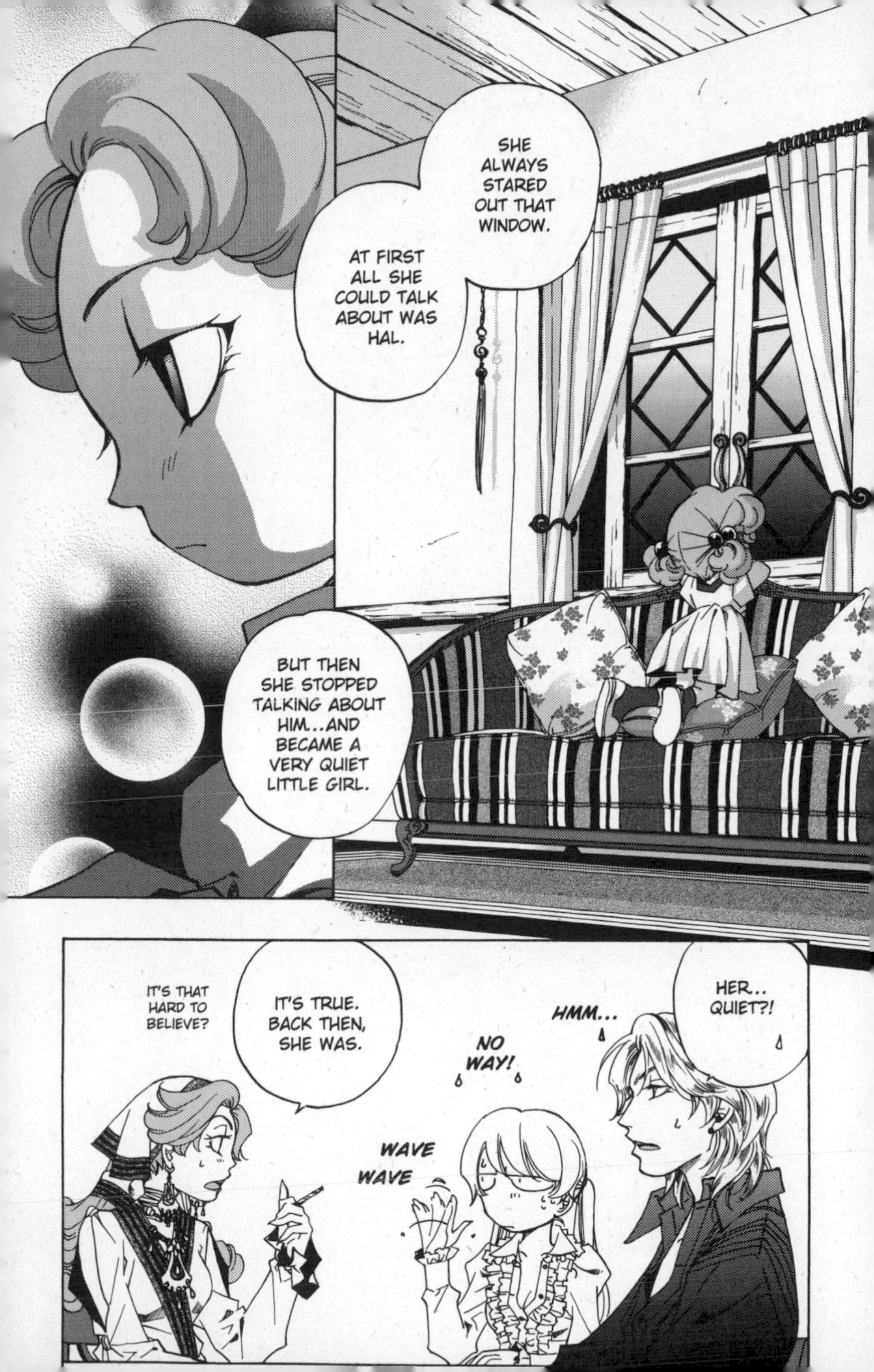
SHE ALWAYS STARED OUT THAT WINDOW.
AT FIRST ALL SHE COULD TALK ABOUT WAS HAL.
BUT THEN SHE STOPPED TALKING ABOUT HIM...AND BECAME A VERY QUIET LITTLE GIRL.
HER.. QUIET?!
HMM...
NO WAY!
WAVE WAVE
IT'S TRUE. BACK THEN, SHE WAS.
IT'S THAT HARD TO BELIEVE?

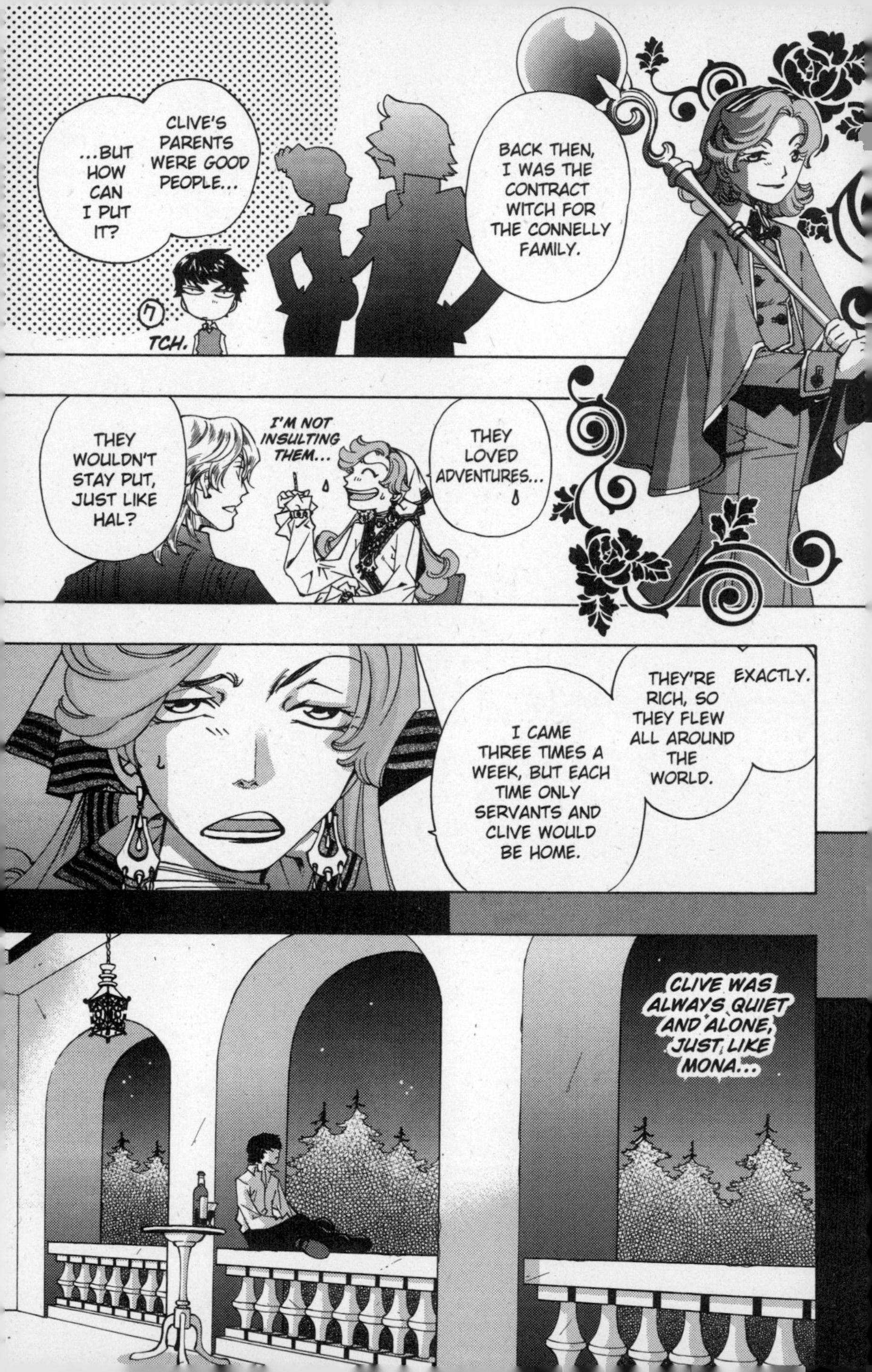
BACK THEN, I WAS THE CONTRACT WITCH FOR THE CONNELLY FAMILY.
CLIVE'S PARENTS WERE GOOD PEOPLE...
...BUT HOW CAN I PUT IT?
TCH.
THEY LOVED ADVENTURES...
I'M NOT INSULTING THEM...
THEY WOULDN'T STAY PUT, JUST LIKE HAL?
EXACTLY.
THEY'RE RICH, SO THEY FLEW ALL AROUND THE WORLD.
I CAME THREE TIMES A WEEK, BUT EACH TIME ONLY SERVANTS AND CLIVE WOULD BE HOME.
CLIVE WAS ALWAYS QUIET AND ALONE, JUST LIKE MONA...

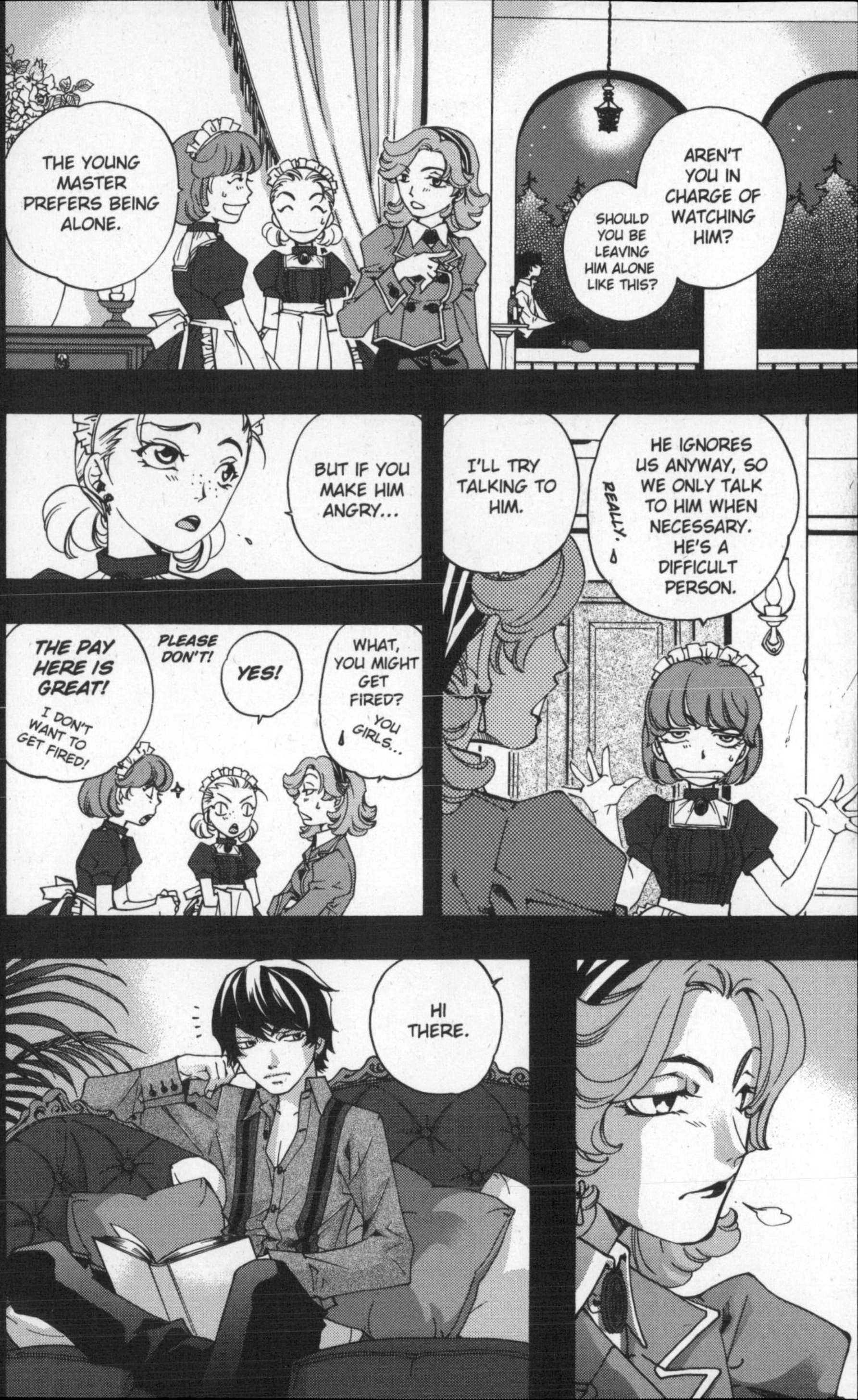
AREN'T YOU IN CHARGE OF WATCHING HIM?
SHOULD YOU BE LEAVING HIM ALONE LIKE THIS?
THE YOUNG MASTER PREFERS BEING ALONE.
I'LL TRY TALKING TO HIM.
HE IGNORES US ANYWAY, SO WE ONLY TALK TO HIM WHEN NECESSARY. HE'S A DIFFICULT PERSON.
REALLY.
BUT IF YOU MAKE HIM ANGRY...
WHAT, YOU MIGHT GET FIRED?
YOU GIRLS...
YES!
PLEASE DON'T!
THE PAY HERE IS GREAT!
I DON'T WANT TO GET FIRED!
HI THERE.

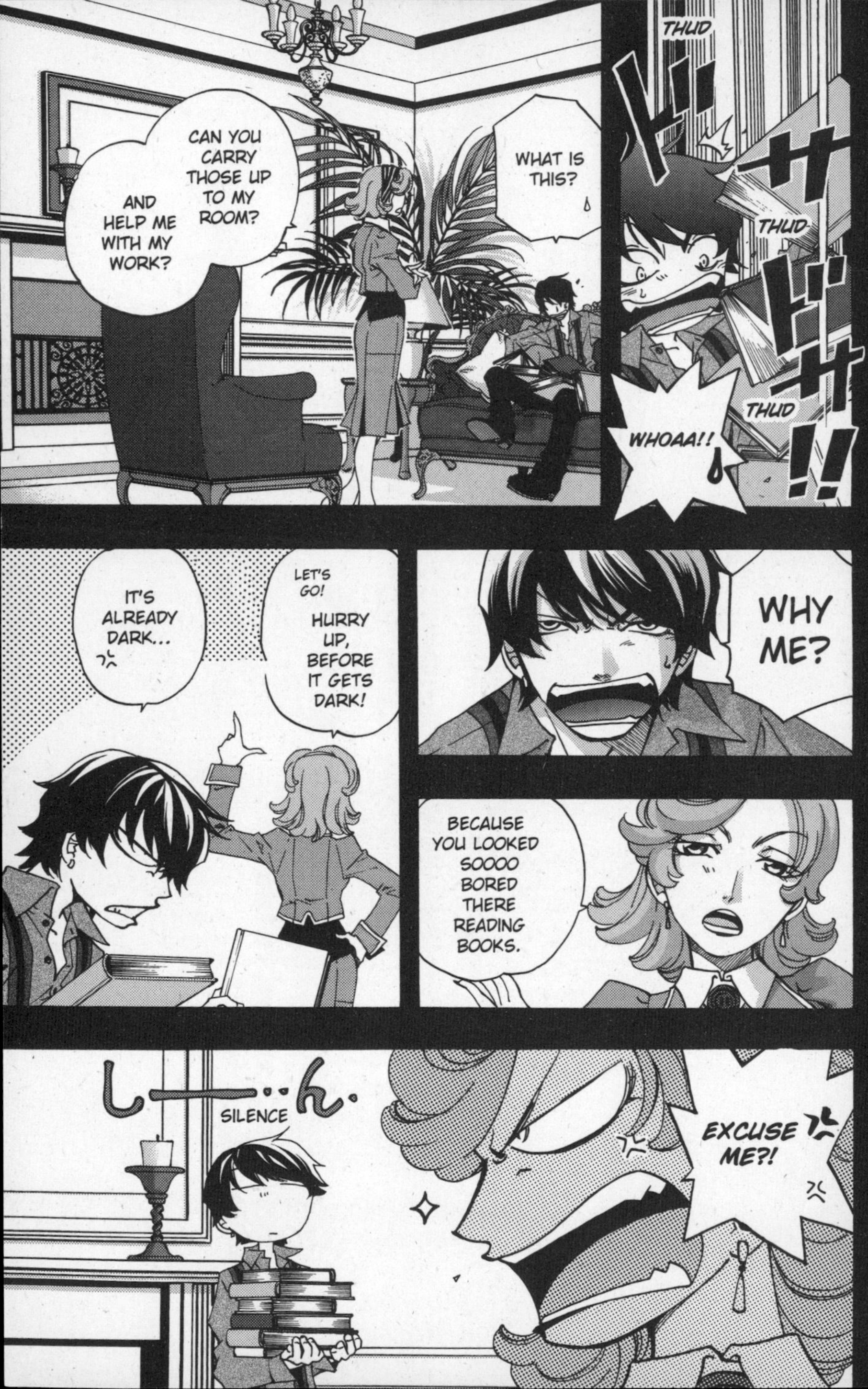
THUD
THUD
THUD
WHOAA!!
!!
WHAT IS THIS?
CAN YOU CARRY THOSE UP TO MY ROOM?
AND HELP ME WITH MY WORK?
WHY ME?
BECAUSE YOU LOOKED SOOOO BORED THERE READING BOOKS.
LET'S GO!
HURRY UP, BEFORE IT GETS DARK!
IT'S ALREADY DARK...
EXCUSE ME?!
しー…ん.
SILENCE

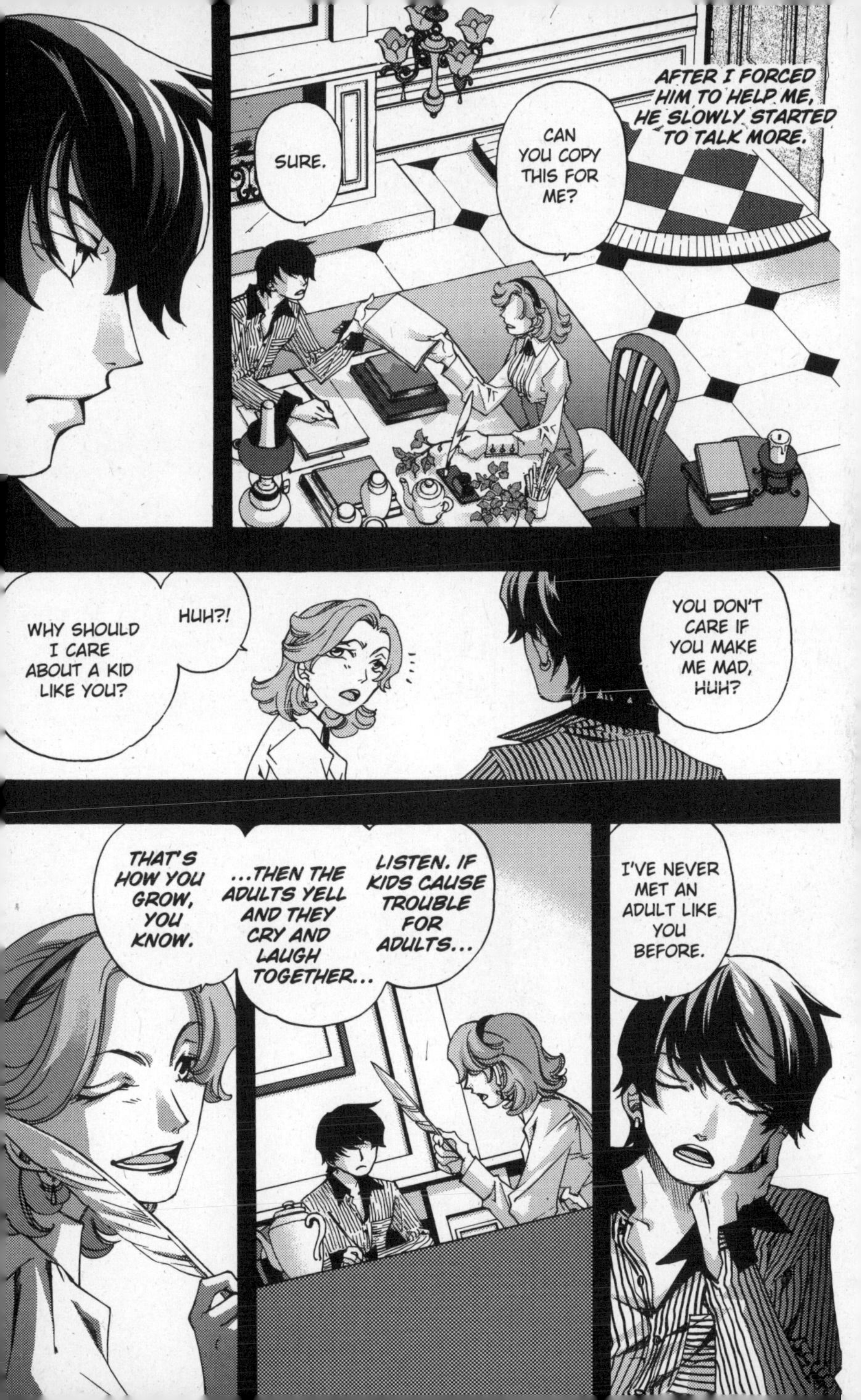
AFTER I FORCED HIM TO HELP ME, HE SLOWLY STARTED TO TALK MORE.
CAN YOU COPY THIS FOR ME?
SURE.
YOU DON'T CARE IF YOU MAKE ME MAD, HUH?
HUH?!
WHY SHOULD I CARE ABOUT A KID LIKE YOU?
I'VE NEVER MET AN ADULT LIKE YOU BEFORE.
LISTEN. IF KIDS CAUSE TROUBLE FOR ADULTS...
...THEN THE ADULTS YELL AND THEY CRY AND LAUGH TOGETHER...
THAT'S HOW YOU GROW, YOU KNOW.

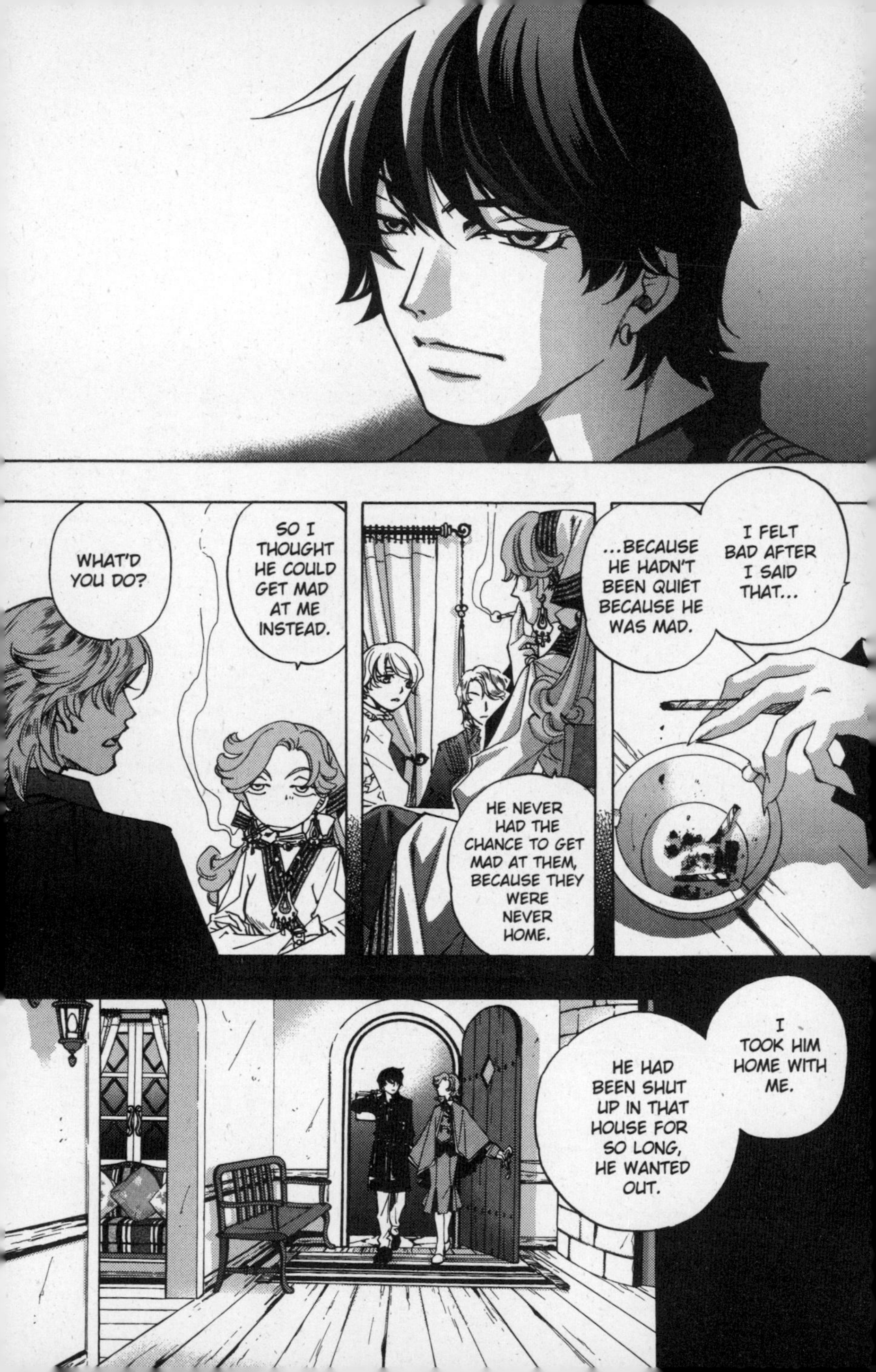
I FELT BAD AFTER I SAID THAT...
...BECAUSE HE HADN'T BEEN QUIET BECAUSE HE WAS MAD.
HE NEVER HAD THE CHANCE TO GET MAD AT THEM, BECAUSE THEY WERE NEVER HOME.
SO I THOUGHT HE COULD GET MAD AT ME INSTEAD.
WHAT'D YOU DO?
I TOOK HIM HOME WITH ME.
HE HAD BEEN SHUT UP IN THAT HOUSE FOR SO LONG, HE WANTED OUT.

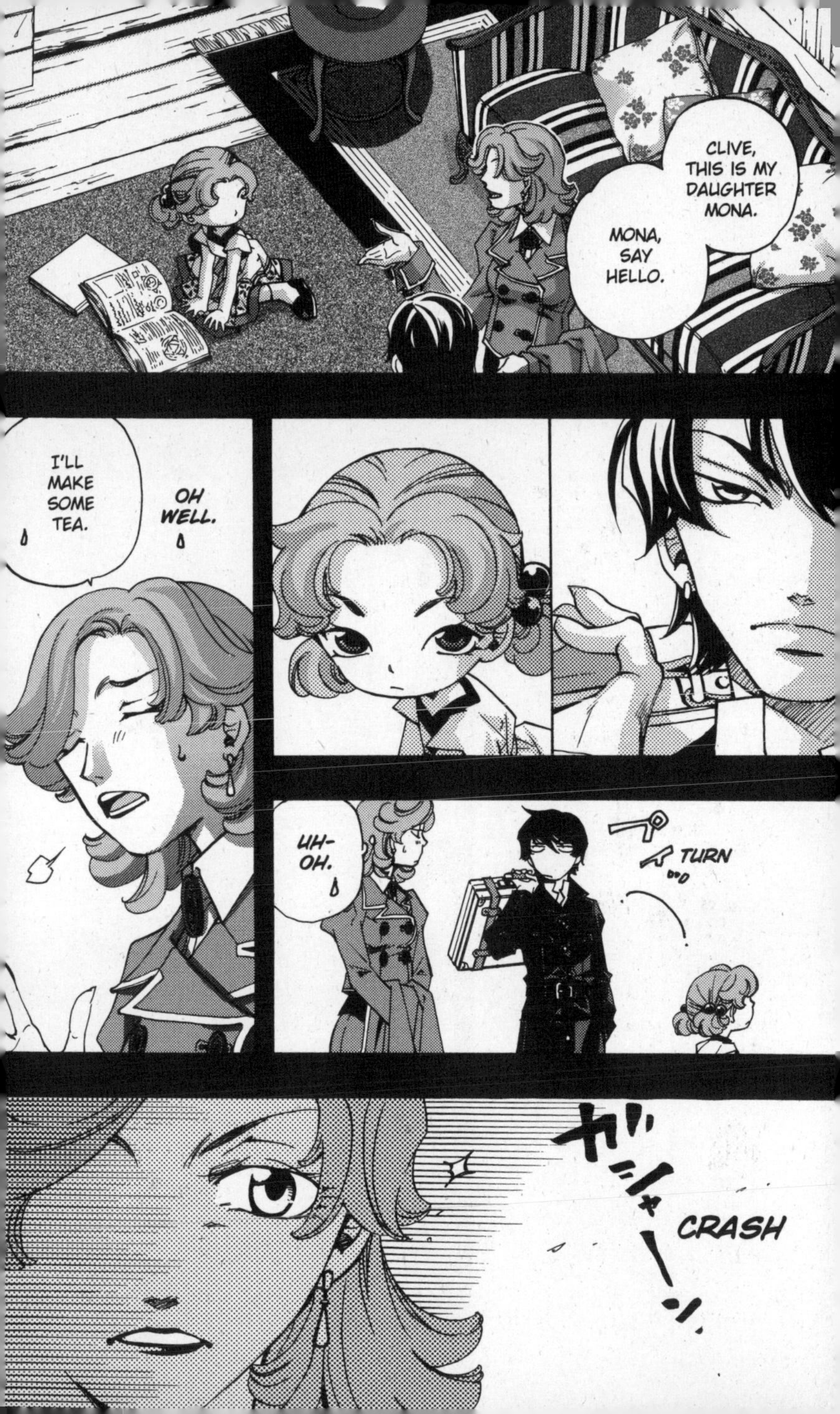
CLIVE, THIS IS MY DAUGHTER MONA.
MONA, SAY HELLO.
TURN
UH-OH.
OH WELL.
I'LL MAKE SOME TEA.
ガシャーン
CRASH

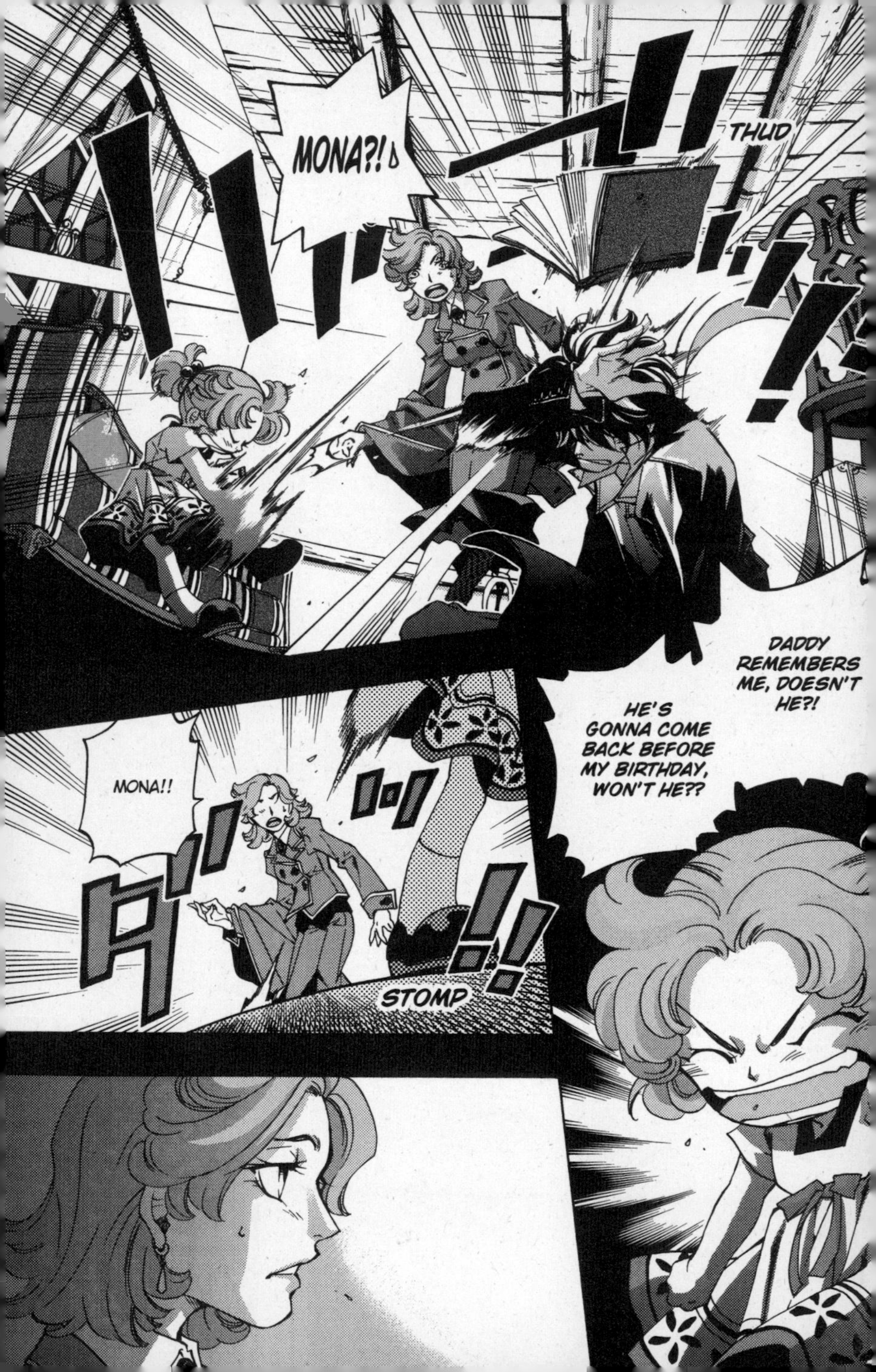
THUD
MONA?!
DADDY REMEMBERS ME, DOESN'T HE?!
HE'S GONNA COME BACK BEFORE MY BIRTHDAY, WON'T HE??
MONA!!
STOMP

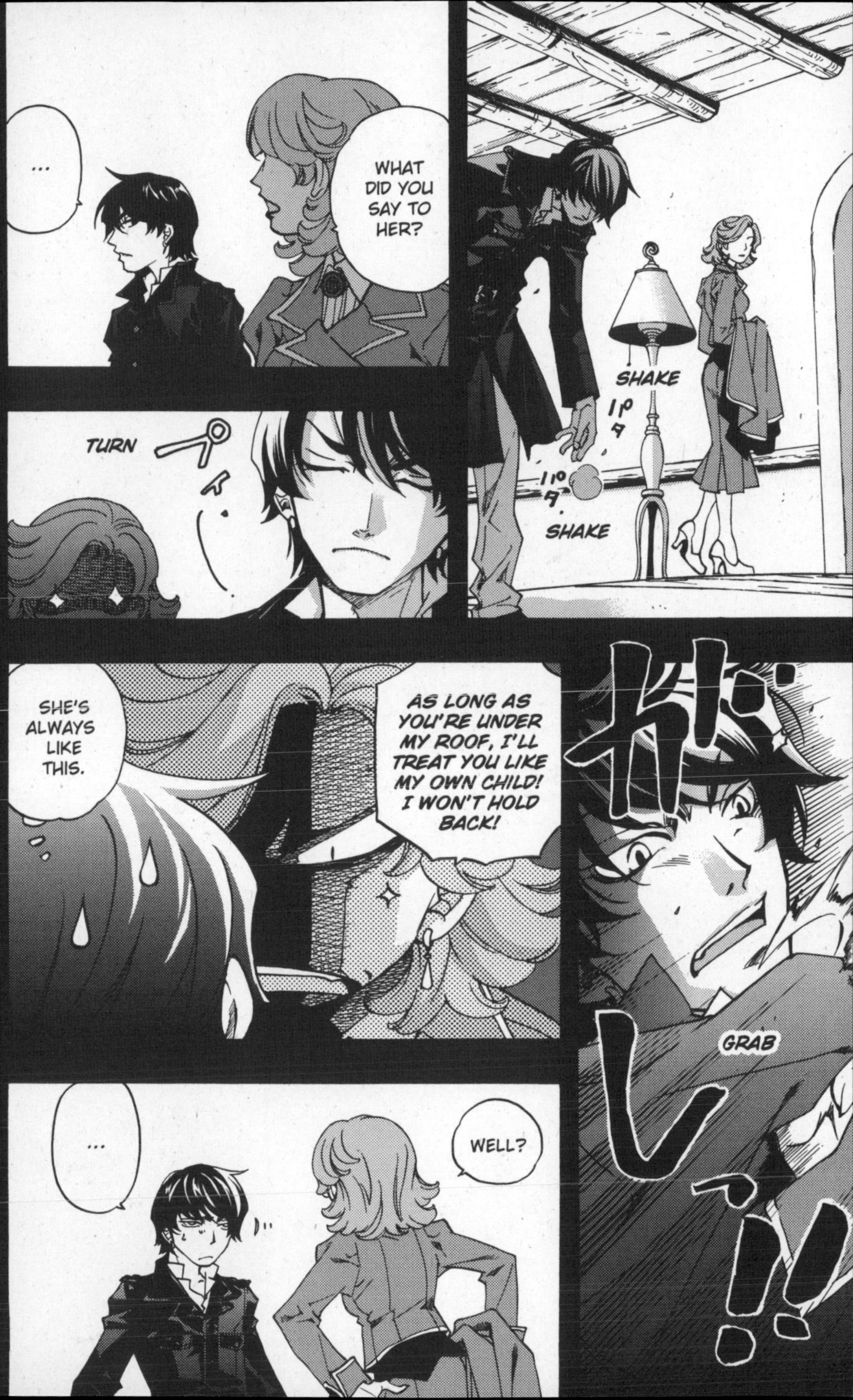
SHAKE
SHAKE
WHAT DID YOU SAY TO HER?
...
TURN
GRAB
AS LONG AS YOU'RE UNDER MY ROOF, I'LL TREAT YOU LIKE MY OWN CHILD! I WON'T HOLD BACK!
SHE'S ALWAYS LIKE THIS.
WELL?
...

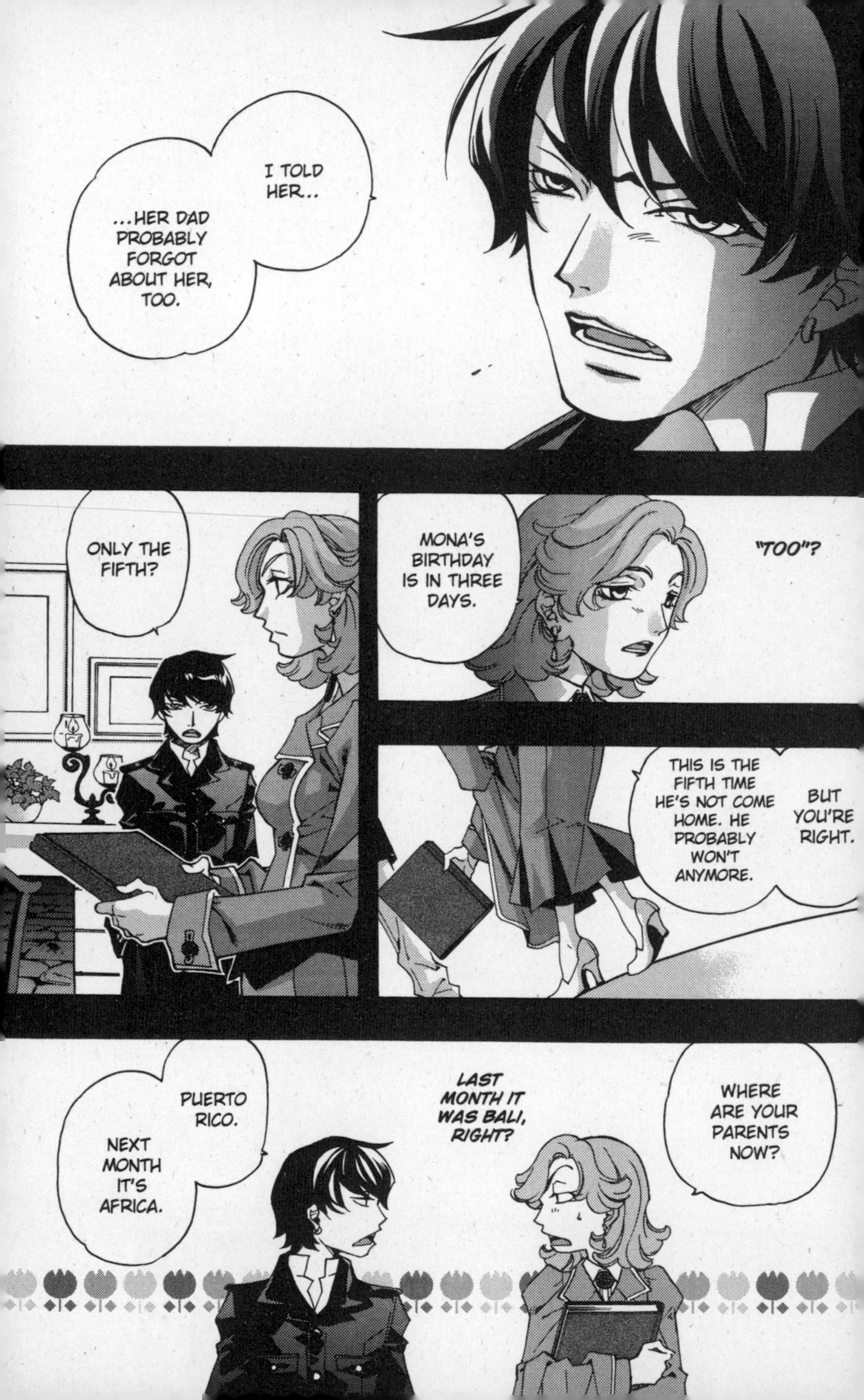
I TOLD HER...
...HER DAD PROBABLY FORGOT ABOUT HER, TOO.
"TOO"?
MONA'S BIRTHDAY IS IN THREE DAYS.
BUT YOU'RE RIGHT.
THIS IS THE FIFTH TIME HE'S NOT COME HOME. HE PROBABLY WON'T ANYMORE.
ONLY THE FIFTH?
WHERE ARE YOUR PARENTS NOW?
LAST MONTH IT WAS BALI, RIGHT?
PUERTO RICO.
NEXT MONTH IT'S AFRICA.

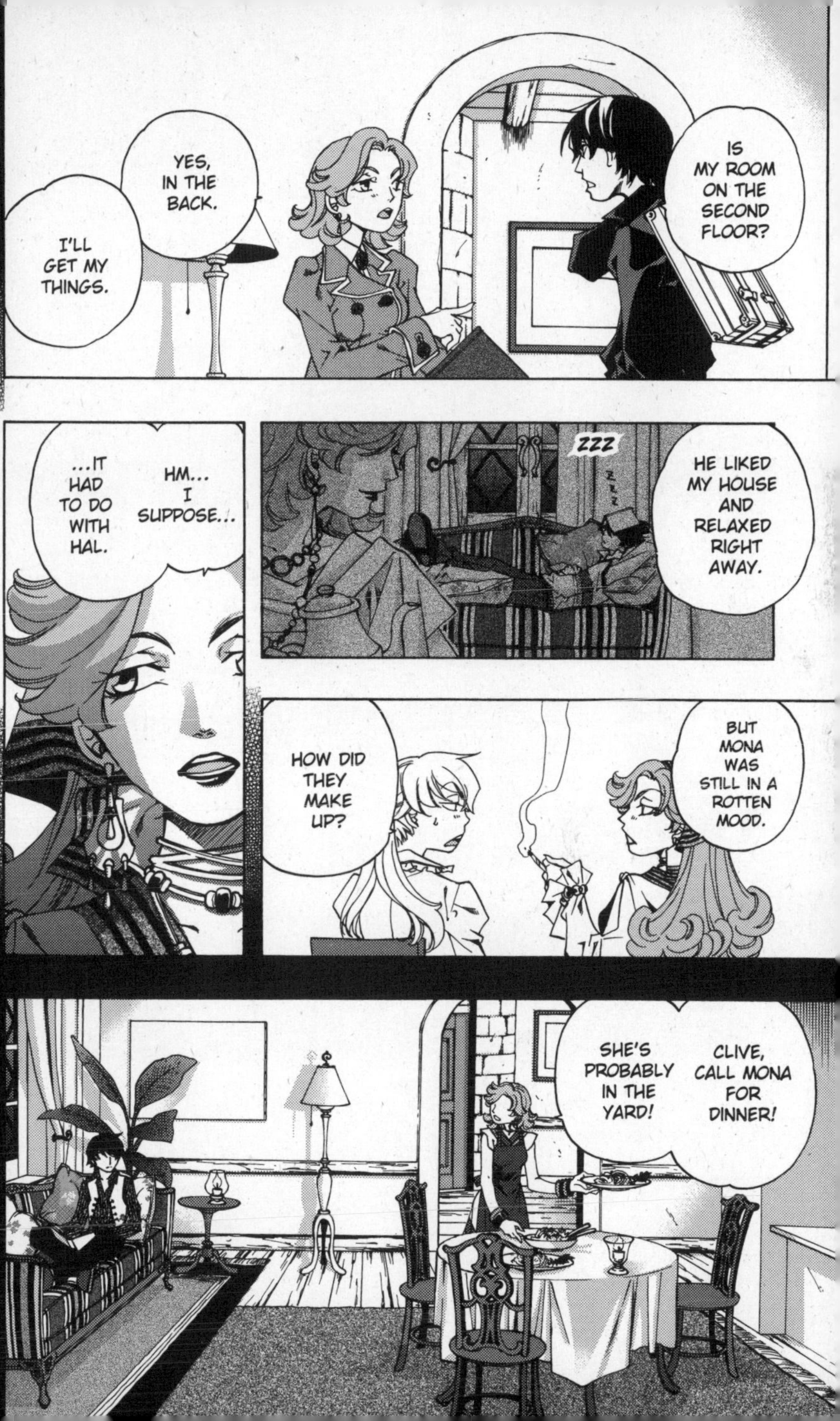
IS MY ROOM ON THE SECOND FLOOR?
YES, IN THE BACK.
I'LL GET MY THINGS.
ZZZ
HE LIKED MY HOUSE AND RELAXED RIGHT AWAY.
BUT MONA WAS STILL IN A ROTTEN MOOD.
HOW DID THEY MAKE UP?
HM... I SUPPOSE...
...IT HAD TO DO WITH HAL.
CLIVE, CALL MONA FOR DINNER!
SHE'S PROBABLY IN THE YARD!

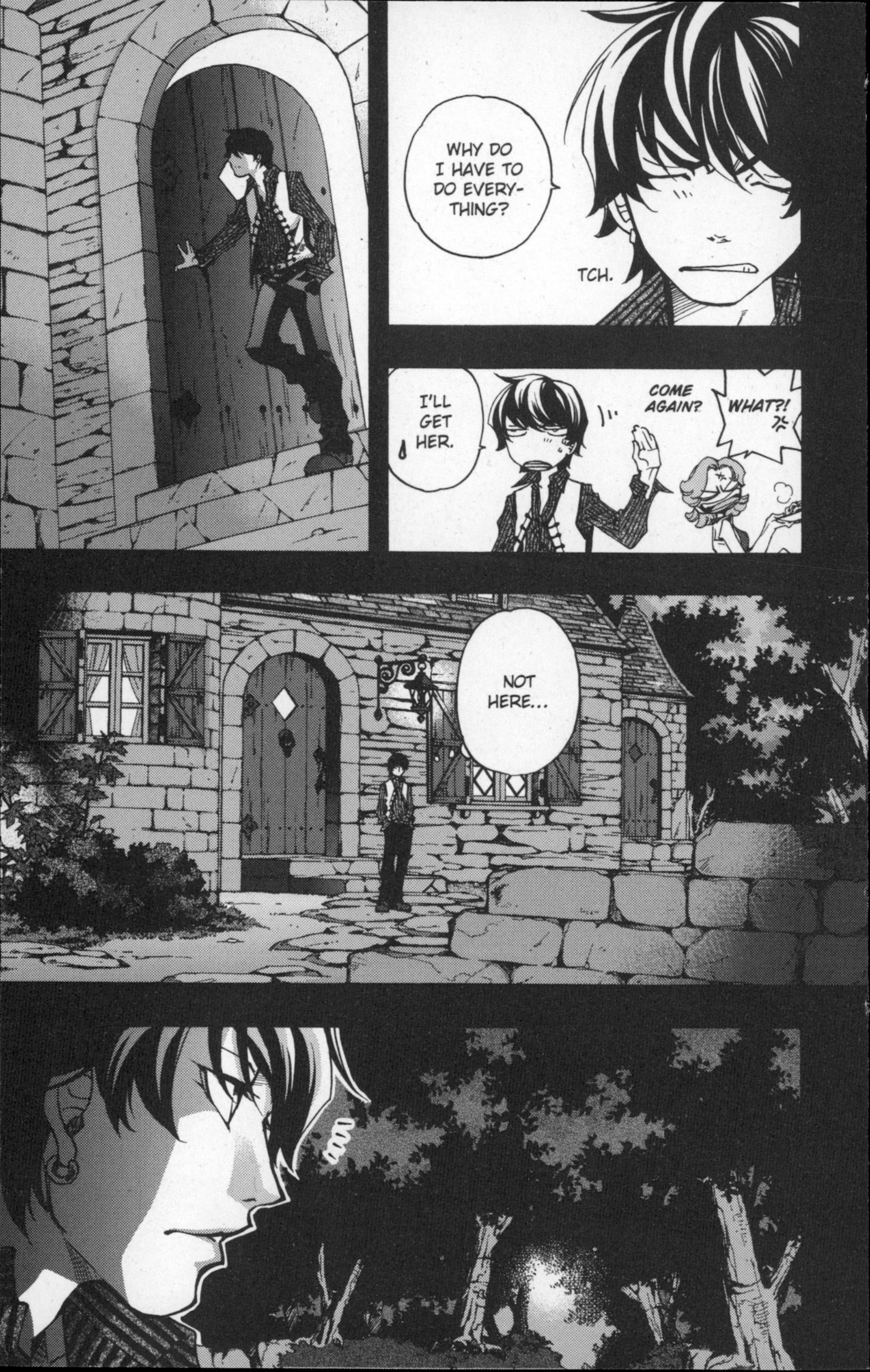
WHY DO I HAVE TO DO EVERYTHING?
TCH.
WHAT?!
COME AGAIN?
I'LL GET HER.
NOT HERE...

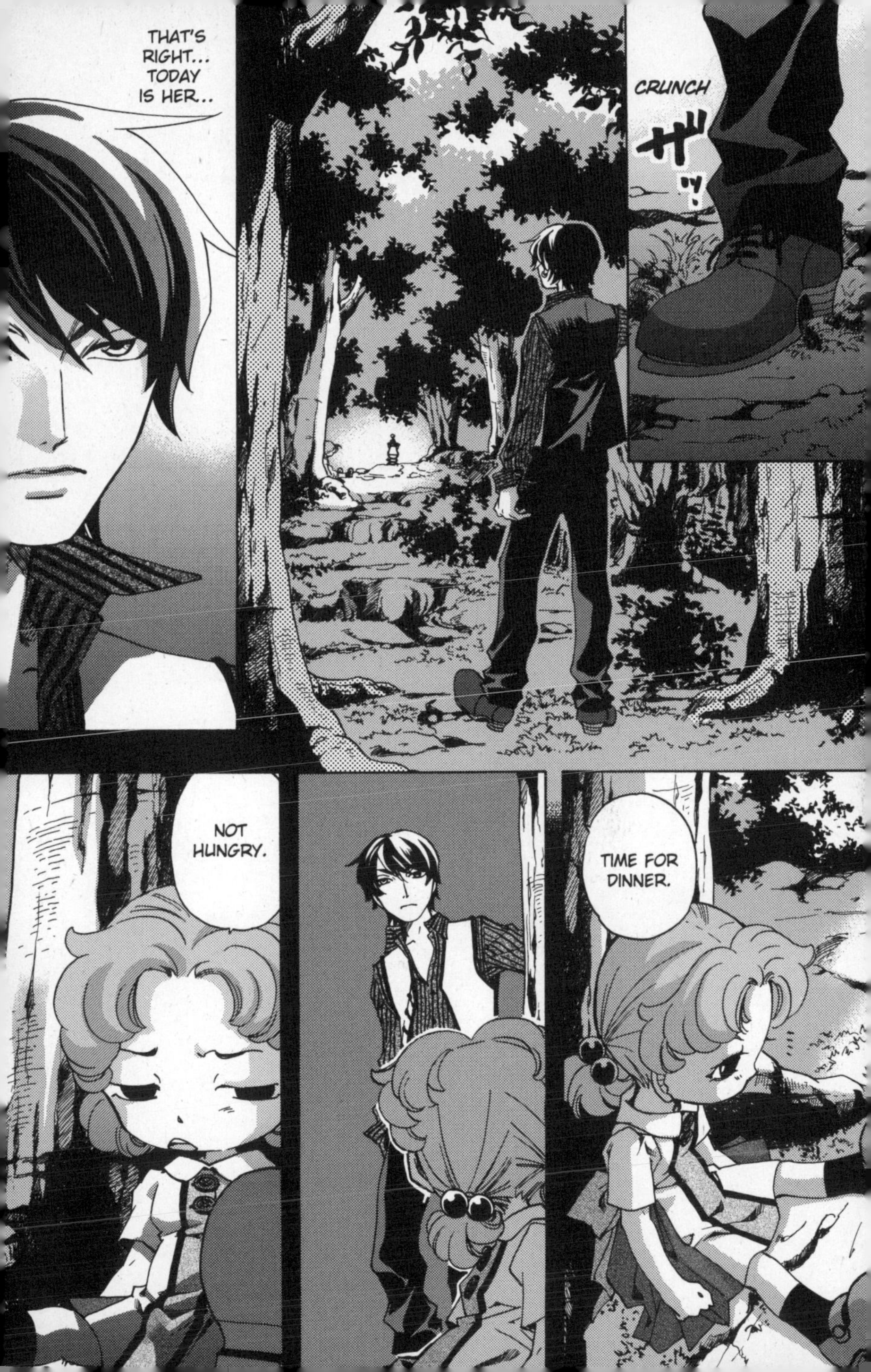
CRUNCH
ザッ
THAT'S RIGHT... TODAY IS HER...
TIME FOR DINNER.
NOT HUNGRY.

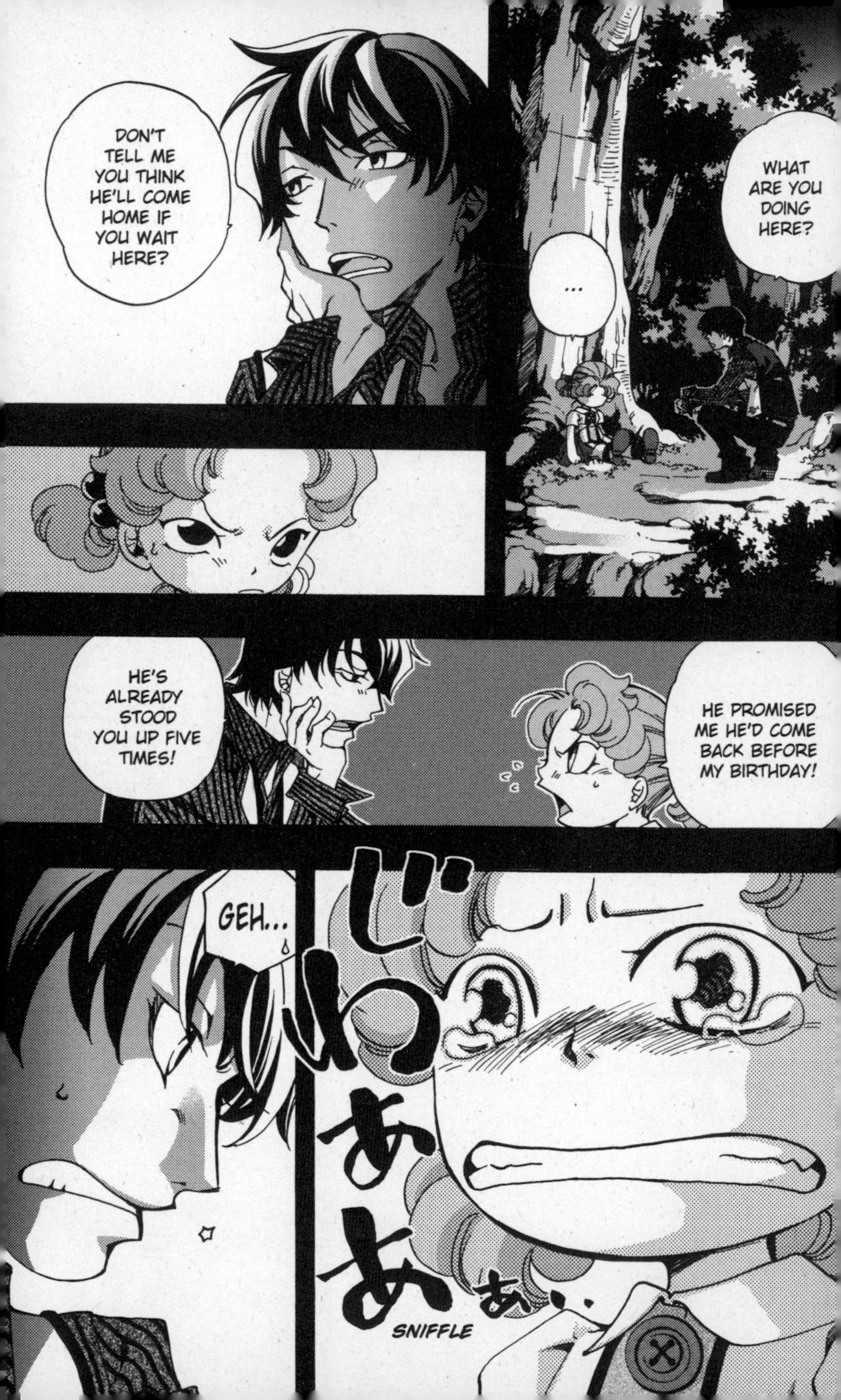
WHAT ARE YOU DOING HERE?
...
DON'T TELL ME YOU THINK HE'LL COME HOME IF YOU WAIT HERE?
HE PROMISED ME HE'D COME BACK BEFORE MY BIRTHDAY!
HE'S ALREADY STOOD YOU UP FIVE TIMES!
じわっ
あああ
SNIFFLE
GEH...

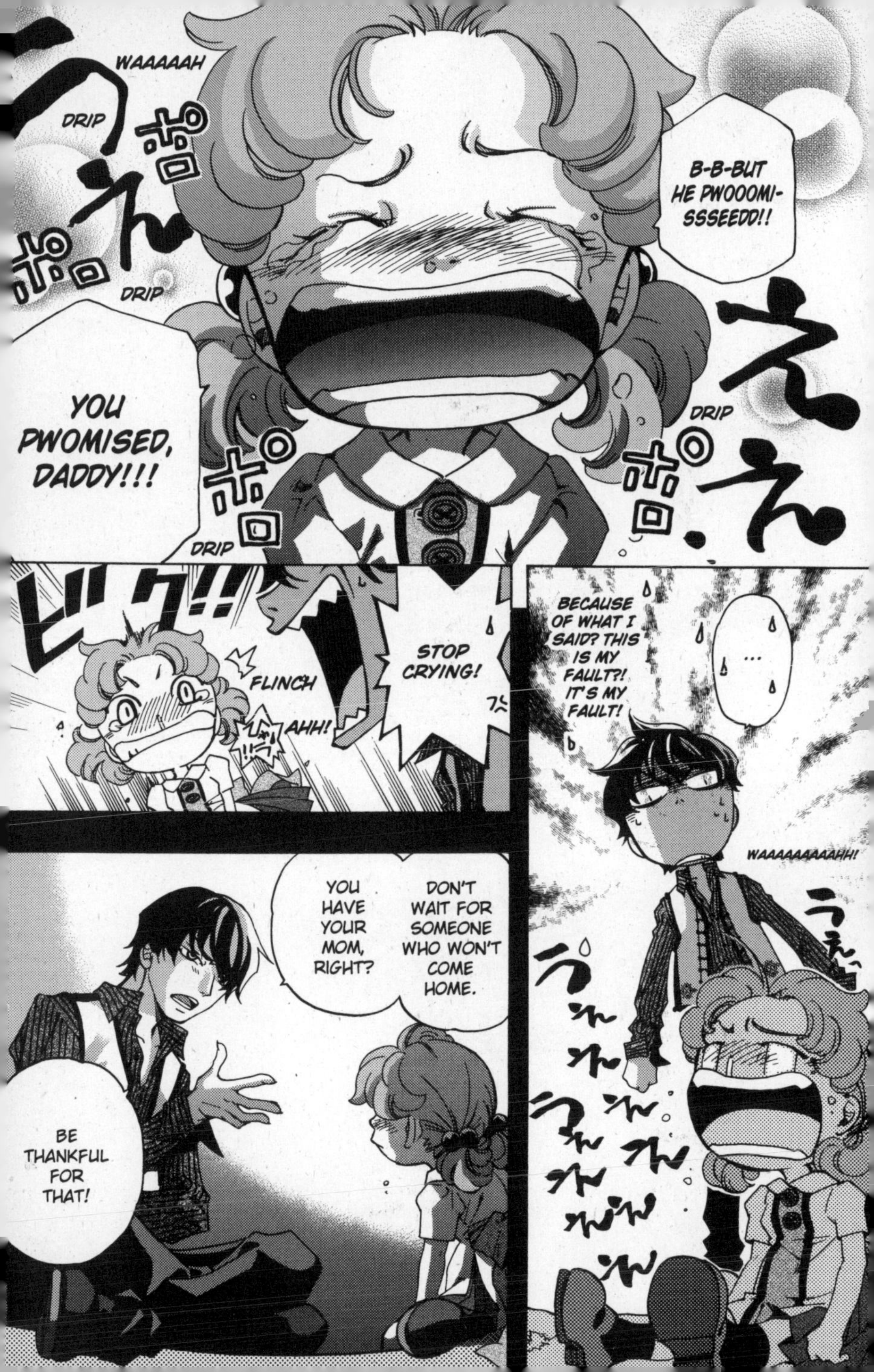
B-B-BUT HE PWOOOMI-SSSEEDD!!
WAAAAAH
DRIP
DRIP
DRIP
YOU PWOMISED, DADDY!!!
DRIP
...
BECAUSE OF WHAT I SAID? THIS IS MY FAULT?! IT'S MY FAULT!
WAAAAAAAAAHH!
STOP CRYING!
FLINCH
AHH!
DON'T WAIT FOR SOMEONE WHO WON'T COME HOME.
YOU HAVE YOUR MOM, RIGHT?
BE THANKFUL FOR THAT!

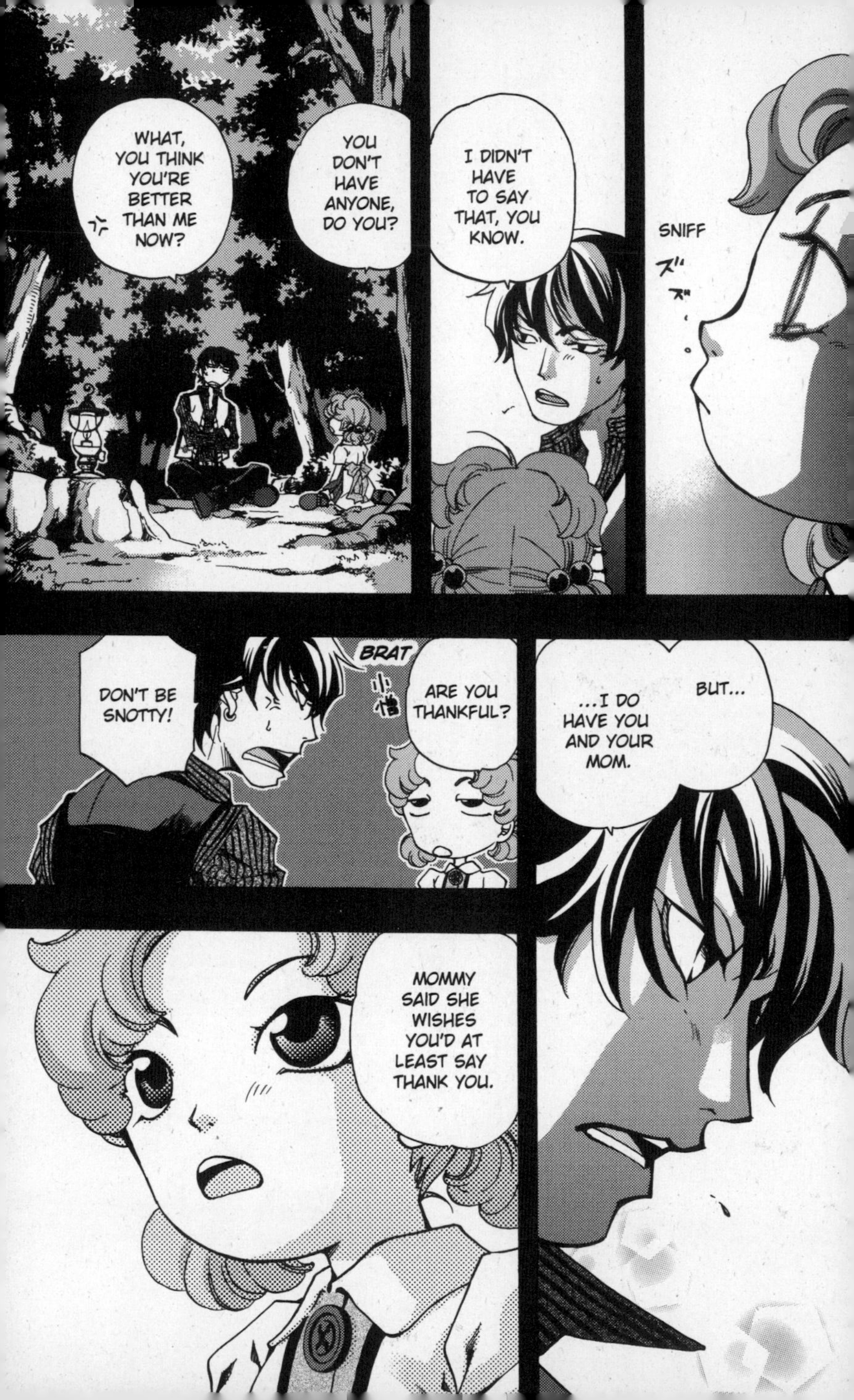
SNIFF
I DIDN'T HAVE TO SAY THAT, YOU KNOW.
YOU DON'T HAVE ANYONE, DO YOU?
WHAT, YOU THINK YOU'RE BETTER THAN ME NOW?
BUT...
...I DO HAVE YOU AND YOUR MOM.
ARE YOU THANKFUL?
BRAT
DON'T BE SNOTTY!
MOMMY SAID SHE WISHES YOU'D AT LEAST SAY THANK YOU.

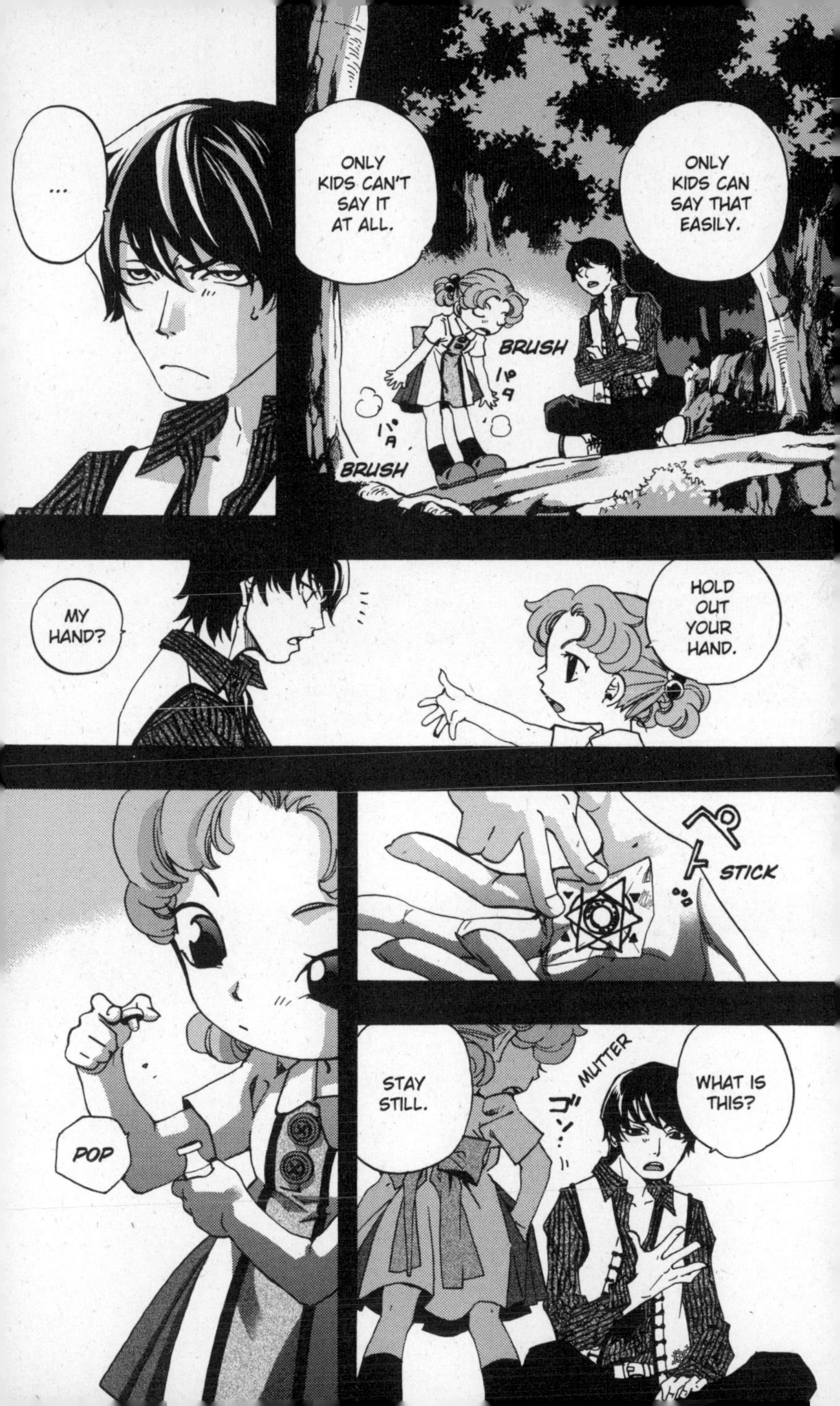

ONLY KIDS CAN SAY THAT EASILY.
ONLY KIDS CAN'T SAY IT AT ALL.
BRUSH
BRUSH
...
HOLD OUT YOUR HAND.
MY HAND?
STICK
WHAT IS THIS?
MUTTER
STAY STILL.
POP

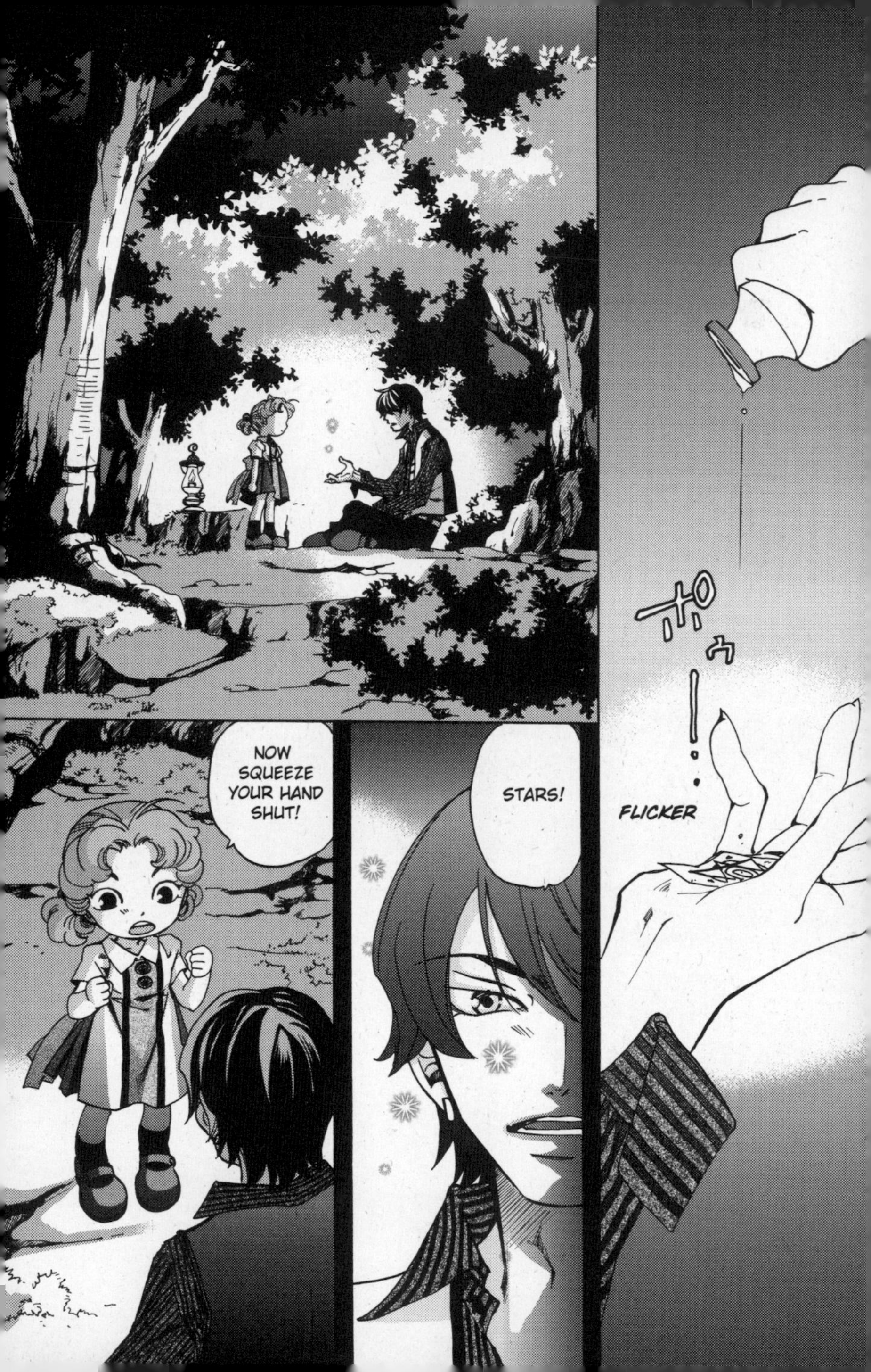
ポゥー!..
FLICKER
STARS!
NOW SQUEEZE YOUR HAND SHUT!

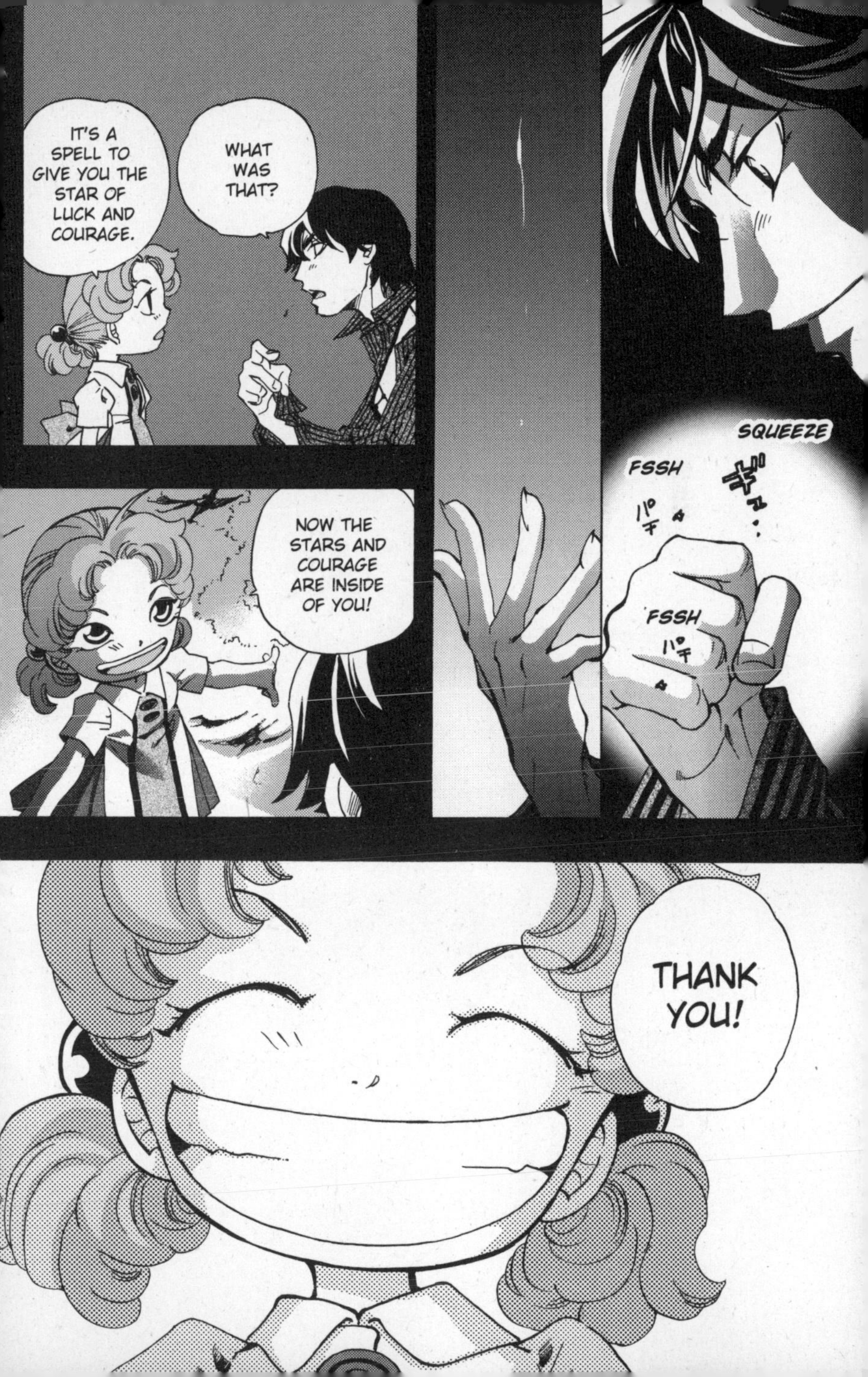
SQUEEZE
ギュ…
FSSH
パチ
FSSH
パチ
WHAT WAS THAT?
IT'S A SPELL TO GIVE YOU THE STAR OF LUCK AND COURAGE.
NOW THE STARS AND COURAGE ARE INSIDE OF YOU!
THANK YOU!

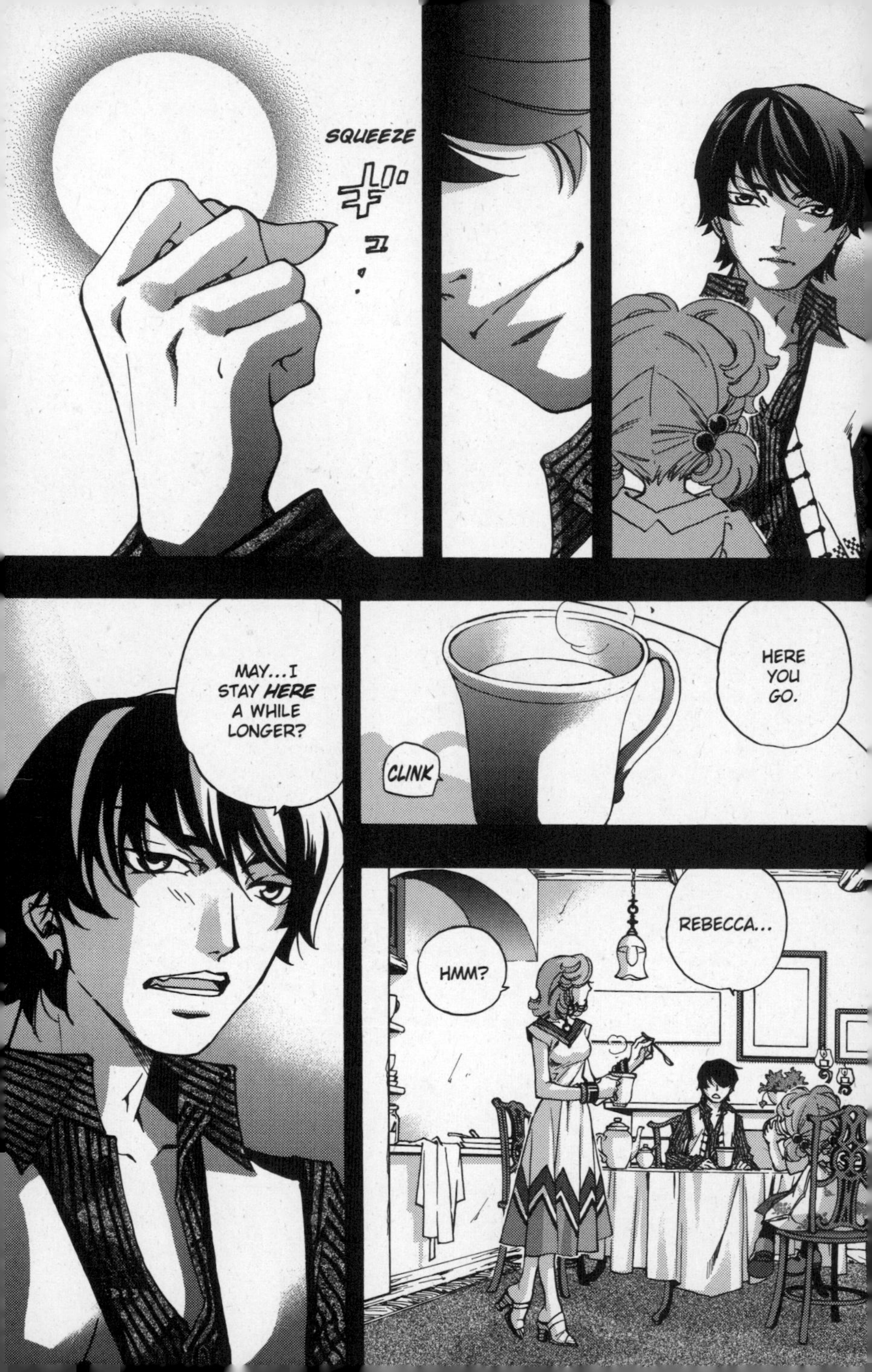
SQUEEZE
HERE YOU GO.
CLINK
REBECCA...
HMM?
MAY... I STAY *HERE* A WHILE LONGER?

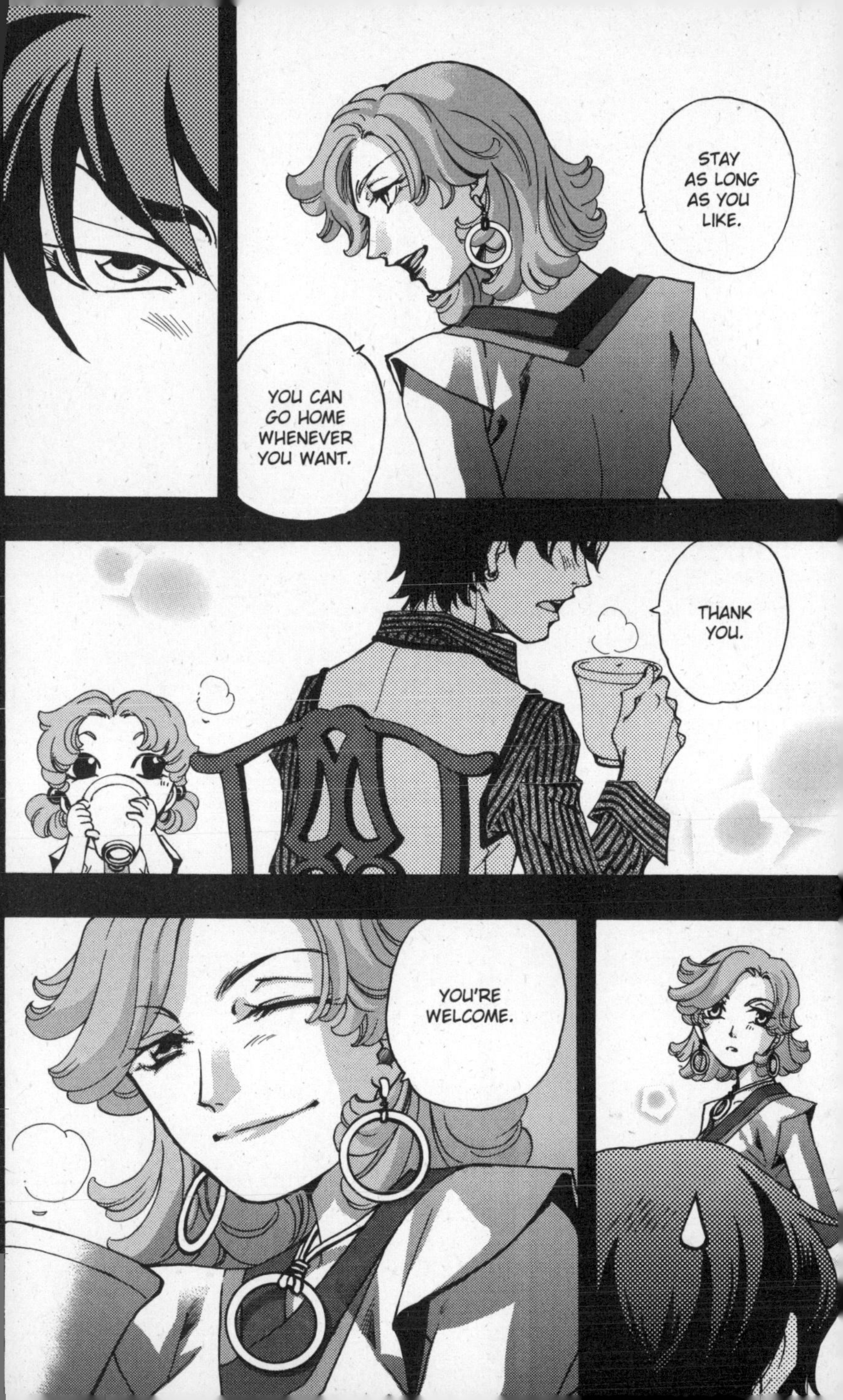
STAY AS LONG AS YOU LIKE.
YOU CAN GO HOME WHENEVER YOU WANT.
THANK YOU.
YOU'RE WELCOME.

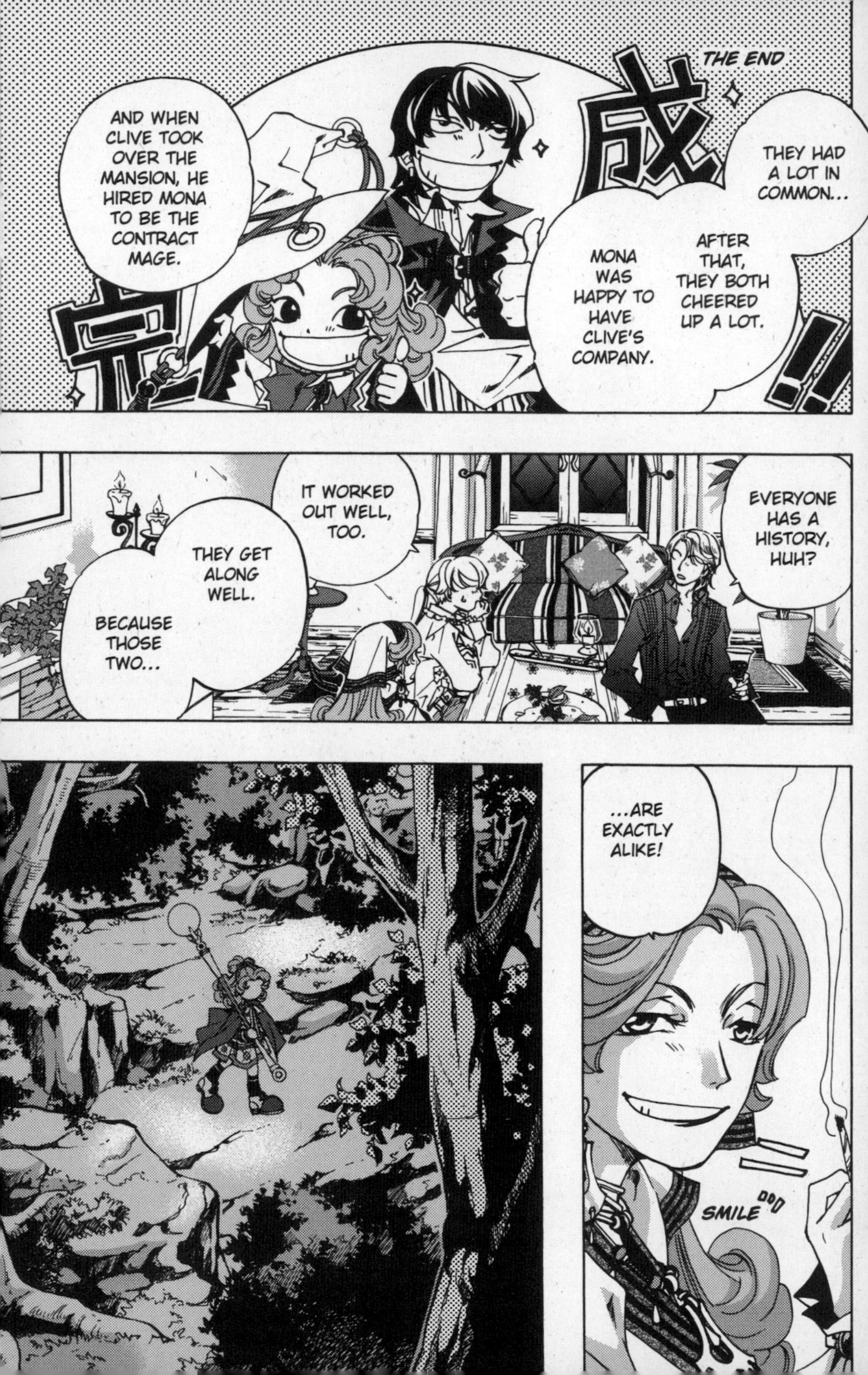
THE END
THEY HAD A LOT IN COMMON...
AFTER THAT, THEY BOTH CHEERED UP A LOT.
MONA WAS HAPPY TO HAVE CLIVE'S COMPANY.
AND WHEN CLIVE TOOK OVER THE MANSION, HE HIRED MONA TO BE THE CONTRACT MAGE.
EVERYONE HAS A HISTORY, HUH?
IT WORKED OUT WELL, TOO.
THEY GET ALONG WELL.
BECAUSE THOSE TWO...
...ARE EXACTLY ALIKE!
SMILE

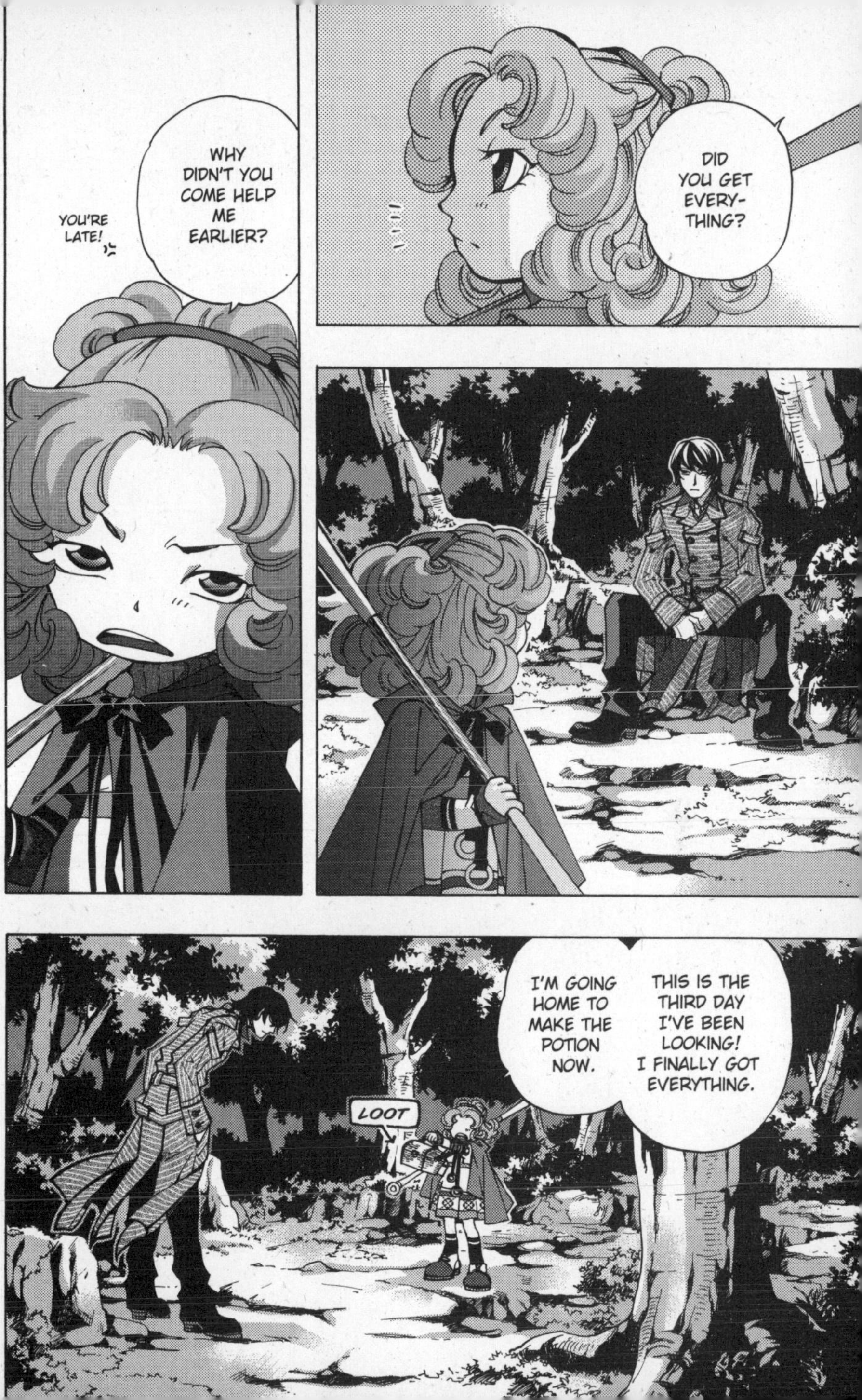
DID YOU GET EVERY-THING?
WHY DIDN'T YOU COME HELP ME EARLIER?
YOU'RE LATE!
THIS IS THE THIRD DAY I'VE BEEN LOOKING! I FINALLY GOT EVERYTHING.
I'M GOING HOME TO MAKE THE POTION NOW.
LOOT

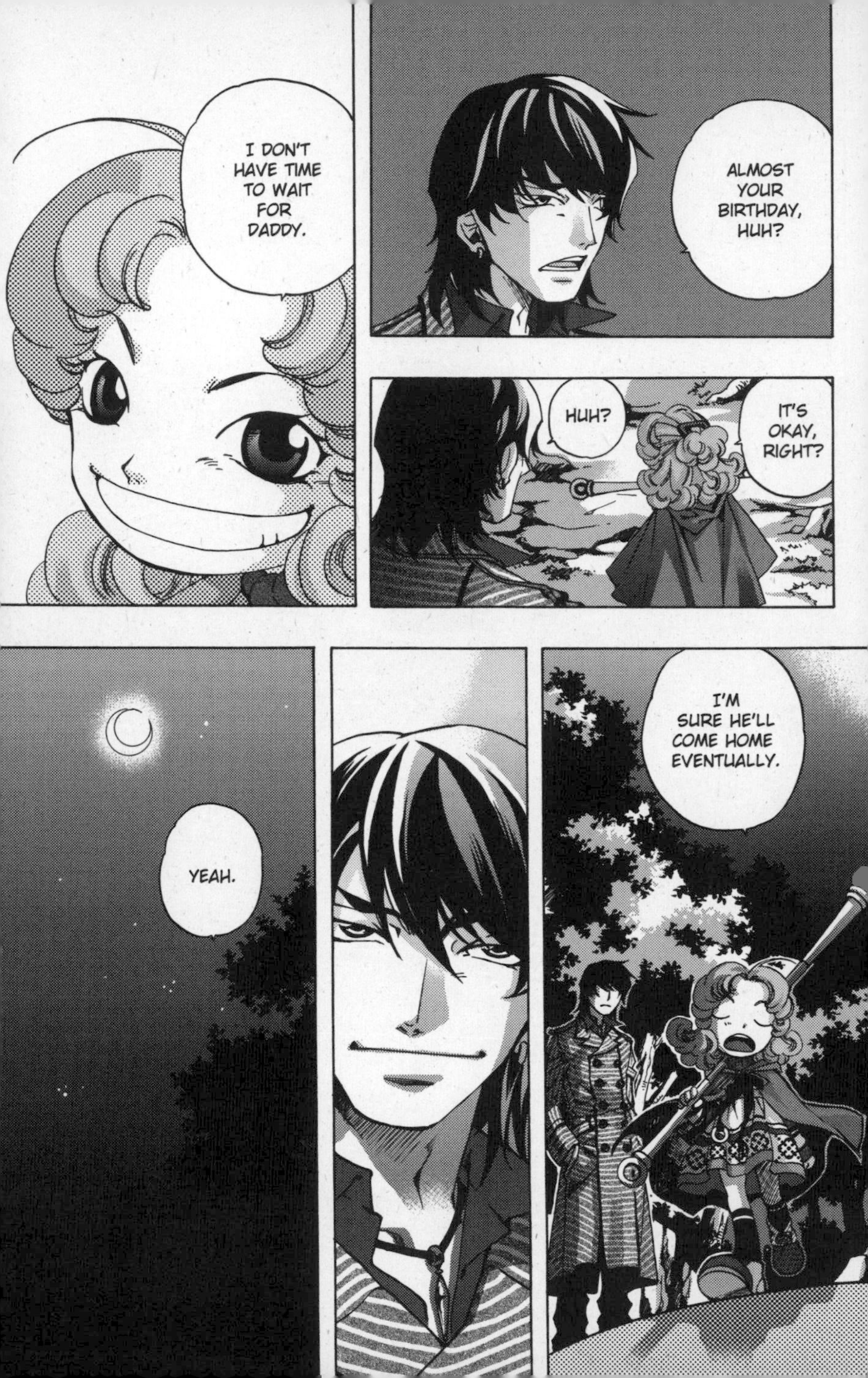
ALMOST YOUR BIRTHDAY, HUH?
IT'S OKAY, RIGHT?
HUH?
I DON'T HAVE TIME TO WAIT FOR DADDY.
I'M SURE HE'LL COME HOME EVENTUALLY.
YEAH.

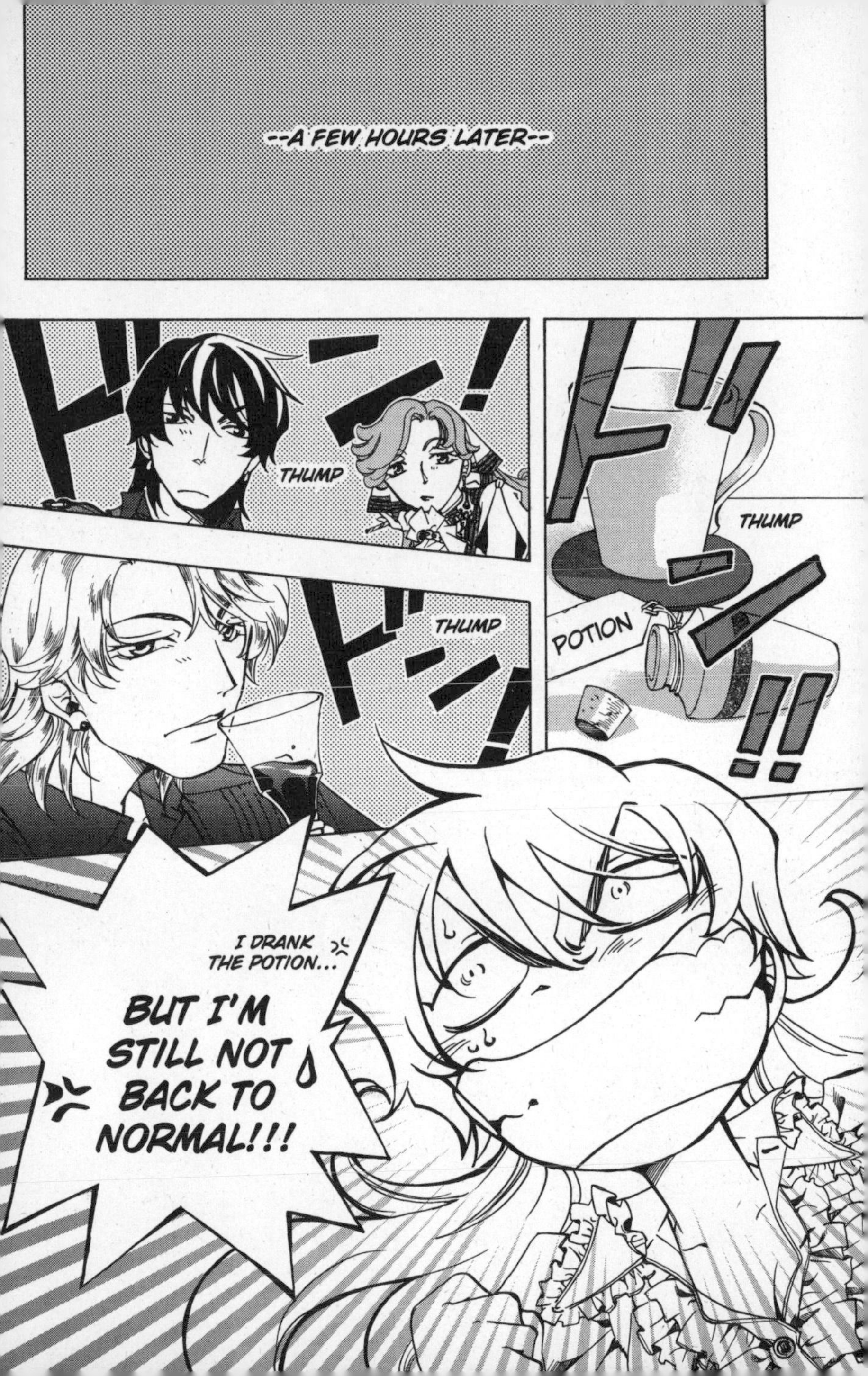
--A FEW HOURS LATER--
THUMP
POTION
THUMP
THUMP
I DRANK THE POTION...
BUT I'M STILL NOT BACK TO NORMAL!!!

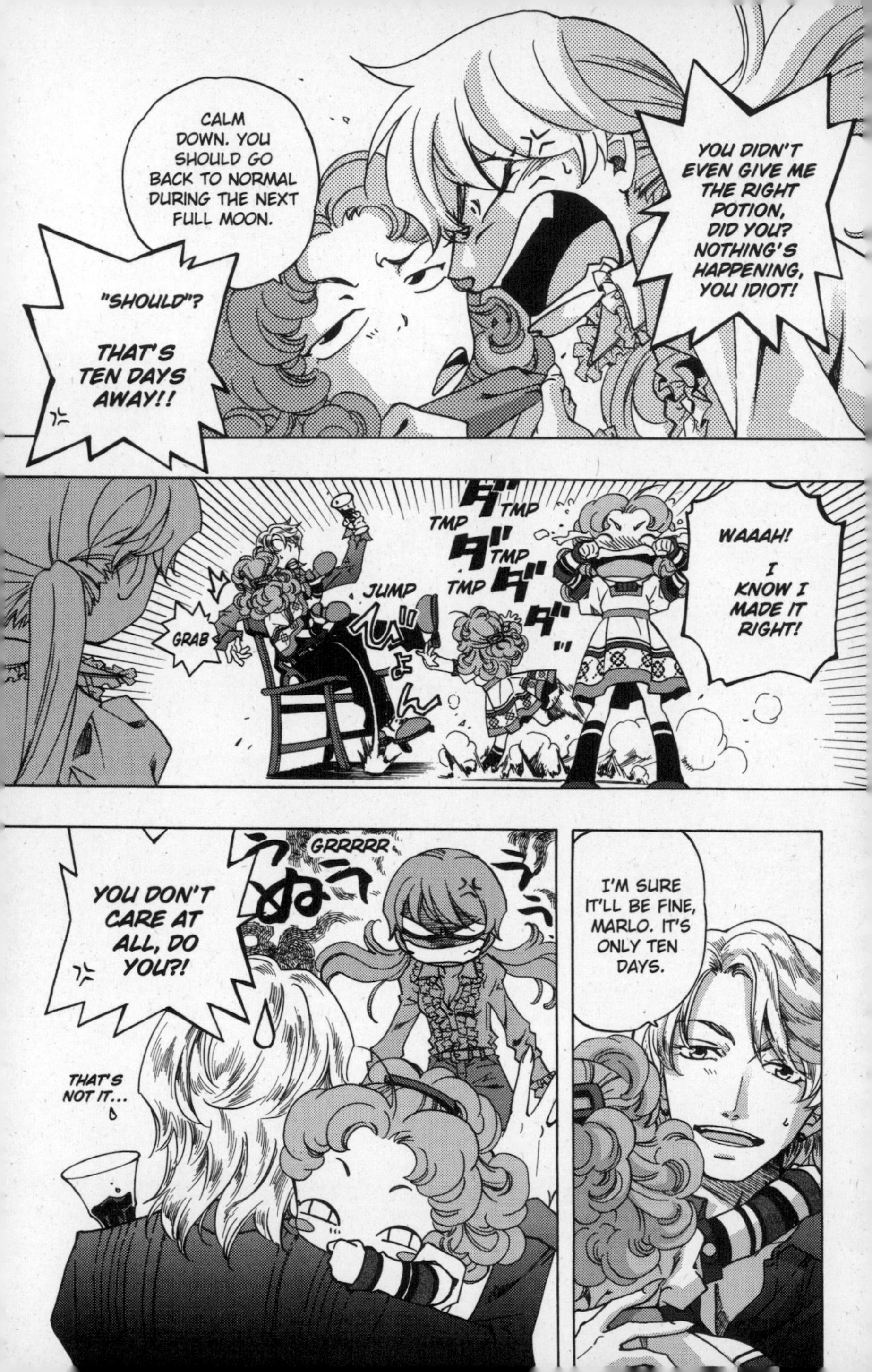
YOU DIDN'T EVEN GIVE ME THE RIGHT POTION, DID YOU? NOTHING'S HAPPENING, YOU IDIOT!
CALM DOWN. YOU SHOULD GO BACK TO NORMAL DURING THE NEXT FULL MOON.
"SHOULD"?
THAT'S TEN DAYS AWAY!!
WAAAH!
I KNOW I MADE IT RIGHT!
TMP TMP
TMP TMP
JUMP
GRAB
I'M SURE IT'LL BE FINE, MARLO. IT'S ONLY TEN DAYS.
GRRRRR
YOU DON'T CARE AT ALL, DO YOU?!
THAT'S NOT IT...

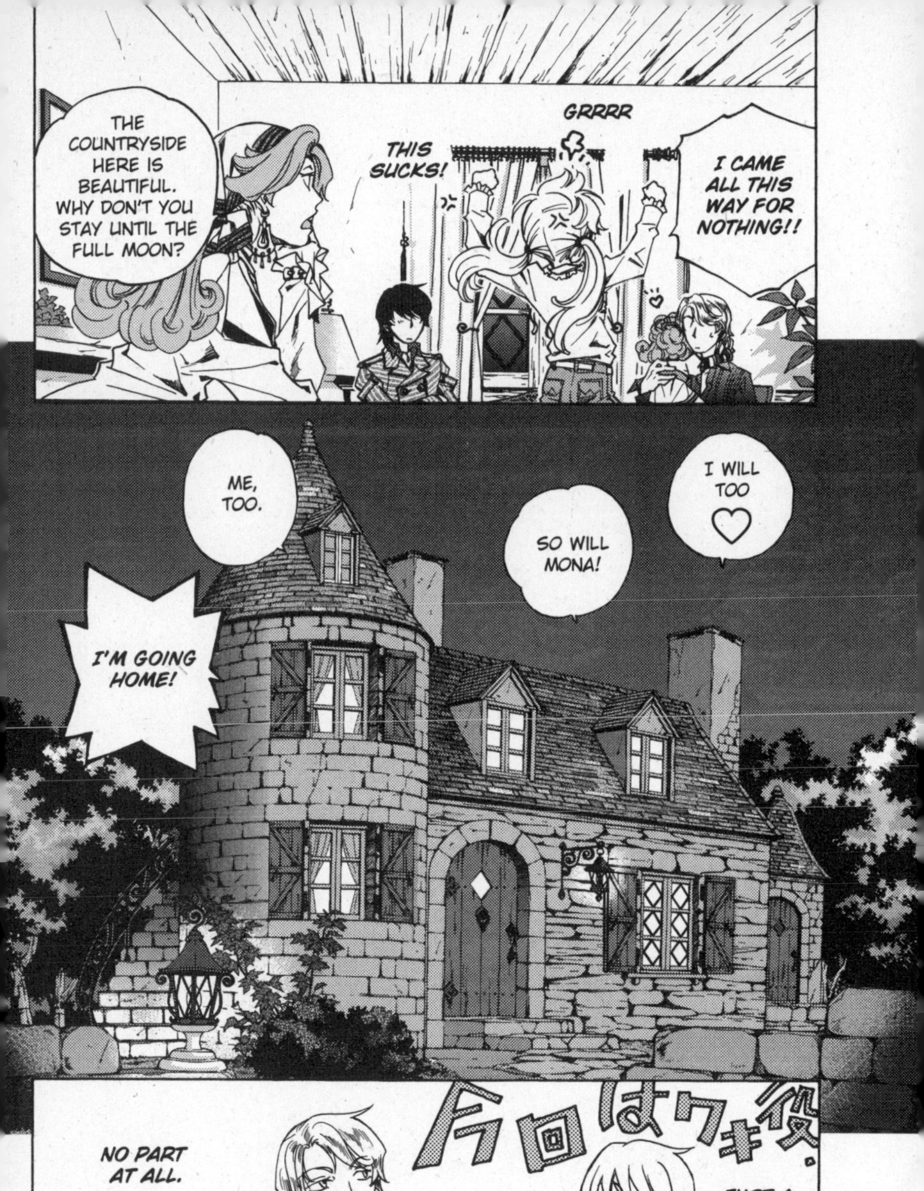
I CAME ALL THIS WAY FOR NOTHING!!
GRRRR
THIS SUCKS!
THE COUNTRYSIDE HERE IS BEAUTIFUL. WHY DON'T YOU STAY UNTIL THE FULL MOON?
I WILL TOO ♡
SO WILL MONA!
ME, TOO.
I'M GOING HOME!
今回はワキ役。
JUST A SUPPORTING ROLE THIS TIME.
NO PART AT ALL.

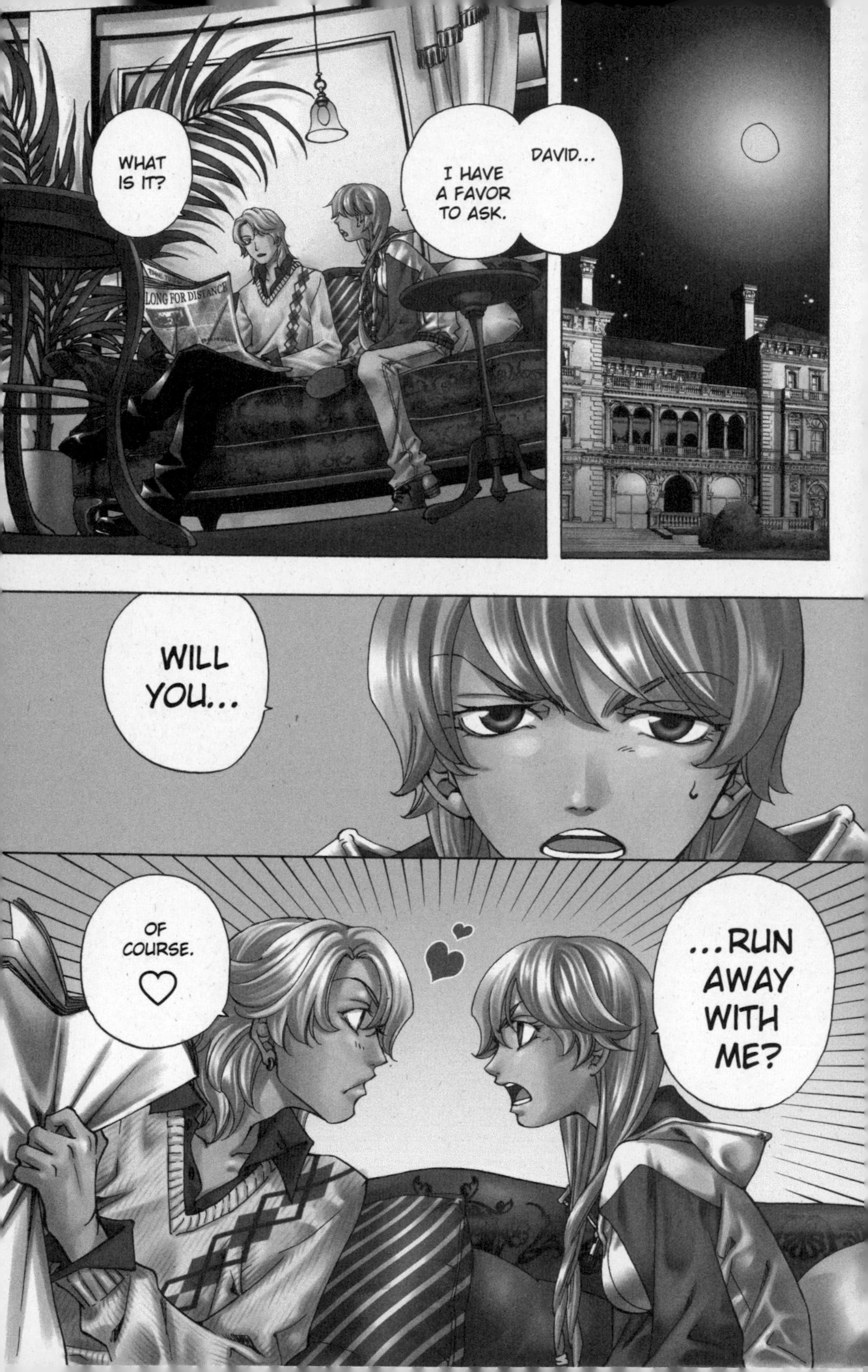
DAVID...
I HAVE A FAVOR TO ASK.
WHAT IS IT?
LONG FOR DISTANCE
WILL YOU...
...RUN AWAY WITH ME?
OF COURSE. ♡

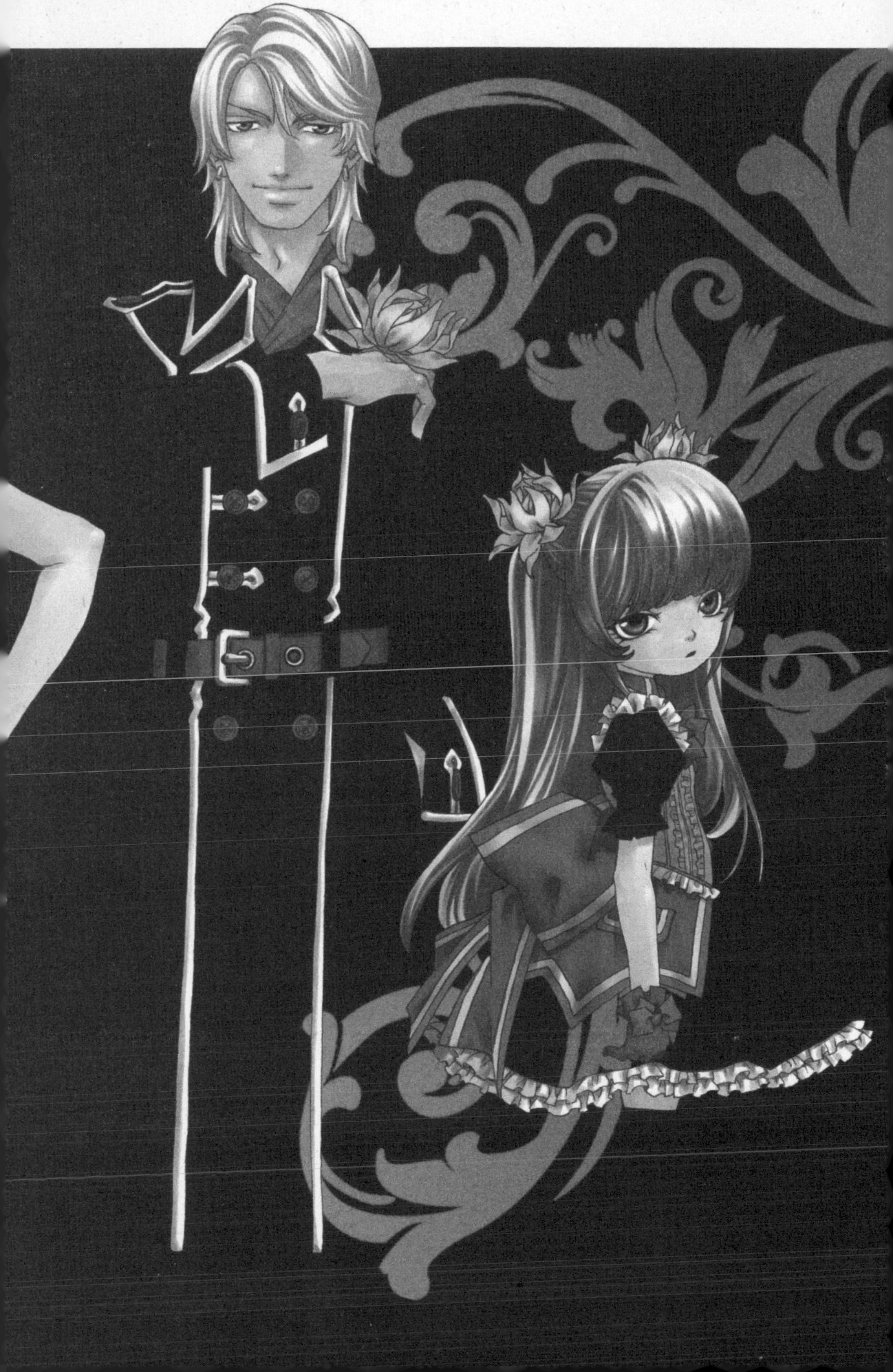

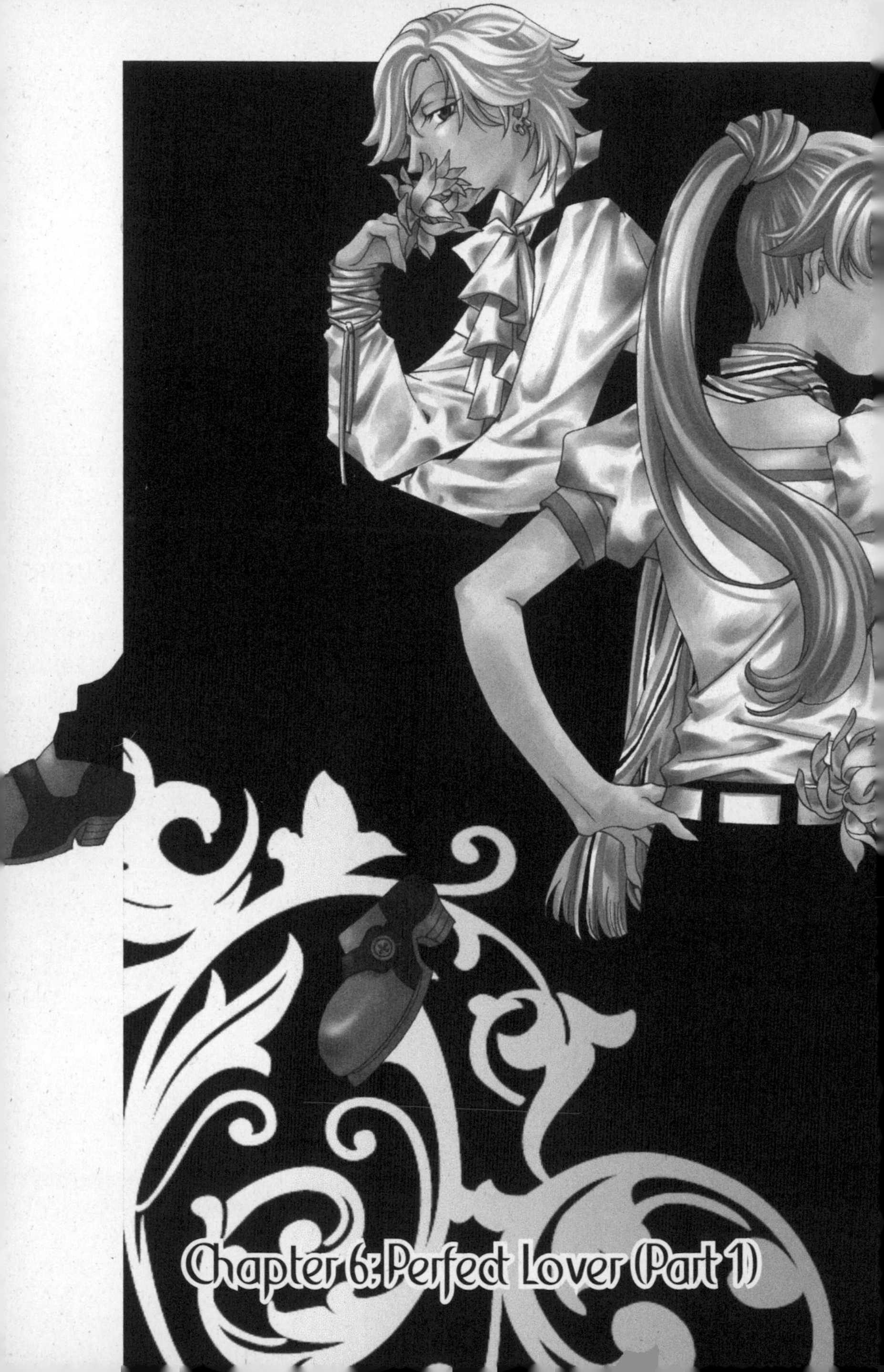
Chapter 6: Perfect Lover (Part 1)

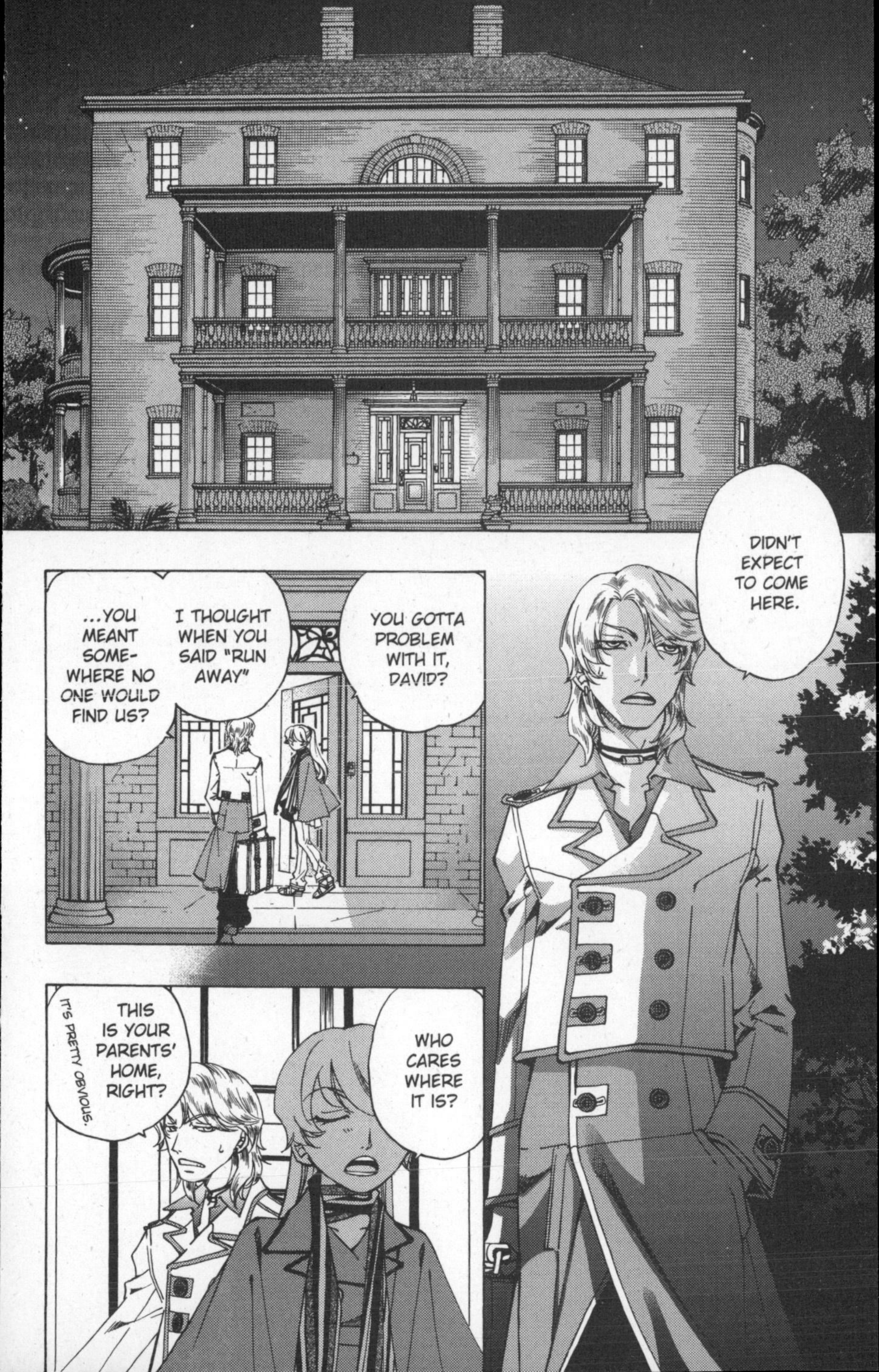
DIDN'T EXPECT TO COME HERE.
YOU GOTTA PROBLEM WITH IT, DAVID?
I THOUGHT WHEN YOU SAID "RUN AWAY"
...YOU MEANT SOME-WHERE NO ONE WOULD FIND US?
THIS IS YOUR PARENTS' HOME, RIGHT?
IT'S PRETTY OBVIOUS.
WHO CARES WHERE IT IS?

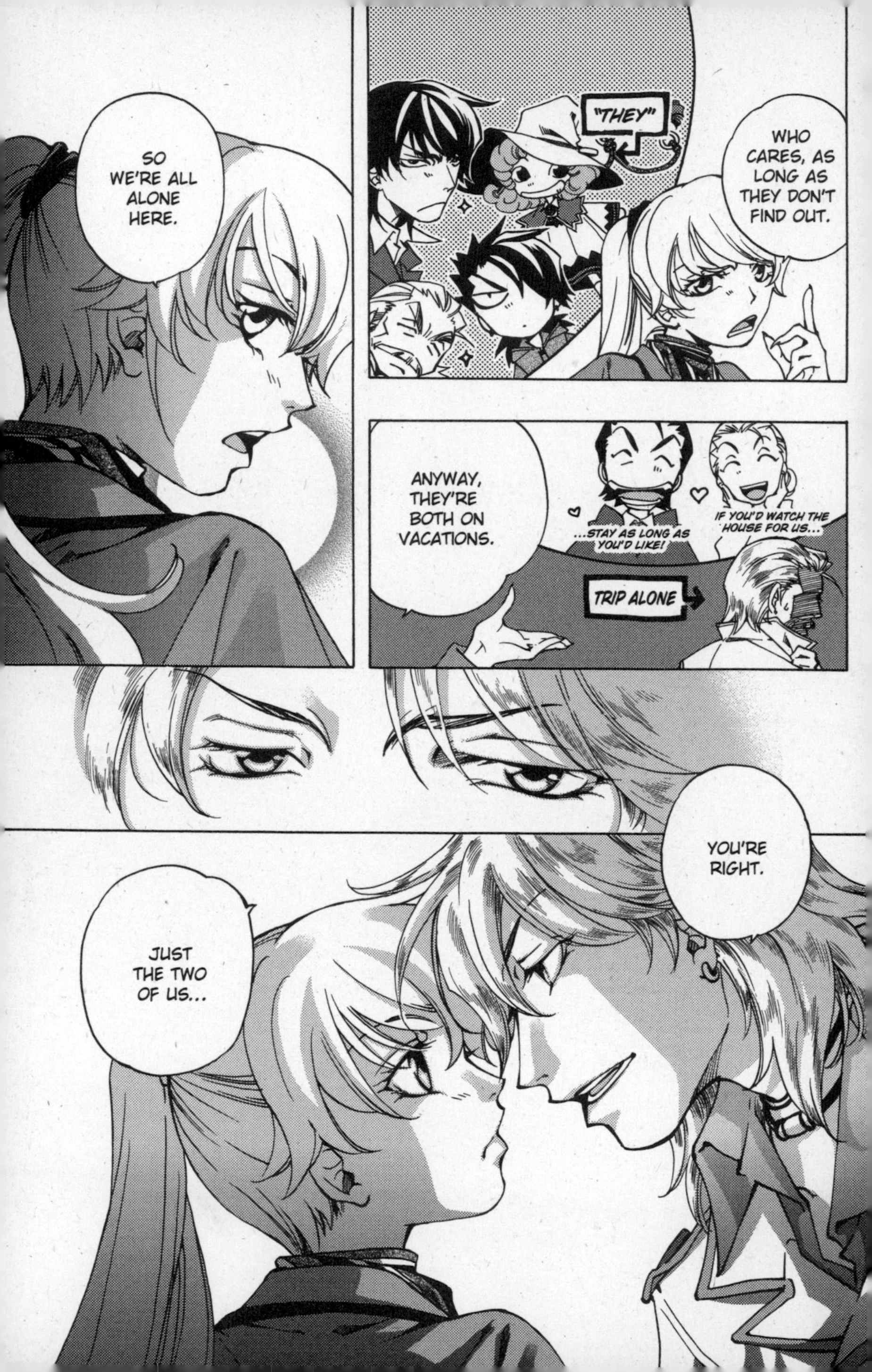
"THEY"
WHO CARES, AS LONG AS THEY DON'T FIND OUT.
ANYWAY, THEY'RE BOTH ON VACATIONS.
IF YOU'D WATCH THE HOUSE FOR US...
...STAY AS LONG AS YOU'D LIKE!
TRIP ALONE
SO WE'RE ALL ALONE HERE.
YOU'RE RIGHT.
JUST THE TWO OF US...

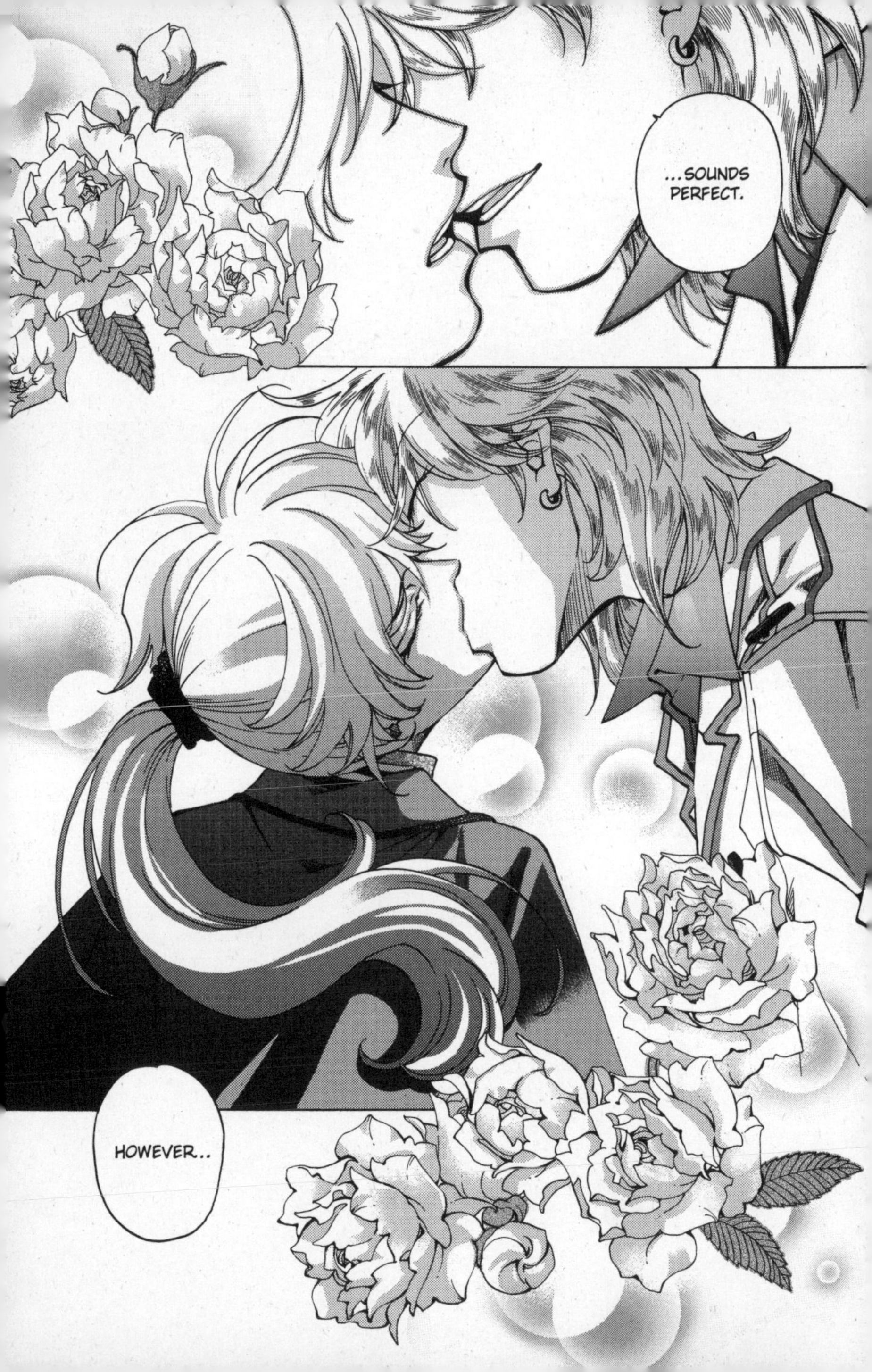
...SOUNDS PERFECT.
HOWEVER...

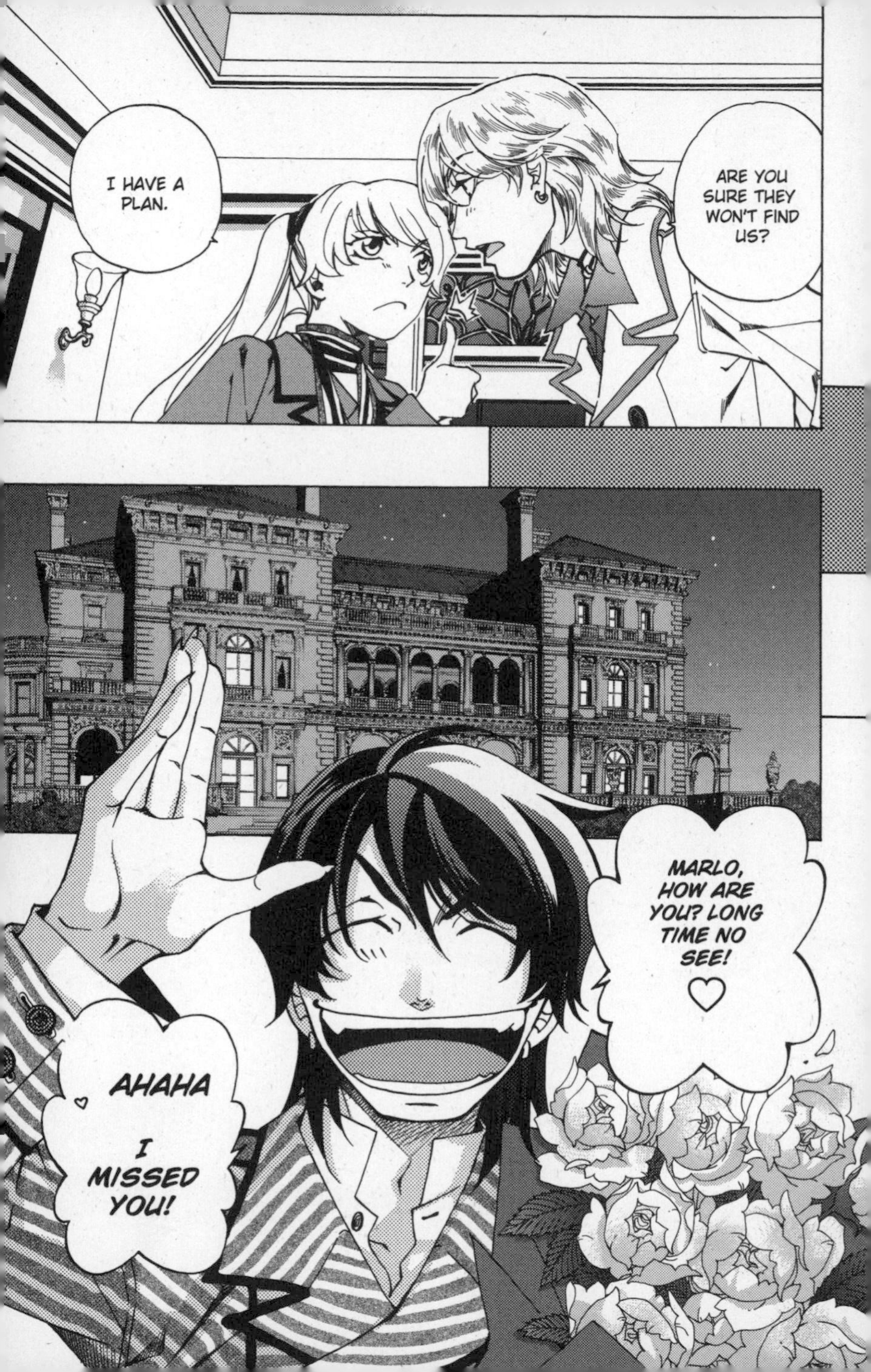
ARE YOU SURE THEY WON'T FIND US?
I HAVE A PLAN.
MARLO, HOW ARE YOU? LONG TIME NO SEE! ♥
AHAHA ♥
I MISSED YOU!

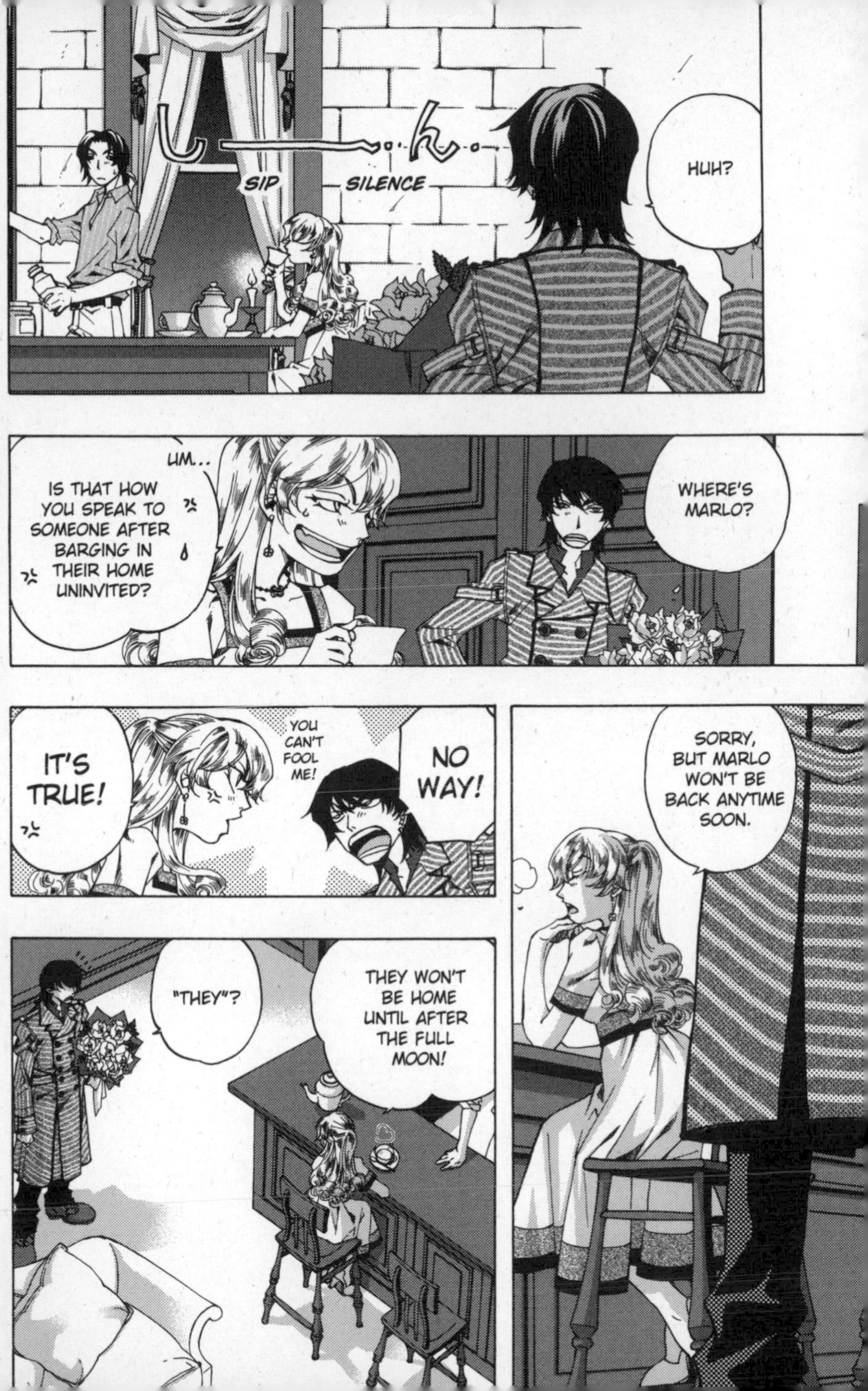
HUH?
SILENCE
SIP
WHERE'S MARLO?
UM...
IS THAT HOW YOU SPEAK TO SOMEONE AFTER BARGING IN THEIR HOME UNINVITED?
SORRY, BUT MARLO WON'T BE BACK ANYTIME SOON.
NO WAY!
YOU CAN'T FOOL ME!
IT'S TRUE!
THEY WON'T BE HOME UNTIL AFTER THE FULL MOON!
"THEY"?

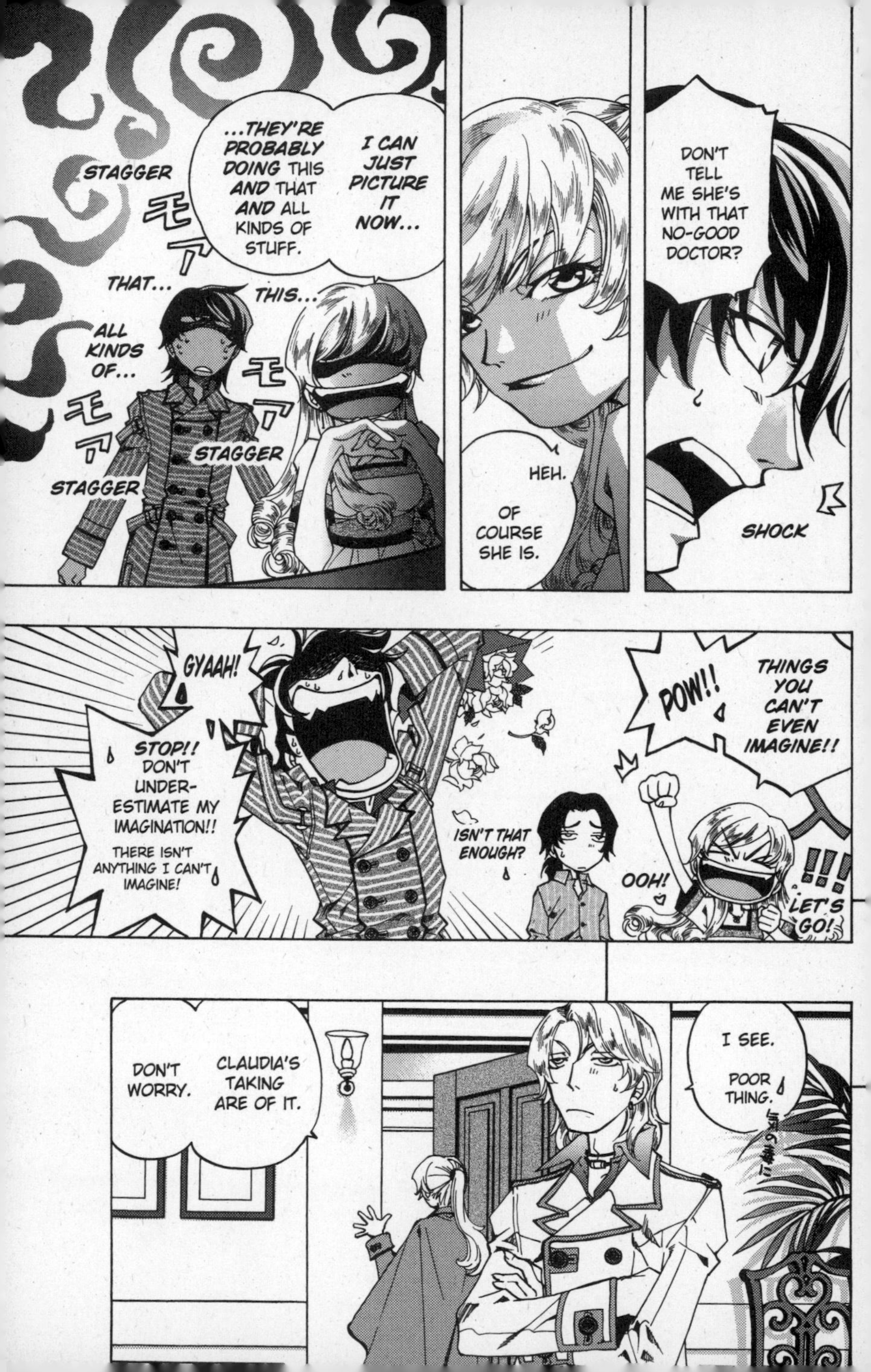
DON'T TELL ME SHE'S WITH THAT NO-GOOD DOCTOR?
SHOCK
HEH.
OF COURSE SHE IS.
I CAN JUST PICTURE IT NOW...
...THEY'RE PROBABLY DOING THIS AND THAT AND ALL KINDS OF STUFF.
STAGGER
THIS...
THAT...
ALL KINDS OF...
STAGGER
STAGGER
THINGS YOU CAN'T EVEN IMAGINE!!
POW!!
!!!
LET'S GO!
OOH!
ISN'T THAT ENOUGH?
GYAAH!
STOP!! DON'T UNDER-ESTIMATE MY IMAGINATION!!
THERE ISN'T ANYTHING I CAN'T IMAGINE!
I SEE.
POOR THING.
気の毒に
CLAUDIA'S TAKING ARE OF IT.
DON'T WORRY.

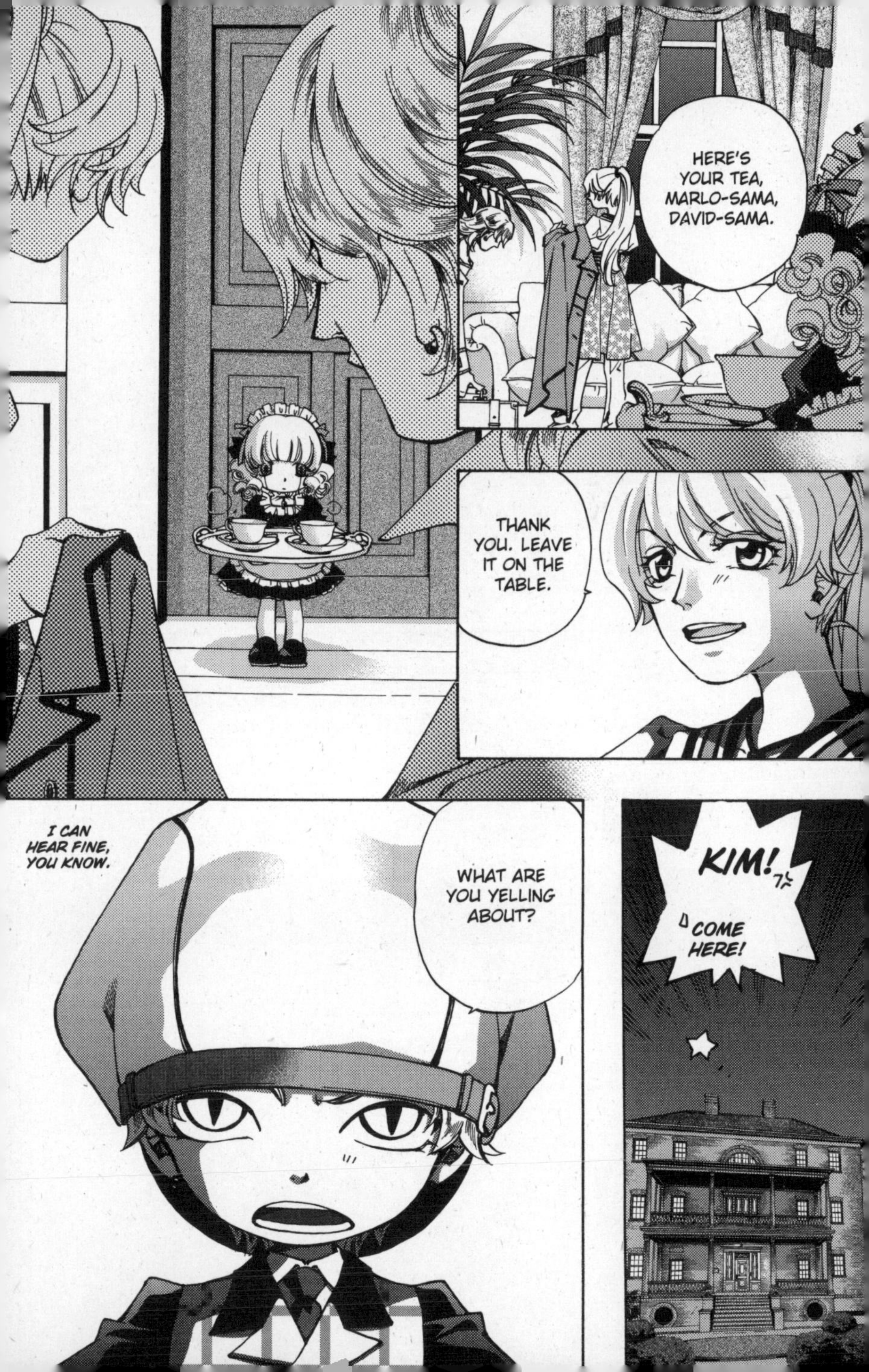
HERE'S YOUR TEA, MARLO-SAMA, DAVID-SAMA.
THANK YOU. LEAVE IT ON THE TABLE.
KIM!
COME HERE!
WHAT ARE YOU YELLING ABOUT?
I CAN HEAR FINE, YOU KNOW.

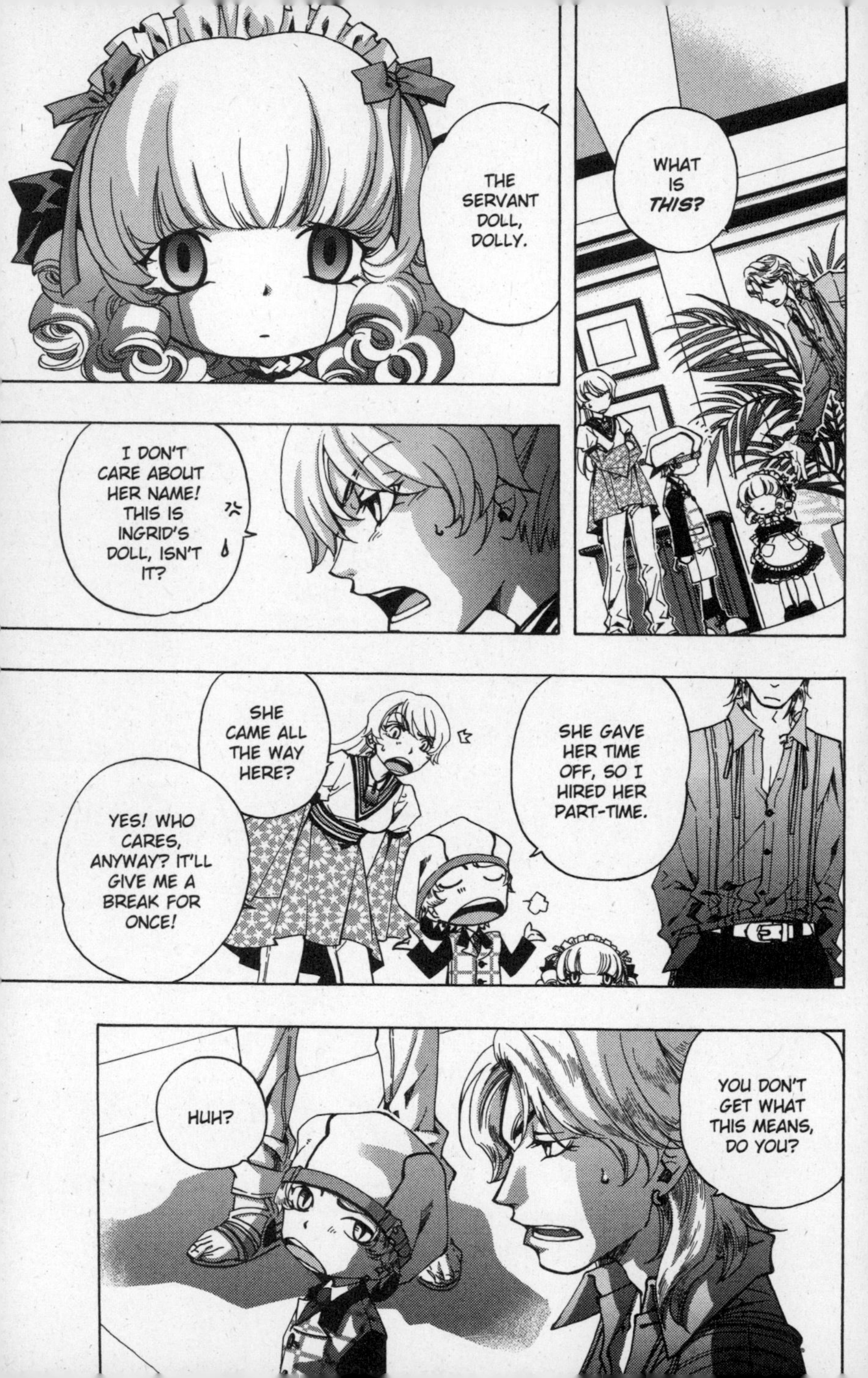
WHAT IS THIS?
THE SERVANT DOLL, DOLLY.
I DON'T CARE ABOUT HER NAME! THIS IS INGRID'S DOLL, ISN'T IT?
SHE GAVE HER TIME OFF, SO I HIRED HER PART-TIME.
SHE CAME ALL THE WAY HERE?
YES! WHO CARES, ANYWAY? IT'LL GIVE ME A BREAK FOR ONCE!
YOU DON'T GET WHAT THIS MEANS, DO YOU?
HUH?

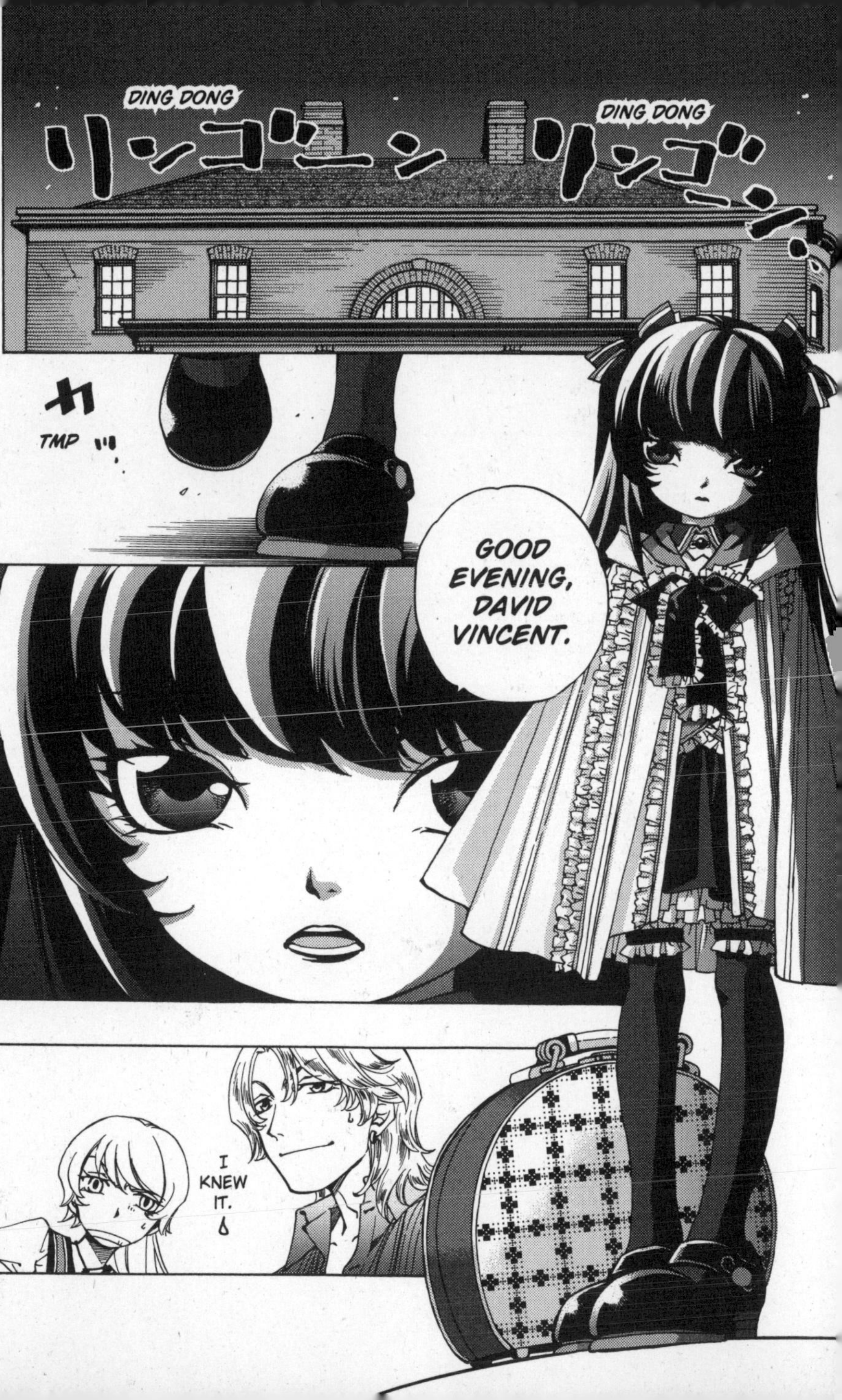
DING DONG
リンゴーン
DING DONG
リンゴーン
カ
TMP
GOOD EVENING, DAVID VINCENT.
I KNEW IT.

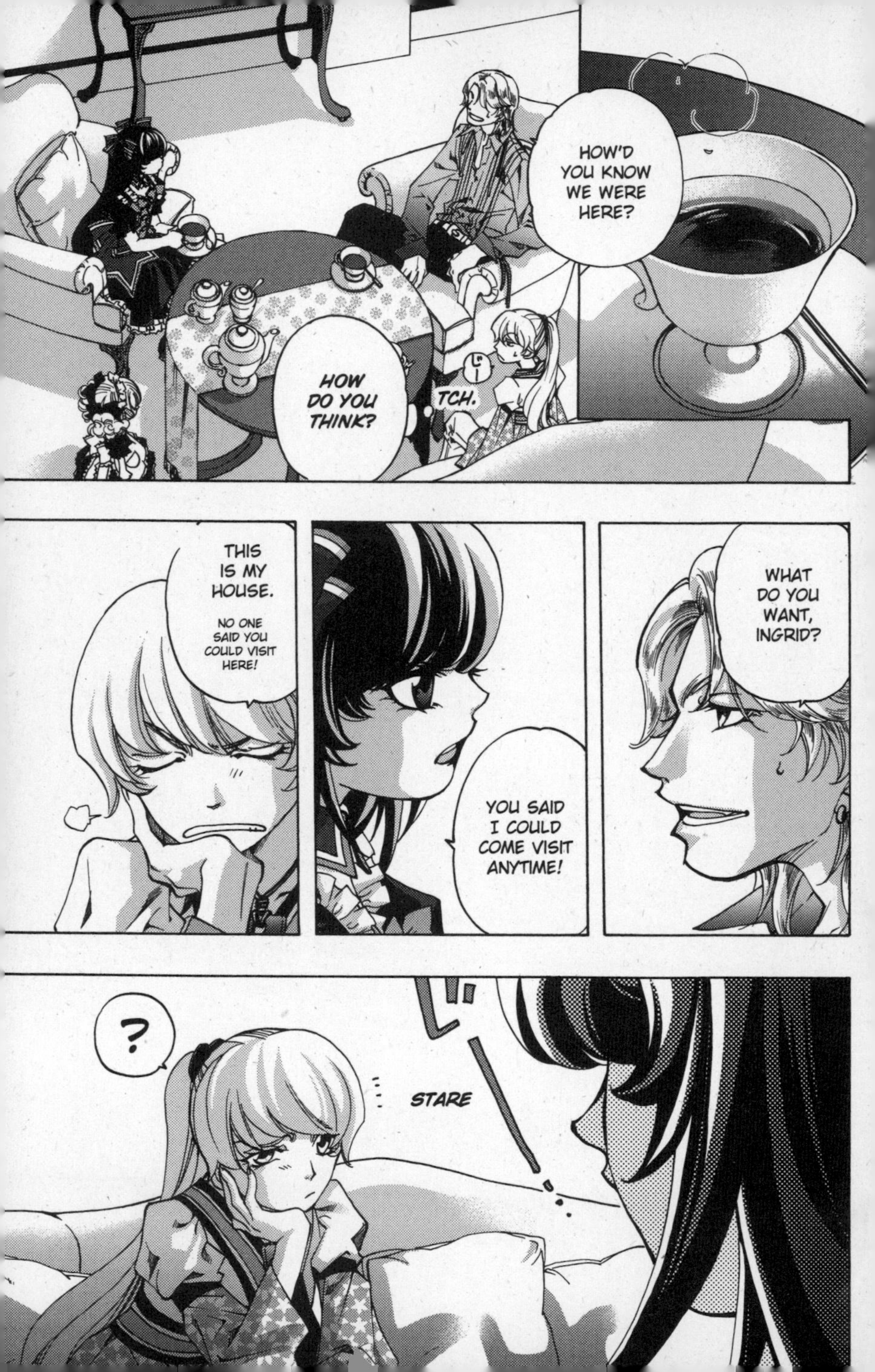
HOW'D YOU KNOW WE WERE HERE?
HOW DO YOU THINK?
TCH.
WHAT DO YOU WANT, INGRID?
YOU SAID I COULD COME VISIT ANYTIME!
THIS IS MY HOUSE.
NO ONE SAID YOU COULD VISIT HERE!
?
STARE

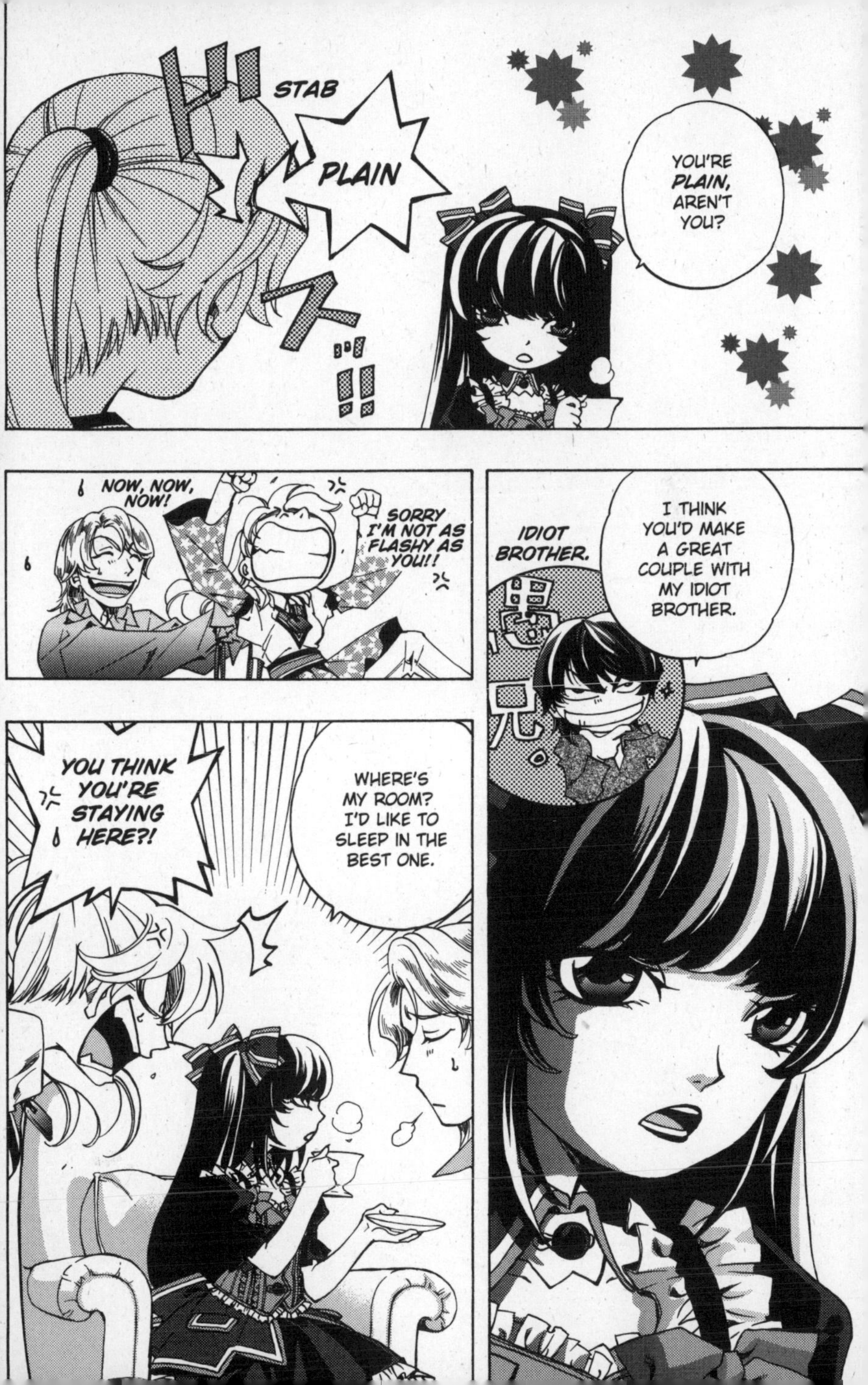
YOU'RE PLAIN, AREN'T YOU?
STAB
PLAIN
!!
I THINK YOU'D MAKE A GREAT COUPLE WITH MY IDIOT BROTHER.
IDIOT BROTHER.
SORRY I'M NOT AS FLASHY AS YOU!!
NOW, NOW, NOW!
WHERE'S MY ROOM? I'D LIKE TO SLEEP IN THE BEST ONE.
YOU THINK YOU'RE STAYING HERE?!

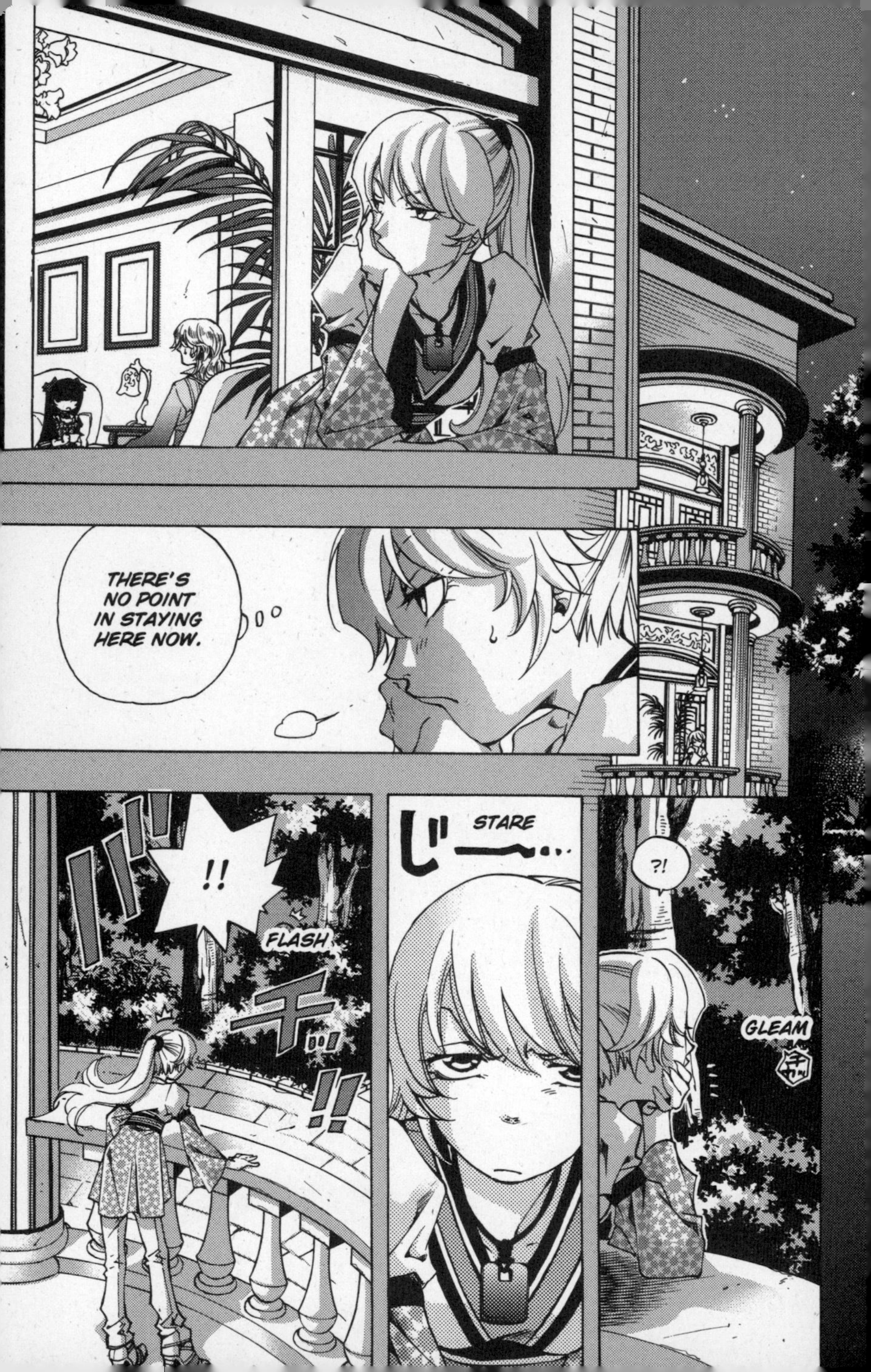
THERE'S NO POINT IN STAYING HERE NOW.
STARE
?!
GLEAM
!!
FLASH

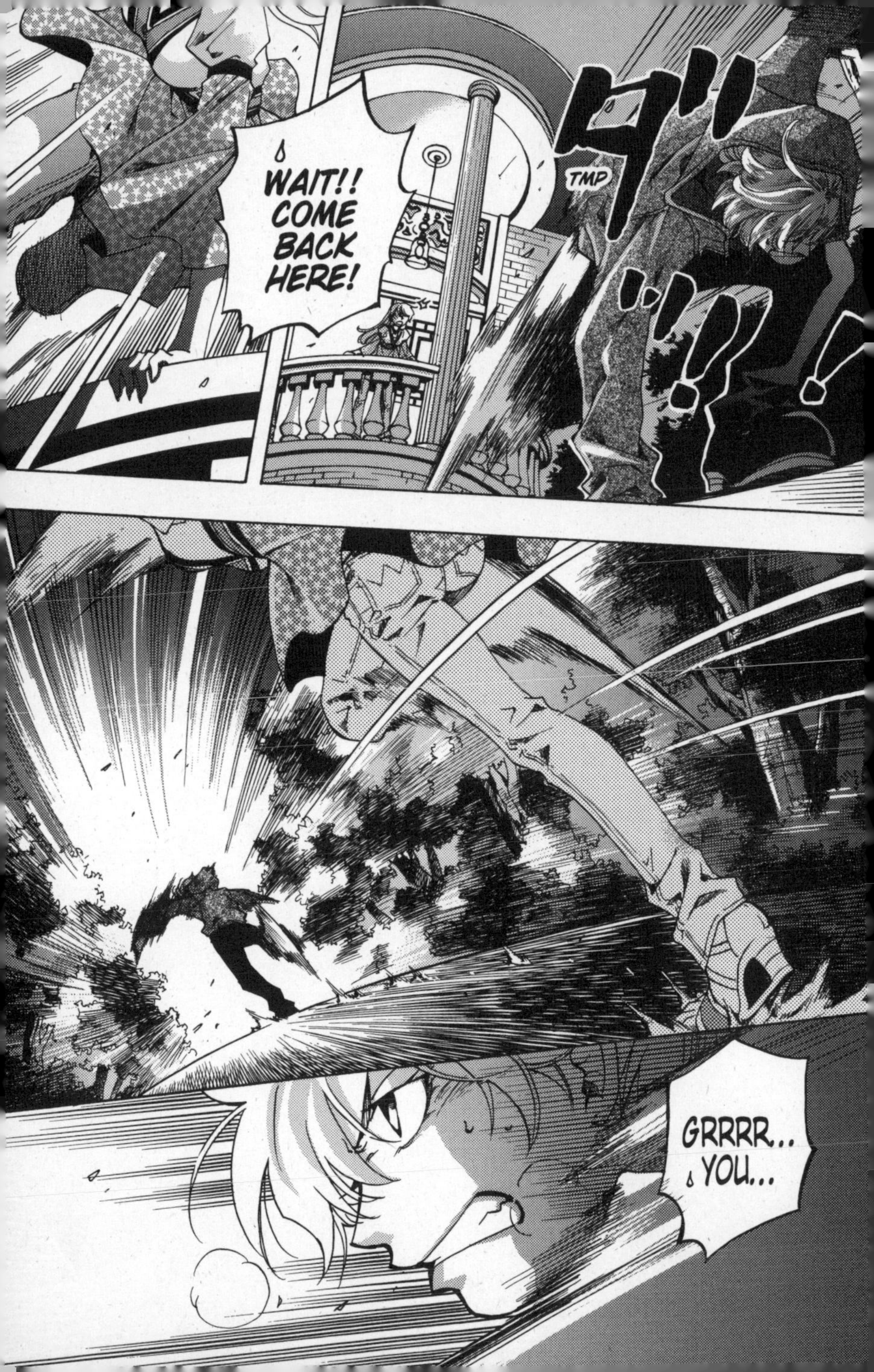
TMP
WAIT!! COME BACK HERE!
GRRRR... YOU...

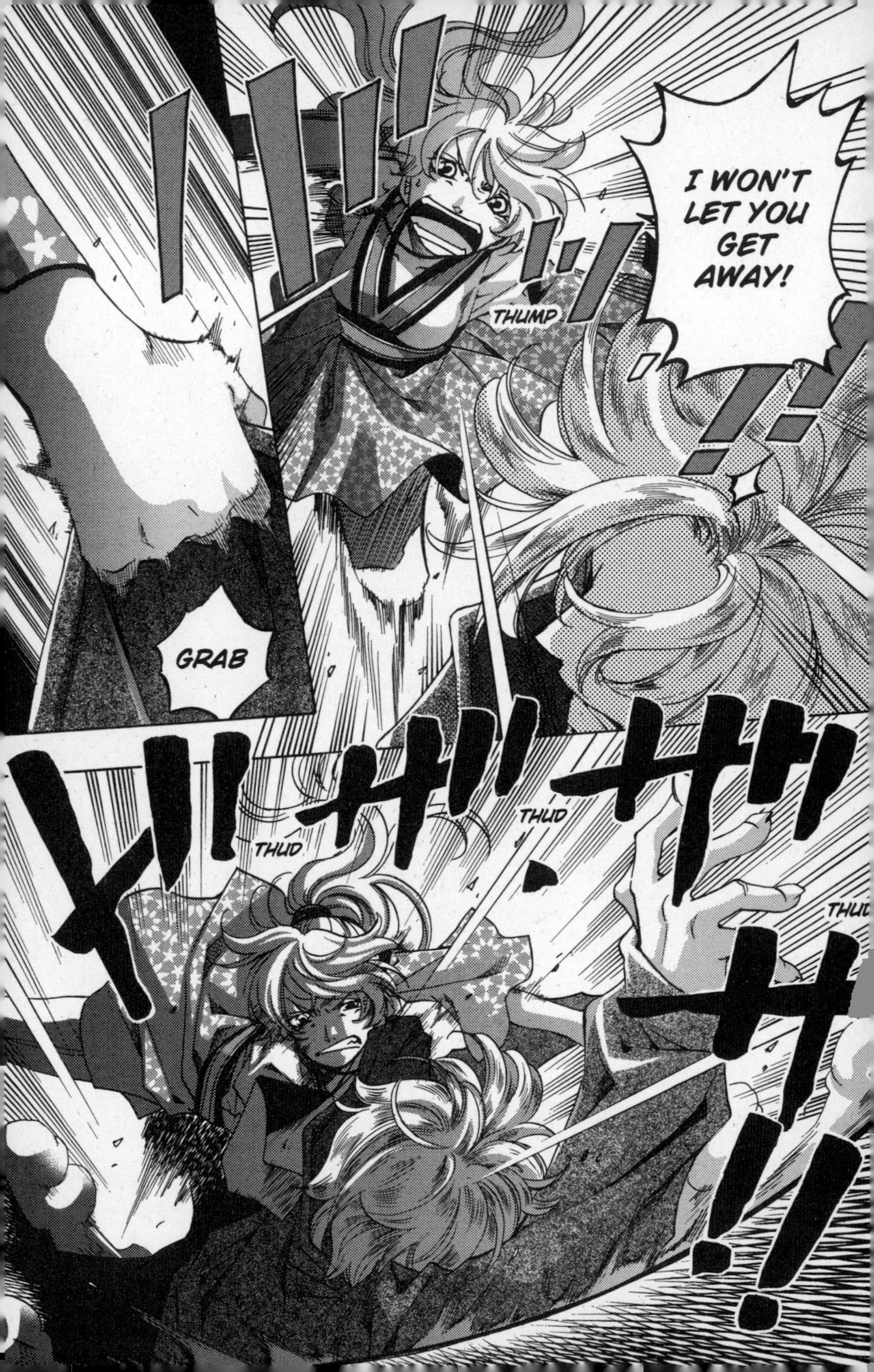
I WON'T LET YOU GET AWAY!
THUMP
GRAB
THUD
THUD
THUD

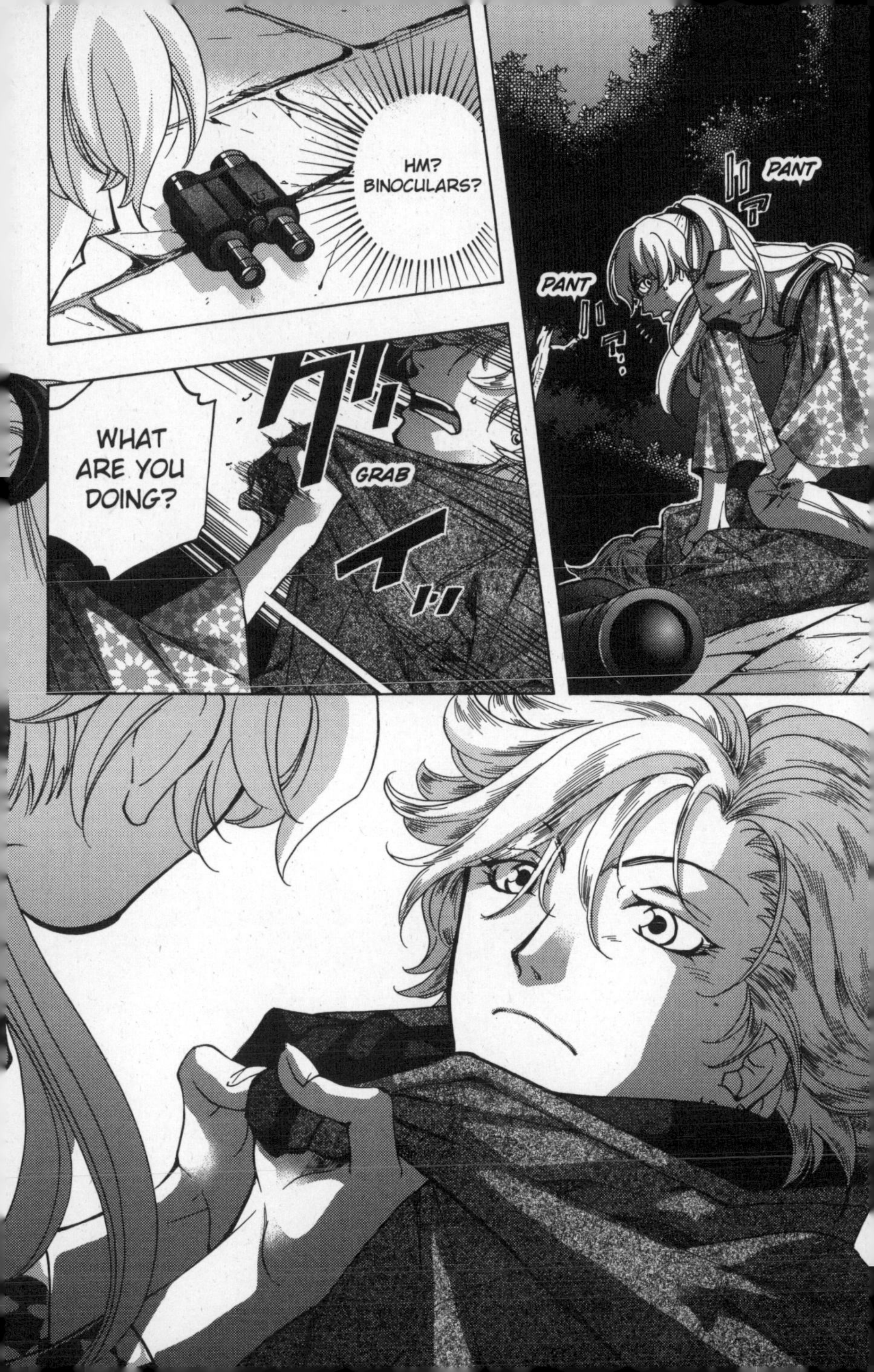
PANT
PANT
HM? BINOCULARS?
WHAT ARE YOU DOING?
GRAB

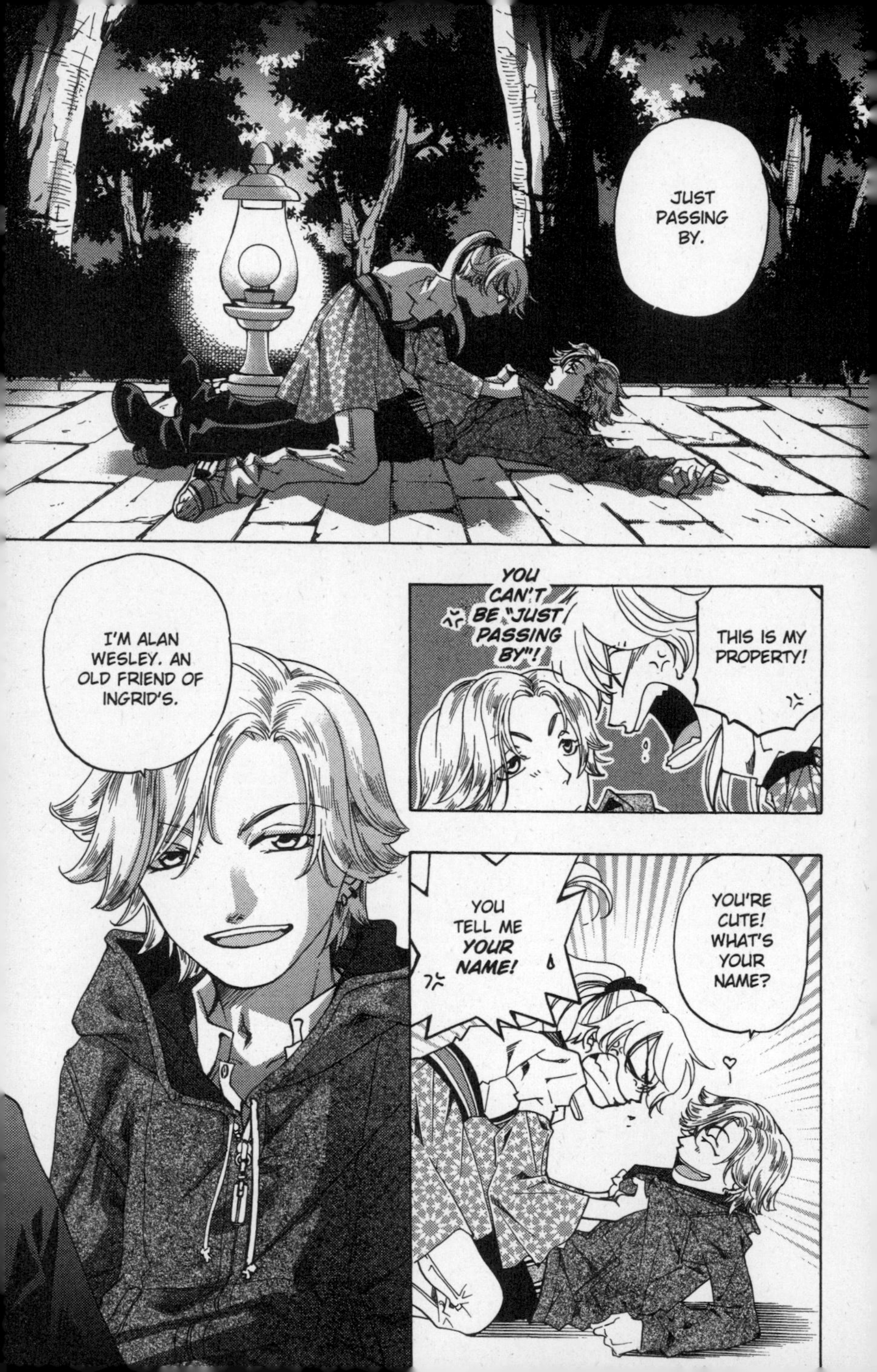
JUST PASSING BY.
YOU CAN'T BE "JUST PASSING BY"!
THIS IS MY PROPERTY!
YOU'RE CUTE! WHAT'S YOUR NAME?
YOU TELL ME *YOUR NAME!*
I'M ALAN WESLEY. AN OLD FRIEND OF INGRID'S.

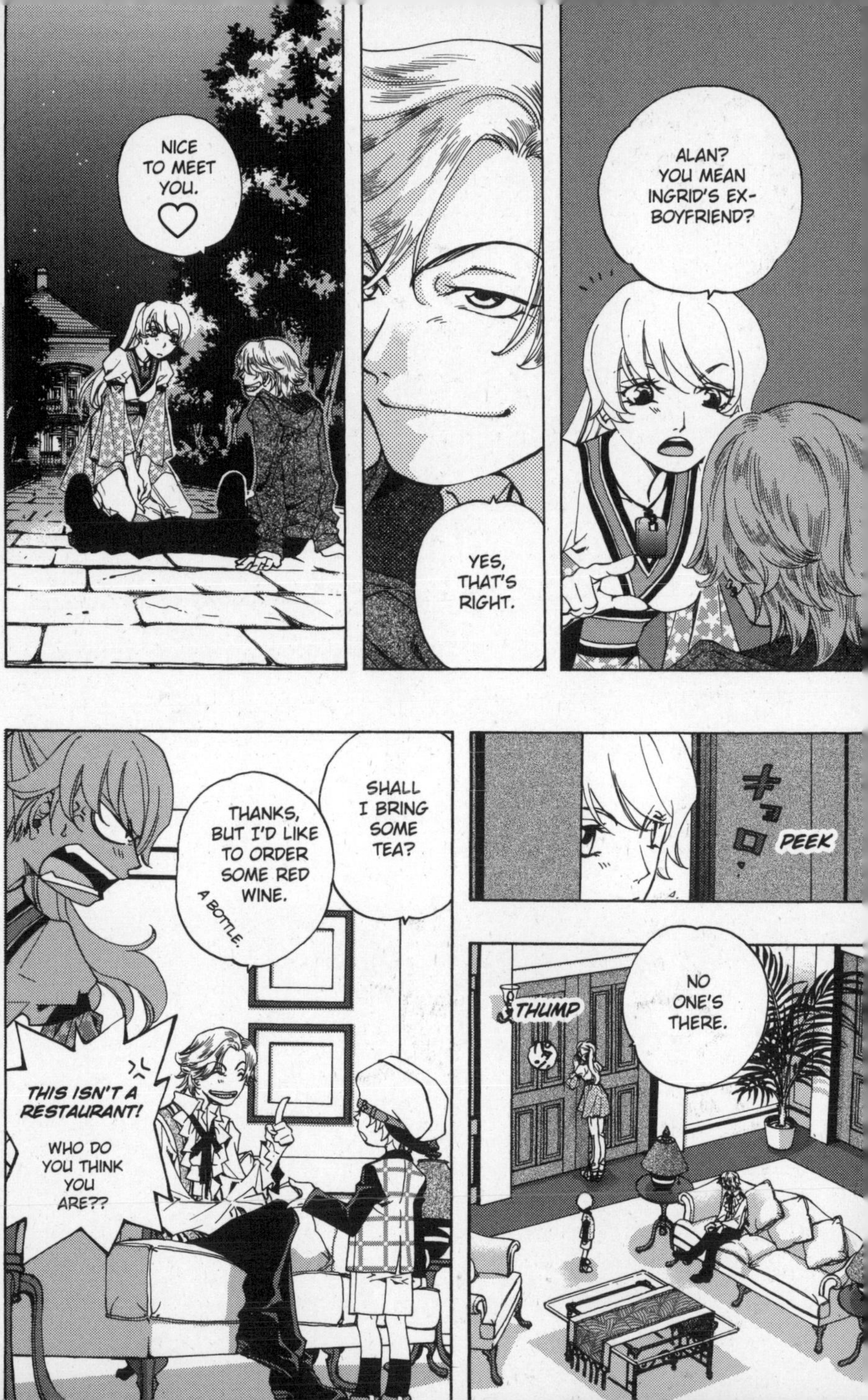
ALAN? YOU MEAN INGRID'S EX-BOYFRIEND?
YES, THAT'S RIGHT.
NICE TO MEET YOU. ♡
PEEK
THUMP
NO ONE'S THERE.
SHALL I BRING SOME TEA?
THANKS, BUT I'D LIKE TO ORDER SOME RED WINE.
A BOTTLE.
THIS ISN'T A RESTAURANT!
WHO DO YOU THINK YOU ARE??

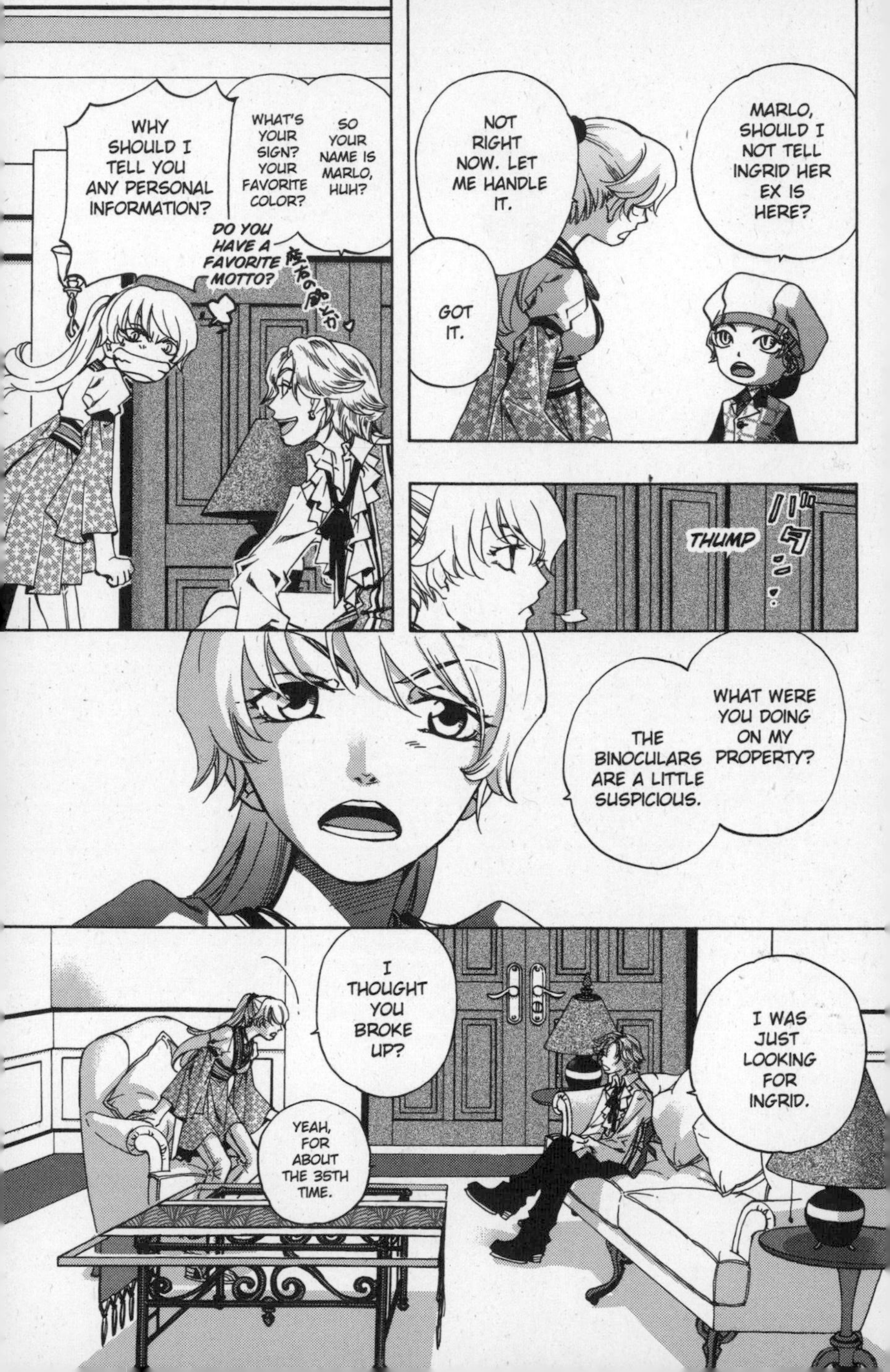
MARLO, SHOULD I NOT TELL INGRID HER EX IS HERE?
NOT RIGHT NOW. LET ME HANDLE IT.
GOT IT.
THUMP
SO YOUR NAME IS MARLO, HUH?
WHAT'S YOUR SIGN? YOUR FAVORITE COLOR?
WHY SHOULD I TELL YOU ANY PERSONAL INFORMATION?
DO YOU HAVE A FAVORITE MOTTO?
WHAT WERE YOU DOING ON MY PROPERTY?
THE BINOCULARS ARE A LITTLE SUSPICIOUS.
I WAS JUST LOOKING FOR INGRID.
I THOUGHT YOU BROKE UP?
YEAH, FOR ABOUT THE 35TH TIME.

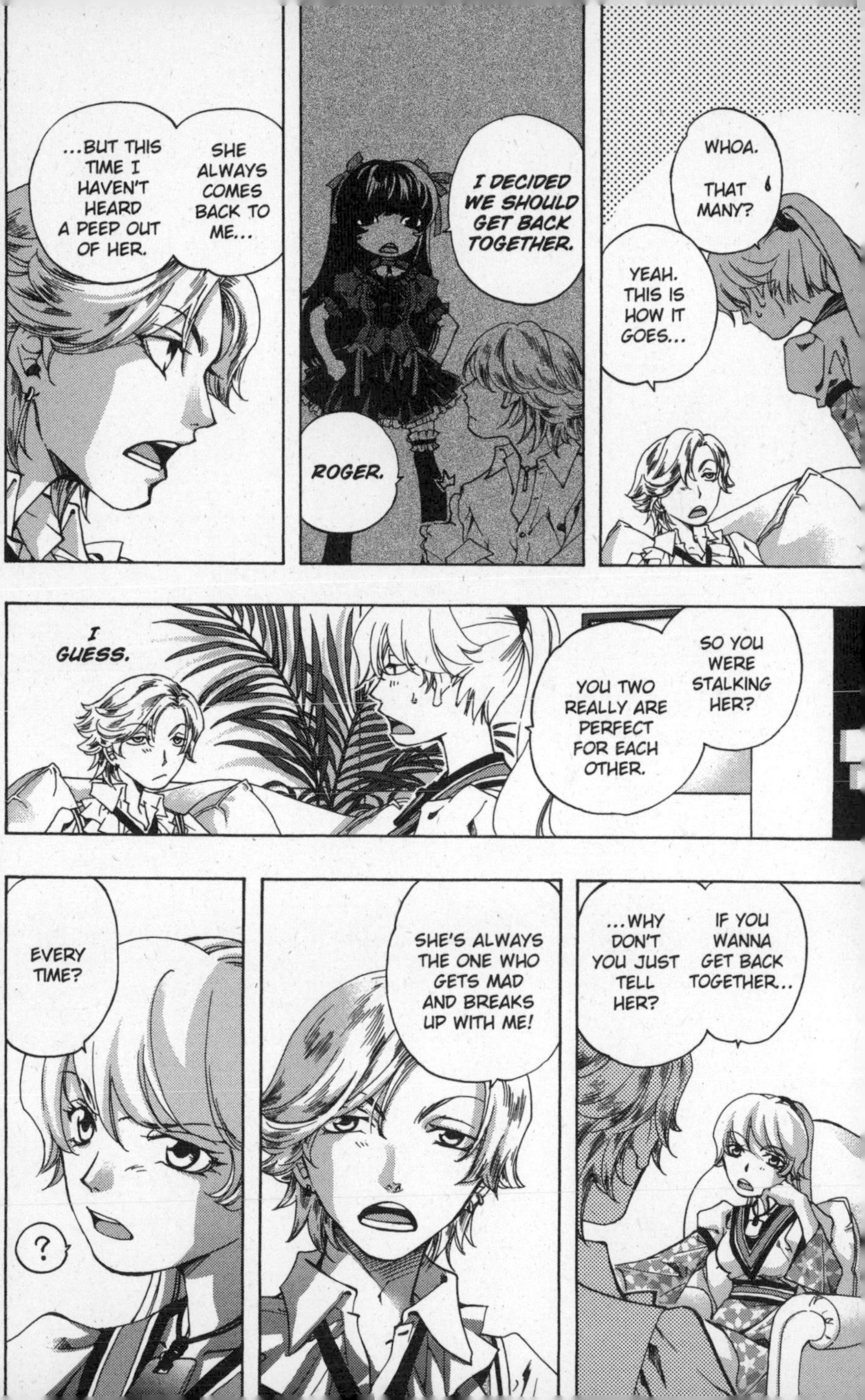
WHOA. THAT MANY?
YEAH. THIS IS HOW IT GOES...
I DECIDED WE SHOULD GET BACK TOGETHER.
ROGER.
SHE ALWAYS COMES BACK TO ME...
...BUT THIS TIME I HAVEN'T HEARD A PEEP OUT OF HER.
SO YOU WERE STALKING HER?
YOU TWO REALLY ARE PERFECT FOR EACH OTHER.
I GUESS.
IF YOU WANNA GET BACK TOGETHER...
...WHY DON'T YOU JUST TELL HER?
SHE'S ALWAYS THE ONE WHO GETS MAD AND BREAKS UP WITH ME!
EVERY TIME?
?

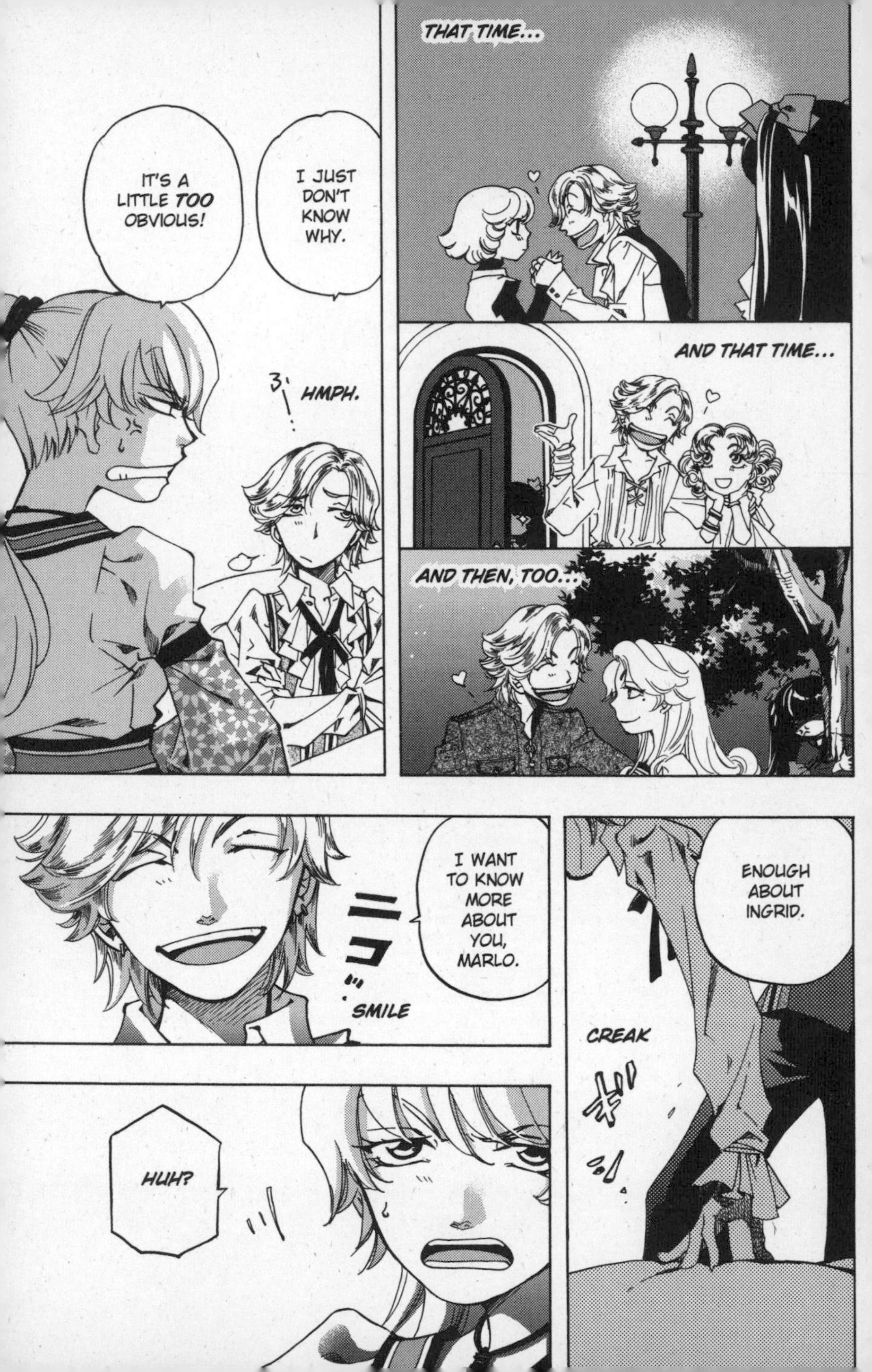
THAT TIME...
AND THAT TIME...
AND THEN, TOO...
I JUST DON'T KNOW WHY.
IT'S A LITTLE TOO OBVIOUS!
HMPH.
ENOUGH ABOUT INGRID.
CREAK
I WANT TO KNOW MORE ABOUT YOU, MARLO.
SMILE
HUH?

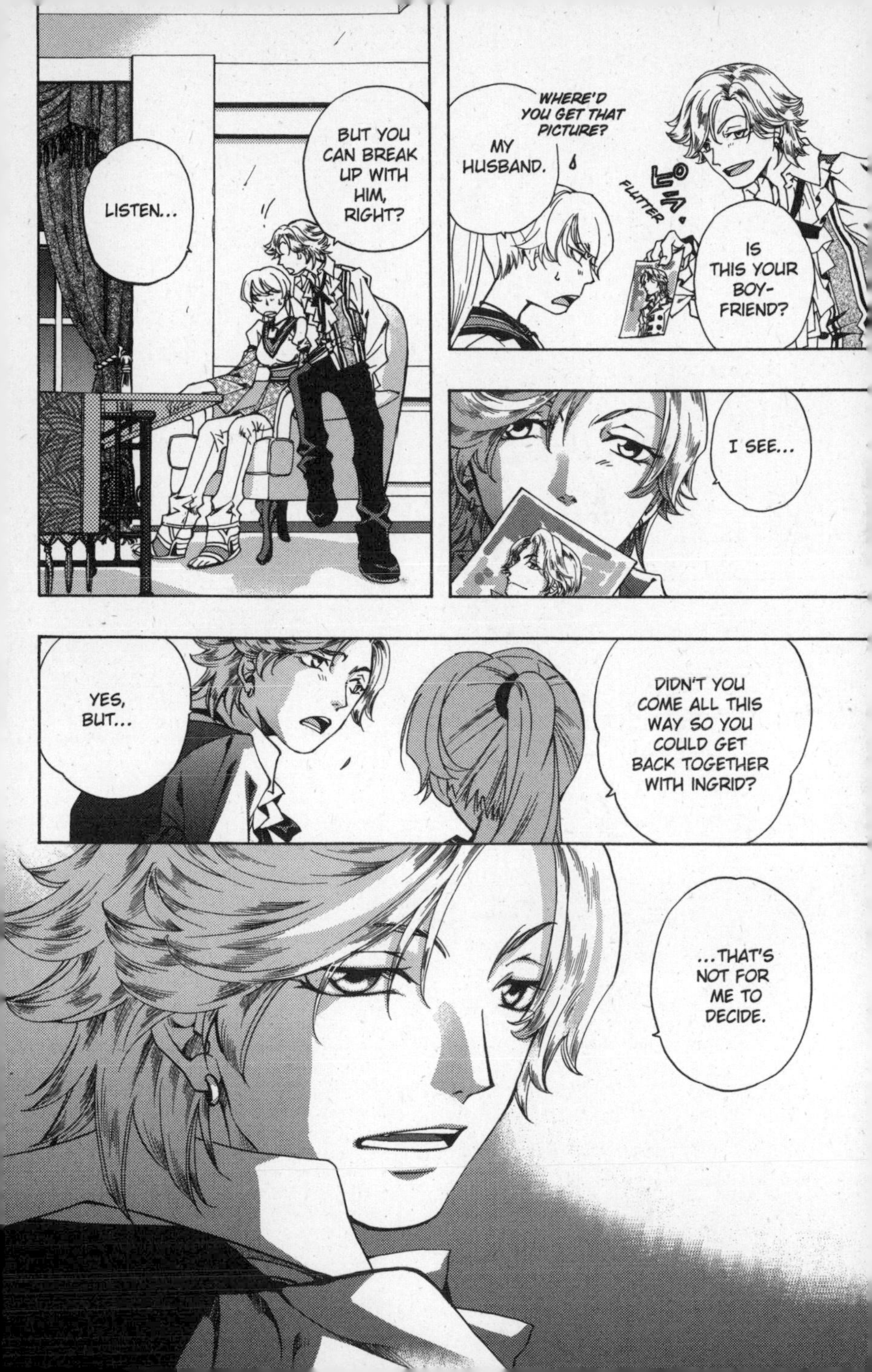
IS THIS YOUR BOY-FRIEND?
FLUTTER
WHERE'D YOU GET THAT PICTURE?
MY HUSBAND.
I SEE...
BUT YOU CAN BREAK UP WITH HIM, RIGHT?
LISTEN...
DIDN'T YOU COME ALL THIS WAY SO YOU COULD GET BACK TOGETHER WITH INGRID?
YES, BUT...
...THAT'S NOT FOR ME TO DECIDE.

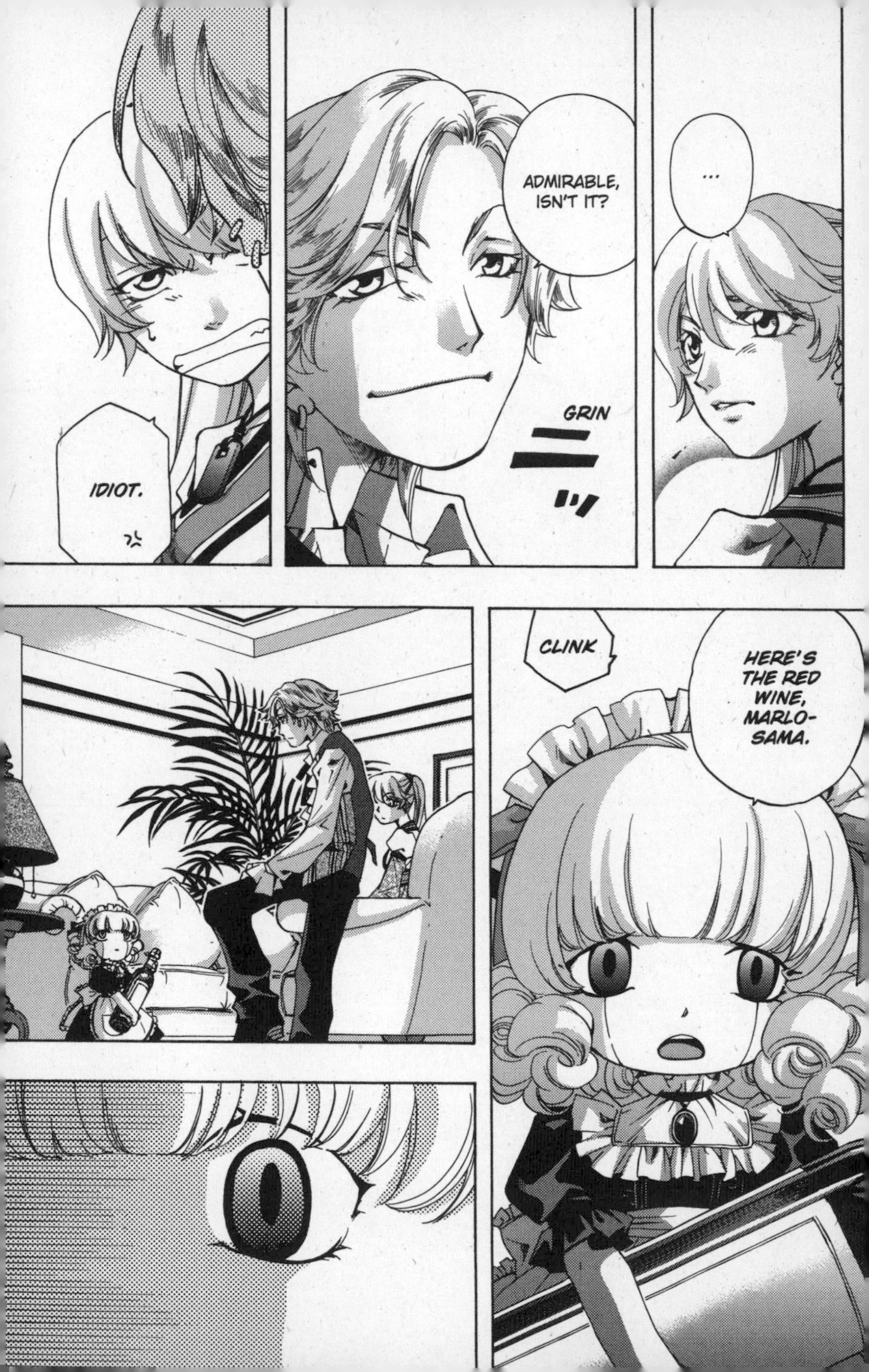
...
ADMIRABLE, ISN'T IT?
GRIN
IDIOT.
HERE'S THE RED WINE, MARLO-SAMA.
CLINK

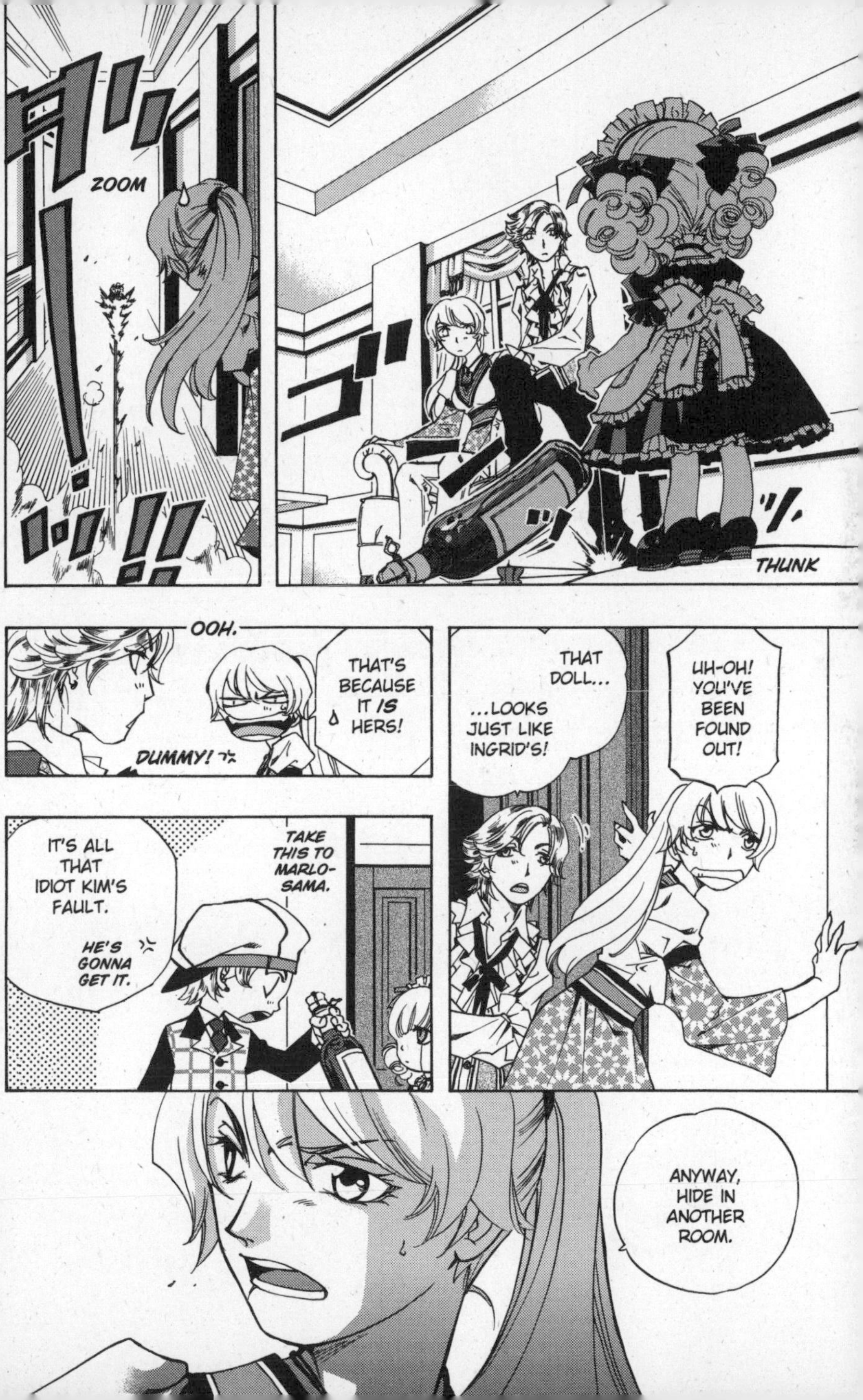
THUNK
ZOOM
UH-OH! YOU'VE BEEN FOUND OUT!
THAT DOLL...
...LOOKS JUST LIKE INGRID'S!
OOH.
THAT'S BECAUSE IT IS HERS!
DUMMY!
TAKE THIS TO MARLO-SAMA.
IT'S ALL THAT IDIOT KIM'S FAULT.
HE'S GONNA GET IT.
ANYWAY, HIDE IN ANOTHER ROOM.

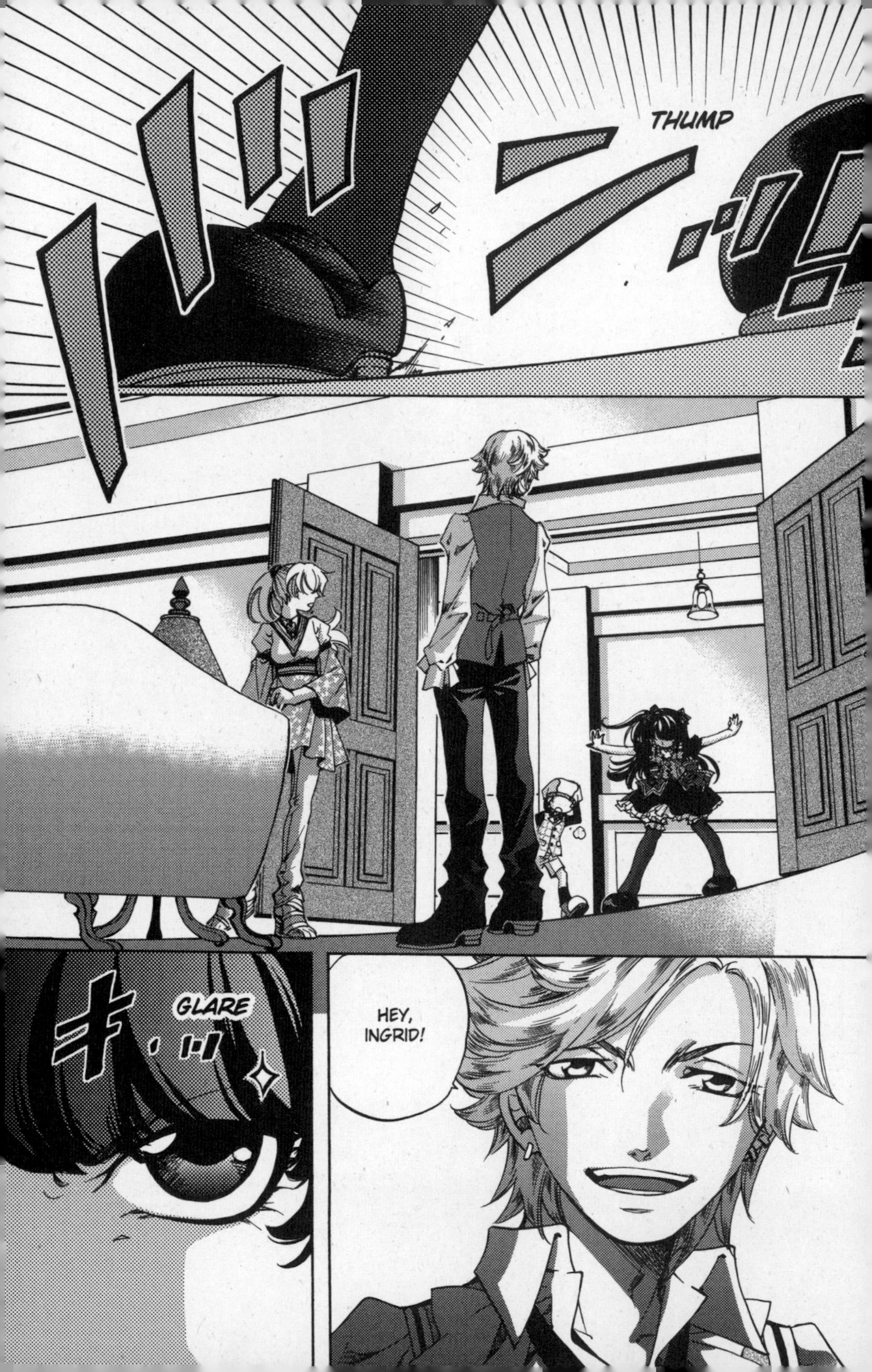
THUMP
HEY, INGRID!
GLARE

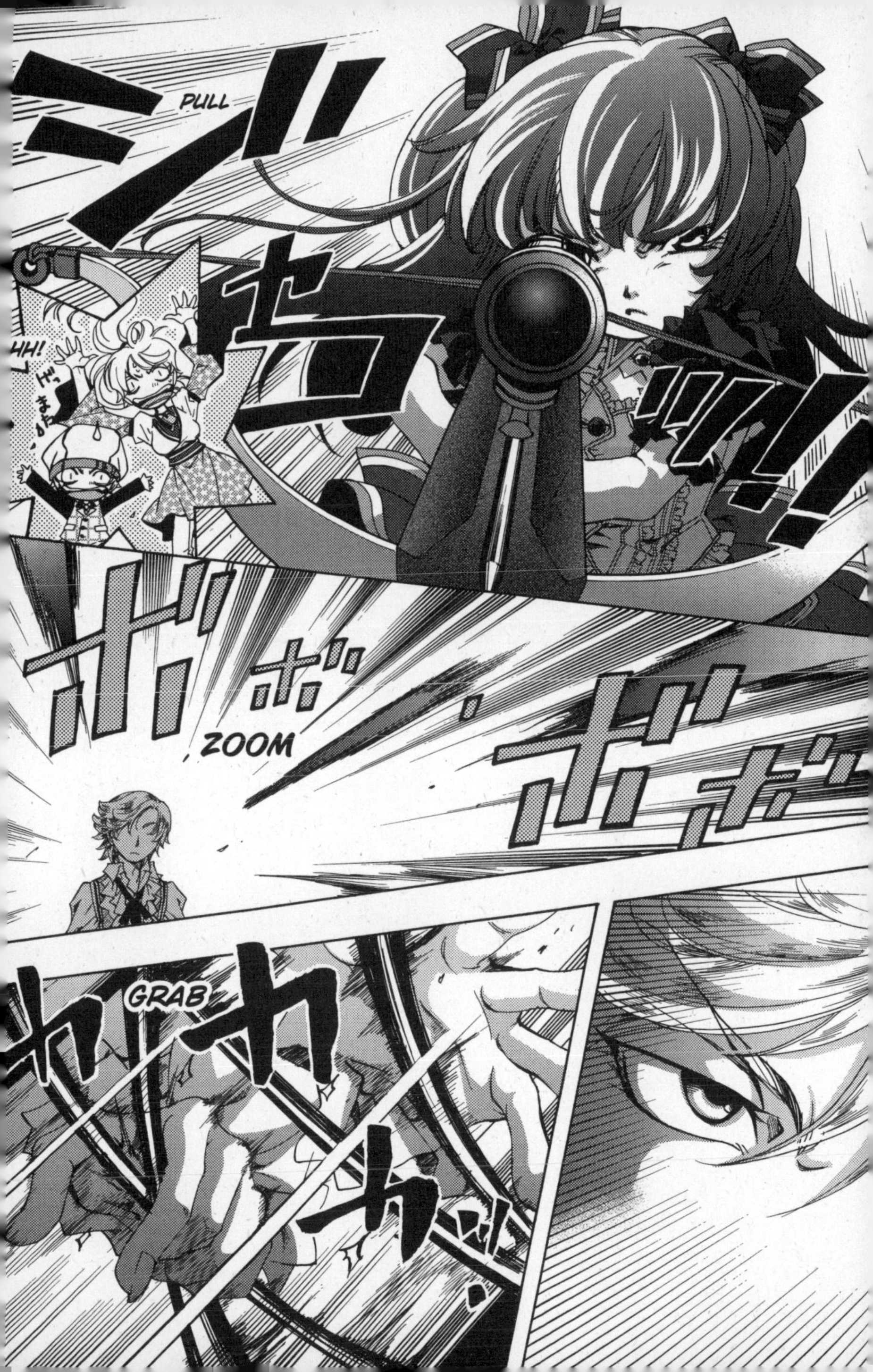
PULL
HH!
ZOOM
GRAB

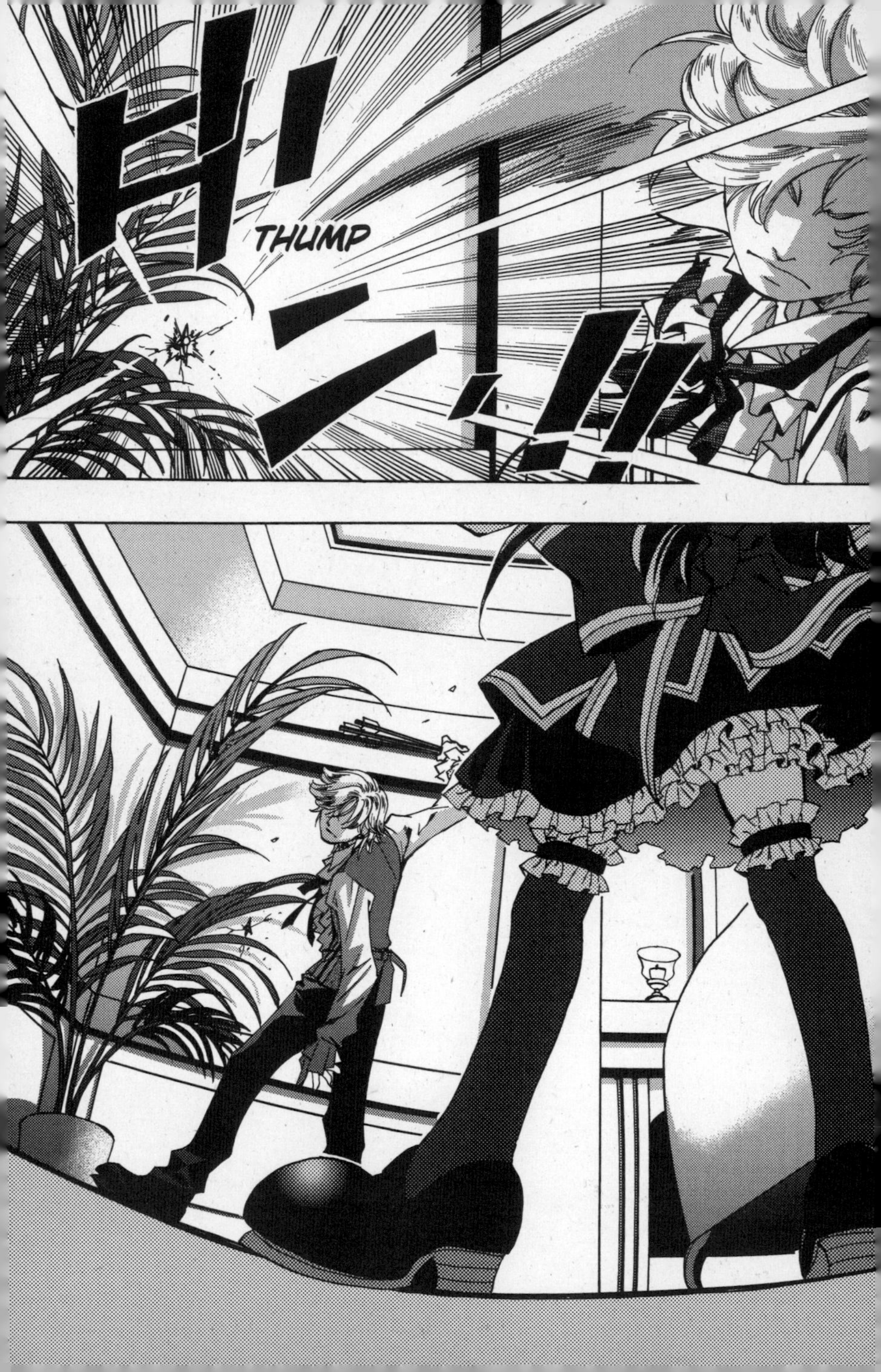
THUMP

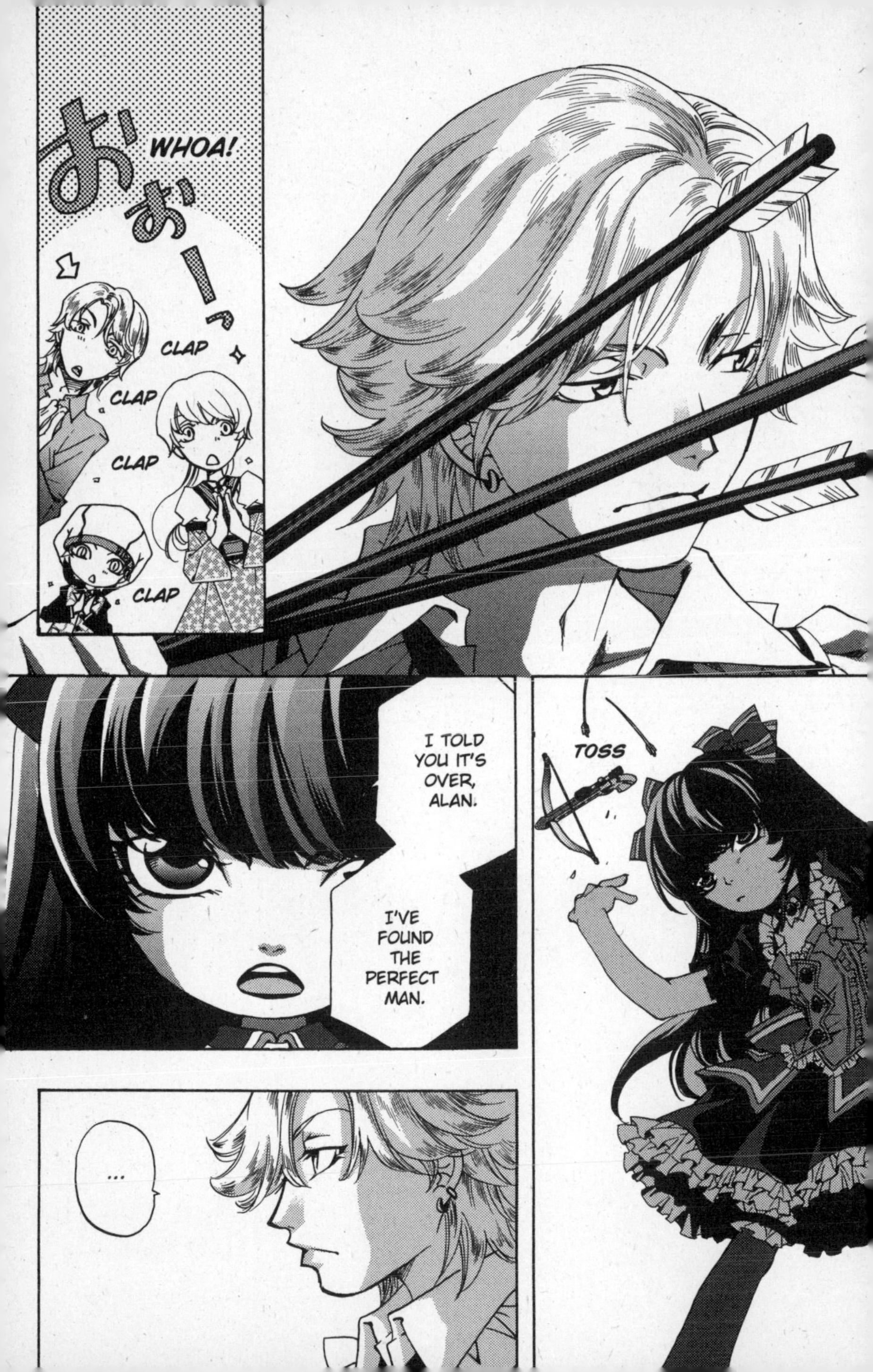
おぉー!
WHOA!
CLAP
CLAP
CLAP
CLAP
TOSS
I TOLD YOU IT'S OVER, ALAN.
I'VE FOUND THE PERFECT MAN.
...

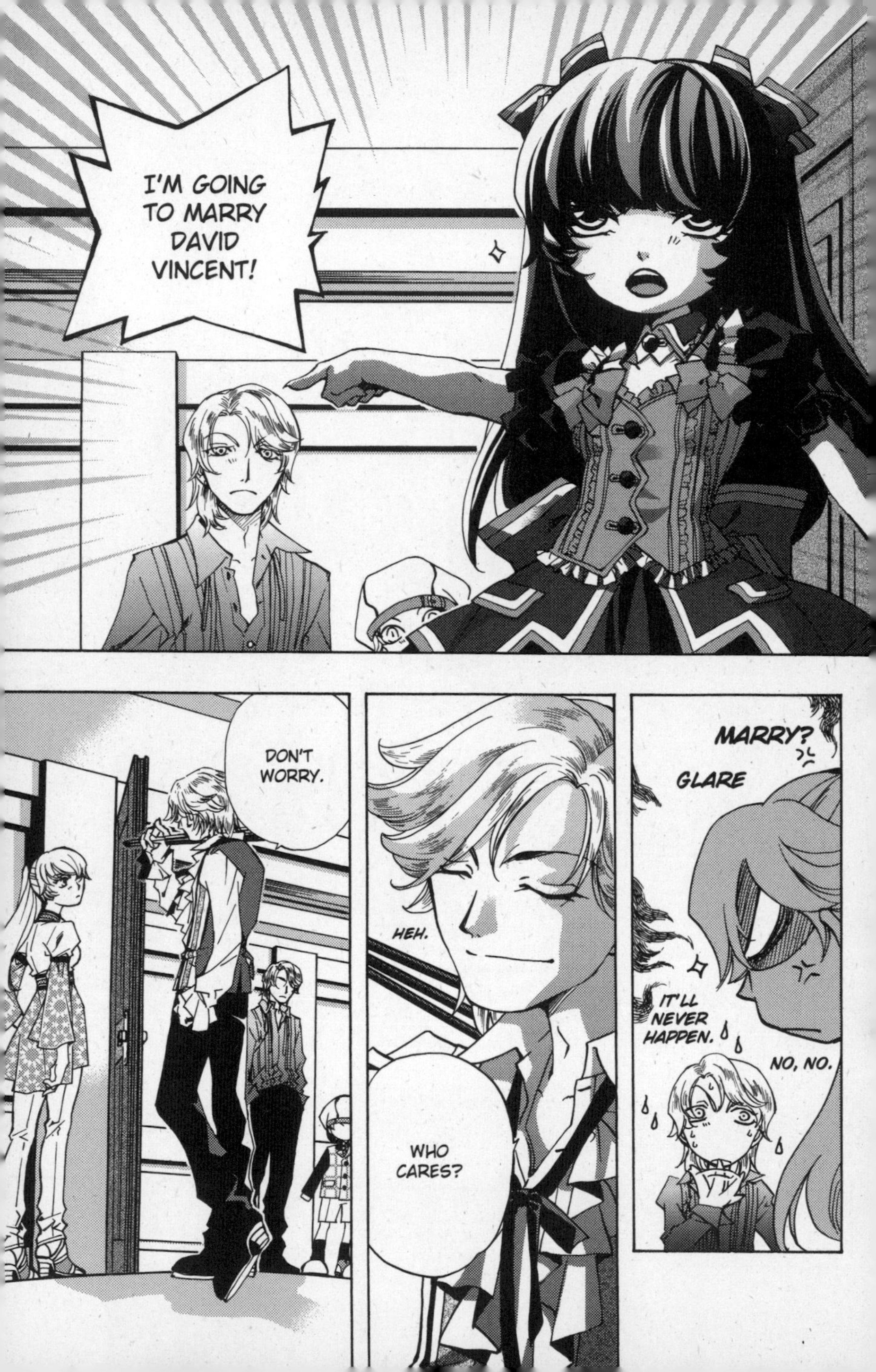
I'M GOING TO MARRY DAVID VINCENT!
MARRY?
GLARE
IT'LL NEVER HAPPEN.
NO, NO.
HEH.
WHO CARES?
DON'T WORRY.

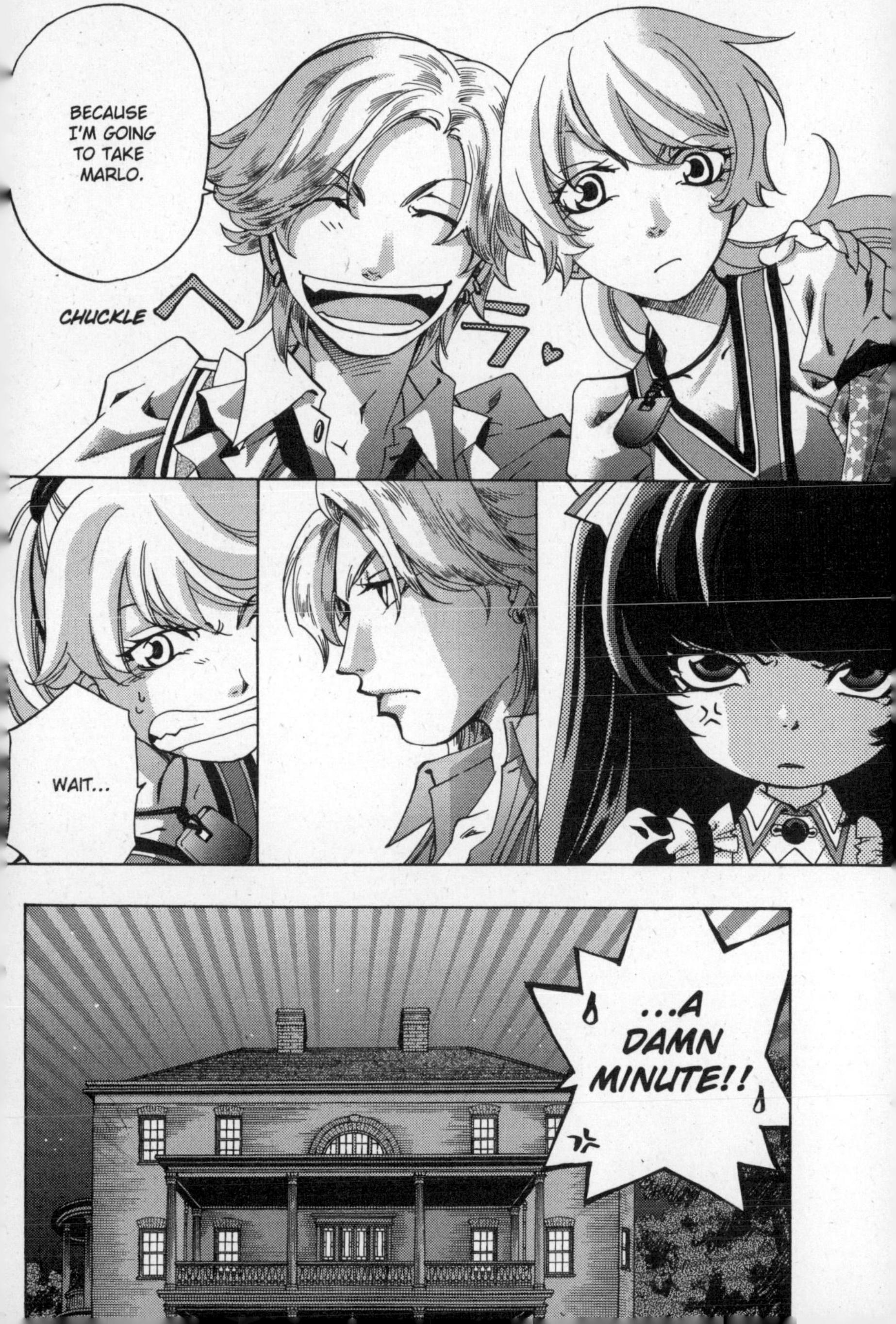
BECAUSE I'M GOING TO TAKE MARLO.
CHUCKLE
WAIT...
...A DAMN MINUTE!!

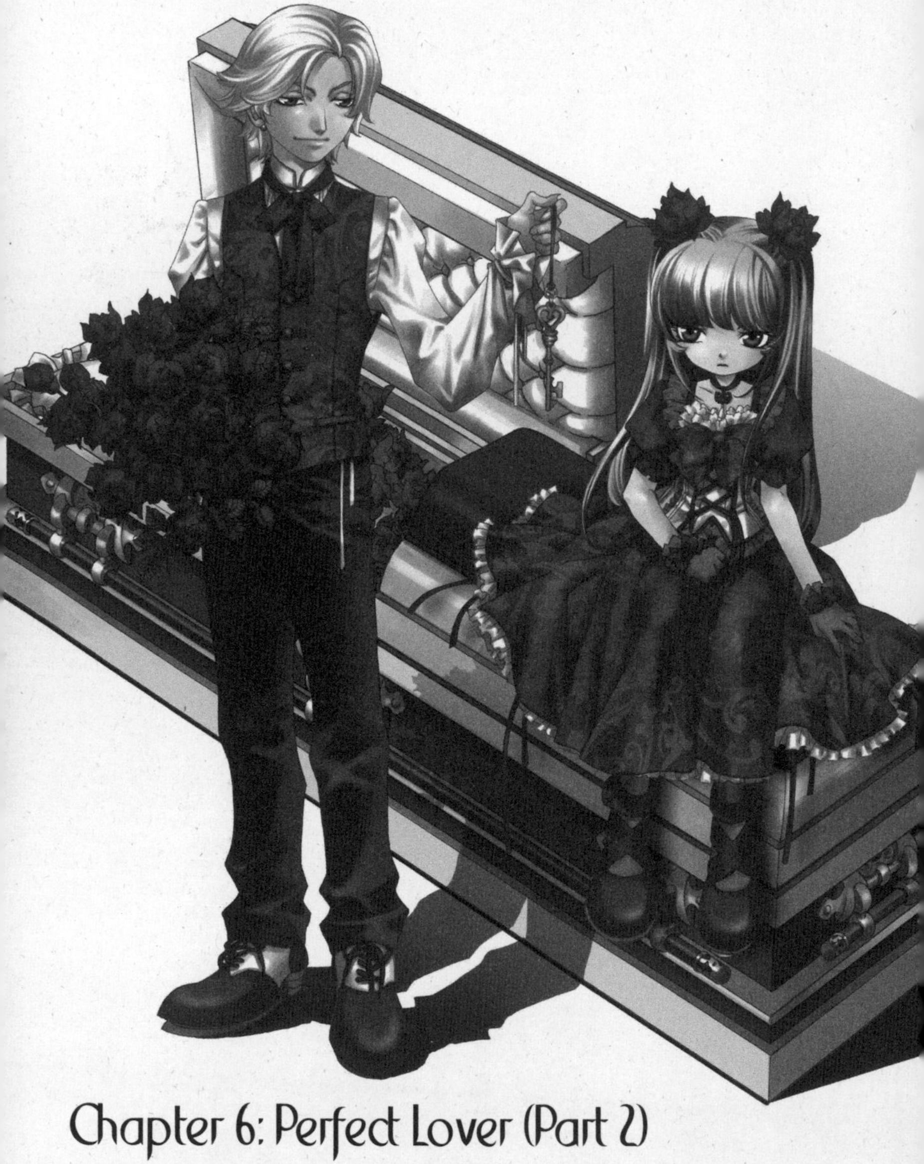

Chapter 6: Perfect Lover (Part 2)

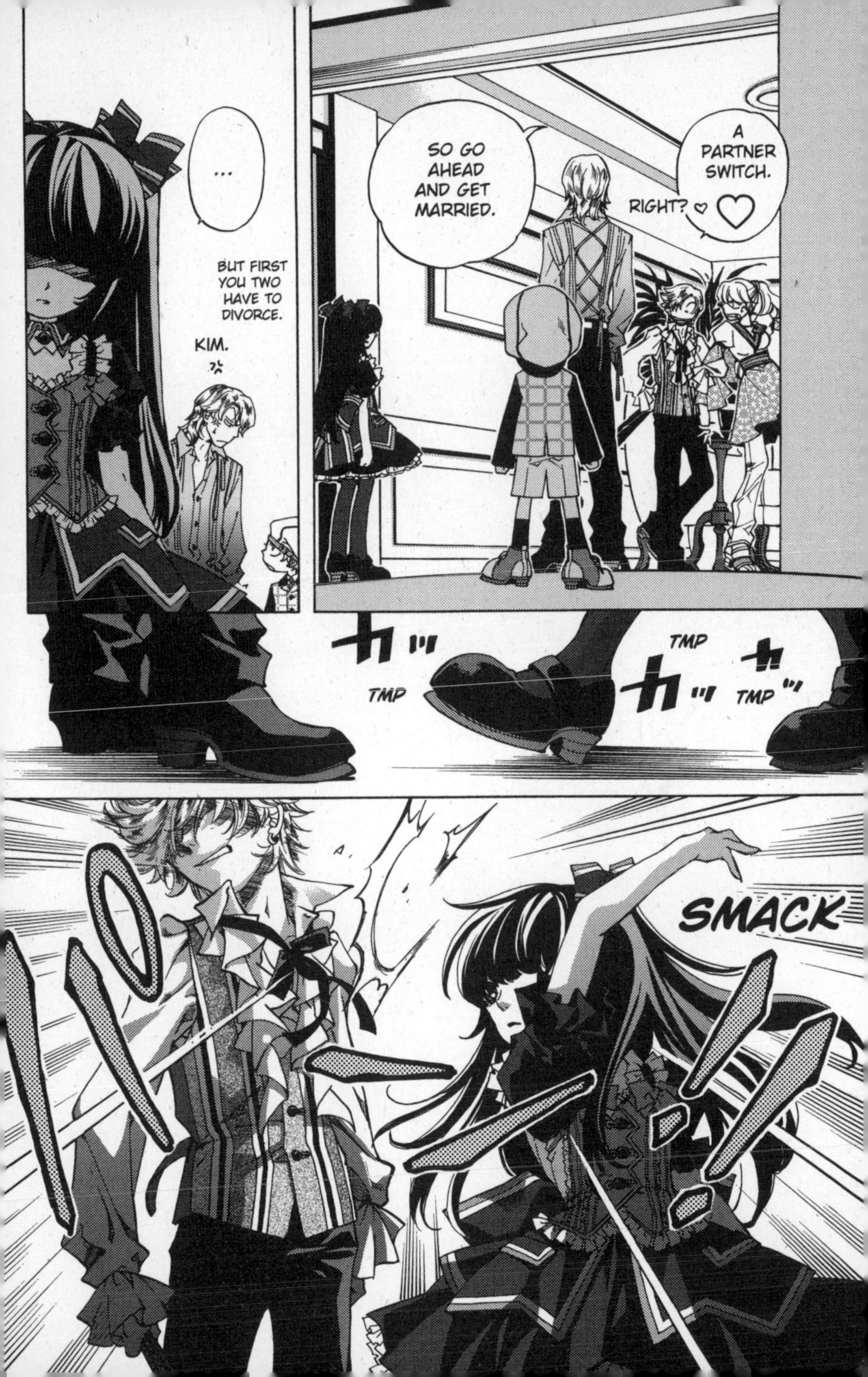
A PARTNER SWITCH.
RIGHT? ♡
SO GO AHEAD AND GET MARRIED.
...
BUT FIRST YOU TWO HAVE TO DIVORCE.
KIM.
カッ
TMP
カッ
TMP
カッ
TMP
SMACK

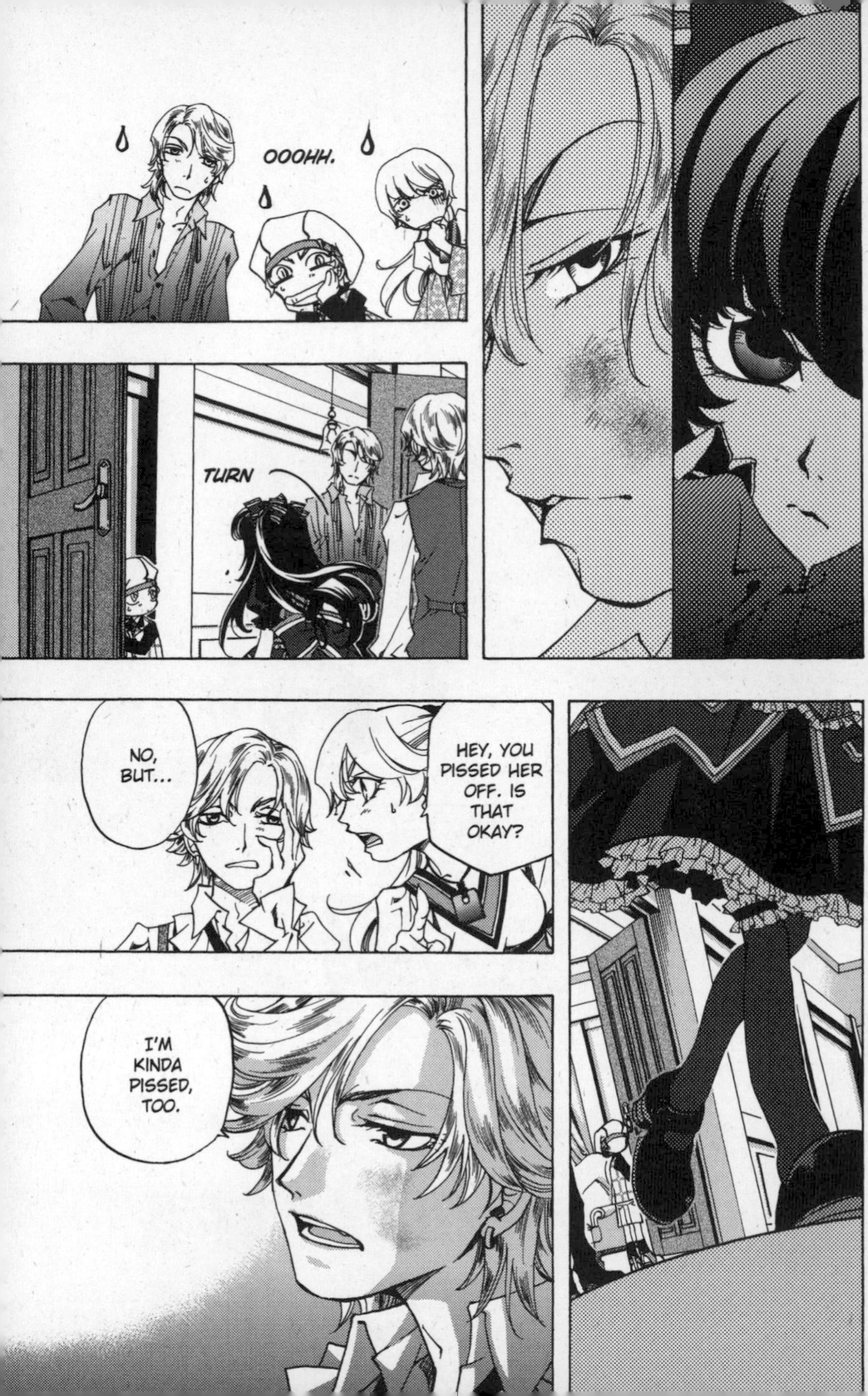
OOOHH.
TURN
HEY, YOU PISSED HER OFF. IS THAT OKAY?
NO, BUT...
I'M KINDA PISSED, TOO.

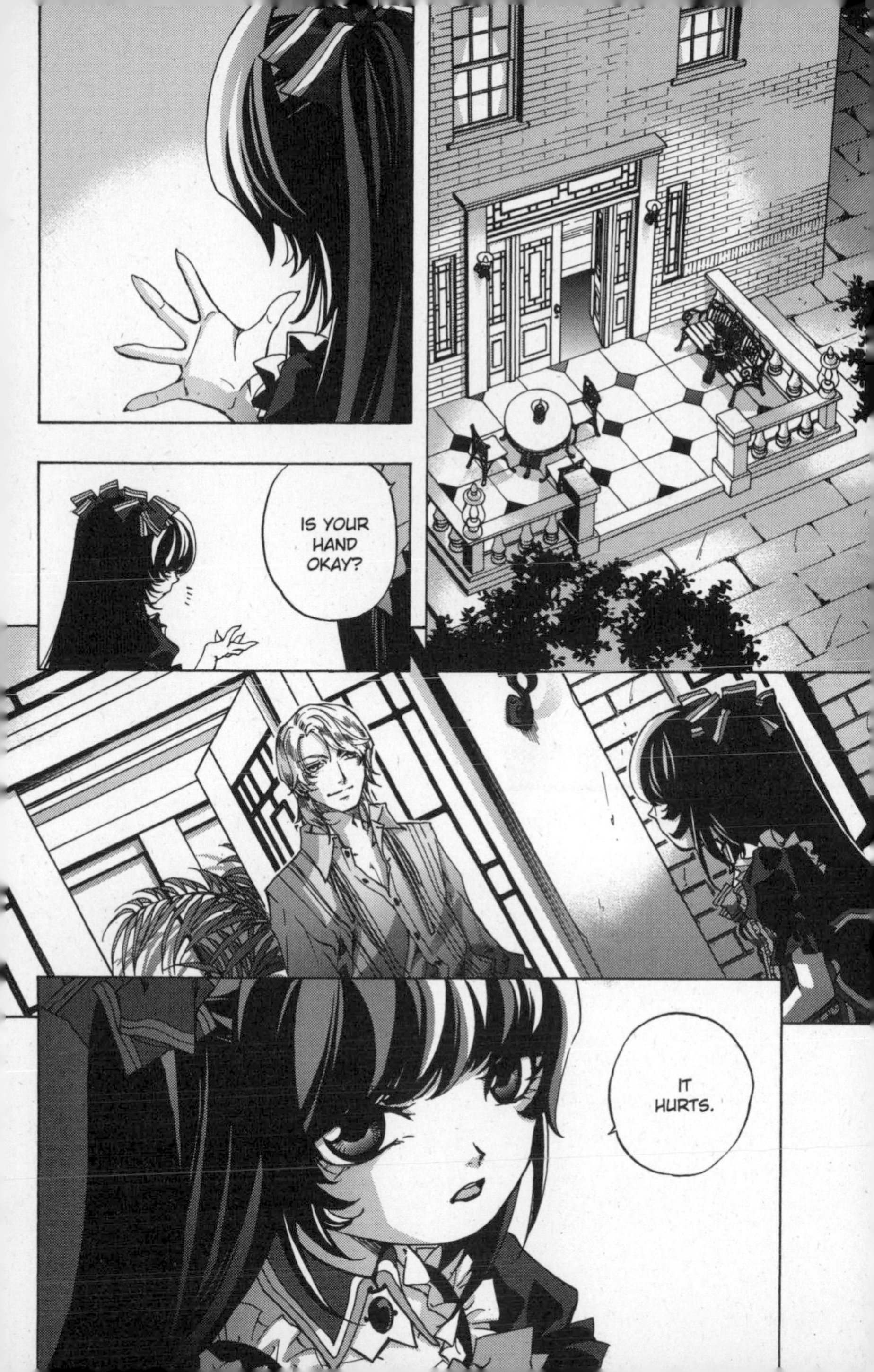
IS YOUR HAND OKAY?
IT HURTS.

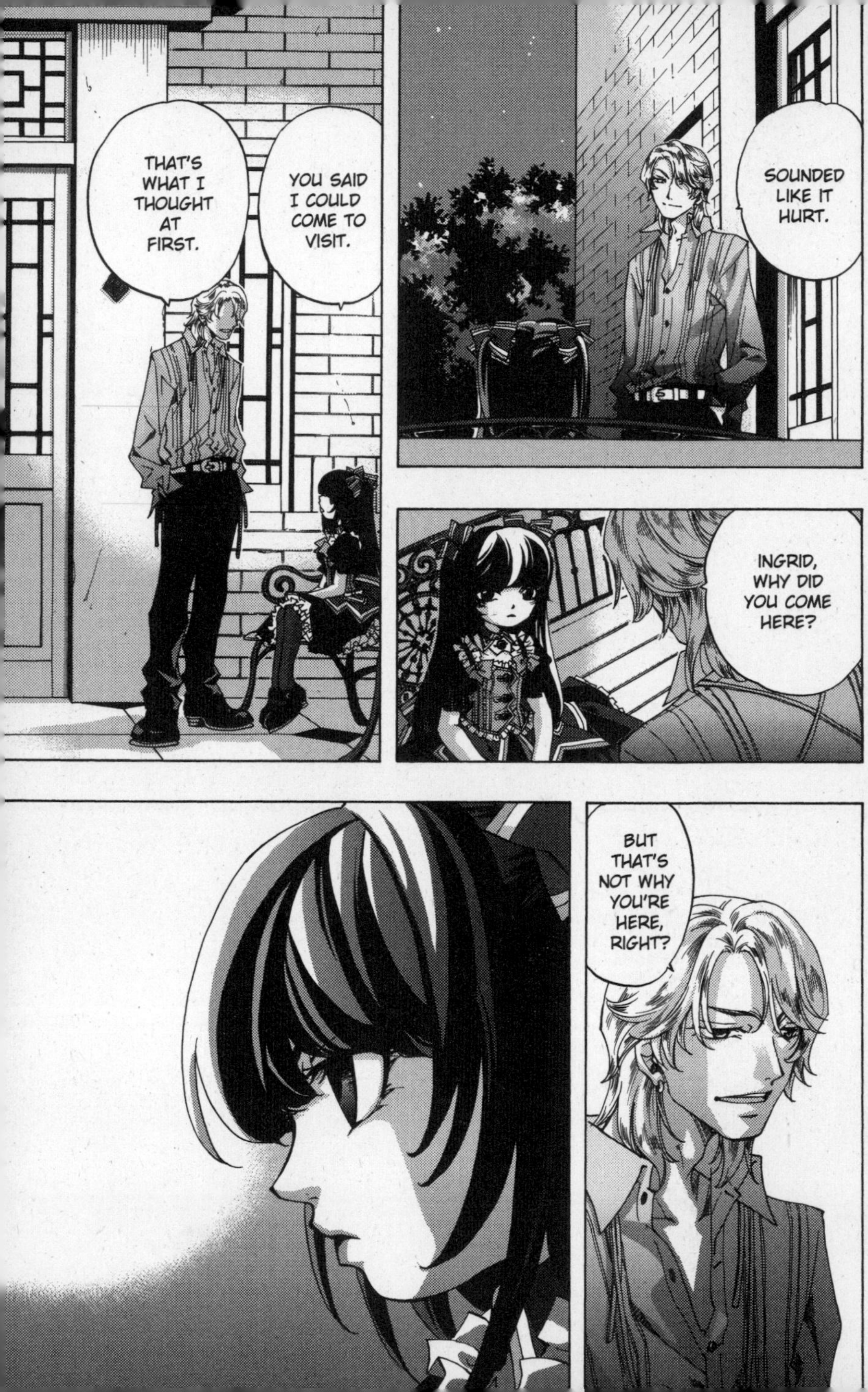

SOUNDED LIKE IT HURT.
INGRID, WHY DID YOU COME HERE?
YOU SAID I COULD COME TO VISIT.
THAT'S WHAT I THOUGHT AT FIRST.
BUT THAT'S NOT WHY YOU'RE HERE, RIGHT?

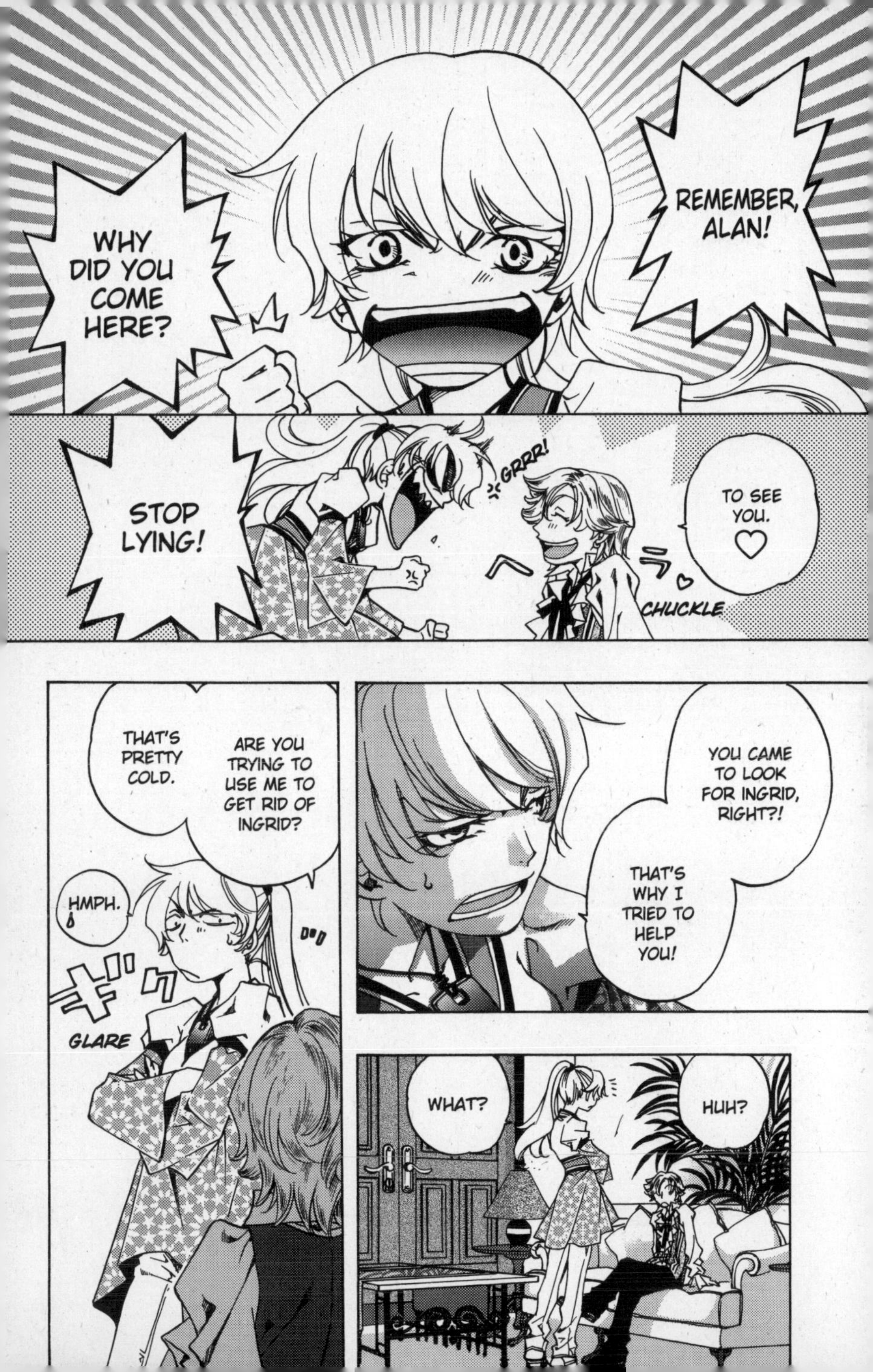
REMEMBER, ALAN!
WHY DID YOU COME HERE?
TO SEE YOU. ♥
CHUCKLE
GRRR!
STOP LYING!
YOU CAME TO LOOK FOR INGRID, RIGHT?!
THAT'S WHY I TRIED TO HELP YOU!
HUH?
WHAT?
THAT'S PRETTY COLD. ARE YOU TRYING TO USE ME TO GET RID OF INGRID?
HMPH.
GLARE

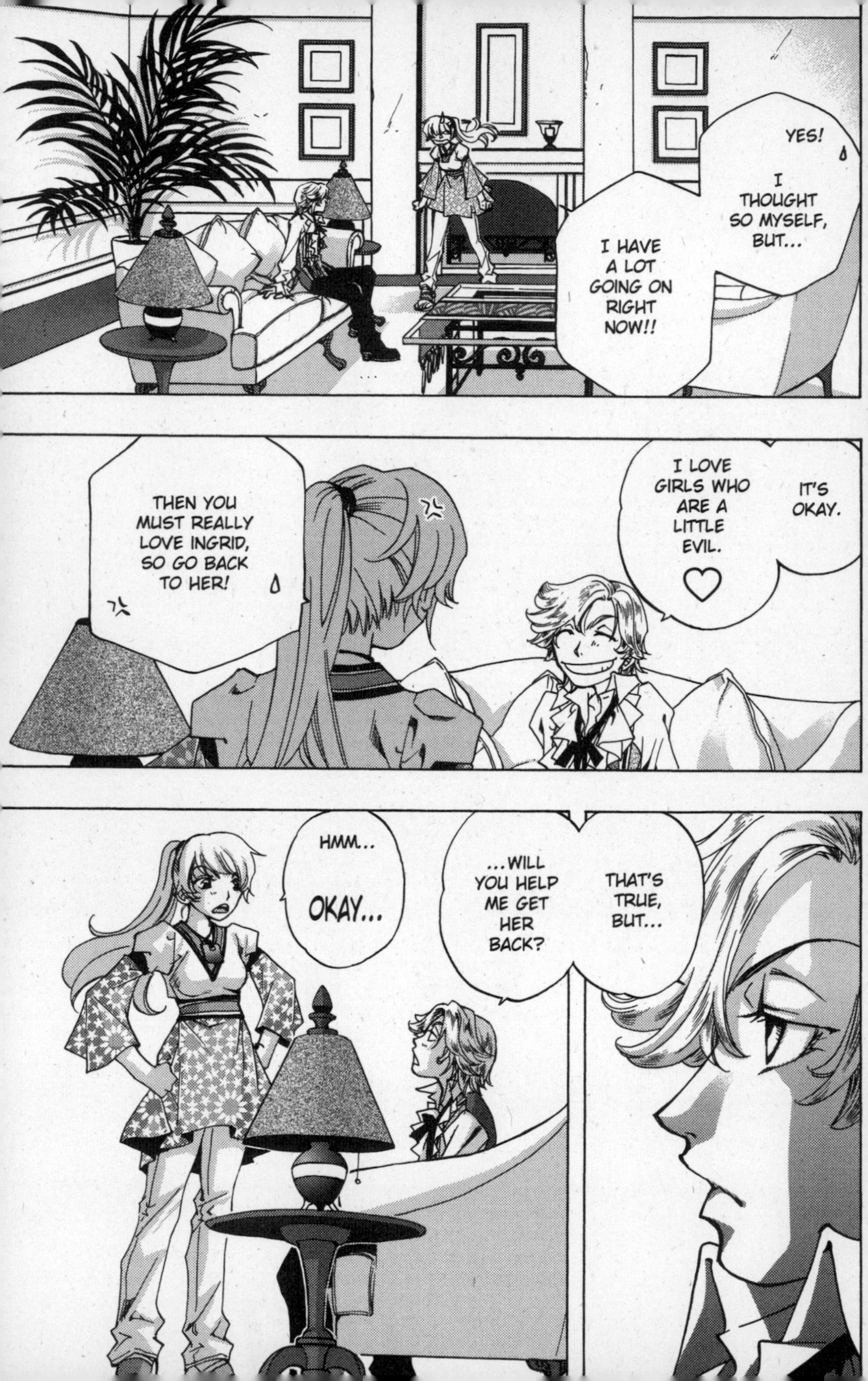
YES!
I THOUGHT SO MYSELF, BUT...
I HAVE A LOT GOING ON RIGHT NOW!!
IT'S OKAY.
I LOVE GIRLS WHO ARE A LITTLE EVIL. ♥
THEN YOU MUST REALLY LOVE INGRID, SO GO BACK TO HER!
THAT'S TRUE, BUT...
...WILL YOU HELP ME GET HER BACK?
HMM...
OKAY...

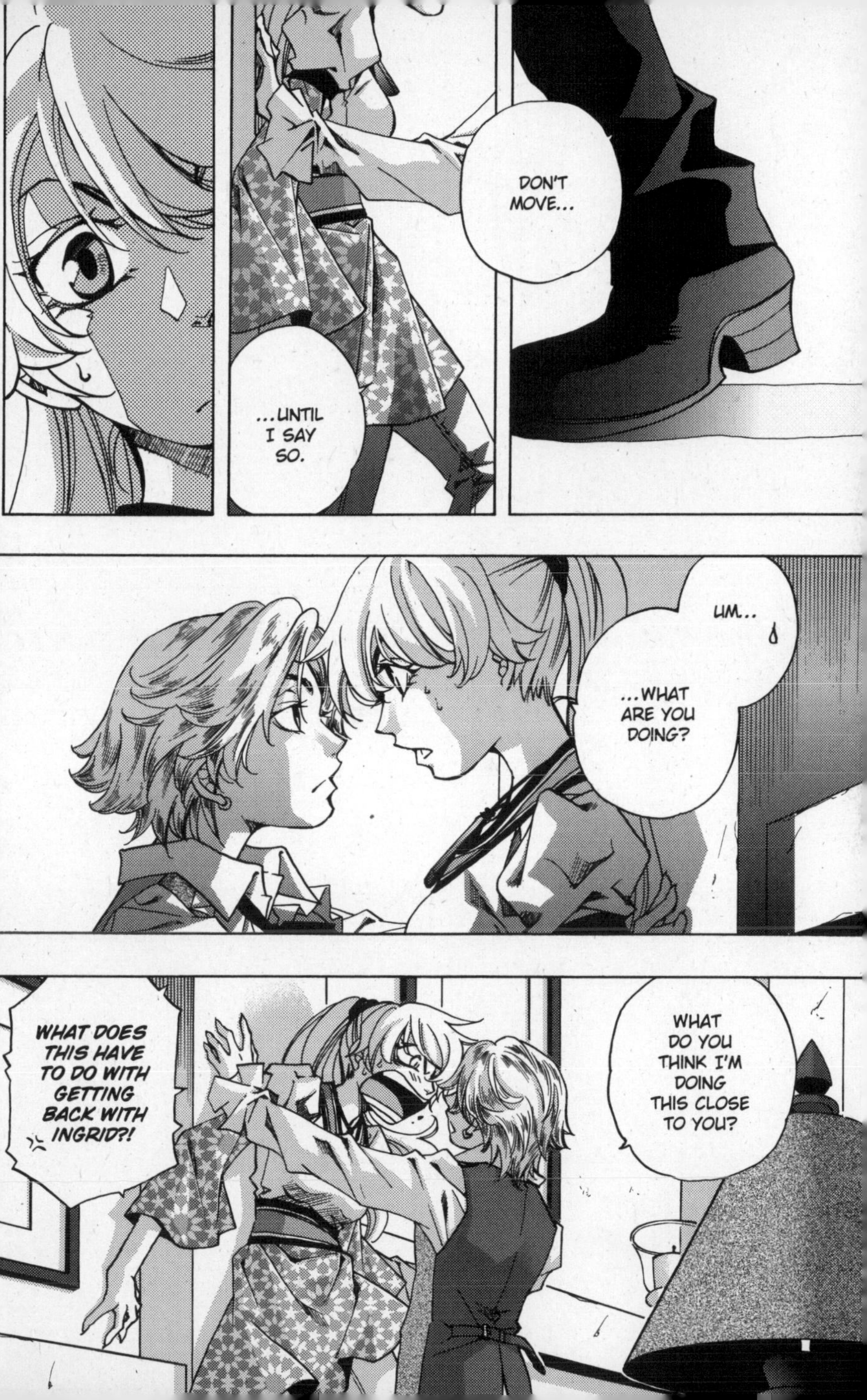
DON'T MOVE...
...UNTIL I SAY SO.
UM...
...WHAT ARE YOU DOING?
WHAT DO YOU THINK I'M DOING THIS CLOSE TO YOU?
WHAT DOES THIS HAVE TO DO WITH GETTING BACK WITH INGRID?!

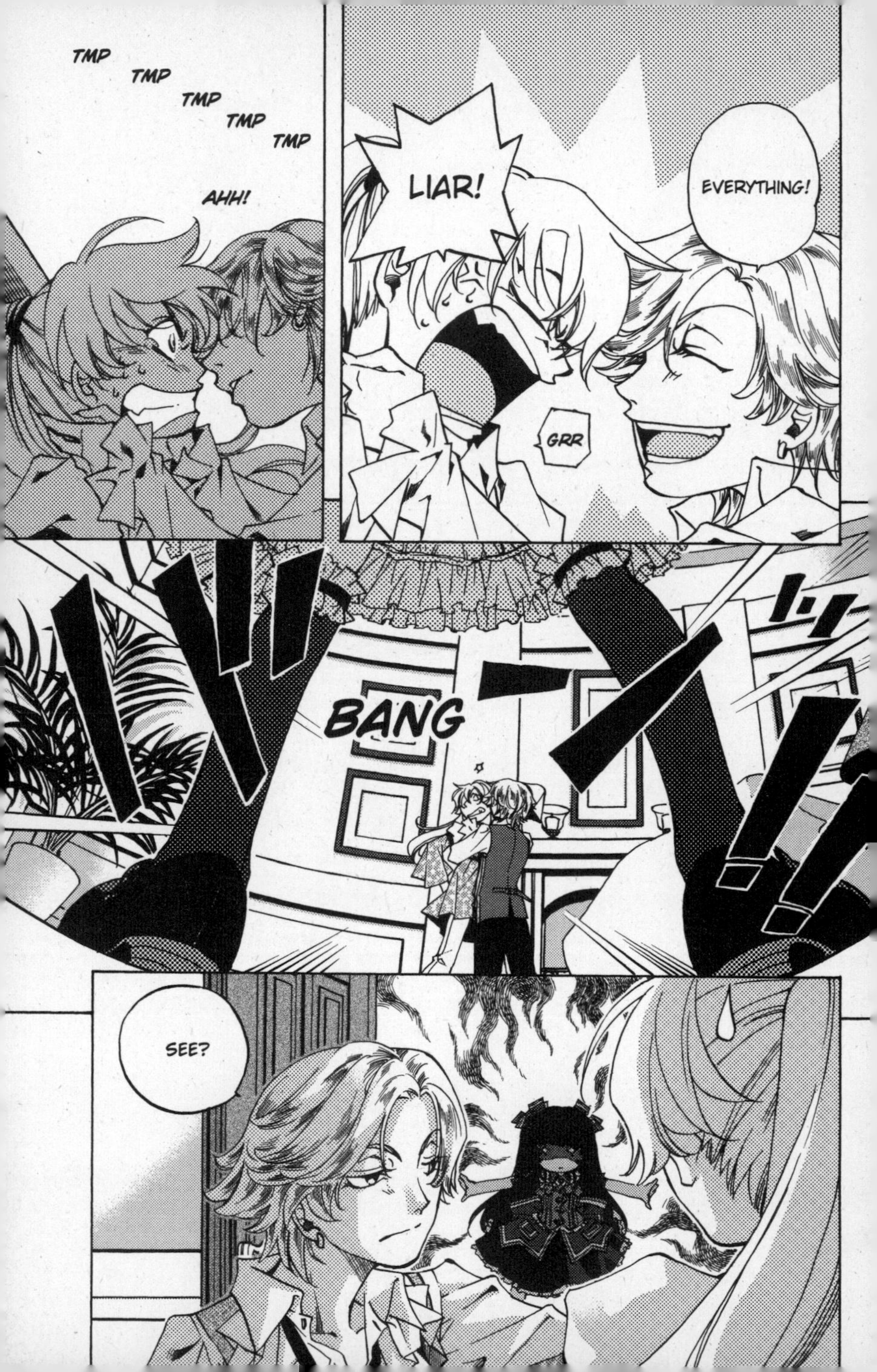
EVERYTHING!
LIAR!
GRR
TMP
TMP
TMP
TMP
TMP
AHH!
BANG
SEE?

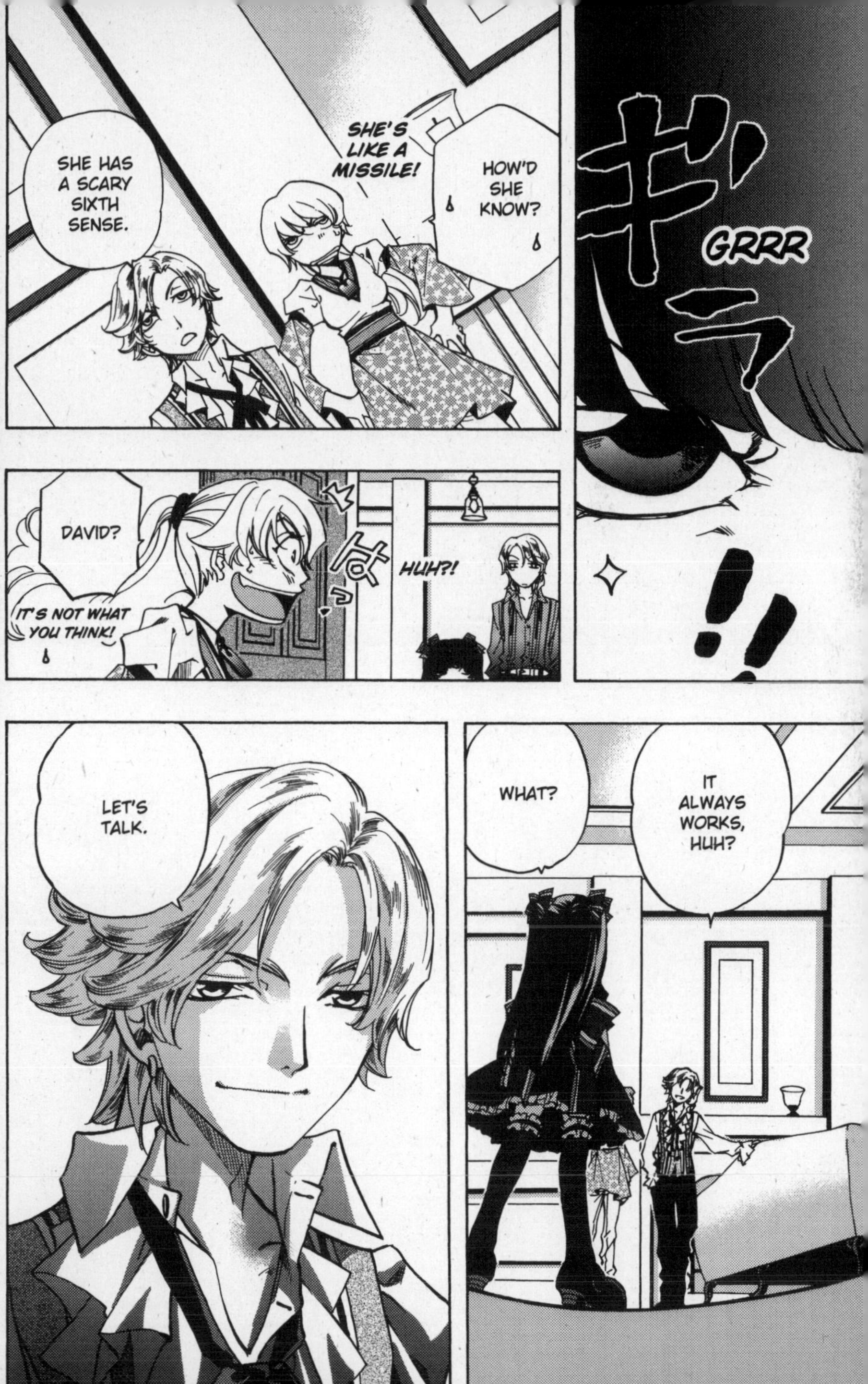
ギラ
GRRR
!!
HOW'D SHE KNOW?
SHE'S LIKE A MISSILE!
SHE HAS A SCARY SIXTH SENSE.
はっ
HUH?!
DAVID?
IT'S NOT WHAT YOU THINK!
IT ALWAYS WORKS, HUH?
WHAT?
LET'S TALK.

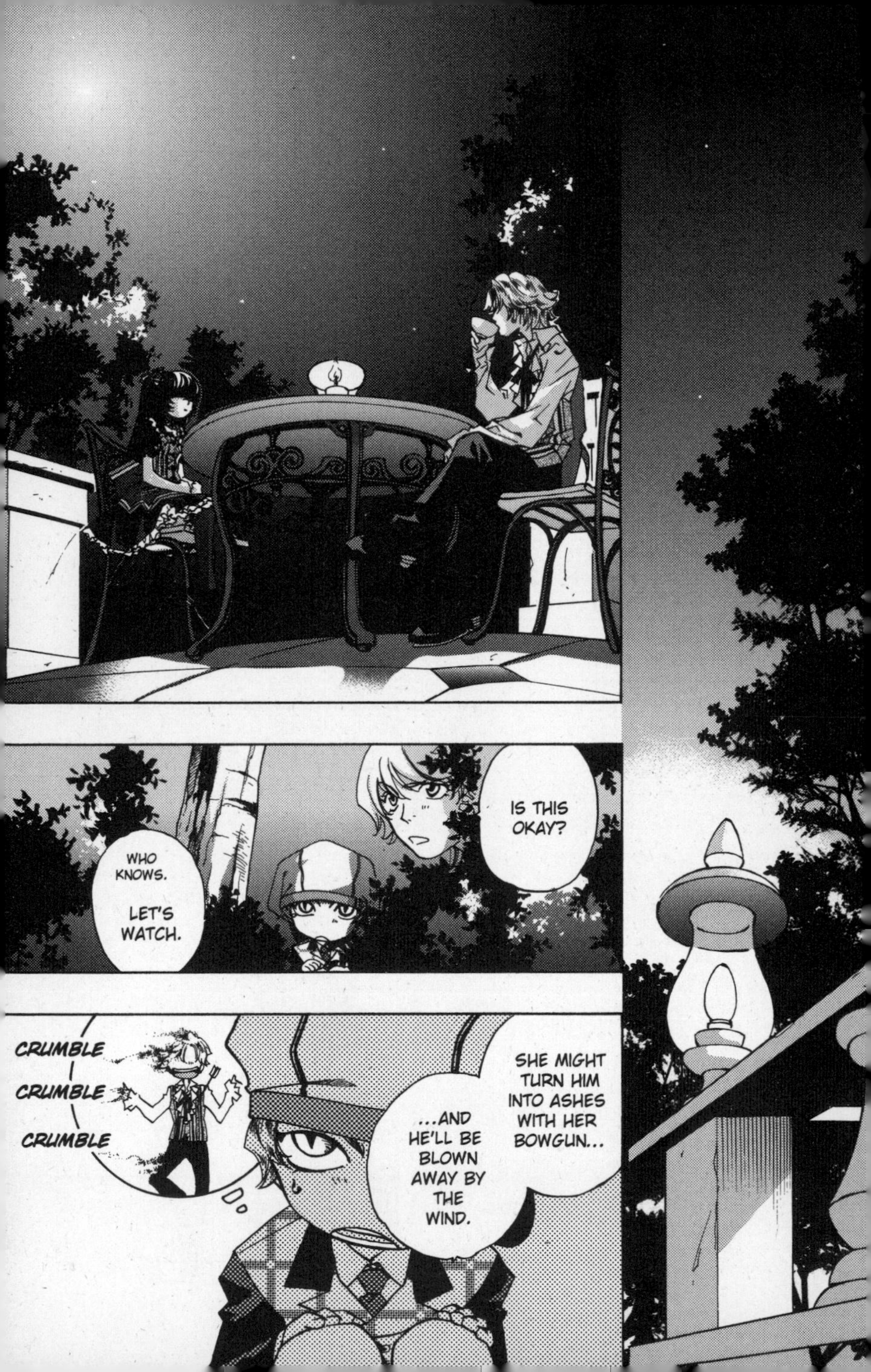
IS THIS OKAY?
WHO KNOWS.
LET'S WATCH.
SHE MIGHT TURN HIM INTO ASHES WITH HER BOWGUN...
...AND HE'LL BE BLOWN AWAY BY THE WIND.
CRUMBLE
CRUMBLE
CRUMBLE

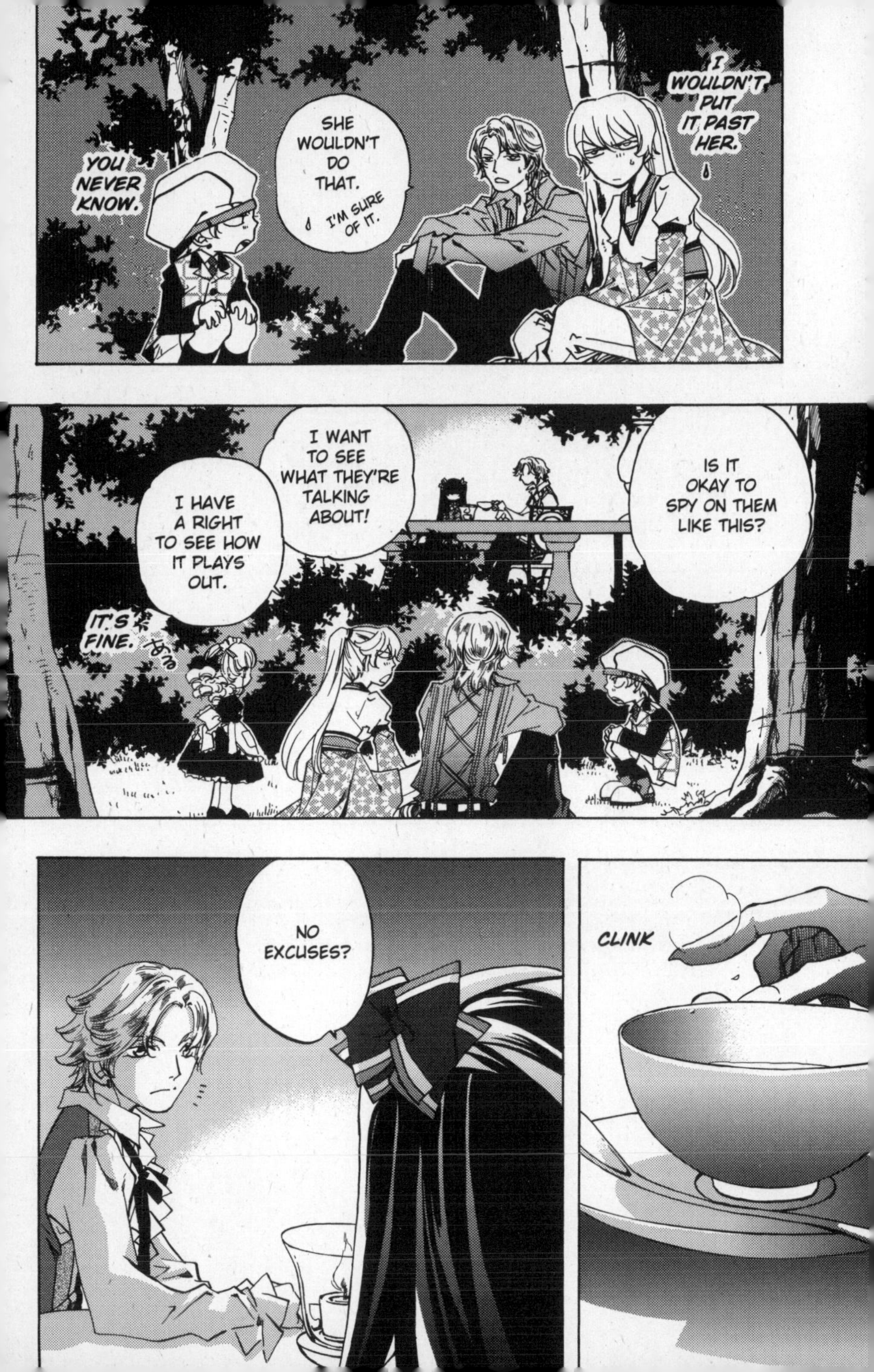
I WOULDN'T PUT IT PAST HER.
SHE WOULDN'T DO THAT.
I'M SURE OF IT.
YOU NEVER KNOW.
IS IT OKAY TO SPY ON THEM LIKE THIS?
I WANT TO SEE WHAT THEY'RE TALKING ABOUT!
I HAVE A RIGHT TO SEE HOW IT PLAYS OUT.
IT'S FINE.
CLINK
NO EXCUSES?

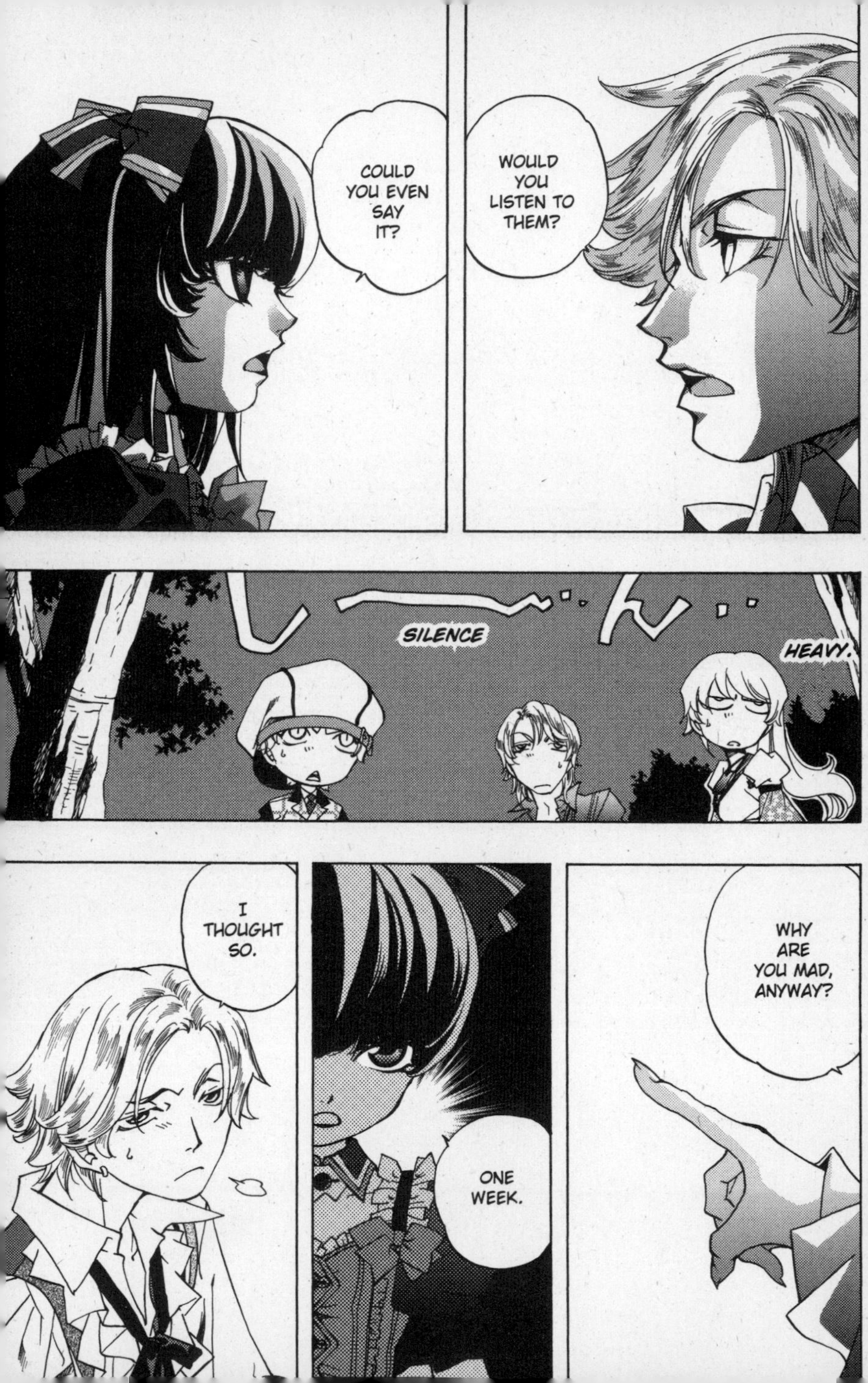
WOULD YOU LISTEN TO THEM?
COULD YOU EVEN SAY IT?
しーん
SILENCE
HEAVY.
WHY ARE YOU MAD, ANYWAY?
ONE WEEK.
I THOUGHT SO.

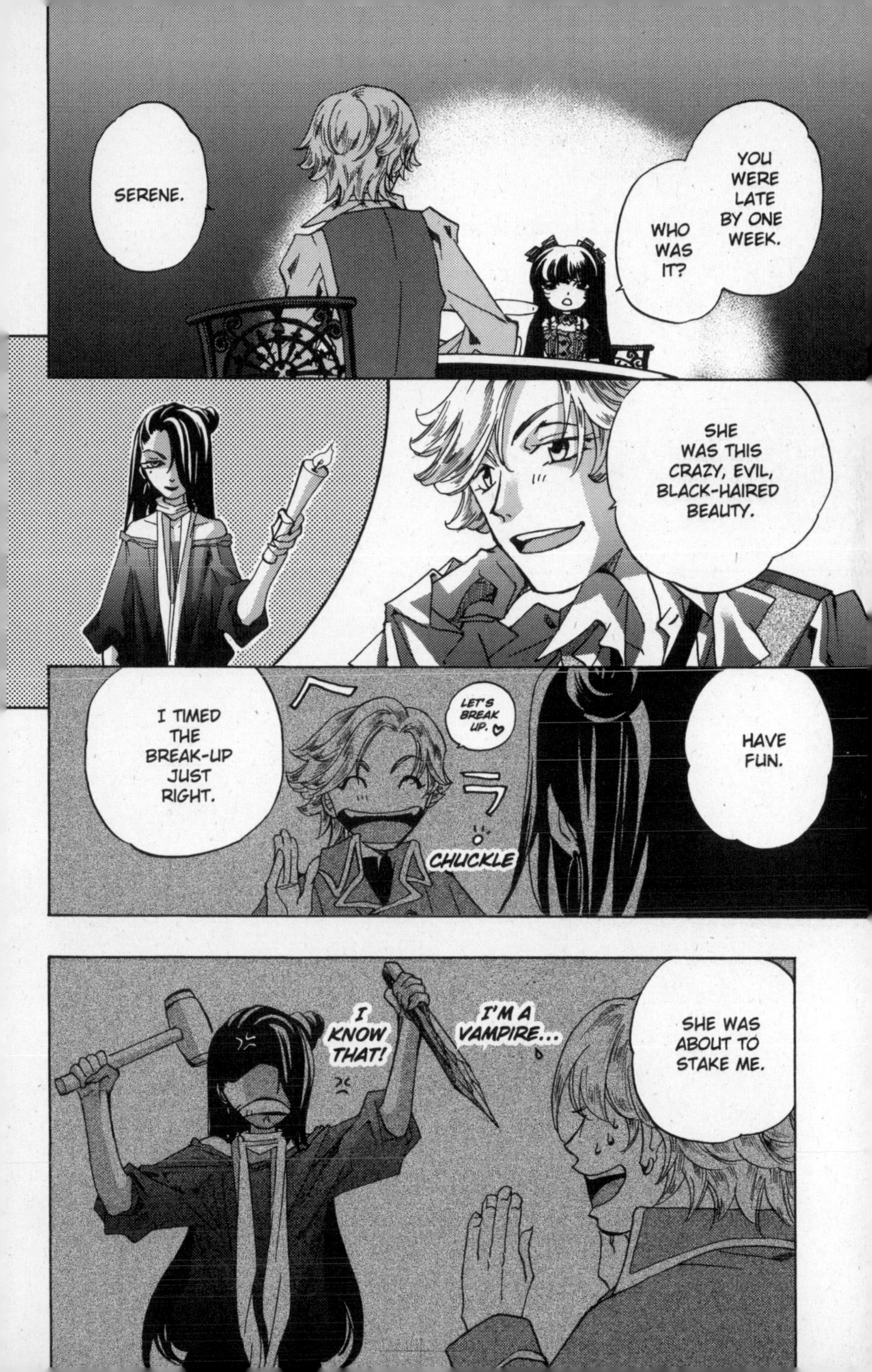
YOU WERE LATE BY ONE WEEK.
WHO WAS IT?
SERENE.
SHE WAS THIS CRAZY, EVIL, BLACK-HAIRED BEAUTY.
HAVE FUN.
LET'S BREAK UP. ♡
CHUCKLE
I TIMED THE BREAK-UP JUST RIGHT.
SHE WAS ABOUT TO STAKE ME.
I'M A VAMPIRE...
I KNOW THAT!

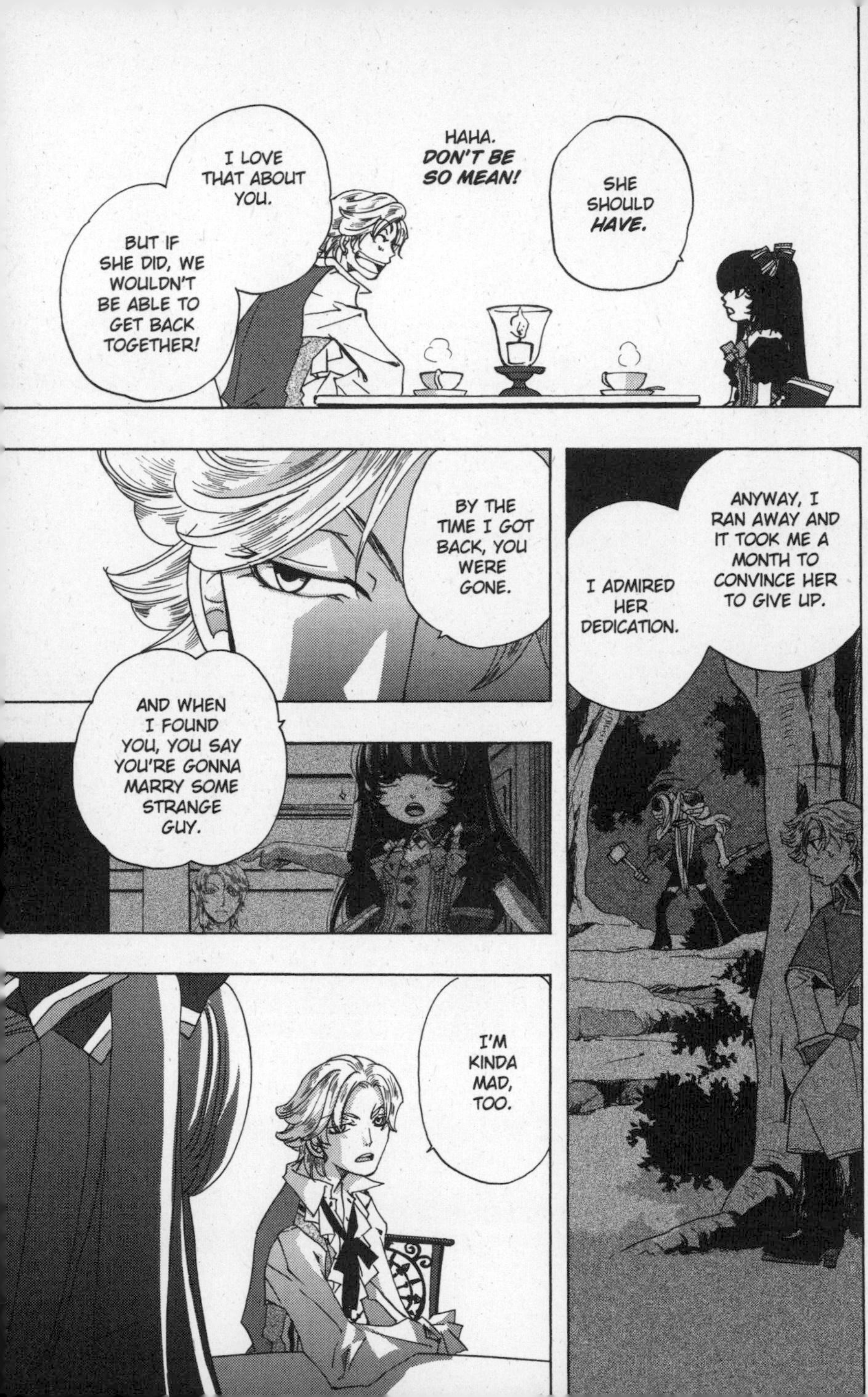
SHE SHOULD *HAVE.*
HAHA. *DON'T BE SO MEAN!*
I LOVE THAT ABOUT YOU.
BUT IF SHE DID, WE WOULDN'T BE ABLE TO GET BACK TOGETHER!
ANYWAY, I RAN AWAY AND IT TOOK ME A MONTH TO CONVINCE HER TO GIVE UP.
I ADMIRED HER DEDICATION.
BY THE TIME I GOT BACK, YOU WERE GONE.
AND WHEN I FOUND YOU, YOU SAY YOU'RE GONNA MARRY SOME STRANGE GUY.
I'M KINDA MAD, TOO.

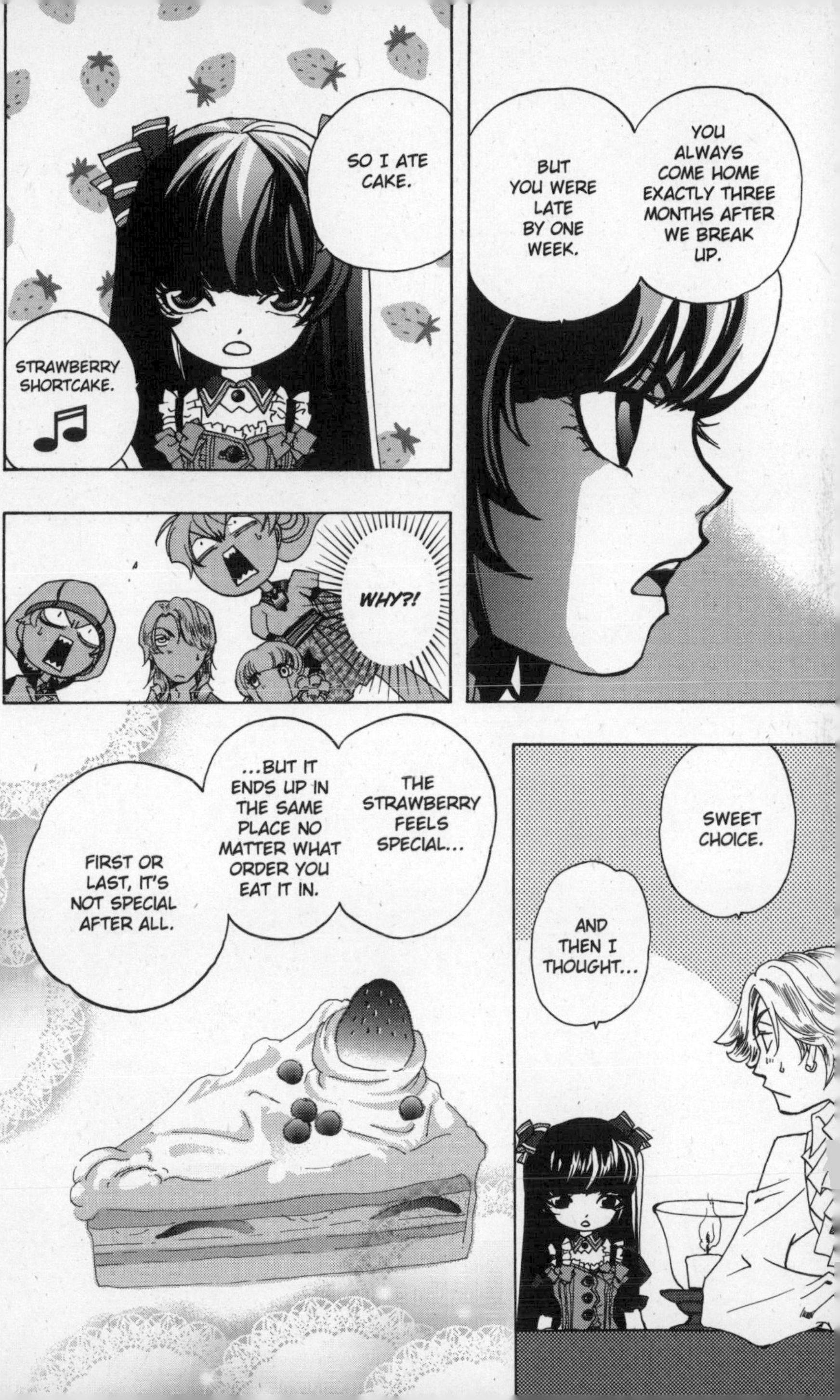
YOU ALWAYS COME HOME EXACTLY THREE MONTHS AFTER WE BREAK UP.
BUT YOU WERE LATE BY ONE WEEK.
SO I ATE CAKE.
STRAWBERRY SHORTCAKE. ♫
WHY?!
SWEET CHOICE.
AND THEN I THOUGHT...
THE STRAWBERRY FEELS SPECIAL...
...BUT IT ENDS UP IN THE SAME PLACE NO MATTER WHAT ORDER YOU EAT IT IN.
FIRST OR LAST, IT'S NOT SPECIAL AFTER ALL.

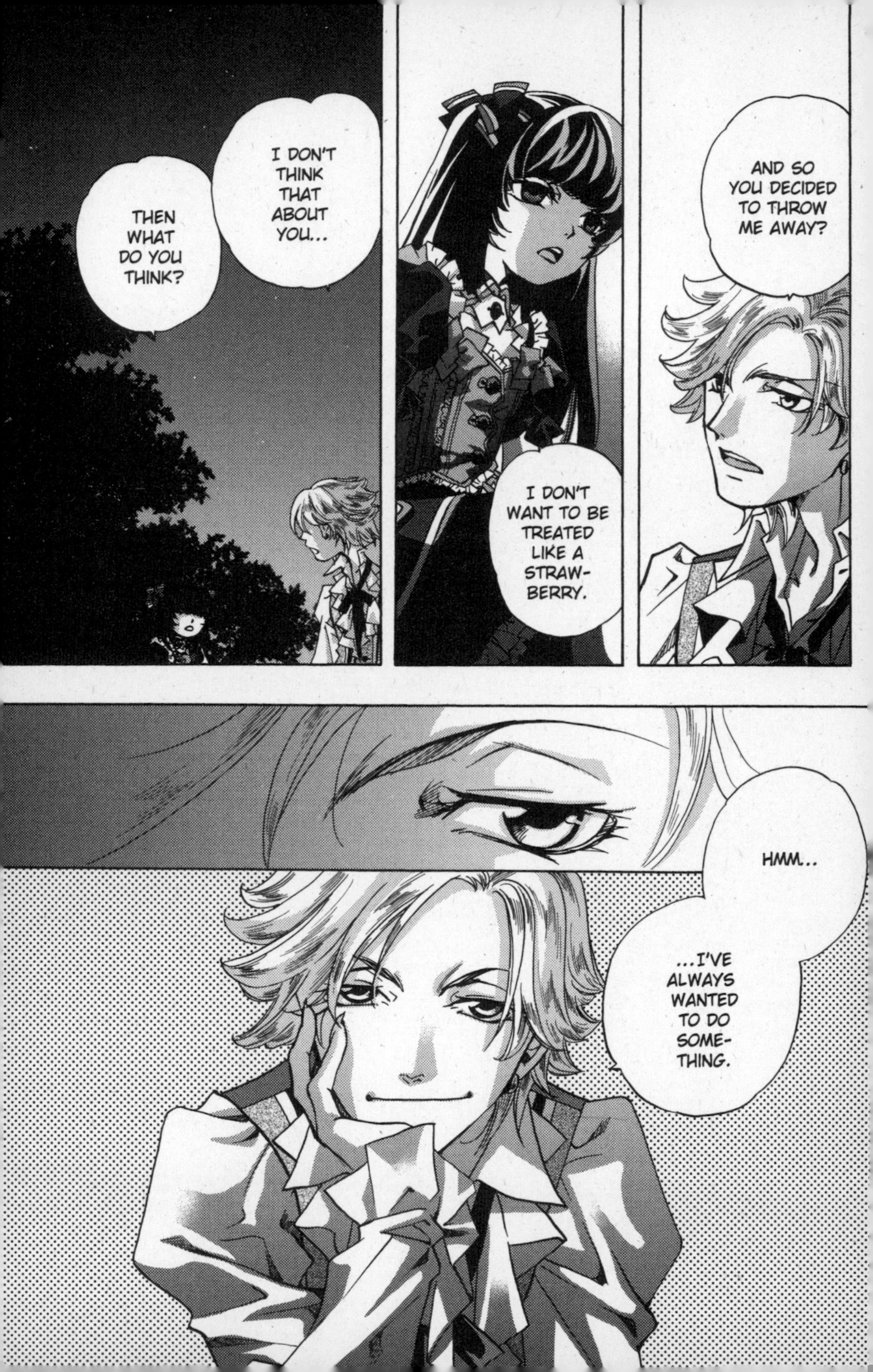
AND SO YOU DECIDED TO THROW ME AWAY?
I DON'T WANT TO BE TREATED LIKE A STRAW-BERRY.
I DON'T THINK THAT ABOUT YOU...
THEN WHAT DO YOU THINK?
HMM..
...I'VE ALWAYS WANTED TO DO SOME-THING.

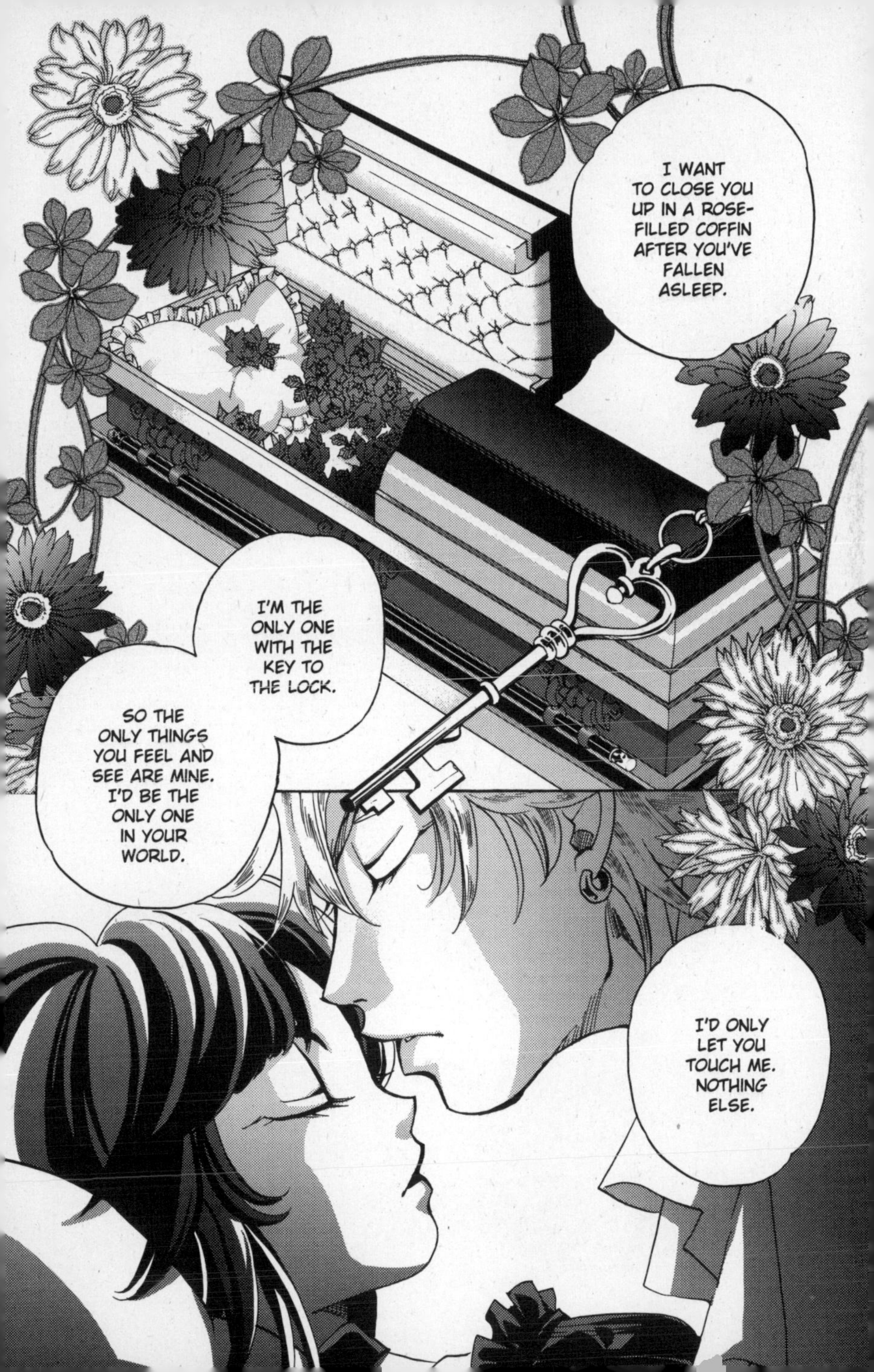
I WANT TO CLOSE YOU UP IN A ROSE-FILLED COFFIN AFTER YOU'VE FALLEN ASLEEP.
I'M THE ONLY ONE WITH THE KEY TO THE LOCK.
SO THE ONLY THINGS YOU FEEL AND SEE ARE MINE. I'D BE THE ONLY ONE IN YOUR WORLD.
I'D ONLY LET YOU TOUCH ME. NOTHING ELSE.

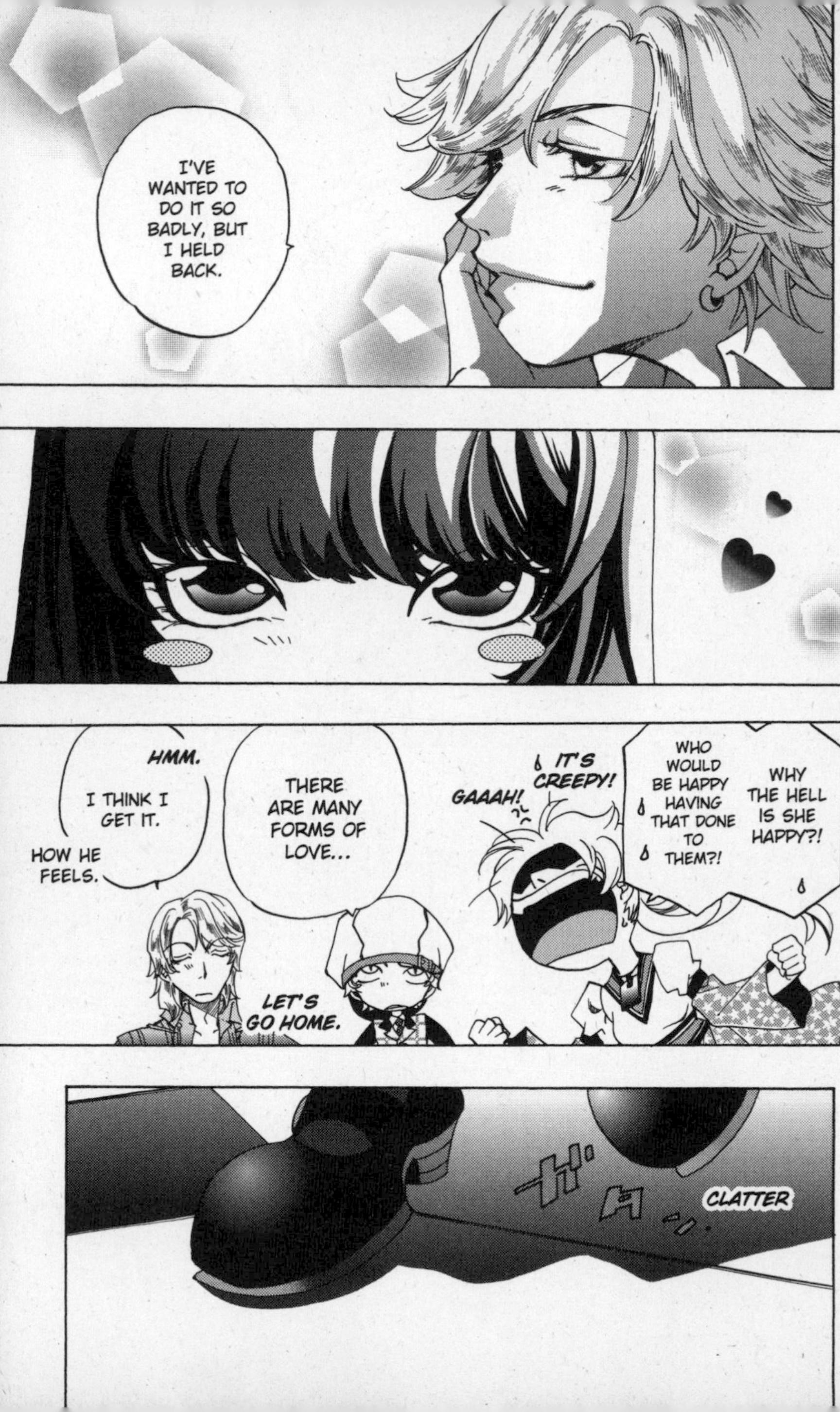
I'VE WANTED TO DO IT SO BADLY, BUT I HELD BACK.
WHY THE HELL IS SHE HAPPY?!
WHO WOULD BE HAPPY HAVING THAT DONE TO THEM?!
IT'S CREEPY!
GAAAH!
THERE ARE MANY FORMS OF LOVE...
HMM.
I THINK I GET IT.
HOW HE FEELS.
LET'S GO HOME.
CLATTER

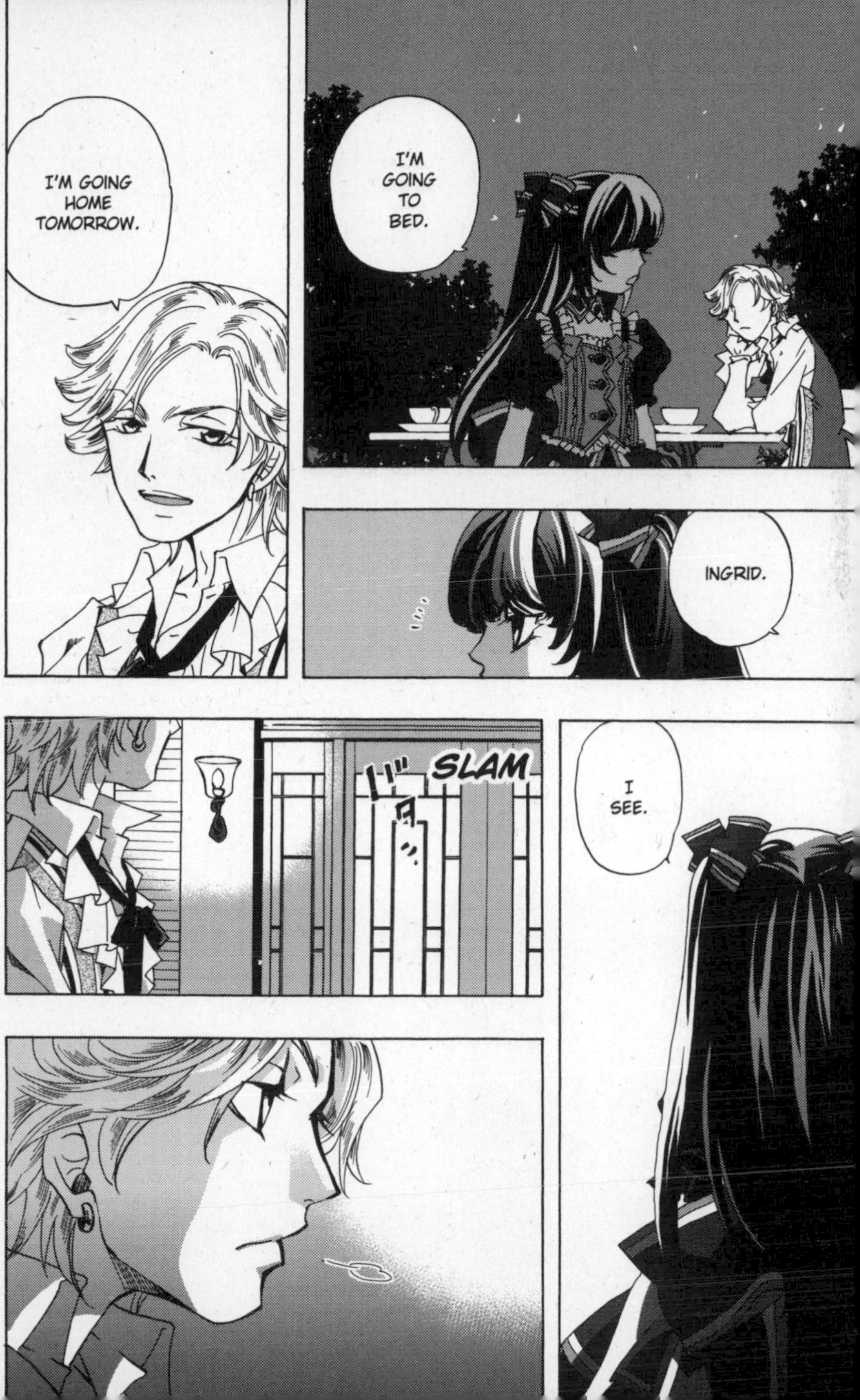
I'M GOING TO BED.
INGRID.
I'M GOING HOME TOMORROW.
I SEE.
SLAM

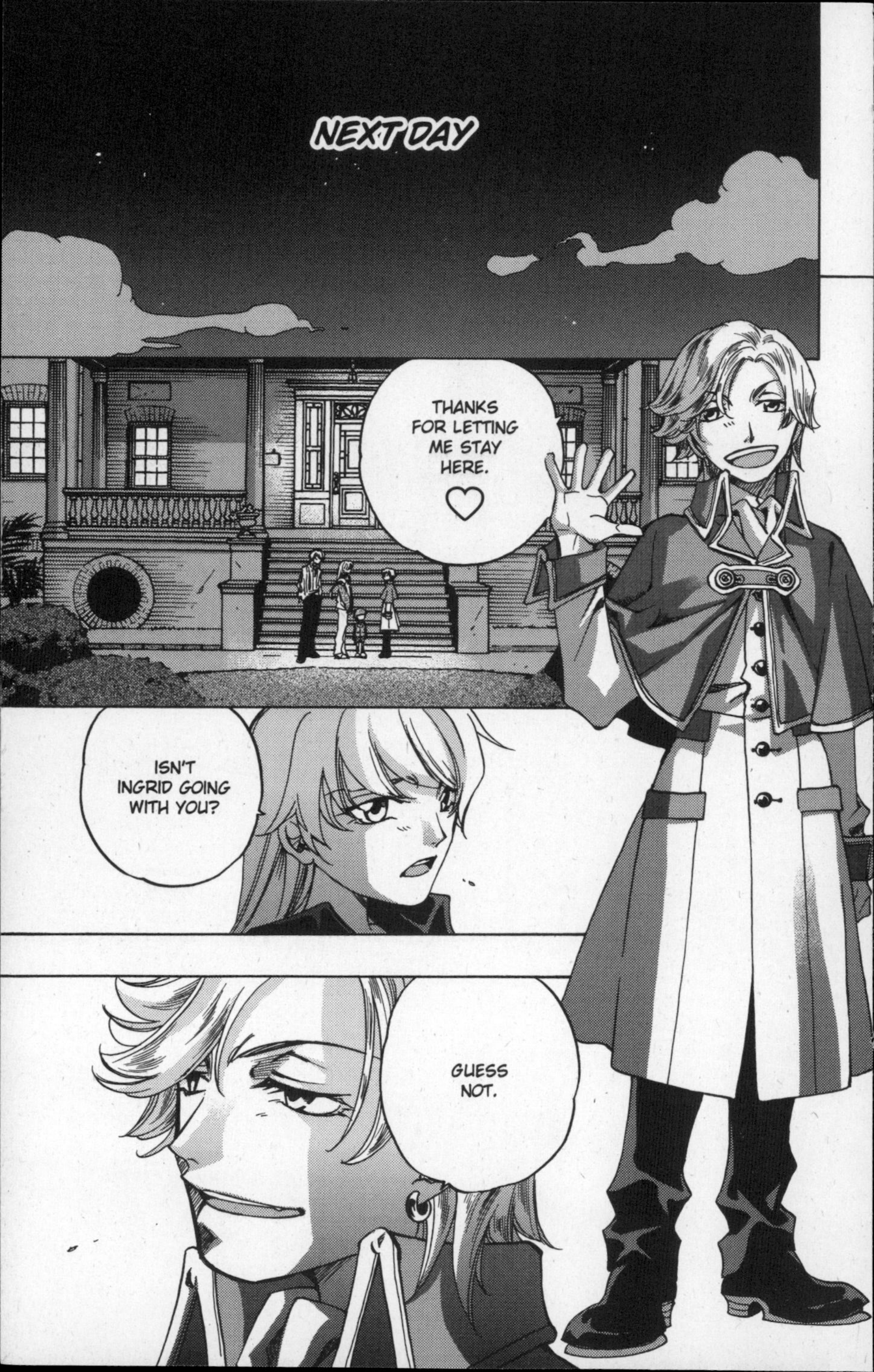
NEXT DAY
THANKS FOR LETTING ME STAY HERE. ♡
ISN'T INGRID GOING WITH YOU?
GUESS NOT.

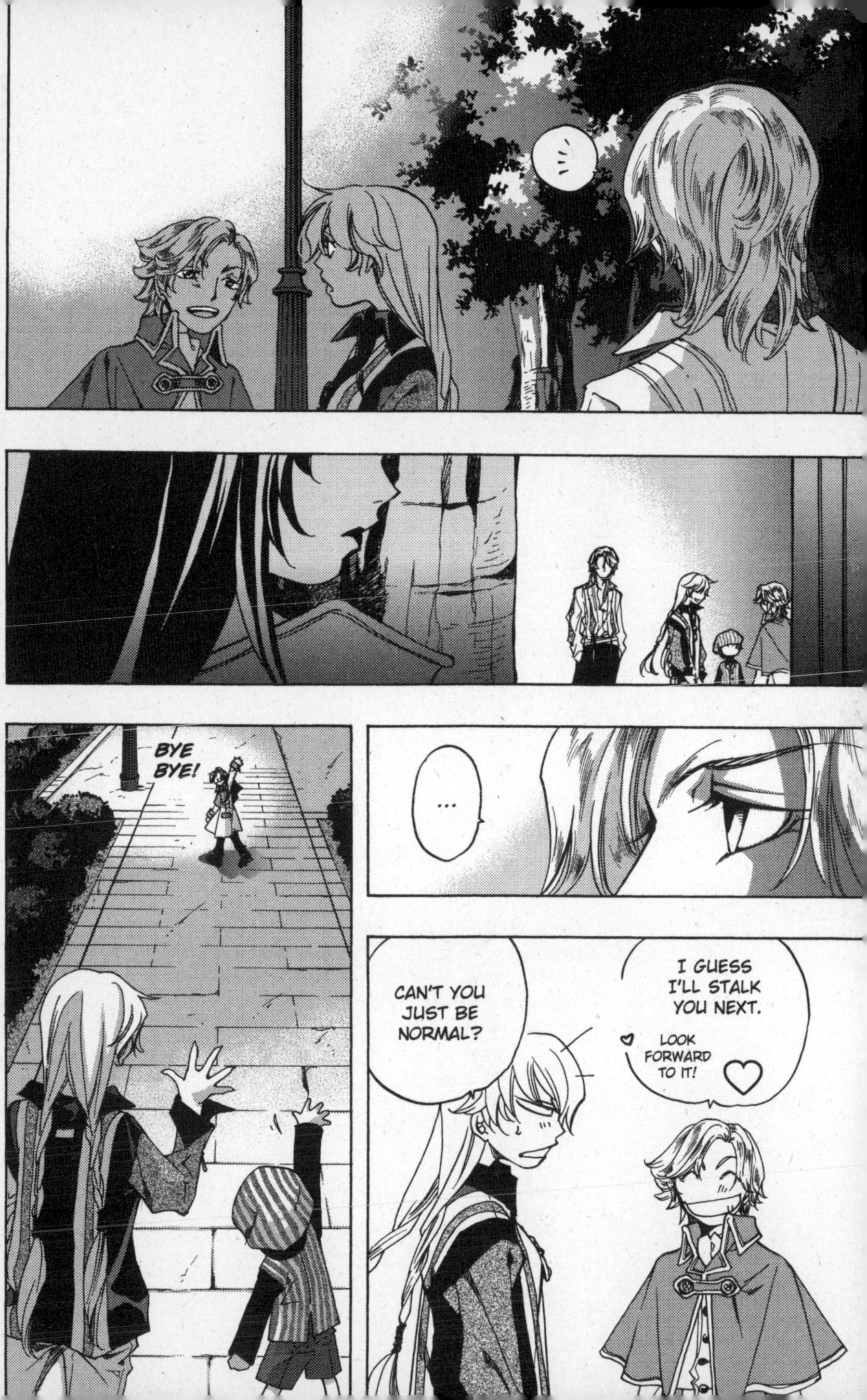
...
I GUESS I'LL STALK YOU NEXT.
LOOK FORWARD TO IT!
CAN'T YOU JUST BE NORMAL?
BYE BYE!

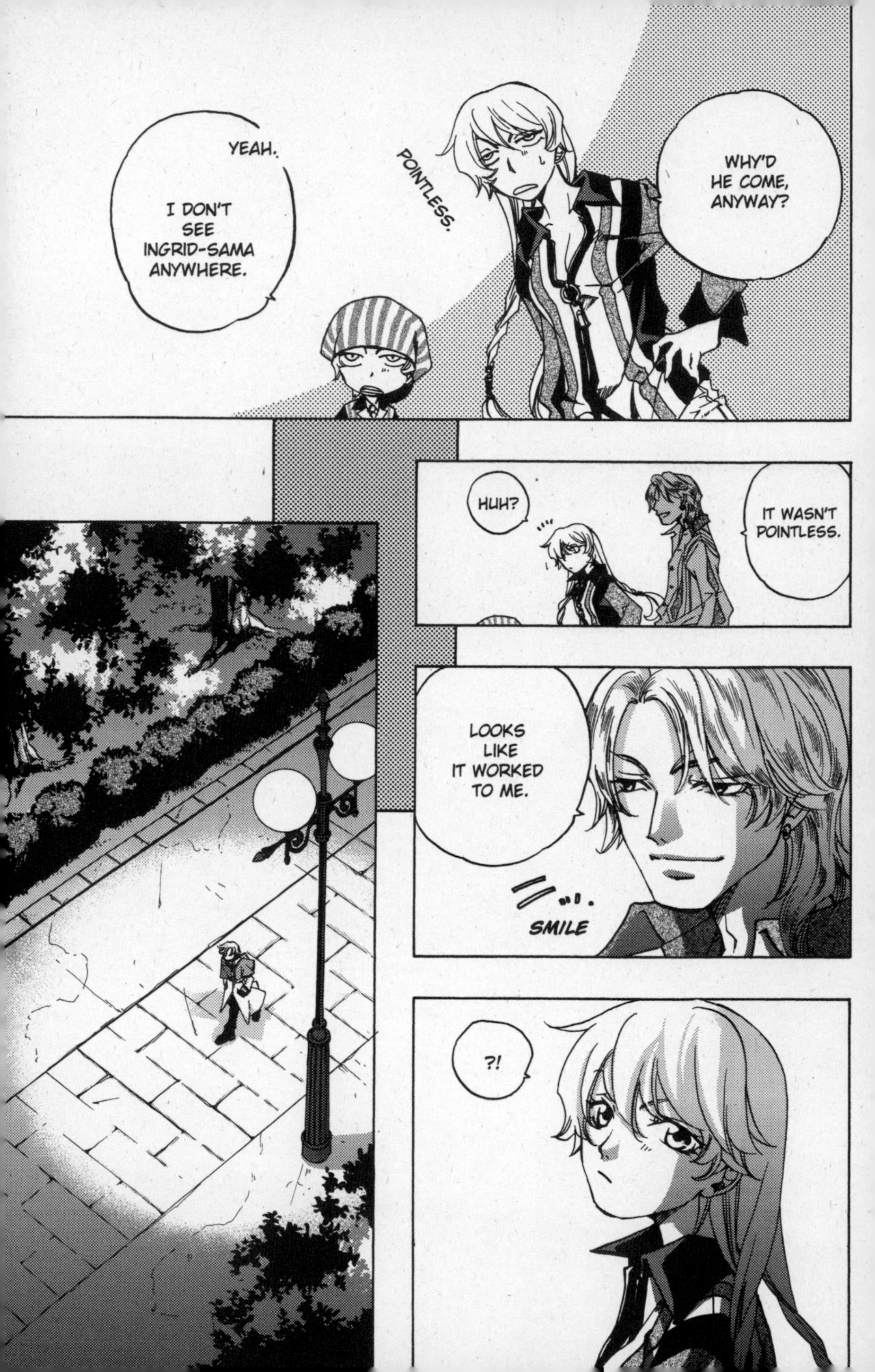
WHY'D HE COME, ANYWAY?
POINTLESS.
YEAH.
I DON'T SEE INGRID-SAMA ANYWHERE.
IT WASN'T POINTLESS.
HUH?
LOOKS LIKE IT WORKED TO ME.
SMILE
?!

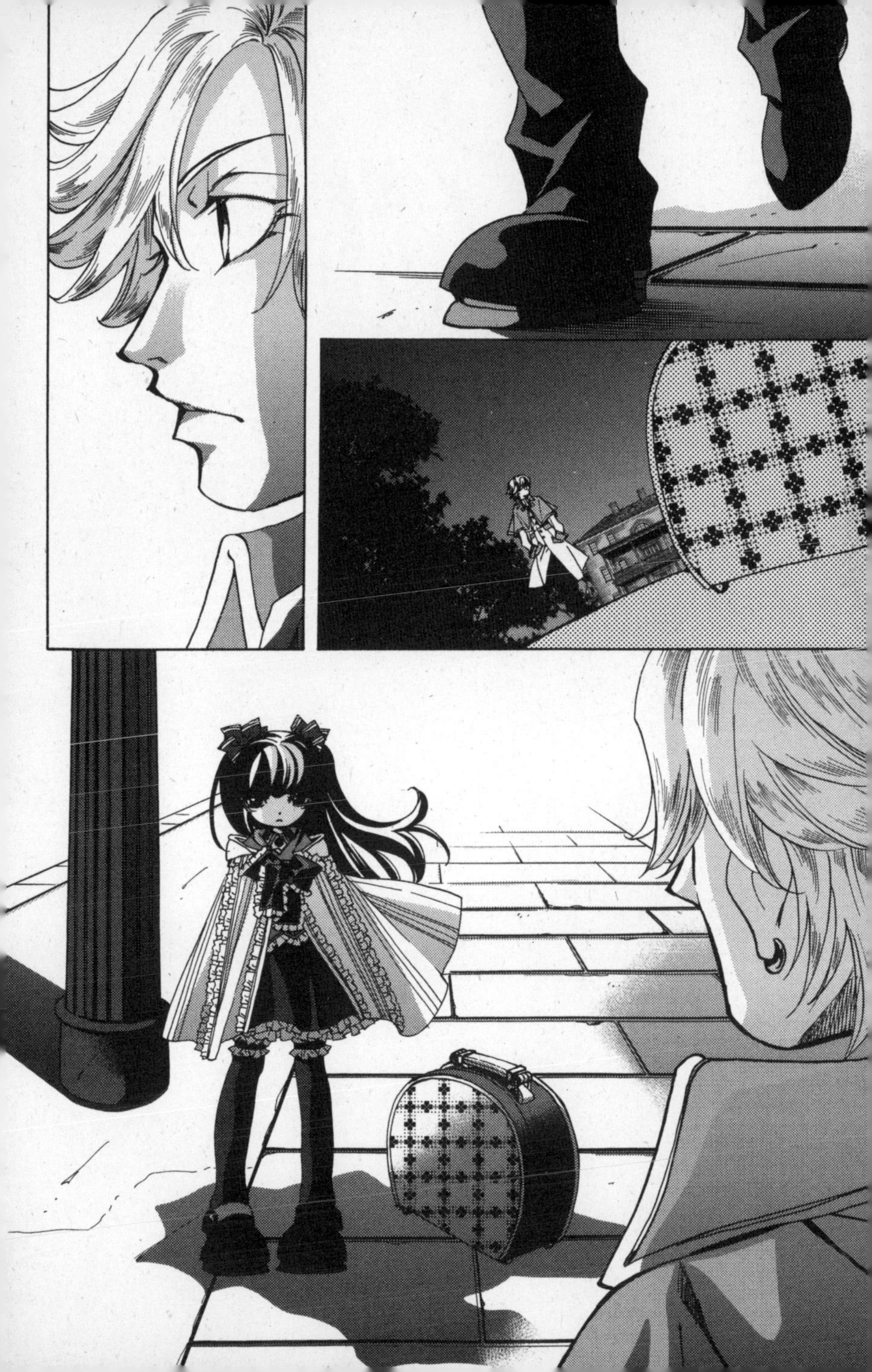

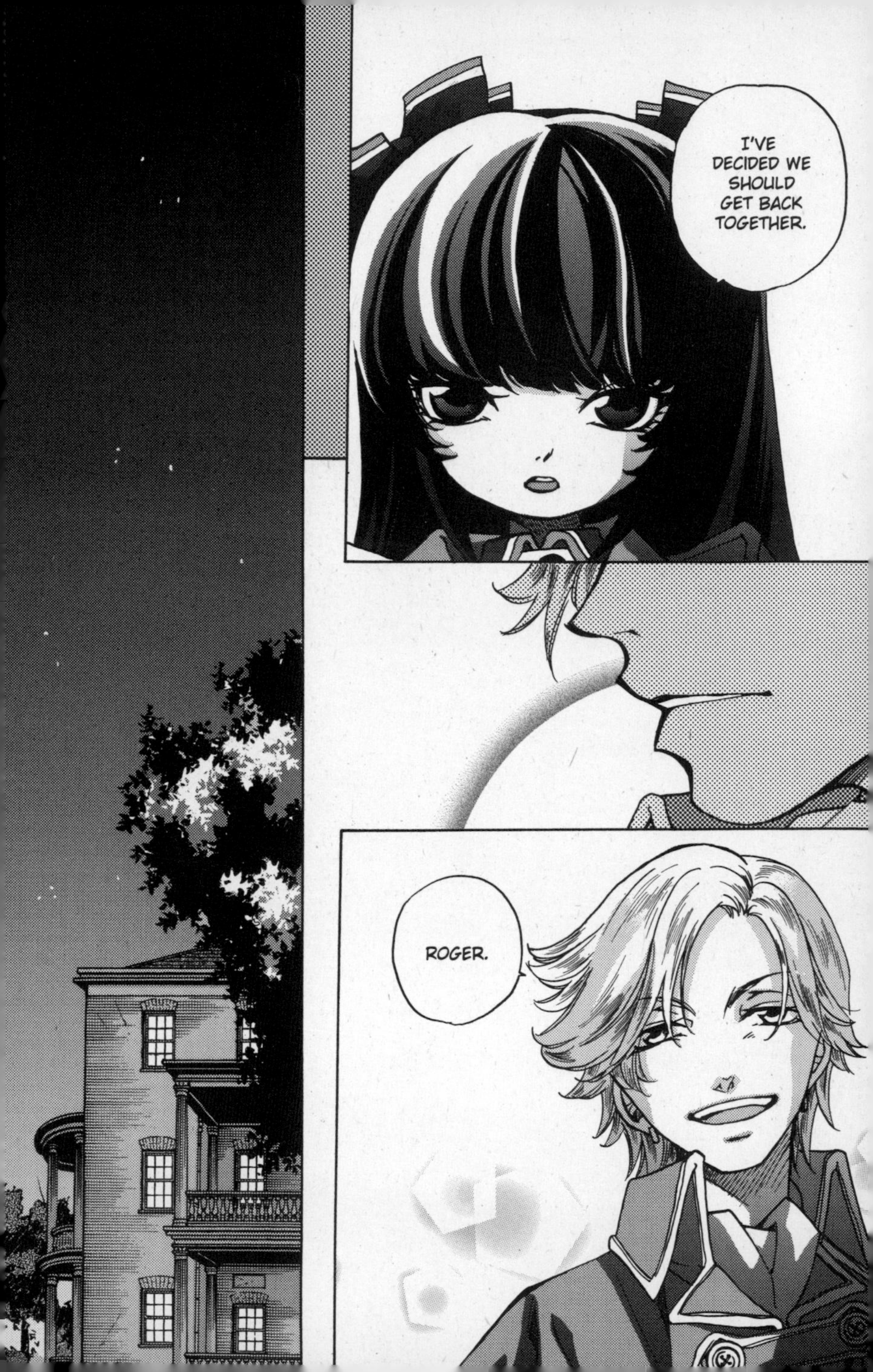
I'VE DECIDED WE SHOULD GET BACK TOGETHER.
ROGER.

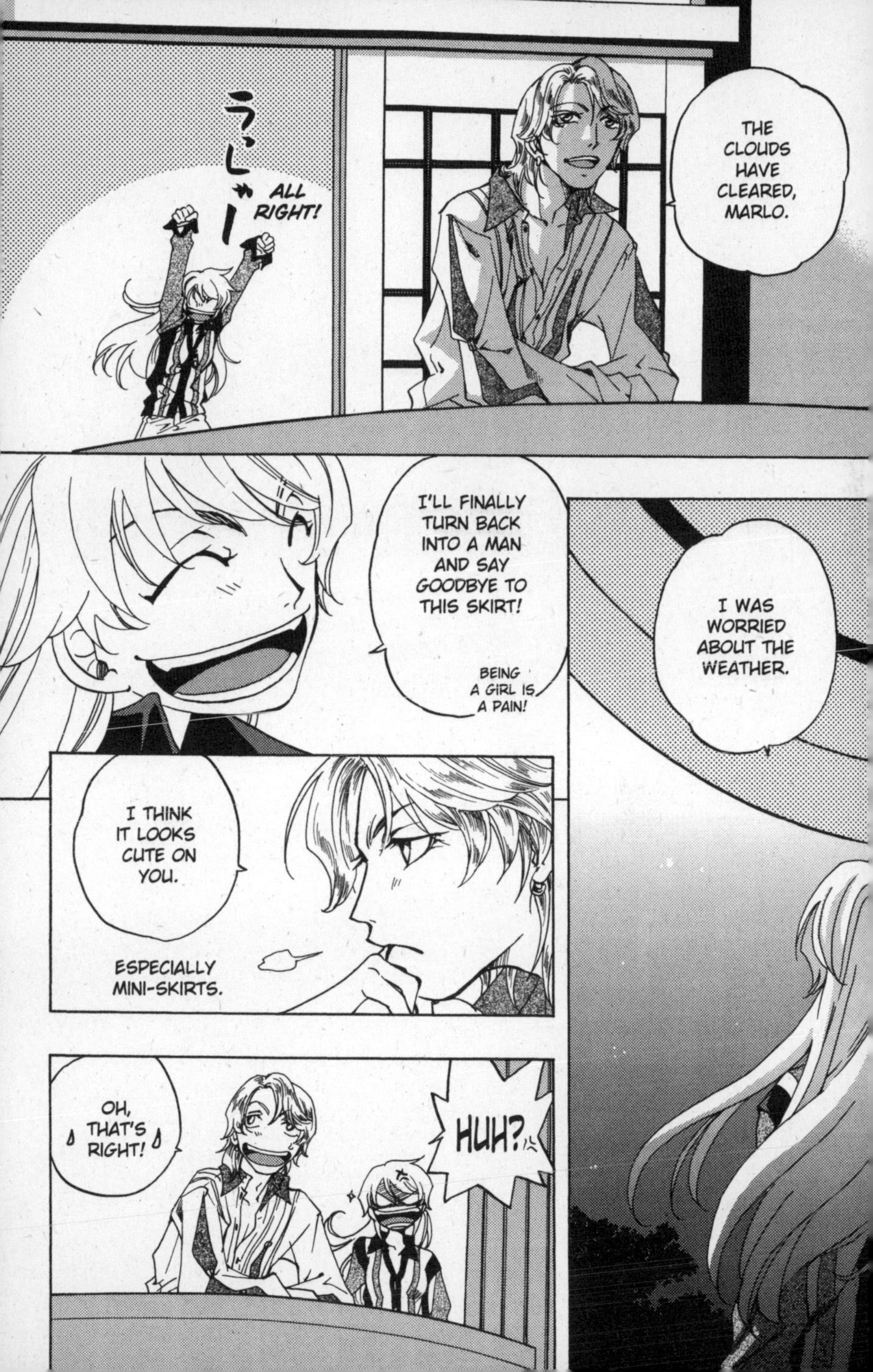
THE CLOUDS HAVE CLEARED, MARLO.
うしゃー
ALL RIGHT!
I WAS WORRIED ABOUT THE WEATHER.
I'LL FINALLY TURN BACK INTO A MAN AND SAY GOODBYE TO THIS SKIRT!
BEING A GIRL IS A PAIN!
I THINK IT LOOKS CUTE ON YOU.
ESPECIALLY MINI-SKIRTS.
HUH?!
OH, THAT'S RIGHT!

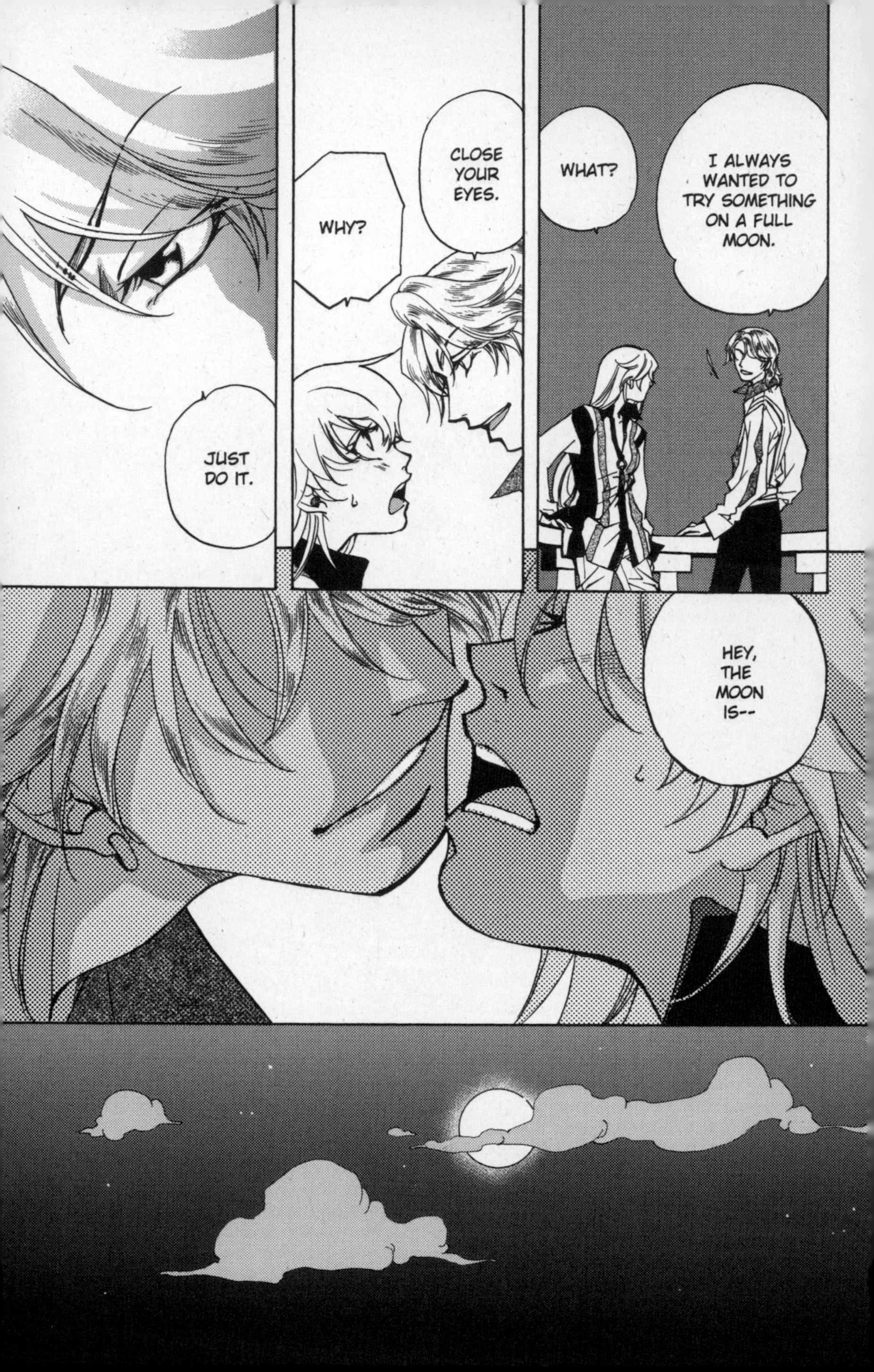
I ALWAYS WANTED TO TRY SOMETHING ON A FULL MOON.
WHAT?
CLOSE YOUR EYES.
WHY?
JUST DO IT.
HEY, THE MOON IS--

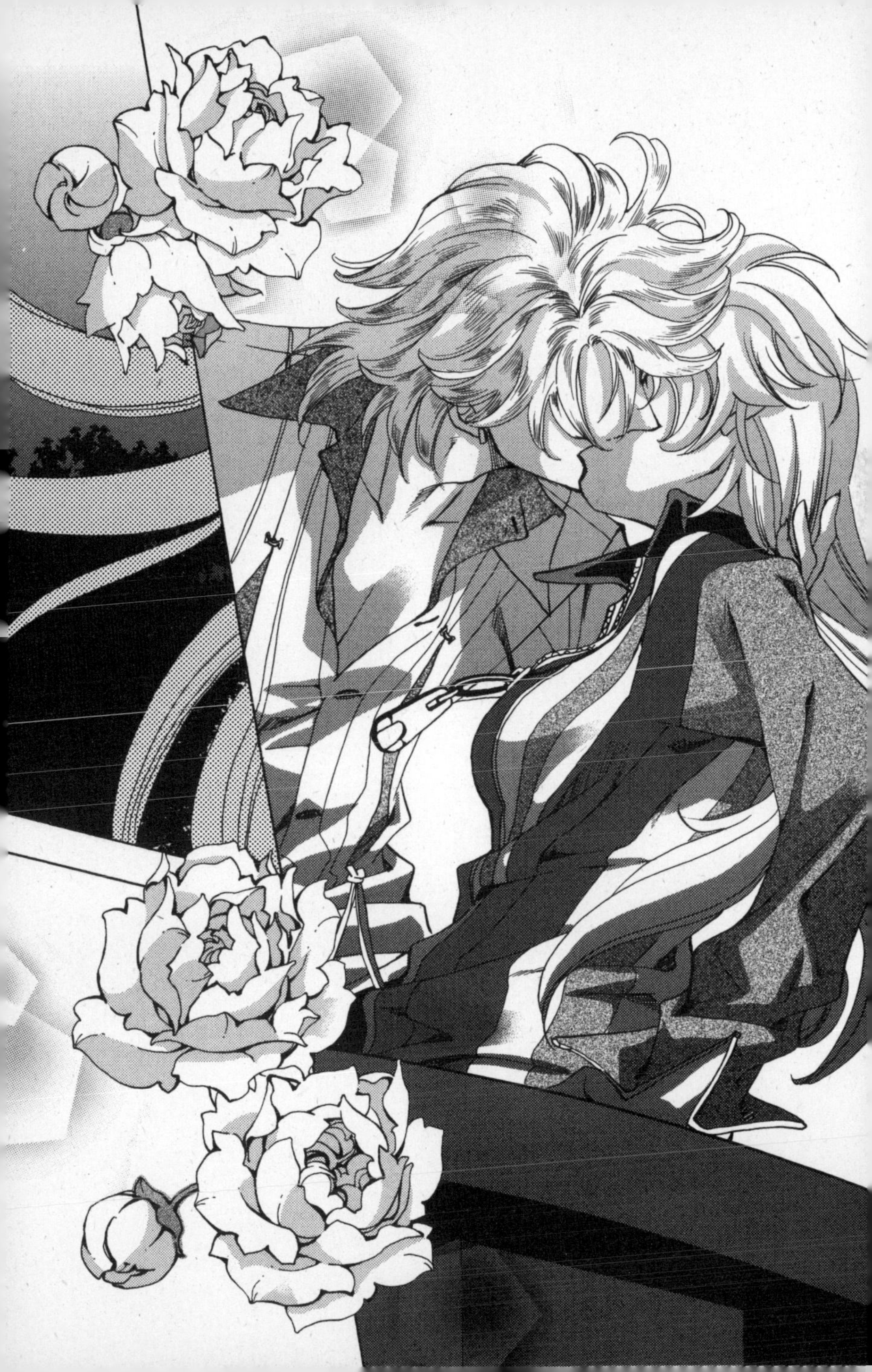

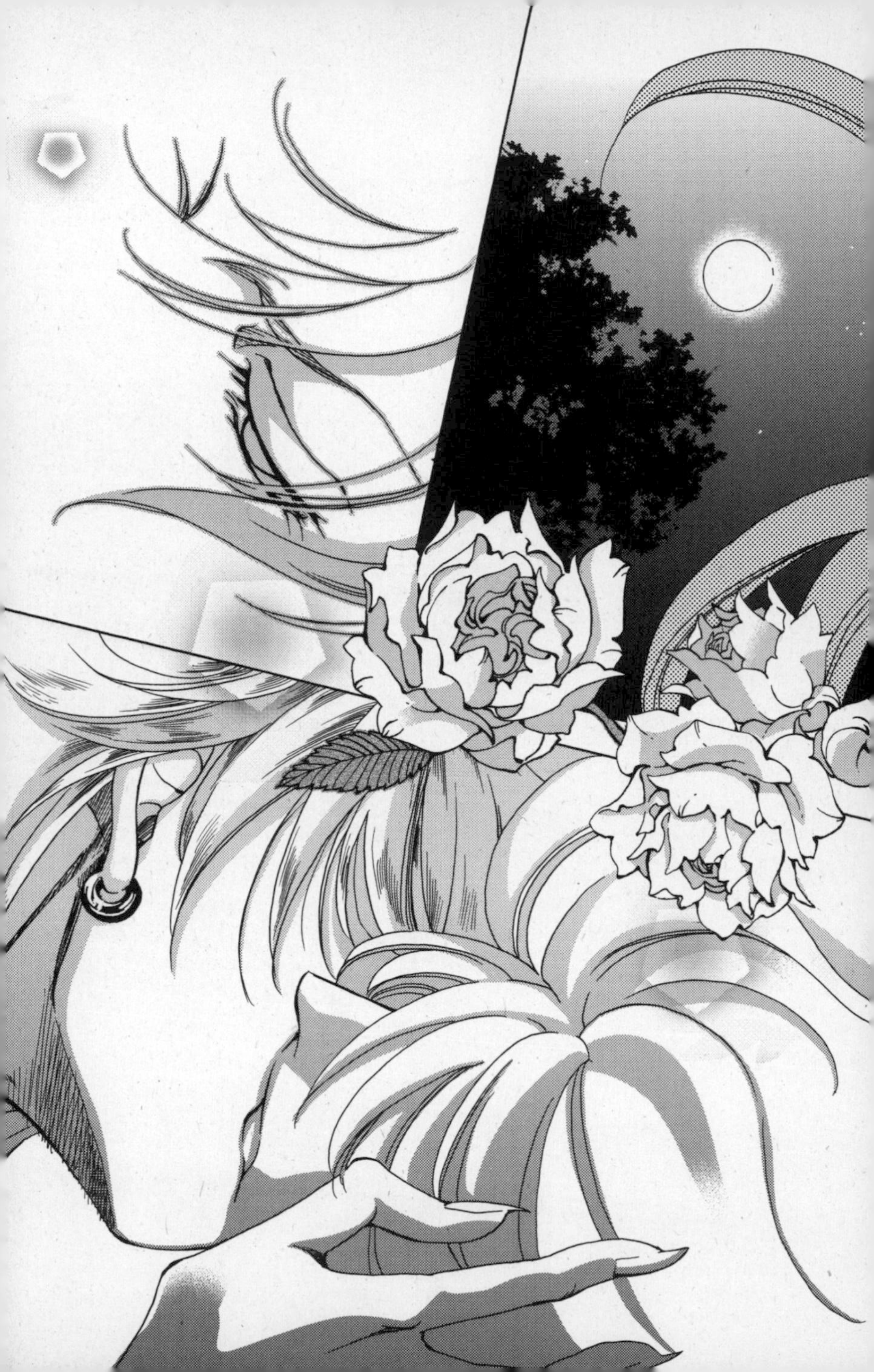

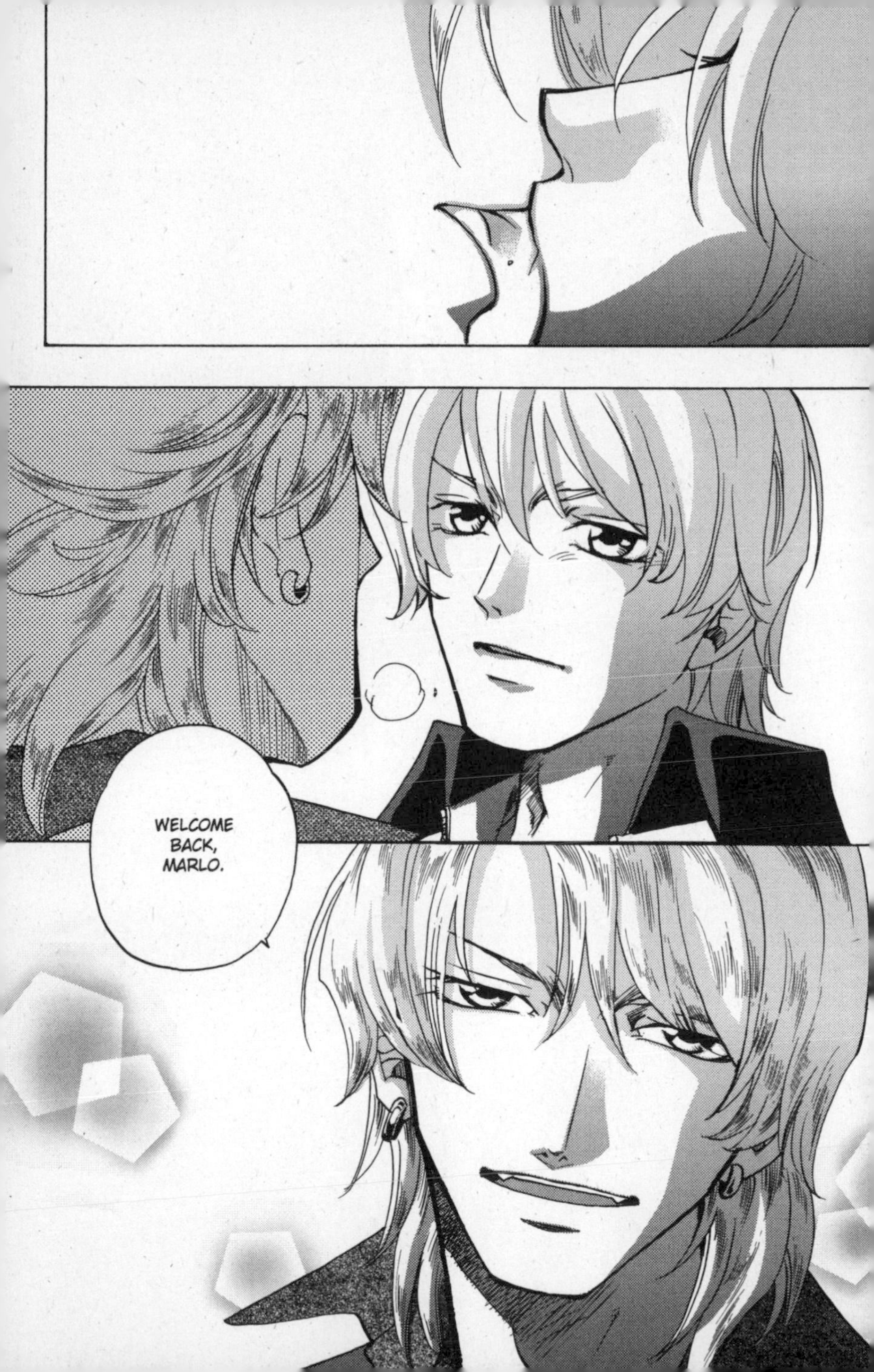
WELCOME BACK, MARLO.

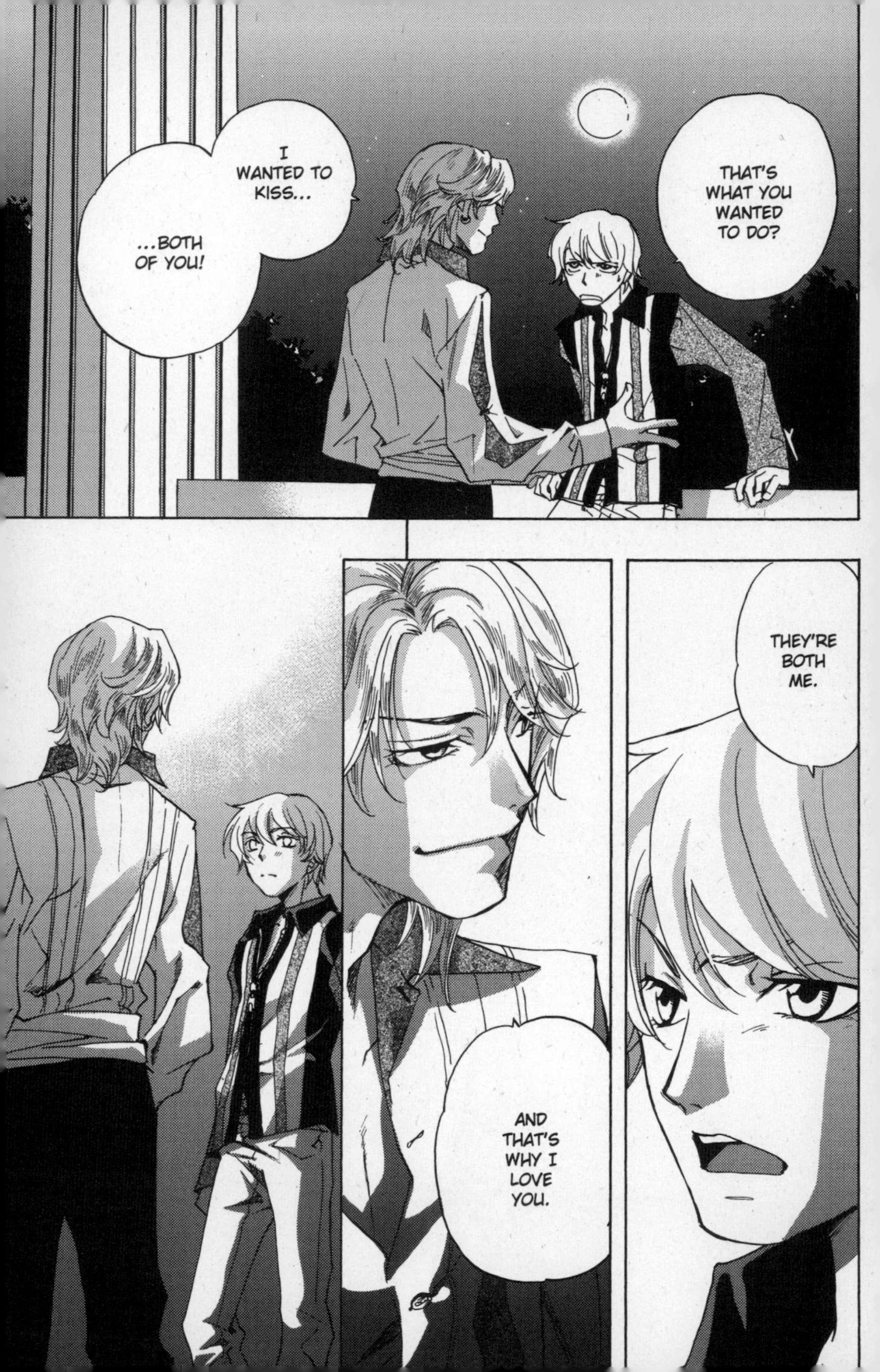
THAT'S WHAT YOU WANTED TO DO?
I WANTED TO KISS...
...BOTH OF YOU!
THEY'RE BOTH ME.
AND THAT'S WHY I LOVE YOU.

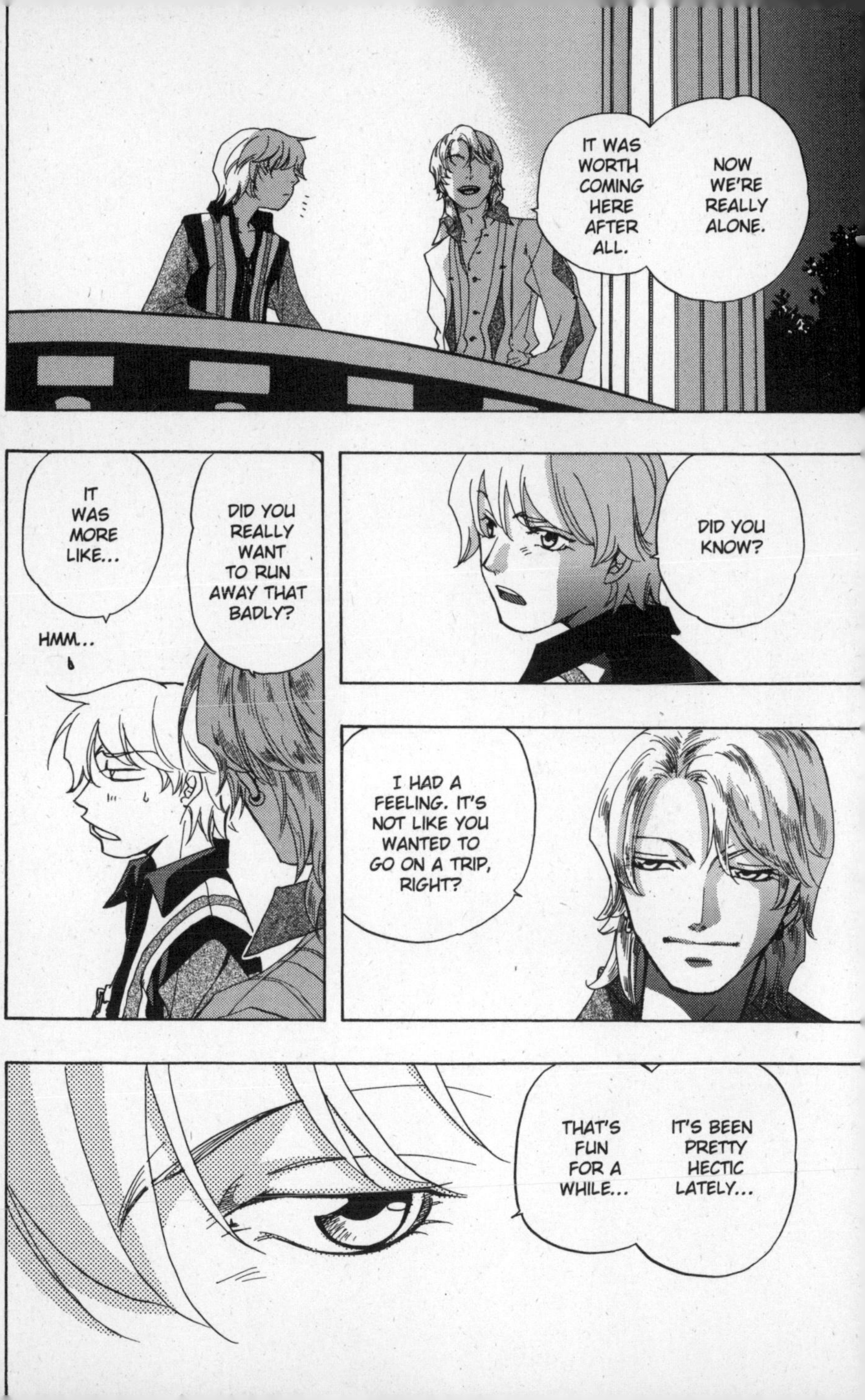
NOW WE'RE REALLY ALONE.
IT WAS WORTH COMING HERE AFTER ALL.
DID YOU KNOW?
I HAD A FEELING. IT'S NOT LIKE YOU WANTED TO GO ON A TRIP, RIGHT?
DID YOU REALLY WANT TO RUN AWAY THAT BADLY?
IT WAS MORE LIKE...
HMM...
IT'S BEEN PRETTY HECTIC LATELY...
THAT'S FUN FOR A WHILE...

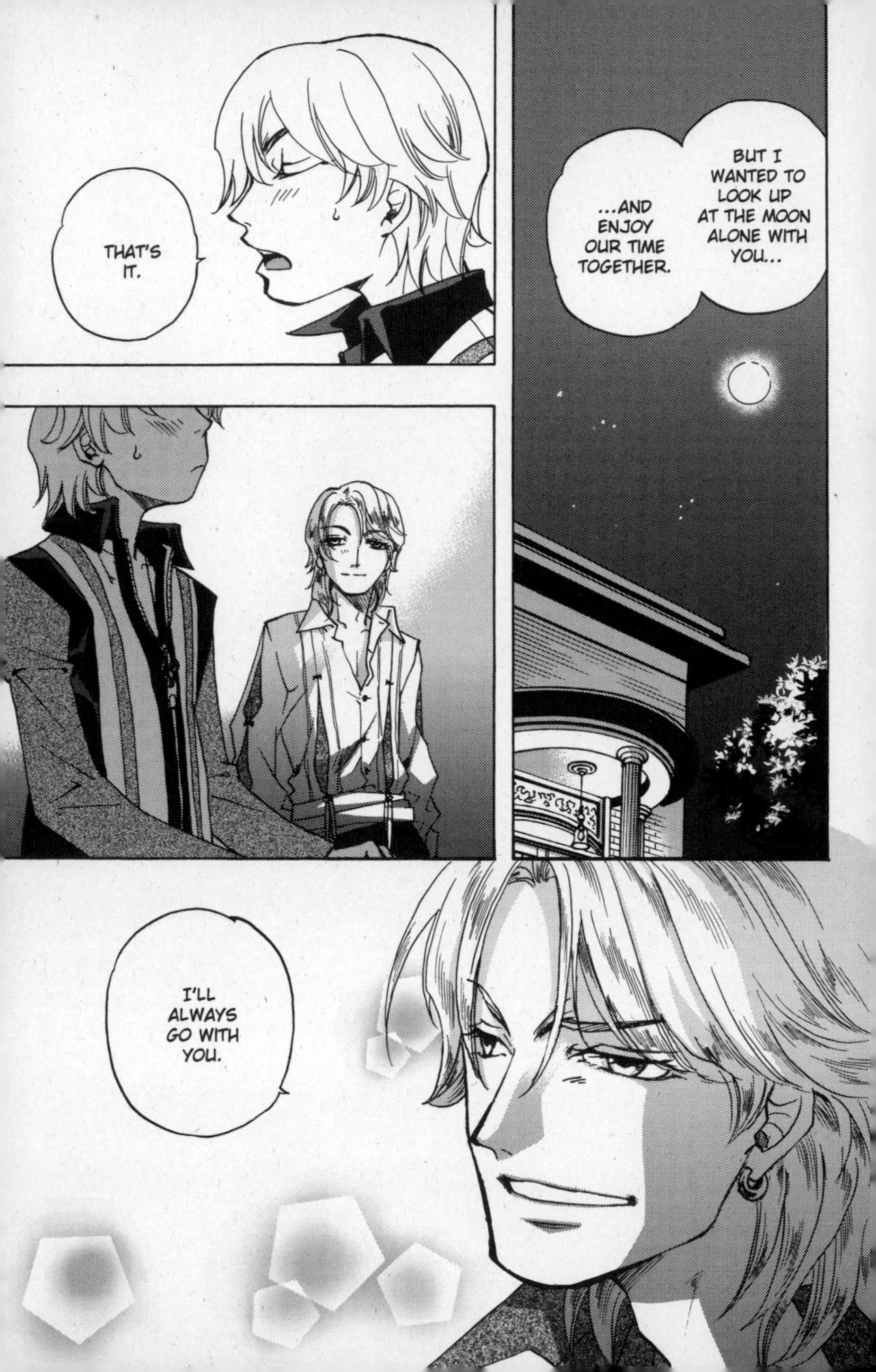
BUT I WANTED TO LOOK UP AT THE MOON ALONE WITH YOU...
...AND ENJOY OUR TIME TOGETHER.
THAT'S IT.
I'LL ALWAYS GO WITH YOU.

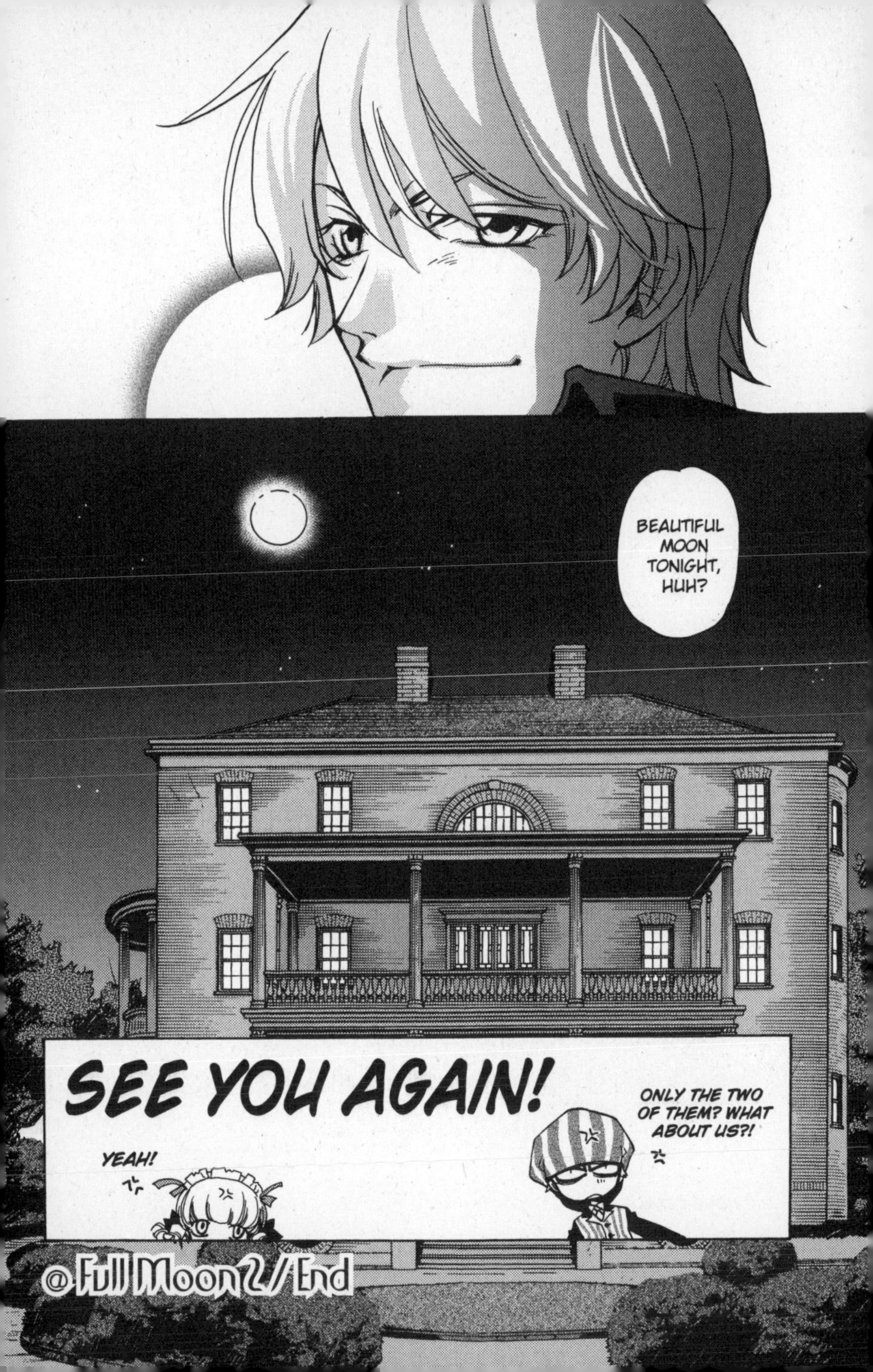
BEAUTIFUL MOON TONIGHT, HUH?
SEE YOU AGAIN!
ONLY THE TWO OF THEM? WHAT ABOUT US?!
YEAH!
@ Full Moon 2 / End

AFTER TALK
@FULL MOON VOL 2

THANKS FOR BUYING @ FULL MOON VOLUME 2!

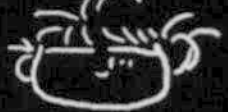

AFTER A LONG YEAR, VOLUME 2 IS FINALLY FINISHED. THANK YOU FOR ALL THE COMMENTS YOU SENT REGARDING VOLUME 1. (^ ^) THE COMMENT I RECEIVED THE MOST WAS "THE ART CHANGED, BUT THE FEEL OF THE STORY IS THE SAME SO I LIKED IT." THAT MADE ME FEEL BETTER. PHEW.

I TRIED TO WRITE THE STORY WITH THE SAME FEEL TO IT AS THE PREQUEL, "FULL MOON NI SASAYAITE."

I'M GLAD THAT CAME ACROSS TO THE READERS.

REGARDING THE ART, IT'S NOT AS IF MY STYLE CHANGED SUDDENLY, IT JUST CHANGED NATURALLY AND GRADUALLY OVER TIME, AND I'M SURE IT WILL CHANGE MORE IN THE FUTURE.

I FELT LIKE I HAD TO WORK HARD AT MAKING THE STORY GO IN A GOOD DIRECTION AS WELL.

I'M SURE THERE WERE MANY OF YOU WHO PREFERRED THE ART OF THE PREVIOUS FULL MOON SERIES, BUT I HOPE YOU ALSO ENJOYED THIS ART STYLE AS WELL.

I RECEIVED MANY COMMENTS FROM READERS SAYING THEY LIKED THE NEW ART STYLE, SO I SUPPOSE IT'S JUST A MATTER OF TASTE. SORRY ABOUT THAT. M(_ _)M

I JUST HOPE THAT YOU ENJOY IT. (^ ^)

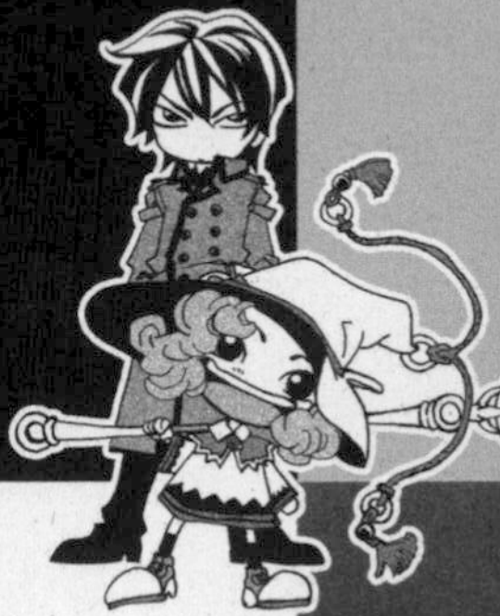

THIS IS SUDDEN, BUT...

UNFORTUNATELY THE MAGAZINE -MICHAO!- HAS BEEN CANCELLED.

THERE WERE SOME PROBLEMS WITHIN THE COMPANY. THAT MEANS THE STATUS OF @FULL MOON IS UP IN THE AIR. IT'S REALLY A SHAME, BECAUSE WE WERE PLANNING A THIRD VOLUME.

I'M FRUSTRATED BECAUSE I WAS LOOKING FORWARD TO WRITING ABOUT THESE NEW CHARACTERS.

HOWEVER, IT'S OUT OF MY POWER, SO I JUST HAVE TO SEE HOW THE SITUATION TURNS OUT. I HOPE I HAVE THE OPPORTUNITY TO CHALLENGE MYSELF WITH THIS MANGA AGAIN SOMEDAY. PLEASE KEEP READING IF THAT HAPPENS. (T_T)

FOR MORE DETAILS, PLEASE CHECK OUT MY HOME PAGE.

HTTP://WWW.SANAMI-MATOH.COM

I HOPE TO SEE YOU AGAIN!

A Kodansha Comics Trade Paperback Original

@ *Full Moon* volume 2 copyright © 2009 Sanami Matoh
English translation copyright © 2012 Sanami Matoh

Published in the United States by Kodansha Comics, an imprint of Kodansha USA Publishing, LLC, New York.

Publication rights for this English edition arranged through Kodansha Ltd, Tokyo.

First published in Japan in 2009 by Kodansha Ltd., Tokyo, as Full Moon-ni Sasayaite, volume 2.

ISBN 978-1-935429-21-0

Printed in the United States of America.

www.kodanshacomics.com

9 8 7 6 5 4 3 2 1
Translator: Mari Morimoto
Lettering: Dave Sharpe

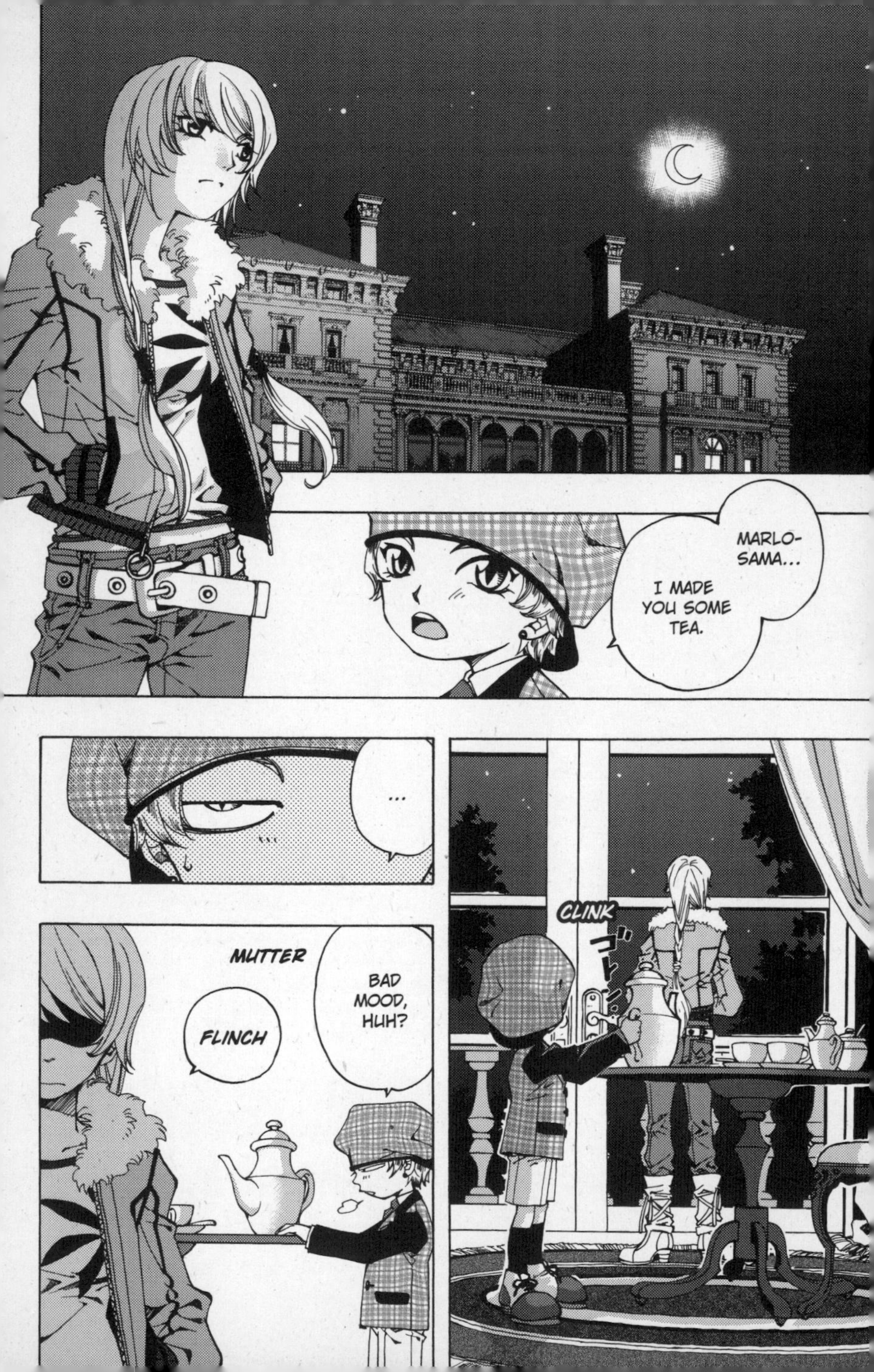
MARLO-SAMA...
I MADE YOU SOME TEA.
CLINK
ゴトッ
...
BAD MOOD, HUH?
MUTTER
FLINCH

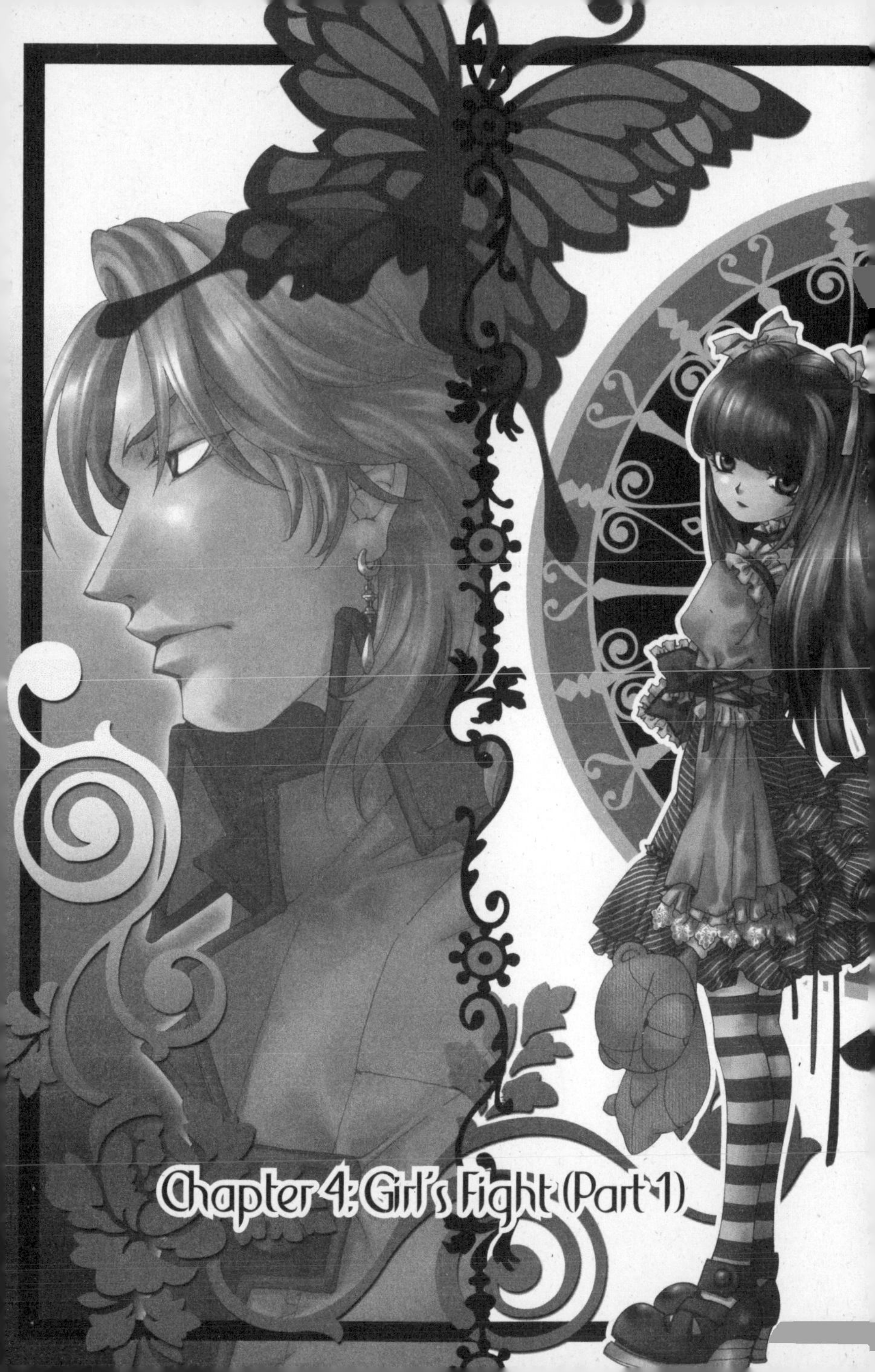
Chapter 4: Girl's Fight (Part 1)

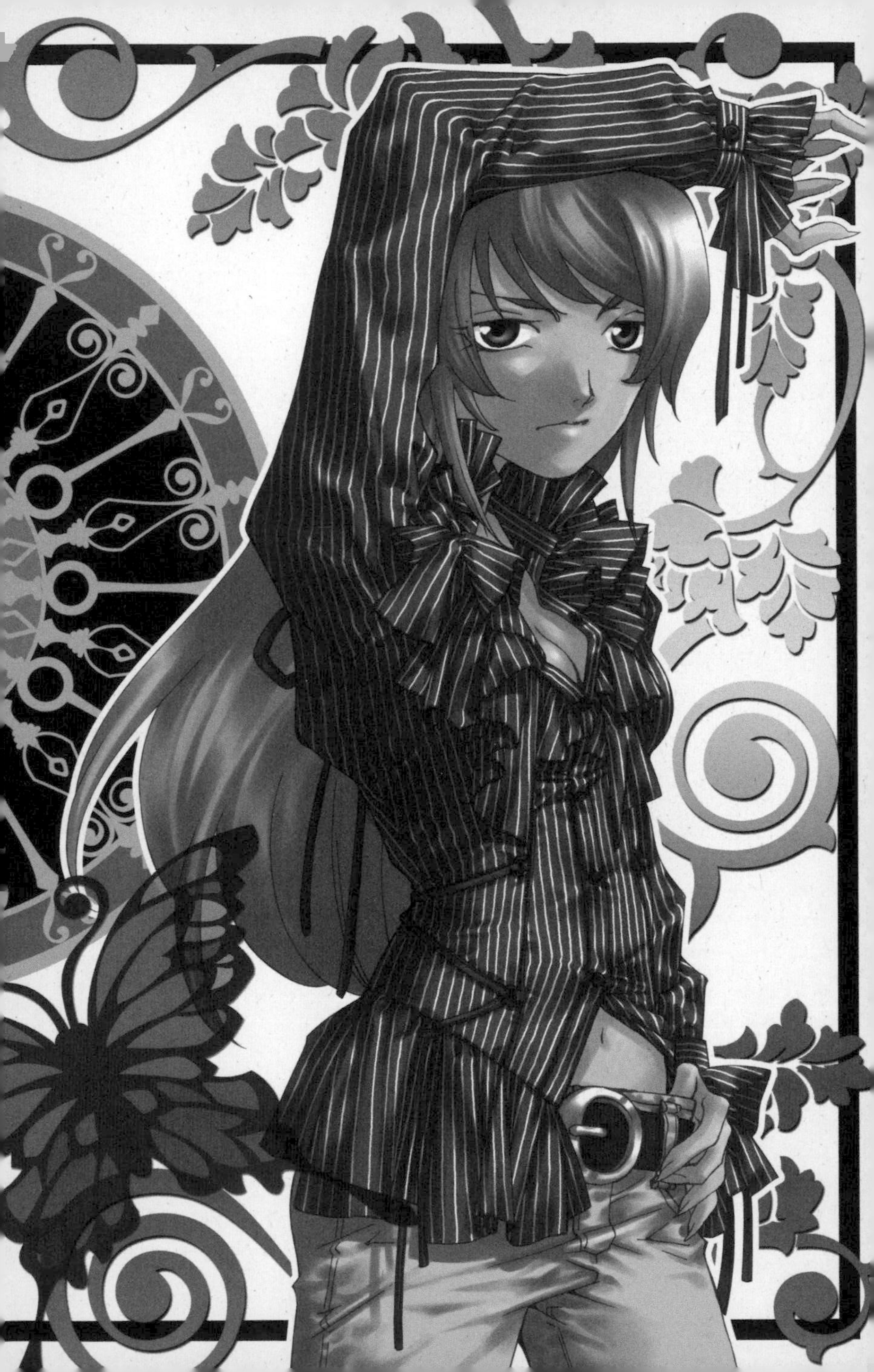

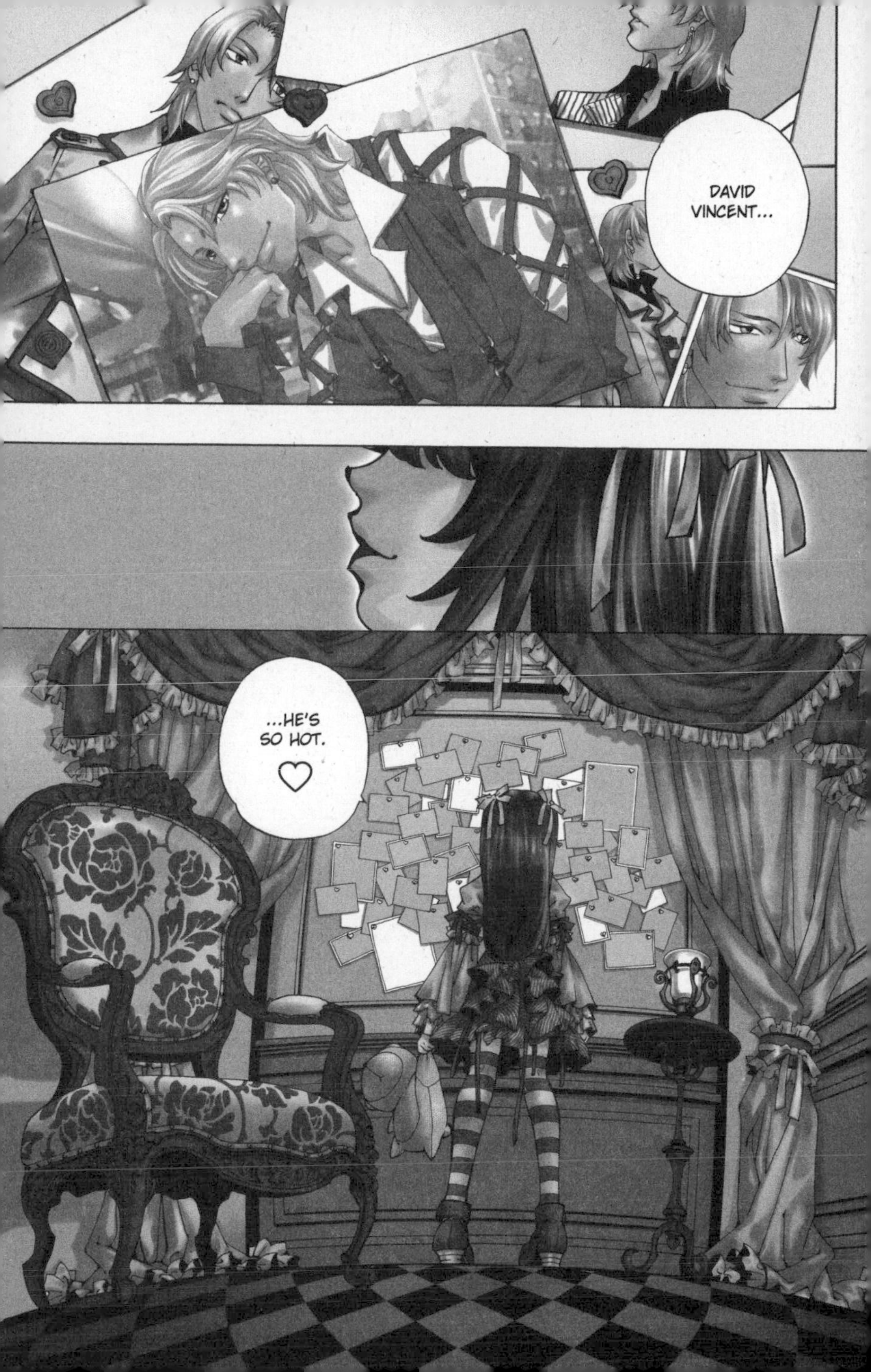
DAVID VINCENT...
...HE'S SO HOT. ♡

@Full Moon
~2~

Contents

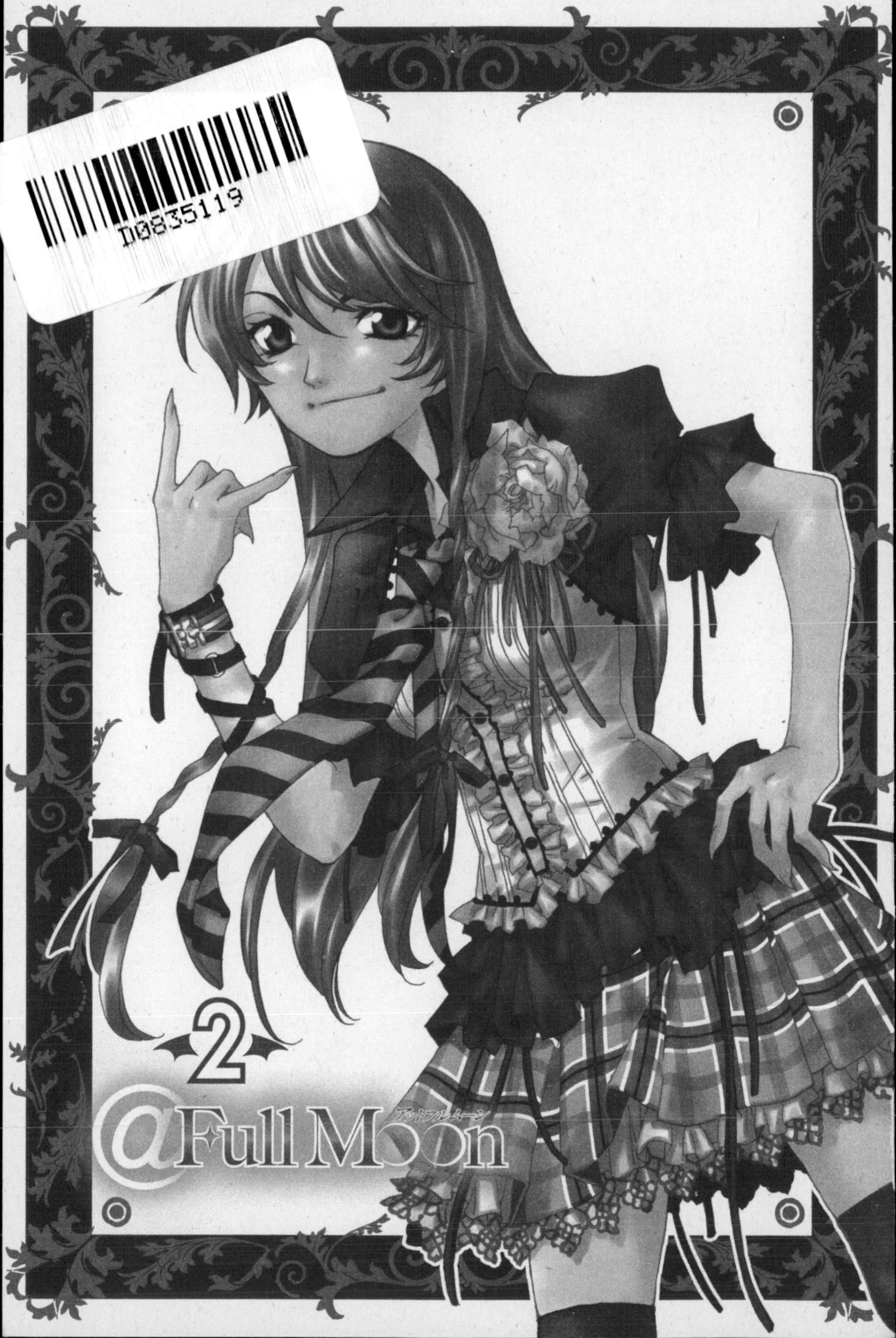
2
@Full Moon
アットフルムーン